MW01678521

Teaching Secondary School Mathematics

A RESOURCE BOOK

(Second Edition, Updated)

Edited by
Lee Peng Yee
Lee Ngan Hoe
Mathematics and Mathematics Education
National Institute of Education
Nanyang Technological University
Singapore

Mc Graw Hill

Singapore • Boston • Burr Ridge, IL • Dubuque, IA • Madison, WI • New York • San Francisco
St. Louis • Bangkok • Kuala Lumpur • Lisbon • London • Madrid • Mexico City
Milan • Montreal • New Delhi • Seoul • Sydney • Taipei • Toronto

The McGraw·Hill Companies

Teaching Secondary School Mathematics
A Resource Book
(*Second Edition, Updated*)

McGraw Hill Education

Copyright © 2009 by McGraw-Hill Education (Asia). All rights reserved. No part of this publication may be reproduced or distributed in any form or by any means, or stored in a data base or retrieval system, without the prior written permission of the publisher.

10 9 8
CTP SLP
20 14 13

When ordering this title, use ISBN 978-007-126849-3 or MHID 007-126849-9

Printed in Singapore

Contents

Preface to the First Edition

This book evolved from a set of course notes compiled by past and present lecturers teaching the postgraduate diploma secondary (PGDE (Sec)) mathematics methodology course at the National Institute of Education. It is the product of conscious and tireless effort put in by the PGDE (Sec) team to provide useful resource materials for trainee students.

The first version of the book was put together in 1997. Meant for internal circulation only, it was based on a modest set of resource materials on the teaching of various topics compiled by a team of five lecturers. In 1999, another set of supplementary notes was compiled to incorporate information and communication technology, thinking skills, assessment, lesson planning and other related theories.

In July 2000, the two sets of notes were combined into one book with major revision to reflect the new initiatives in education and the philosophy of the team of lecturers then teaching the course.

The book went through two printings in 2003 and 2004 respectively with limited distribution.

Now, the PGDE (Sec) team has decided to publish the book formally.

Many of the chapters in Part I have been revised. New chapters have also been added. These chapters are: *Teaching of Algebra* (Yeap Ban Har), *Teaching of Counting* (Tay Eng Guan), *Teaching of Functions* (Eric Fredrick Wood), *Teaching of Higher Algebra* (Fan Lianghuo), *Teaching of Matrices* (Martyn Quigley, Yeo Boon Wooi Joseph) and *Teaching of Trigonometry* (Wong Khoon Yoong).

It is hoped that some of the chapters in the book here will provide basic reading materials for various fundamental issues in mathematics education. My appreciation to Dr Kho Tek Hong and Dr Fong Ho Kheong, for their permission to include their papers on the model method in this book. The illustration on p. 12[1] in Chapter 1 was drawn by Yeap Ban Har. The fractal image on the cover is designed by Eric Fredrick Wood.

[1] This illustration appears on p. 4 of the current edition.

I would like to thank past and present staff of the Mathematics and Mathematics Education Academic Group who have contributed in one way or another to the contents of this book. They are:

Ang Keng Cheng
Awyong Poh Wah
Berinderjeet Kaur
Chua Kwee Gek
Dawn Ng Kit Ee
Eric Fredrick Wood
Fan Lianghuo
Ho Juan Beng
John Cheung Yiu Lin
Joseph Yeo Boon Wooi
Joseph Yeo Kai Kow
Koay Phong Lee
Lee Ngan Hoe
Leong Yew Hoong
Lim-Teo Suat Khoh
Martyn Quigley
Ng Wee Leng
Quek Khiok Seng
Spario Soon Yu Tiong
Tay Eng Guan
Toh Tin Lam
Wong Khoon Yoong
Yap Sook Fwe
Yeap Ban Har

Also, I thank other staff of the Academic Group who have helped to make this book possible by providing ideas, suggestions, advice and encouragement. Finally, I acknowledge once again the work done by the PGDE (Sec) team over the years. Without their contribution, publication of this book would not have been possible.

Editor
July 2005

About the cover: The image displayed on the cover is based on a collection of points called the Mandelbrot Set. In 1976 the French mathematician Benoit Mandelbrot coined the word "fractal" to describe these strange objects which can actually have fractional dimensions. The image here is produced by examining how many times a number, represented by a point in the complex plane, has to be squared before it iterates to a fixed point and then colouring the point differently depending on the number of iterations taken. This design represents a tiny section of the Mandelbrot Set magnified many thousand of times.

Preface to the Second Edition

Teaching Secondary School Mathematics: A Resource Book has been used in its present form since 2003 as a main reference for the Postgraduate Diploma in Education (Secondary Education) at the National Institute of Education, Singapore, in training secondary school teachers in Singapore. It is now revised and published as Volume Two of the Singapore Mathematics Education Series. The objective of the series is to document how our teachers are being trained in Singapore.

In this edition, a new chapter on problem solving has been added. The last two chapters on algebra by Kho Tek Hong and Fong Ho Kheong respectively in the first edition are now replaced by a single chapter. In some cases, it is difficult to attribute a chapter to a single or multiple authors. We have made an attempt to do so. Obviously, we did not acknowledge all the contributions from our colleagues, past or present, in making the book what it is now. Here we would like to acknowledge once again their contribution.

We are also grateful to the staff of the University of Auckland, New Zealand, who are the first to use the book in their teaching outside Singapore and provided us with valuable feedback. The book is now updated to be in line with the latest 2007 syllabus, recently implemented in schools in Singapore. The major difference in the 2007 syllabus at the secondary school level is not so much in the content but in the approaches. As in Volume One of the series, *Teaching Primary School Mathematics: A Resource Book*, the present book covers the following four aspects: syllabus (standards) and concepts, teaching approaches and ideas, common errors and learning difficulties, and sample activities. We hope that this book will be useful not only to pre-service teachers but also to in-service teachers, mathematics educators, parents and anyone interested in mathematics education.

Lee Peng Yee
Editor
Mathematics and Mathematics Education
National Institute of Education
Nanyang Technological University
Singapore
August 2007

Contributing Authors

Ang Keng Cheng received his B.Sc. (Hons) and PhD degrees in Applied Mathematics from the University of Adelaide (Australia). He is currently an Associate Professor of Mathematics at the National Institute of Education, Nanyang Technological University, Singapore. His primary interest in research encompasses mathematical modelling in various biological and medical settings, as well as numerical methods for partial differential equations. He is the author of several papers dealing with modelling of blood flow through arterial structures and which have appeared in journals in biomedical engineering, computers and simulation, engineering science and medicine. In addition, he has also published a number of papers relating to the teaching of mathematics in journals such as *The Mathematics Educator, Teaching Mathematics and Its Applications* and the *International Journal of Mathematical Education in Science and Technology*.

Chua Boon Liang is a lecturer with the Mathematics and Mathematics Education Academic Group, National Institute of Education, Nanyang Technological University, Singapore. With over ten years of experience as a secondary school teacher and head of the mathematics department, he currently teaches mathematics education courses for pre-service teachers at both primary and secondary school level. He is interested in helping secondary school teachers inspire their students to develop an appreciation for the beauty and power of mathematics through the learning and applications of mathematics.

Fan Lianghuo (PhD) is an Associate Professor with the Mathematics and Mathematics Education Academic Group, National Institute of Education, Nanyang Technological University, Singapore. He has taught at both school and university levels. His research interest includes mathematics assessment, teacher professional development, curriculum studies and textbook development, algorithm of polynomial algebra, and educational policy and sociology. He has authored and co-authored many publications in these areas, including *How Chinese Learn Mathematics* (2004, World Scientific) and a research paper on textbook analysis in *Educational Studies in Mathematics*. He recently completed, as principal investigator, a mathematics assessment project funded by the Ministry of Education of Singapore through the Centre for Research in Pedagogy and Practice (CRPP), National Institute of Education.

Ho Juan Beng was the Project Director of the Secondary Mathematics Project. The project was set up by the Ministry of Education, Singapore, to produce textbooks for the Normal Technical stream. He was also a member of the subject committee for the mathematics curriculum in the 1980s. He was a lecturer at the National Institute of Education, Singapore, before he retired in 2000.

Berinderjeet Kaur is an Associate Professor of Mathematics Education at the National Institute of Education in Singapore. She began her career as a secondary school mathematics teacher. She taught in secondary schools for eight years before joining the National Institute of Education in 1988. Since then, she has been actively involved in the education of teachers and heads of departments. Her primary research interests are in the areas of pedagogy, mathematical problem solving, and comparative studies. She has been involved in numerous international studies of mathematics education. As the President of the Association of Mathematics Educators (2002, 2004–), she has also been actively involved in the professional development of mathematics teachers in Singapore and is the founding chairperson of the Mathematics Teachers' Conference series that started in 2005.

Kho Tek Hong (PhD) is a Principal Curriculum Specialist with the Curriculum Planning and Development Division of the Ministry of Education, Singapore. He was the Project Director of the Primary Mathematics Project (PMP) from 1980 to 1996. The PMP was set up by the Curriculum Development Institute of Singapore (CDIS) with the aim of producing good instructional materials for the teaching and learning of primary mathematics. Dr Kho and his team members developed the model drawing method to help students visualise and conceptualise abstract mathematical relationships and various problem structures through pictorial representations.

Lee Ngan Hoe (PhD) is an Assistant Professor with the Mathematics and Mathematics Education Academic Group, National Institute of Education, Nanyang Technological University, Singapore. His research covers primary and secondary mathematics teaching, mathematics teacher training, the teaching of thinking, and the role of the family in mathematics learning.

Leong Yew Hoong (PhD) is an Assistant Professor with the Mathematics and Mathematics Education Academic Group, National Institute of Education, Nanyang Technological University, Singapore. His mathematics teaching experience includes stints at different levels and contexts – in secondary schools, junior colleges, and polytechnics. He continues to be interested in the work of school-teaching through his research in the complexities involved in the classroom teaching of mathematics.

Lim-Teo Suat Khoh (PhD) is an Associate Professor and the Dean/Academic of the National Institute of Education, Nanyang Technological University, Singapore. She was formerly the Head of the Mathematics and Mathematics Education Academic Group. She has been a mathematics educator for nearly 30 years and a mathematics teacher educator for 20 years. Her earlier research interests are in general mathematics education, especially the learning of geometry and algebra at the secondary school level. Her current research and development interests are in mathematics teacher education, particularly in the development of primary teachers' mathematics pedagogical content knowledge.

Ng Kit Ee Dawn is a lecturer with the Mathematics and Mathematics Education Academic Group, National Institute of Education, Singapore. She is currently finishing her PhD in Mathematics Education. Her research interests include the use of metacognitive strategies in small group interactions during problem solving, mathematical knowledge application in Project Work, and the impact of use of real-world contextualised tasks on mathematical learning.

Ng Wee Leng (PhD) is an Assistant Professor with the Mathematics and Mathematics Education Academic Group, National Institute of Education, Singapore. Prior to this, he was an Assistant Director of the Ministry of Education, Singapore. His research interests include the use of technology in the teaching and learning of mathematics and the role of ancient Chinese mathematics in the mathematics curriculum.

Soon Yu Tiong Spario graduated with a PhD in Mathematics and a Postgraduate Diploma in Education (PGDE). He was a faculty member at the National Institute of Education, Singapore, and is currently chief consultant at a private learning centre.

Tay Eng Guan is an Associate Professor with the Mathematics and Mathematics Education Academic Group of the National Institute of Education at Nanyang Technological University, Singapore. He obtained his PhD in Mathematics (Graph Theory) from the National University of Singapore. Dr Tay continues to do research in Graph Theory as well as in Mathematics Education and has had papers published in international scientific journals in both areas. Dr Tay has taught in Singapore junior colleges and also served a stint at the Ministry of Education. He is co-author of four book on Combinatorics and Graph Theory at the H3 and undergraduate levels.

Toh Tin Lam is an Assistant Professor with the Mathematics and Mathematics Education Academic Group, National Institute of Education, Nanyang Technological University, Singapore. He obtained his PhD in Mathematics (Henstock-stochastic integral) from the National University of Singapore. Dr Toh continues to do research in mathematics as well as in mathematics education. He has papers published in international scientific journals in both areas. Dr Toh has taught in junior colleges in Singapore and was head of the mathematics department at the junior college level before he joined the National Institute of Education.

Martyn Quigley lectured at the University of Brunei Darussalam before joining the National Institute of Education, Singapore, for three years, from 2001 to 2004. He taught in the Postgraduate Diploma in Education (PGDE) (Secondary) programme while at the National Institute of Education.

Wong Khoon Yoong (PhD) is an Associate Professor with the Mathematics and Mathematics Education Academic Group, National Institute of Education, Nanyang Technological University, Singapore. His research covers many aspects of general education and mathematics education, including learning and teaching theories and strategies, comparative study of mathematics curriculum, problem-solving heuristics, ICT in mathematics education, and teacher education. His experience as a mathematics teacher and educator spans five countries, namely Australia, Brunei Darussalam, Malaysia, Philippines and Singapore.

Eric Fredrick Wood was a lecturer at the National Institute of Education from 2002 to 2005. He has since retired, and travels between his residences in London and Ontario. He designed the cover of the first edition of this volume.

Yap Sook Fwe (PhD) is a faculty member of the Mathematics and Mathematics Education Academic Group, National Institute of Education, Nanyang Technological University, Singapore. Her research interest includes statistics and statistics education.

Previously a teacher and Head of Department in several Singapore schools, Yeap Ban Har (PhD) now teaches mathematics education courses at NIE. He also sits on the editorial board of *The Mathematics Educator*, the official publication of the Association of Mathematics Educators, Singapore. Well-versed in the areas of problem solving, problem posing and lesson study, Yeap has conducted numerous professional development courses for teachers in Singapore and other parts of Asia as well as in South Africa, United Arab Emirates, Chile and the United States of America.

Yeo Boon Wooi Joseph (MEd) is a lecturer with the Mathematics and Mathematics Education Group at the National Institute of Education, Nanyang Technology University, Singapore. He has a First Class Honours in mathematics and a Distinction for his Postgraduate Diploma in Education. He has taught students from both government and independent schools for eight years and is currently training pre-service teachers. His research interest includes mathematical problem solving involving puzzles, mathematical and logical games, and mathematical investigations, and using computers in the teaching and learning of mathematics.

Yeo Kai Kow Joseph (PhD) is an Assistant Professor with the Mathematics and Mathematics Education Academic Group, National Institute of Education, Nanyang Technological University, Singapore. At present, he is involved in training pre-service and in-service mathematics teachers at the primary and secondary levels and has also conducted numerous professional development courses for teachers in Singapore. Before joining the National Institute of Education, he held the post of Vice Principal and Head of Mathematics Department in secondary schools. He was part of the team at the Research and Evaluation Branch in the Ministry of Education between 1998 and 2000. His research interests include mathematical problem solving at the primary and secondary levels, mathematics pedagogical content knowledge of teachers and mathematics anxiety.

Introduction

Teaching Mathematics

Lim-Teo Suat Khoh

Mathematics education is a fascinating and expanding field of study wherein researchers and educationists try to understand the workings of the learners' minds and hearts as they go through their journey of engaging with mathematics. It is the mathematics teachers, the practitioners, however, who apply such understanding to the practical task of guiding and helping their students along this journey. Students may regard learning mathematics as an exciting adventure or a boring necessity to be tolerated or (worse), as a series of confusing and mystifying but meaningless activities. Their attitudes towards learning mathematics often depend on their accumulated experiences in mathematics lessons and teachers who are the authors and designers of these experiences contribute in no small way to the formation of these attitudes.

It is thus necessary for mathematics teachers to prepare for the mathematical encounters of their students with high standards of professionalism. While acknowledging that methodology courses will not be able to create a natural flair for teaching, they can provide the knowledge base and skills necessary for teachers to do a credible job as professionals. This resource book is intended to be used in conjunction with a methodology course for beginning mathematics teachers, to help them develop their knowledge and master skills for teaching mathematics at the secondary school level.

PRINCIPLES FOR MATHEMATICS TEACHING

The basic approach taken in each of the chapters on teaching topics is based on the premise that effective mathematics teachers need to have the following:

i. a good grasp of learning theories and pedagogical principles to enable them to understand how students learn mathematics,
ii. a true and deep understanding of the discipline and processes of mathematics since they are guiding and inspiring their students to engage with the discipline, and
iii. a repertoire of skills and methods for designing and conducting effective mathematics lessons.

First, it is necessary for beginning secondary mathematics teachers, who are likely to be very successful mathematics learners themselves, to have an awareness of the mathematical difficulties which many of their students face. Freudenthal (1980) makes the point that "knowing a piece of mathematics too well may be a serious impediment to teaching it decently as long as the teacher is unconscious about the learning process that produced his excellence". Much of this awareness will be learned through experiences with students, through observation and reflection, and developed over time. However, beginning teachers can be provided with the knowledge of learning theories and research findings to form a basis which they will verify or modify through observations and reflections during their practice of teaching. Such understanding will also provide a theoretical foundation on which the practice of planning and conducting mathematics lessons is based.

Secondly, a sound understanding of the concepts in the mathematics curriculum and the underlying principles and procedures which form the structure of the mathematics discipline is necessary if the teacher is to be the guide and facilitator of learning. The mathematics teacher is not someone who is just able to explain how to carry out certain mathematical procedures but one who understands the concepts behind the procedures, the usefulness of and connections between the topics being taught, and the mathematical thinking processes which are being fostered through the learning of the concepts and procedures associated with a particular topic. A lack of such understanding often results in didactic and procedure-oriented teaching where students are instructed to merely follow set steps without deviation because the teacher may be reluctant to allow mathematical explorations that will likely go beyond the limits of his or her expertise. Moreover, it takes a strong teacher with a good understanding of the connections between various mathematics topics to capitalise on unexpected moments or situations during lessons to guide the students to mathematics beyond what is planned.

While beginning secondary mathematics teachers often acquire their own mathematical knowledge and understanding outside of teacher preparation programmes, mathematics methodology courses require them to revisit the curriculum topics of the level which they will be teaching. This is necessary for three reasons: First, even for those who have read university mathematics, undergraduate mathematics courses may not provide a deep understanding of secondary curriculum topics. Moreover, some topics, such as geometry, feature largely in the secondary mathematics curriculum but rarely at higher levels. Secondly, the beginning mathematics teacher may not have taken many courses in mathematics at the university level or perhaps have taken very functional mathematics such as engineering mathematics or business mathematics. Often, the result is that they may not have revisited the topics that they will be teaching in secondary school and their understanding is typically very functional without a deep examination of the meaning of concepts and procedures. The approach is thus not to provide more tertiary-level mathematics but rather a closer examination of key ideas and curriculum topics at the secondary level from the perspective of teaching the topic. This is best done by integrating the study of mathematics with the teaching of that area of the discipline.

Finally, although all mathematics teachers would have been secondary mathematics students in their own time, they may not have encountered or appreciated effective and alternative methods of helping students construct and understand concepts. Moreover, today's students and the current school and social environment may be very different. Consequently, teachers need to be exposed to different methods and approaches for facilitating mathematics learning. Although no teaching strategy or approach is guaranteed to be successful, there are yet many strong teaching ideas and methods which have been tested and found effective. It is useful for beginning teachers to be exposed to such approaches and as professionals, they should examine the suggested strategies critically so that they are able to experiment with them and adapt them to their own teaching style rather than implementing them wholesale.

The three components discussed above will contribute towards the planning of mathematics lessons and the following chapters, which focus on the teaching of topics in mathematics, will cover these three components. As a resource book for teachers, the third component with suggested teaching and learning activities and resource materials will, in general, occupy the largest portion of each chapter. It must be noted, however, that the contents of these three components are evolving and as the growing field and new research findings generate new understanding and insights, resulting in new ideas and possibilities, the knowledge base will need to be continually modified and improved.

FRAMEWORK FOR MATHEMATICS CURRICULUM IN SINGAPORE

The previous section articulated the three main components of a mathematics methodology course in general. Mathematics teaching is carried out within a particular social-national context, and the setting of this book is the context of the Singapore education system.

The Singapore mathematics curriculum framework

Since the release of the Third International Mathematics and Science Study (TIMSS) results in 1996, Singapore's mathematics education has been in the limelight due to the strong performance of her students. From the national viewpoint, mathematical competence is seen as a fundamental necessity among her young citizens because of its foundational role in developing a workforce for a technological and knowledge-based economy. Singapore's education system places a premium on mathematics and, other than English and one mother tongue language, mathematics is the only other compulsory subject up to the end of ten years of compulsory education. The mathematics curriculum is established and regulated by the Curriculum Planning and Development Division (CPDD) of the Ministry of Education. The content and level at which topics have to be taught is determined by syllabus committees and reviewed periodically.

Since 1991, the framework of the Singapore mathematics curriculum has been articulated in a pentagon model as given in Figure I-1. Mathematics departments in schools are well aware that "the primary aim of the mathematics curriculum is to enable students to develop their ability in mathematical problem solving" (Ministry of Education, 2000) and that the attainment of this aim is dependent on the five inter-related components of Concepts, Skills, Processes, Attitudes and Metacognition.

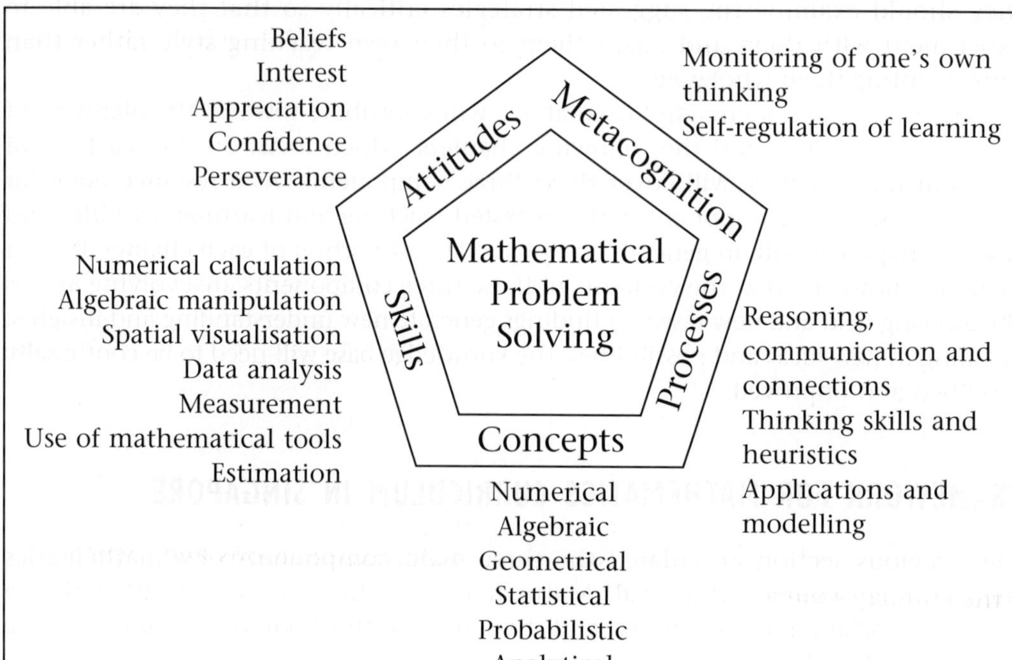

Figure I-1 Framework of the mathematics curriculum (Ministry of Education, 2006).

Concepts refer to the basic mathematical knowledge and *Skills* refer to topic related manipulative skills. Both concepts and skills are needed for solving mathematical problems, whether in daily living or, at higher levels, for professional needs. *Processes* refer to the thinking skills and heuristics which are applicable to problem solving while *Metacognition* refers to the ability to monitor one's own thinking processes in problem solving. *Attitudes* refer to the affective aspects of mathematics learning such as appreciation, enjoyment and having confidence in doing mathematics.

Developing in students a sound understanding of the basic concepts and skills which are internalised and consolidated through practice is an underlying principle in mathematics teaching. Nevertheless, the development of concepts and skills need to be partnered with processes and metacognition in order to develop our students into mathematical problem solvers. As two chopsticks need to be equally strong to function effectively as a pair, these two areas must assume equal importance with the teacher and the learner. Also, if learners are able to use their concepts and skills with processes to solve problems, the motivation for learning will increase and they will then be better able to appreciate the power of mathematics.

However, in a very examination-oriented culture, it is easy to forget the other areas besides concepts and skills, especially the affective aspects in learning mathematics. Many students go through their school days learning mathematics but acquire neither confidence in applying it nor enjoyment in engaging with mathematics. Moreover, they often have no idea why they need to learn various topics of secondary mathematics except to pass examinations. Save for a few, many students are reluctant to understand the "whys" of formulae or to make meaning of concepts, preferring to apply short-cut procedures without understanding the context or constraints because "it is not required for examinations".

Also, while the objective of learning heuristics and metacognition is to enable our students to become better problem solvers, there is a tendency for heuristics to be taught as basic skills and for students to be drilled to recognise given problems within certain categories and simply apply particular heuristics for that particular type of problem. This is especially so in the last year of primary school where the underlying objective of teaching is more to prepare pupils for the high stakes Primary School Leaving Examination (PSLE) than the mathematical development of the learners. At the secondary level, teachers have often resorted to quick or superficial explanations of procedures and concepts because approaches which nurture questioning and making sense of concepts are time-consuming and teachers thus run the risk of not covering the syllabus in time for examinations. There seems to be a misconception that sufficient drill and practice will enable students to recognise the types of problems encountered in examinations and, hence, apply the correct sequence of procedures to solve them. This practice does run counter to the objective of developing in students the ability to explore and use heuristics in non-routine problem solving. Such methods, which are the result of seeing teaching as an examination preparation exercise as opposed to an enabling process to help students engage in real learning, are unlikely to nurture the spirit of innovation and enterprise.

We need to understand that the objective of achieving high examination scores in mathematics should be largely aligned with the objective of mathematical development because examinations are (or should be) an assessment of whether we have achieved our curriculum objectives. The time invested in helping students learn well may be rewarded; they may need fewer subsequent remedial classes.

However, it is also true that doing well in timed examinations is not completely synonymous with true mathematics learning. Unfortunately, it is the examination scores which are quantifiable and recognised by various stakeholders, namely, students, parents, school leaders, employers and the society. There are methods whereby teachers can work with their students to achieve good examination scores but the mathematics is not well learned. Mathematics teachers have to decide for themselves whether they will choose to put time and energy into ensuring good mathematical learning, with the objective of also achieving good examination results.

Mathematics teachers must also be mindful that the mathematics concepts and skills in the curriculum are not static. Even as mathematics expands and evolves, the concepts and skills which our students need to master are ever changing. For example, technology makes obsolete the need to be able to do complicated computations or plot accurate graphs by hand. As argued in Lim (2002), most of the mathematics one needs for day-to-day living is in the primary school curriculum and this leaves the secondary mathematics teachers the more difficult task of justifying to their students the need to study trigonometry or solve quadratic equations.

On the other hand, the mathematical thinking processes, such as logical reasoning and systematic analysis of problems, are skills which will stand our students in good stead in whatever career they embark on. Experience has shown that it is the mathematical way of thinking which remains with us longer than any of the more advanced content we learn, unless we use such content on a very regular basis.

It is fruitless to impose an artificial dichotomy between concepts/skills and mathematical thinking processes but it is important to note that teachers do tend to place more emphasis on teaching the syllabus content, that is, the concepts and skills. This is perhaps because the content is more easily spelt out in terms of the concepts and skills to be mastered under each topic whereas the processes are infused into different topics and have to be inculcated over many topics and over time. In addition, it is far easier to assess whether a student has mastered the concepts and skills as compared to the less tangible thinking processes. Nevertheless, we certainly need to find curriculum time and space to develop mathematical thinking in our students and it is precisely because such processes may have been neglected that the syllabus document clearly articulates the components of processes and metacognition.

The objectives of the curriculum as described above seek to develop the mathematical ability of students in a holistic way and mathematics teachers must consider them seriously since they are to be the deliverers of the curriculum. As people who have advanced levels of engagement with mathematics, mathematics teachers should have the passion for mathematics as a discipline of study and the desire to develop mathematical ability and enthusiasm in their students. Because there will certainly be some conflicts between different objectives of the curriculum and the stakeholders from time to time and under different circumstances, it is essential for mathematics teachers to reflect upon and formulate their own principles and philosophy for guiding practice.

CONCLUSION

Teaching mathematics is a challenging yet fulfilling adventure, much as engaging with mathematics itself is a very human endeavour. Both the learning and teaching of mathematics require perseverance and commitment. The discipline itself, which encourages systematic thinking and logical reasoning, will stand mathematics teachers in good stead when they analyse the components of teaching each topic and to plan their lessons in a systematic and coherent way. Teachers need to be constantly re-examining their own understanding of concepts and skills and processes as they prepare to teach them to their students.

In the previous sections in this chapter, we have discussed three large areas or requirements for mathematics teaching as well as a fourth area of teaching in the context of Singapore. The knowledge base anchored on these four areas is fundamental for teachers to function as professionals. However, much as *attitudes* form an important part in mathematics learning, the value system which teachers carry is what determines their standing as true professionals. As role models for their students, teachers need to show enthusiasm for learning and commitment towards student learning. They need to be constantly reflecting upon their practice with a view to improving their teaching for the sake of their students.

Mathematics teacher preparation courses can thus have a curriculum based on all these components of an effective mathematics teacher and such a curriculum can be represented by another pentagon as in Figure I-2, with the central principle of developing a reflective professional.

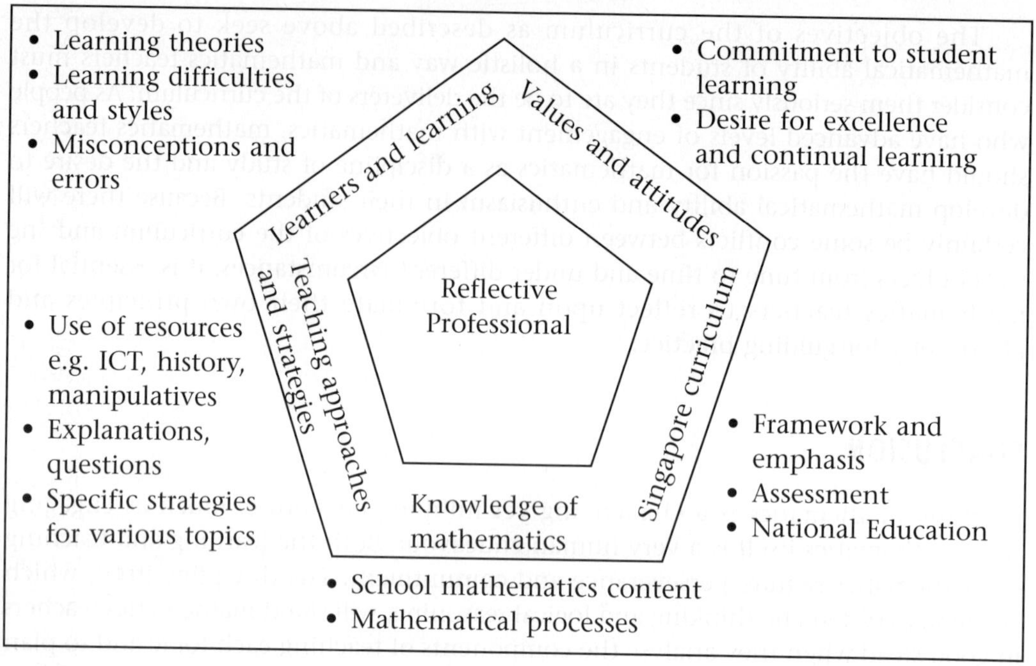

Figure I-2 Framework of teacher preparation

Besides being a possible framework for a teacher preparation curriculum, the above framework serves as a good reminder of the different components which contribute to effective mathematics teaching and can be useful as you go through the next chapters.

REFERENCES

Freudenthal, H. (1980). Major problems of mathematics education, in *Proceedings of the Fourth International Congress on Mathematical Education*. Boston, MA: Birkhäuser.

Lim, S.K. (2002). Mathematics education within the formal Singapore education system: Where do we go from here? In *Mathematics Education for a Knowledge-based Era: Proceedings of Second East Asia Regional Conference on Mathematics Education*. Singapore: National Institute of Education.

Ministry of Education. (2000). Mathematics syllabus – Lower secondary. Singapore: Curriculum Planning and Development Division, Ministry of Education.

Ministry of Education. (2006). A guide to teaching and learning of O-level Mathematics 2007, Singapore: Ministry of Education, Curriculum Planning and Development Division.

Part I

Teaching of Specific Topics

Chapter 1

Teaching of Arithmetic

Lee Ngan Hoe

> Mathematics is the queen of the sciences, and arithmetic the queen of mathematics.
>
> Gauss (1777–1855)

Arithmetic, taken from the Greek word *arithmetike*, means "the art of counting" (Johnson, 1994, p. 152). Davis, Hersh, and Marchisotto (1995, p. 6) described arithmetic as the science of quantity, concerned with numbers of various sorts, and the rules for operations with numbers, and the situations in daily life where these operations are used.

DEVELOPMENT OF ARITHMETICAL CONCEPTS IN SINGAPORE SCHOOL MATHEMATICS

The Singapore mathematics syllabus (Ministry of Education, 2006) includes the following topics:

- Real numbers
- Approximation and estimation
- Standard form
- Ratio, rate and proportion
- Percentage
- Speed
- Everyday mathematics

The following topics/concepts are not covered in the primary mathematics syllabus:

- Whole numbers beyond 10 million
- Use of inequality symbols such as <, >, ≤, ≥
- Lowest common multiple (L.C.M.) and highest common factor (H.C.F.) (knowledge of common multiples and common factors is covered)
- Multiplication and division of fractions involving mixed numbers
- Decimals beyond 3 decimal places
- Recurring decimals
- Multiplication of a decimal with a decimal
- Division of a decimal by a decimal
- Real numbers such as negative numbers, rational and irrational numbers, and terminologies such as integers and natural numbers
- Significant figures
- Standard form
- Inverse proportion
- Simple financial transactions beyond problems involving discounts, Goods and Services Tax (GST), and simple interest

SOME LEARNING DIFFICULTIES AND MISCONCEPTIONS

- Lack of understanding of algorithms
  For example, why do we "invert and multiply" when dividing fractions?

- Limited understanding of concepts
  For example, fractions are viewed as parts of a whole, not as numbers (on the number line).
- Interference from other topics or wrong inferences
  For example, multiplication makes bigger and division makes smaller or $x < y$ implies that $-x < -y$.
- Confusion over rules
  For example, $-2(-3) = (-2) \times (-3)$ is often confused with $-2-3$.

GENERAL TEACHING APPROACHES

Spiral curriculum

Many of the arithmetical concepts covered in secondary school mathematics are an extension of those learned in primary school mathematics. It is helpful to then extend students' understanding from primary school mathematics when introducing these concepts in secondary school mathematics. The following is an example of how to do so.

Introduction of the real number line: Though not all primary mathematics textbooks use the number line to develop early number concepts, the idea of counting on and counting backwards is widely used in the teaching of whole numbers.

Subtract 3 from 10.

(Source: Ministry of Education, 1997, p. 49.)

By redrawing steps used in counting as points on a line for counting backwards, the idea of negative numbers and number line will evolve as a natural extension of students' earlier understanding of whole numbers. Similarly, the counting backwards technique will also introduce students to the technique of subtracting a larger whole number from a smaller whole number.

Problem solving

The Singapore mathematics curriculum is a problem-solving one. Problem solving should not be restricted to the applying of learned concepts only. It can also be emphasised for development of mathematical skills and concepts, as illustrated below.

Multiplication and division of negative numbers

There are many ways that the multiplication and division of negative numbers can be taught; some may be preferred more than others by teachers. The following example uses the problem-solving heuristic – looking for patterns – to aid students to arrive at the rule:

> Examine the following number sentences.
> Look at the pattern and then complete the number sentences.

$3 \times 4 = 12$ (– ?)
$3 \times 3 = 9$
$3 \times 2 = 6$
$3 \times 1 =$ ___
$3 \times 0 =$ ___
$3 \times (-1) =$ ___
$3 \times (-2) =$ ___
$3 \times (-3) =$ ___
$3 \times (-4) =$ ___

→ Commutative Law →

$(-4) \times 3 =$ ___ (+ ?)
$(-4) \times 2 =$ ___
$(-4) \times 1 =$ ___
$(-4) \times 0 =$ ___
$(-4) \times (-1) =$ ___
$(-4) \times (-2) =$ ___
$(-4) \times (-3) =$ ___
$(-4) \times (-4) =$ ___

From the above pattern, complete the following:

(positive number) × (positive number) = (______________ number)
(positive number) × (negative number) = (______________ number)
(negative number) × (positive number) = (______________ number)
(negative number) × (negative number) = (______________ number)

What happens when we divide? Explain.

The activity not only gets students to view problem-solving heuristics as a means for acquiring concepts and skills, but also emphasises the importance of applying Polya's four-step problem-solving model (Polya, 1945) to extend and refine learning. The last question is an example of how Polya's last step in the problem-solving model encourages the solvers to "look back" and examine the solution and see what else they have accomplished and what they can use the result for.

Thinking skills

The learning of mathematics lends itself well to the acquisition of higher-order thinking skills. However, teachers often concentrate on the teaching of the actual mathematics content so much so that although higher-order thinking skills are applied to acquire the mathematics concepts and skills, the learning of the thinking skills often has to take a backseat. As such skills are also essential to preparing students for life-long learning, it helps to make the learning of such skills explicit (Chang and Cheah, 2002). The following illustrates how the teaching of inductive thinking can be made explicit as the learning of mathematics lends well to the development of such a skill.

Rule for finding L.C.M. of two numbers using prime factorisation:

In learning the concept of L.C.M., students are usually taught to first list the multiples of each of the two numbers and then identify the smallest of their common multiples. As this method can be tedious, it is quickly replaced by the prime factorisation method and the repeated division method (sometimes called the "staircase" method). However, explanations are not often adequately provided for the use of these methods. The repeated division method may be seen as a "shortcut" of the prime factorisation method but why does the prime factorisation method work? By getting students to observe the prime factorisation of pairs of numbers and the prime factorisation of their L.C.M., they will be encouraged to predict the rule, and then to verify the rule using different numbers:

For each pair of numbers below, perform prime factorisation for each number. Find their L.C.M. using the listing method and perform prime factorisation of the L.C.M.

a. $4 = 2^2$
$6 = 2 \times 3$
L.C.M. of 4 and 6 is <u>12</u>.
<u>12</u> $= 2^2 \times 3$

b. 15 =
18 =
L.C.M. of 15 and 18 is ____.
____ = ____

What is the relationship between the prime factors of the L.C.M. and the prime factors of the pair of numbers? Can you predict a rule for finding the

L.C.M. of a pair of numbers using prime factorisation? Choose two other numbers and find their L.C.M. using the listing method, then use your rule to check if it works on your new pair of numbers.

It is helpful to remind the students at the end of the lesson that they have learnt how to carry out inductive thinking: observing for patterns, predicting a rule, and then verifying the rule.

National Education

The use of contexts in the teaching and learning of mathematics has long been recognised to have aided students in sense-making when doing mathematics. Given the fact that National Education is to involve all teachers and to be infused across curriculum, the use of National Education related contexts for the teaching and learning of mathematics certainly helps to address both pedagogical and National Education objectives (Tan and Goh, 2003).

Ratio and rate

Many secondary students are unclear of the differences between ratio and rate. However, it is important that they know what the differences are, as these concepts are the foundation for higher mathematics, such as circular measure (covered in Additional Mathematics).

Refer to Table 1-1 and get the students to try out the exercise. Question prompts should then be used to check for students' understanding before they proceed to work with the table:

- What is a census?
- Why are there five columns in the table?

Ask the students to interpret the numbers in the table:

- What do you think each number in the table represents? Do you think that they are ratios? Explain.
- What does the phrase "Males per 1,000 females" at the top-right of the table mean?
- Based on the 2000 census, what is the total number of males per 1,000 females in Singapore? Would you consider such a number a ratio? Explain.

Table 1-1 Sex ratio by ethnic group (males per 1,000 females)

Census year	Total	Chinese	Malays	Indians	Others
1871	3,266	6,307	1,268	4,844	1,723
1881	3,089	5,112	1,281	3,943	1,282
1891	3,209	4,680	1,383	4,216	1,192
1901	2,951	3,871	1,279	4,129	1,094
1911	2,453	2,790	1,172	4,914	1,379
1921	2,044	2,123	1,230	5,021	1,429
1931	1,713	1,656	1,161	5,372	1,357
1947	1,217	1,132	1,208	2,998	1,107
1957	1,117	1,039	1,101	2,257	1,094
1970	1,049	1,017	1,036	1,518	1,071
1980	1,032	1,014	1,036	1,277	991
1990	1,026	1,012	1,041	1,181	937
2000	998	989	1,012	1,092	885

Note: Figures from 1980 onwards refer to Singapore residents only.
Source: Singapore Department of Statistics, www.singstat.gov.sg/keystats//people.html.

The teacher can then address some of the National Education related issues:

- How has the sex ratio changed over the years?
- What could have caused the change to take place?
- Is there a difference in the way the sex ratio changed for the various ethnic groups? Explain.
- Do you think the way the sex ratio is changing will continue? Why?
- Do you have a part to play? Explain.

Next, get the students to appreciate the role mathematical tools play in the communication of information by asking:

- Do you think that the use of ratio is the best way to convey the information? Explain.

Games

Mathematical games sometimes provide joy in the most mundane task. This is particularly so when it comes to arithmetic. By the time students go on to secondary schools, they would have possibly worked on thousands of exercises, causing many of them to loathe practice exercises even if they know that they need the practice. Arithmetic games add an element of fun and surprise to the otherwise monotonous exercise. Using electronically generated games saves teachers the trouble of having to create such games regularly themselves. A good website to start with is http://puzzlemaker.school.discovery.com/, which also allows the creation of new arithmetic puzzles on-line. Teachers might also want to encourage students to create their own games, and a mathematics game day can be organised to showcase these games as well as create joy in the learning of mathematics.

SOME ACTIVITIES FOR TEACHERS

Different uses of whole numbers

Class organisation: Group work (groups of approximately three to five people)

Materials: A set of newspaper

Description: Each group is given a set of newspaper. Members are to scan through the newspaper and perform the following tasks.

a. List the whole numbers used in the newspaper, stating in each case the role that the number serves in the context of their use in the newspaper.
b. Classify the different uses of the whole numbers.
c. State how many different and distinct uses of whole numbers there are.

Rationale: This activity is to sensitise the teachers to the way numbers are used in the mathematics classroom. This is to enable teachers to have a better appreciation of the ambiguities that sometimes arise from the vocabulary used in mathematics, posing possible obstacles to students' learning. It also takes the teachers through an explicit process (shown below) of carrying out a classification exercise (c-l-u-e) (Fogarty & Bellanca, 1986).

- collect data,
- label similar items in a group,
- use patterns to add other groups, and
- evaluate patterns used.

A possible classification of different uses of whole numbers is given by Verschaffel and De Corte (1996):

- to quantify (cardinal aspect),
- to identify (ordinal aspect),
- to measure (measure aspect),
- to reckon (reckoning aspect), and
- to name (non-numerical aspect).

Classification of numbers

Class organisation: Group work (groups of approximately three to five students)

Description: Assign one or two of the following categories of numbers to each group.

- Whole numbers
- Natural numbers
- Integers
- Fractions
- Decimals
- Rational and irrational numbers
- Algebraic numbers
- Real numbers
- Complex numbers
- Prime numbers
- Transcendental numbers

For each of the category of numbers, explain and provide examples to illustrate the terminology, and where conventional notations exist, state the set notation.

Rationale: This activity not only gets teachers to revisit the various categories of numbers covered in both primary and secondary mathematics syllabus, it also introduces to the teachers other number classifications used in mathematics. It provides the teachers with a fuller picture of number classification so as to enhance their understanding of the relationship between these numbers. This would help the teachers to get students to relate their learning to a bigger picture, and thus promote a more holistic rather than piecemeal understanding of their mathematical learning. The chapter on Numbers by Buxton (1985) could be used for background reading.

Some arithmetical questions for discussion

Class organisation: Group work (groups of approximately three to five students)

Description: Each group will be assigned one of the following questions for discussion.

a. Show that $\sqrt{2}$ is irrational.
   Can you show that $\sqrt{3}$ is irrational?
   Next, can you show that $\sqrt{p}$, where p is a prime number, is irrational?

b. Express $0.\dot{2}4\dot{3}$ as a fraction.
   Is $0.\dot{9} = 1$? Explain.

c. What is $\frac{0}{1}$?

   What is $\frac{1}{0}$?

   What is $\frac{0}{0}$? So, what is $\frac{a}{a}$?

   What do you understand by "no answer" versus "cannot be solved", and "well defined" versus "undefined"?

d. Is 1 a prime number? Why?
   Is 3427 a prime number? How do you know?
   How many prime numbers are there? Can you prove your answer?

Rationale: This activity is to encourage the teachers to examine some issues that are closely related to the secondary mathematics syllabus. The issues, though not within the syllabus, can be tackled by the teachers and the mathematically inclined students. The experience will provide the teachers with some necessary background knowledge to handle such issues when they are raised by students during a mathematics class.

SOME ACTIVITIES FOR STUDENTS

A matter of percentage

Class organisation: Pair work

Description: Students work in pairs to answer the following questions. State whether each of the following is True (T) or False (F). Explain your answer.

- A is $\frac{3}{4}$ of B means B is $\frac{4}{3}$ of A.
- A is $\frac{3}{4}$ % of B means B is $\frac{4}{3}$ % of A.
- If A is 5% more than B, then B is 5% less than A.
- If A increases by 8% and then decreases by 8%, then the result is equal to A.
- If A increases by 10% and then further increases by 5%, the overall increase is 15% of A.
- A is given a 5% increase followed by a 10% decrease. This is the same as when A is given a 10% decrease followed by a 5% increase.
- In a class, the ratio of the number of boys to the number of girls is 3:4. The number of boys is 75% of the number of students of the class.
- The number of boys in a class is 45% and the number of girls is 55%. This means the number of girls is 10% more than the number of boys.
- The number of boys in a class is 45% and the number of girls is 55%. This means that the number of girls is more than the number of boys by 10% of the class.
- In a class, there are 20% more girls than boys. This means 60% of the class are girls and 40% are boys.

Rationale: In this activity, students are asked to examine some questions related to percentage. These questions are derived from some of the common misconceptions that students have from primary mathematics knowledge. This exercise serves as a way for teachers to address some of these misconceptions before further developing the topic of percentage.

Arithmetic fallacies

Classroom organisation: Group work (groups of approximately three to five students)

Description: Each group will be asked to examine two of the following fallacies explaining why each of the argument is wrong.

- The fallacy of the ring
  A lady goes to a jeweller to buy a ring. She pays $100 for the ring. The next day, she returns to the shop, saying that she wants to exchange the ring for another one. She then picks a $200 ring. When the jeweller asks for $100 more, she points out that she has paid him $100 the day before, and has just returned him a ring worth $100, so she does not owe him anything. Why is this so?

- To prove that $30 = $29
  Three men dine in a restaurant. The bill is $30 and each man hands the waiter $10.

Later, the cashier realises that there has been a mistake, the bill is \$25. The waiter is asked to return the men \$5. But it suddenly occurs to him that \$5 will be hard to divide among three people, so he keeps \$2 for himself and returns each of the men \$1. This means the men pay \$9 each, making it a total of \$27, and plus the \$2 the waiter keeps, the final amount is \$29. Where has the extra dollar gone? Or are we forced to conclude that \$30 = \$29?

- The fallacy that 25p = 24p
  Two women make their living by selling apples. A sells hers for 3 a penny, B for 2 a penny. They sell 30 apples a day each, earning 10p and 15p a day respectively. One day, woman A falls sick and asks woman B to sell her apples for her. Woman B sells the apples at 5 for 2p (3 a penny + 2 a penny). When she has finished selling all the apples, she is dismayed to find she only has 24p instead of the expected 25p. Why is this so?

- The printer's dilemma
  A printer is asked to print 200 books at the rate of 20 books per day. He prints the first 100 books quickly, at the rate of 30 books per day. He reasons that he needs to print the next 100 books at 10 books per day to complete the assignment on time since the average of 10 and 30 is 20, the required rate. To his dismay, he completes the assignment late. What has gone wrong?

Rationale: Fallacies force students to relook and examine inaccurate arguments with a critical eye. The experience helps students to better evaluate their own arguments in problem solving.

The Singa's will

Class organisation: Group work (groups of approximately three to five students)

Description: Each group is to spend some time reading the following story about the Singa's will and then answer the questions that follow.

> Singa, an old man living on an island, dies and leaves 11 horses to his three sons. His will specifies that $\frac{1}{2}$ of the horses should go to his eldest son, $\frac{1}{4}$ to his second son, and $\frac{1}{6}$ to his youngest son. His sons cannot see how they can distribute the horses without cutting some of them up, or selling them and dividing the money, which they do not want to do. So they go to a village elder for advice.

The old man thinks for a while and then says, "I have a horse, I will add it to your 11 to make 12 horses. Now we shall divide them. The eldest son takes $\frac{1}{2}$ of the number of horses, or 6. The second son takes $\frac{1}{4}$, or 3. The youngest son's share is $\frac{1}{6}$, or 2. Because 6 + 3 + 2 = 11, there is 1 horse left over, so I get my horse back.

How could the village elder solve a seemingly impossible problem?
Do you think that the old Singa's will has been executed accordingly? Why?

Rationale: The Singa's will problem is again a case in which students get to evaluate critically the validity of a mathematical argument. In this case, the argument involves the addition of fractions and the fact that fractional parts of a whole should add up to one. However, by asking the students to decide if the will has been executed accordingly, some may raise the issue of ratio instead. In this case, though the fraction of horses received by each son is not what is stated in the will, the ratios the horses should be shared are correct. Given the constraint, would we still consider such an execution of the will to be correct? This will serve as a good discussion point for students as they investigate how different mathematical concepts are used to handle such a situation. [This Singa's will problem is a modification of the rather well-known ancient Singa's will problem. For more on the Bedouin's will problem, refer to Movshovitz-Hadar and Webb, 1998, pp. 40–43]

The students could also be encouraged to pose their own Singa's will problem by looking at other possible sets of fractions that behave in this manner (e.g. $\frac{1}{2}$, $\frac{1}{3}$ and $\frac{1}{9}$). The teacher may also modify the problem; instead of adding a horse, a horse may be removed to solve the problem. For example, the teacher could use the fractions $\frac{1}{2}$, $\frac{1}{3}$ and $\frac{1}{4}$, and 13 camels. As with the earlier case, students could then be encouraged to discover other sets of fractions that could be used for such a case.

I'm like a rational number ...

Class organisation: Individual work followed by class discussion

Description: The teacher will first show the students the following sentence.

I'm like a rational number ...

Students are then given five minutes to reflect on the sentence. They could choose to "strongly disagree", "disagree", "be neutral", "agree" or "strongly agree" with the given statement.

After the students have made their decision, the teacher will designate certain parts of the classroom for students of the same category of response to share why each has chosen the particular response. After the students have finished sharing, the teacher then gets some students of each category of response to share with the whole class the reason for their choice of response.

Rationale: The activity requires the students to relate their mathematical learning to themselves. Through the sharing, the teacher will not only be able to gauge the students' understanding/misconceptions of rational numbers, but also gain a deeper insight to the students' life and their perception of the world in general.

This is an activity which could be conducted after having taught the concept or during an introduction of a lesson for checking of conceptual understanding of rational numbers, providing the teacher with some input as to how the concept has been internalised by the students. Due to the nature of the activity, the teacher could also use this activity for other mathematical concepts, for example, "I'm like a recurring decimal ...".

Excel Activity

FIBONACCI NUMBERS

Leonardo Pisano Fibonacci (1170–1250) published a book called *Liber abaci* ("The Book of Calculation") in 1202. A problem in the third section of *Liber abaci* led to the introduction of the Fibonacci numbers for which Fibonacci is best remembered today:

> A certain man put a pair of rabbits in a place surrounded on all sides by a wall. How many pairs of rabbits can be produced from that pair in a year if it is supposed that every month each pair begets a new pair which from the second month on becomes productive?

The resulting sequence is 1, 1, 2, 3, 5, 8, 13, 21, 34, 55, etc.

1. Enter the first two Fibonacci numbers in A1 and B1.

	A	B	C	D	E	F	G	H
1	1	1						

In cell C1, enter the formula = A1 + B1. Copy cell C1 and paste it in D1, E1 and F1 to form a sequence. This sequence is known as the **Fibonacci sequence**. (The sequence is generated by the formula contained in cell C1.)

What will the next two numbers be in the sequence?
Copy cell C1 and paste it in G1 and H1 to check.

Describe the pattern in this sequence.
The next number in the sequence is found by ______________________________

____.

What type of number is every third number in the Fibonacci sequence?
(Hint: Is the number divisible by 2?)

____.

What do you notice about every fourth number?

____.

Every fifth number?

____.

2. Enter two consecutive Fibonacci numbers (say 1 and 2) in B5 and C5. In cell D5, enter the formula `= B5 + C5`. Copy cell D5 and paste it in E5. In cell C7, enter the formula `= B5 * E5`. In cell D7, enter the formula `C5 * D5`. What are the numbers in cells C7 and D7?

☐ ☐

Key in different pairs of consecutive Fibonacci numbers in B5 and C5. Note the numbers in the cells D5, E5, C7 and D7. Complete the table.

Number in B5	Number in C5	Number in D5	Number in E5	Number in C7	Number in D7
1	2	3	5		

Complete the following.

The number in cell C7 is the product of the numbers in _____ and _____.

The number in cell D7 is the product of the numbers in _____ and _____.

Compare the two products. What can you conclude?

The product of the first and the last terms of four consecutive Fibonacci numbers is

____.

3. In cells B10 and C10, enter any two consecutive Fibonacci numbers, say 1 and 2. In cell D10, enter the formula = B10 + C10.

   In cell C12, enter the formula = C10 ^ 2. In cell C13, enter the formula = B10 * D10.

   Compare the two numbers in C12 and C13. What do you observe?

   ____

   Key in different pairs of consecutive Fibonacci numbers in B10 and C10. Complete the table below.

Number in B10	Number in C10	Number in D10	Number in C12	Number in C13

   Complete the following.

   The number in cell C12 is the ____________ of the number in C10.

   The number in cell C13 is the ____________ of the numbers in B10 and D10.

   Compare the numbers in C12 and C13. What can you conclude?

   The product of the first and the last terms of three consecutive Fibonacci numbers is

   ____.

4. Use `Formula` to enter the ratio of the second Fibonacci number to the first number in cell B15.

   Use `Copy` and `Paste` to enter the ratio of each Fibonacci number to the number preceding it in corresponding cells C15, D15, ..., H15.
   What do you notice about the ratios? Look for a pattern.

5. You have found some mathematical magic about the Fibonacci numbers! Visit the following website and other related links, and write a summary of the appearance of Fibonacci numbers in nature.

   http://www.ee.surrey.ac.uk/Personal/R.Knott/Fibonacci/fibnat.html

Internet Activity

FINDING SMALL PRIME NUMBERS

1. Eratosthenes
   In about 200 B.C., the Greek Eratosthenes devised a procedure called the "Sieve of Eratosthenes" to find primes.
   - Visit the website http://www-groups.dcs.st-and.ac.uk/~history/.
   - Write a brief account of Eratosthenes' contributions to mathematics.

2. Sieve of Eratosthenes
   - Visit the website http://www.utm.edu/research/primes/prove/prove2.html#sieve.
   - Learn about how to find very small prime numbers using the Sieve of Eratosthenes.
   - Apply the method learned on the 100 squares given below to find all the prime numbers less than 100. List the procedure used.

1	2	3	4	5	6	7	8	9	10
11	12	13	14	15	16	17	18	19	20
21	22	23	24	25	26	27	28	29	30
31	32	33	34	35	36	37	38	39	40
41	42	43	44	45	46	47	48	49	50
51	52	53	54	55	56	57	58	59	60
61	62	63	64	65	66	67	68	69	70
71	72	73	74	75	76	77	78	79	80
81	82	83	84	85	86	87	88	89	90
91	92	93	94	95	96	97	98	99	100

3. Trial division

   Another way to determine whether a number is a prime or not is by *trial division.*

   - Show how you would use trial division to determine if 2357 is a prime.

MORE ABOUT PRIME NUMBERS

Visit the website http://www.utm.edu/research/primes/notes/faq/ .
Answer the following questions.

1. Is 1 a prime number? Explain.

2. Are all prime numbers odd numbers? Explain.

3. What is the largest prime number discovered?
   Why do you think people look for such a large number?

4. What is a perfect number?
   How is it related to prime number?

5. Explain the following terms using the *Prime Pages'* glossary.

   - an abundant number, and
   - a deficient number.

   Can an abundant number be a prime number? Explain.
   Can a deficient number be a prime number? Explain.

APPENDIX 1A: LIST OF LARGE NUMBERS

n =	10^{3n} =	American name	European name	SI prefix
3	10^{9}	billion	milliard	giga-
4	10^{12}	trillion	billion	tera-
5	10^{15}	quadrillion	billiard	peta-
6	10^{18}	quintillion	trillion	exa-
7	10^{21}	sextillion	trilliard	zetta-
8	10^{24}	septillion	quadrillion	yotta-
9	10^{27}	octillion	quadrilliard	
10	10^{30}	nonillion	quintillion	
11	10^{33}	decillion	quintilliard	
12	10^{36}	undecillion	sextillion	
13	10^{39}	duodecillion	sextilliard	
14	10^{42}	tredecillion	septillion	
15	10^{45}	quattuordecillion	septilliard	
16	10^{48}	quindecillion	octillion	
17	10^{51}	sexdecillion	octilliard	
18	10^{54}	septendecillion	nonillion	
19	10^{57}	octodecillion	nonilliard	
20	10^{60}	novemdecillion	decillion	
21	10^{63}	vigintillion	decilliard	
22	10^{66}	unvigintillion	undecillion	
23	10^{69}	duovigintillion	undecilliard	
24	10^{72}	trevigintillion	duodecillion	
25	10^{75}	quattuorvigintillion	duodecilliard	
26	10^{78}	quinvigintillion	tredecillion	

n =	10^{3n} =	American name	European name	SI prefix
27	10^{81}	sexvigintillion	tredecilliard	
28	10^{84}	septenvigintillion	quattuordecillion	
29	10^{87}	octovigintillion	quattuordecilliard	
30	10^{90}	novemvigintillion	quindecillion	
31	10^{93}	trigintillion	quindecilliard	
32	10^{96}	untrigintillion	sexdecillion	
33	10^{99}	duotrigintillion	sexdecilliard	

Source: http://www.unc.edu/~rowlett/units/large.html.

REFERENCES

Buxton, L. (1985). *Mathematics for everyone*. NY: Shoken Books.

Chang, S.C.A., & Cheah, Y.M. (Eds.). (2002). *Teachers' handbook on teaching thinking skills across disciplines*. Singapore: Prentice-Hall.

Davis, P.J., Hersh, R., & Marchisotto, E.A. (1995). *The mathematical experience* (Study Edition). Woodbine, NJ: Birkhäuser.

Fogarty, R., & Bellanca, J. (1986). *Teach them thinking mental menus for 24*. Arlington Heights, Il: Skylight.

Johnson, A. (1994). *Classic math – History topics for the classroom*. Palo Alto, CA: Dale Seymour.

Ministry of Education. (1997). *Primary mathematics 1A*. (3rd ed.). Singapore: Ministry of Education.

Ministry of Education. (2006). *Secondary mathematics syllabuses*. Singapore: Ministry of Education.

Mosvshovitz-Hadar, N., & Webb, J. (1998). *One equals zero and other mathematical surprises*. Emeryville, CA: Key Curriculum Press.

Polya, G. (1945). *How to solve it*. (2nd ed.). Princeton, NJ: Princeton University Press.

Sherwood, W. (1999). *Internet activities for math – Challenging*. Westminster, CA: Teacher Created Materials, Inc.

Tan, K.S.S., & Goh, C.B. (Eds.). (2003). *Securing our future*. Singapore: Pearson.

Verschaffel, L., & De Corte, E. (1996). Number & arithmetic. In A.J. Bishop, M.A. Clements, C. Keital, J. Kilpatrick, & C. Laborde (Eds.), *International handbook of mathematics education* (pp. 99–135). Dorechet, the Netherlands: Kluwer Academic Publishers.

Chapter 2

Teaching of Algebra

Yeap Ban Har

Algebra has its roots in the study of general methods for solving equations. The historical development of algebra as a system of symbols provides useful implications for teachers. There are plenty of readings on the history of algebra. See, for example, http://www.algebra.com/algebra/about/history/.

What is algebra? Algebra should arise as a by-product of making arithmetic sensible (Peck and Jencks, 1988). Algebra is conceived as the branch of mathematics that deals with symbolising general numerical relationships and mathematical structures and with operating on those structures (Kieran, 1992). Algebra is a system where general patterns, relationships and procedures are represented in a concise manner using symbols, usually letters of the alphabet. Algebra is a language for describing actions on, and relationships among, quantities (Wagner and Parker, 1993).

Usiskin (1988) summarised the different conceptions of school algebra. He proposed that there are four conceptions of algebra:

- Algebra as generalised arithmetic
  In this conception, variables are thought of as pattern generalisers. For example, the pattern observed below:

$$\begin{aligned} 3 \cdot 5 &= 15 \\ 2 \cdot 5 &= 10 \\ 1 \cdot 5 &= 5 \\ 0 \cdot 5 &= 0 \\ -1 \cdot 5 &= -5 \\ -2 \cdot 5 &= -10 \\ -3 \cdot 5 &= -15 \end{aligned}$$

  can be generalised as $-x \cdot y = -xy$.

At a more advanced level, data on world track records for a specific sporting event (e.g. 100-metre race) over the years can be used to investigate a possible relationship between the world record time and the year it was created. The relationship is then described using variables. This is an example of mathematical modelling.

- Algebra as a way to solve certain types of problems
  In this conception, variables are either unknowns or constants and are used to solve problems, such as the one shown below.

  When 5 is added to twice a number, the sum is 19. Find the number.

  This problem can be solved by constructing the equation $2x + 5 = 19$.

- Algebra as a study of relationships among quantities
  In this conception, a variable stands for a domain value of a function (argument) or stands for a number on which other numbers depend (parameter). For example, we write A = LW to describe the relationship between the area (A) of a rectangle and its length (L) and width (W).

- Algebra as a study of structures
  In this conception, a variable is an arbitrary symbol. When students are asked to factorise $3x^2 - 7x + 2$, they are not generalising from arithmetic. Neither is there a problem to solve or a relationship to describe. This is an example of the use of algebra as a study of structures.

ACTIVITY 1 FOR TEACHERS

Consider each of these and discuss how they are similar to one another and in what ways they are different.

$$A = \frac{1}{2}bh \qquad 3x - 1 = 8 \qquad y = 3x - 1 \qquad a^2 + b^2 = c^2 \qquad n(\frac{1}{n}) = 1$$

In groups, think of examples to illustrate each of Usiskin's four conceptions of school algebra. Do you think these four categories include all the important ideas in algebra that students should learn? If not, identify new conceptions of school algebra.

ALGEBRA IN THE SINGAPORE MATHEMATICS CURRICULUM

This section focuses on key concepts in algebra as depicted in the Singapore mathematics curriculum. The first part of this section provides an overview of algebra and algebraic thinking in the primary school syllabus. The second part isolates components of the curriculum framework that focus on algebra and algebraic thinking. The third part provides an overview on the algebra topics taught in secondary school.

ALGEBRA IN PRIMARY MATHEMATICS

The primary school curriculum in Singapore includes little formal algebra. Students studying Standard Mathematics[1] at the upper primary levels write expressions in one variable as well as simplify and evaluate such expressions.

However, there are aspects of the primary school mathematics curriculum that facilitate algebraic thinking. Two such aspects are (1) the use of the "model method" in solving word problems, and (2) the inclusion of pattern observation. Teachers can capitalise on these in helping students learn algebra in secondary school.

ACTIVITY 2 FOR TEACHERS

Solve each word problem using (1) the "model method", and (2) algebraic equations. Discuss how you could use the "model method" as a bridge to learn the use of algebraic equations in problem solving.

Problem	Using model method	Using algebraic equation
Siti packs her clothes into a suitcase and it weighs 29 kg. Rahim packs his clothes into an identical suitcase and it weighs 11 kg. Siti's clothes are three times as heavy as Rahim's clothes. (a) What is the mass of Rahim's clothes? (b) What is the mass of the suitcase? (SEAB, 2006, p. 18)		

[1] In the upper primary levels, there is content differentiation into Standard Mathematics and Foundation Mathematics. The majority of the students study Standard Mathematics. However, students who have not achieved a basic understanding of the subject are advised to study Foundation Mathematics where the emphasis is on the acquisition of the basics of the subject.

Problem	Using model method	Using algebraic equation
Ahmad and Mei Ling saved $800 altogether. A quarter of Ahmad's savings was $65 more than a fifth of Mei Ling's savings. How much more money than Mei Ling did Ahmad save? (SEAB, 2007, p. 20)		

How can secondary school teachers help lower secondary students link the "model method" and the use of algebraic equations in problem solving?

In Chapter 16, Bruner described the three forms of mathematical concepts as being (1) symbolic, (2) iconic (pictorial), and (3) enactive (concrete). Algebraic equations are symbolic. Some lower secondary students find this abstract. The "model method" uses a pictorial representation of the equations. The example below shows one way of linking the "model method" and algebra (Lee and Yeap, 2002). Refer to Chapter 22 for a further discussion on the "model method" and its links to algebra.

Example: Mr. Wong is four times as old as his son. Ten years ago, the sum of their ages was 60. Find their present ages.

Using the model method

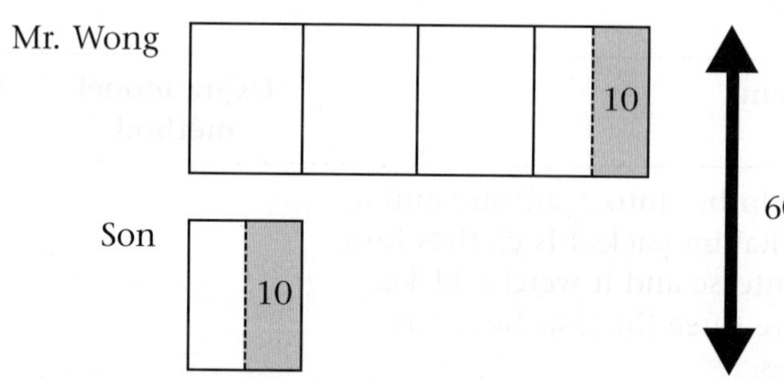

5 units = 60 + 10 + 10 = 80

1 unit = 16

The son is 16 years old and Mr. Wong is 64 years old.

Using the algebraic method

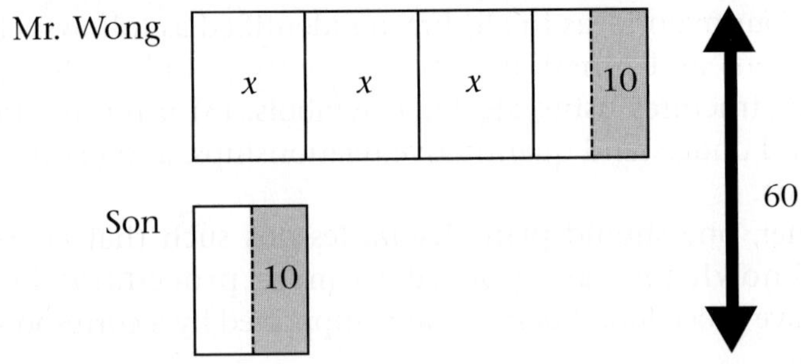

Typically, we write

$$(4x - 10) + (x - 10) = 60$$

$$5x - 20 = 60$$

$$5x = 80$$

The model facilitates an explanation of this step.

$$x = 16$$

Mr. Wong is $4x$ (= 64) years old and his son is x (= 16) years old.

ALGEBRA AND THE SINGAPORE PROBLEM-SOLVING CURRICULUM FRAMEWORK

Why do students learn algebra? Algebra is the language through which most of mathematics is communicated. The Singapore curriculum document does not provide teachers with an explicit focus for algebra teaching and learning. However, an understanding of the curriculum and assessment practices reveals two focus areas. Firstly, students should acquire competent algebraic manipulation skills that are supported by conceptual understanding. Competent manipulation skills do not include manipulating tedious expressions and equations. Instead, students should be encouraged to strive for elegance as they engage in manipulating expressions and equations. Secondly, students should understand the different uses of symbols, usually letters of the alphabet, in algebra.

Both these focus areas culminate in three broad learning outcomes for students. The first is students being able to use the language of algebra to generalise and describe a pattern or a relationship. The second is students using algebra as a problem-solving tool for engaging in simple mathematical modelling process. The third is that, through engagement with patterns, students learn to appreciate the beauty and elegance of mathematics and through engagement with problems and the mathematical modelling process, students come to recognise the power of mathematical tools in real-life applications.

The Principles and Standards for School Mathematics (National Council of Teachers for Mathematics, 2000) provides a clear focus for algebra teaching and learning. The four main ideas in algebra are identified as follows: (1) understanding patterns, relations and functions, (2) representing and analysing mathematical situations and structures using algebraic symbols, (3) using mathematical models to represent and understand quantitative relationships, and (4) analysing change in various contexts.

As a teacher, one should plan algebra lessons such that (1) students develop conceptual knowledge (as opposed to mere procedural knowledge), and (2) students have procedural fluency that is supported by a corresponding conceptual understanding.

Specific concepts

The key ideas in Singapore secondary school algebra include (1) variables, expressions, equations and formulae, (2) algebraic manipulation, and (3) solving equations. These are included in the lower secondary mathematics syllabi as well as mathematics and Additional Mathematics syllabi for the different streams.

In writing expressions, equations and formulae, students should be able to

- use letters to represent generalised numbers, and
- express arithmetic processes algebraically.

In algebraic manipulation, students should be able to

- substitute,
- evaluate,
- expand,
- simplify,
- factorise,
- combine algebraic fractions, and
- change subject of formulae.

In solving equations, students should be able to solve

- linear equations,
- linear inequalities,
- quadratic equations,
- quadratic inequalities,
- cubic equations,
- simultaneous linear equations,
- simultaneous equations with at least one linear equation, and
- fractional equations with numerical and linear denominators.

The Singapore mathematics curriculum is a spiral curriculum. The topics are developed such that the prerequisites are taught at a lower grade level. When the same topic is taught at a higher grade level, it must be an extension, not repetition. The lower secondary and normal streams syllabi are sub-sets of the mathematics O-level syllabus. The Additional Mathematics syllabus is an extension of the mathematics O-level syllabus.

Figure 2-1 shows how the different algebra topics are developed in the Singapore mathematics curriculum.

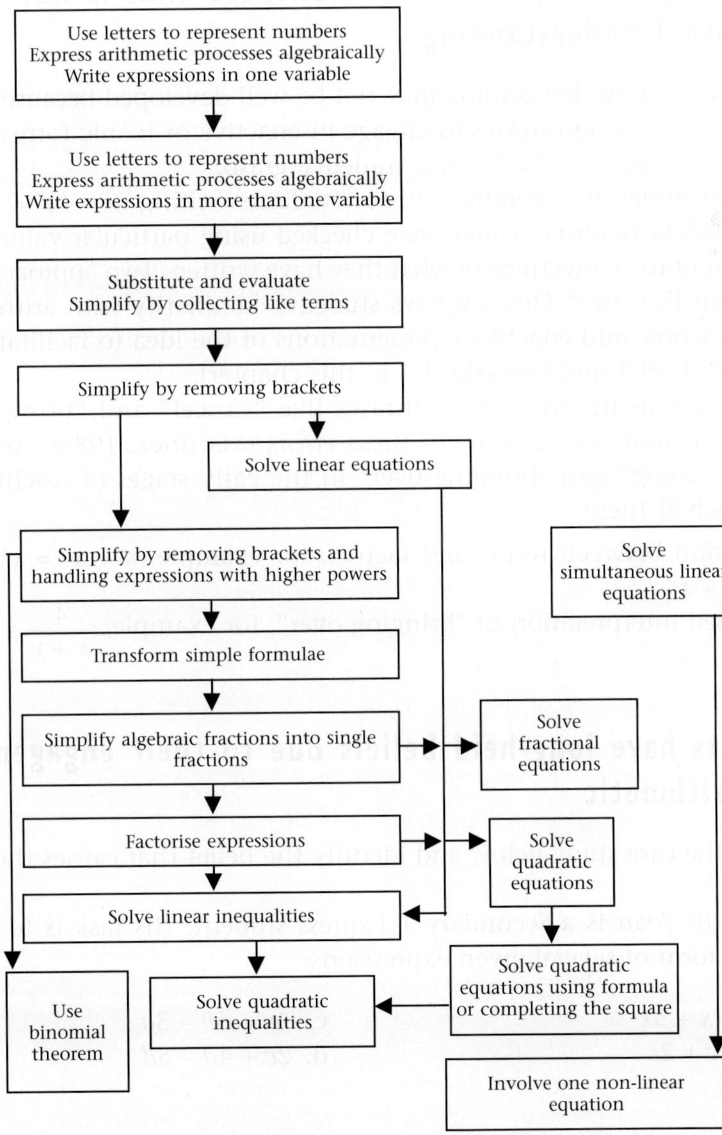

Figure 2-1 Development of topics

COMMON ERRORS

In this section, common errors made by students in algebra tasks are described and discussed. An understanding of students' common errors is helpful in planning instructional strategies to remediate or to prevent them. Three categories of common errors are described here.

Students possess procedural knowledge that is not backed by conceptual understanding

The conceptual understanding may not be well developed because students are not provided with opportunities to engage in enactive or iconic forms of the idea. The symbolic version may be beyond students' grasp.

For example, it is common to see students writing $(a + b)^2 = a^2 + b^2$. Students who are metacognitive would have checked using particular values if they are not confident of the correctness of what they have written. Two approaches are suggested to prevent this error. One employs students' familiarity with arithmetic; the other employs iconic and enactive representations of the idea to facilitate understanding (see Worksheet 1 and Worksheet 4 in this chapter).

Teachers using procedural phrases like "cancel" and "bring over" may find students demonstrating some of these errors (Martinez, 1988). Avoiding shortcuts like "cancelling" and "bringing over" in the early stages of teaching may prevent errors such as these:

- confusion between terms and factors, for example, $x + x^2 = x^3$, $\frac{a + b}{a} = 1 + b$, $-x - x = x^2$.
- confused interpretation of "bringing over", for example, $\frac{4}{x + y} = 1 \Rightarrow 4 = x - y$.

Students have long-held beliefs due to their engagement with arithmetic

Look at the case study below and identify the belief that causes the error.

Case study: Alan is a Secondary 1 Express student. His task is to write down the simplest form of several given expressions.

a. $4x + 7x + 3x$
b. $5c - 7c + 2c$
c. $4a - 6b - 3a$
d. $2c + 4d - 5d$

His answers for the four tasks are (a) $14x$, (b) $0c$, (c) $a - 6b = -5ab$, and (d) $2c - d = 1cd$.

What error pattern did Alan demonstrate?
Predict Alan's answers to this task: Simplify $4 + 3(5x - 1)$.

There are many algebraic situations where letters of the alphabet are used

This causes students to assign different meanings for letters used in algebraic expressions and equations, some of which are incorrect. In Küchemann's test (Küchemann worked on large-scale evaluation of 13- to 15-year-old students' mathematics performance in Britain), students' interpretations of letters in algebra are categorised into four types.

1. Letters evaluated
   Example: $a + 5 = 8$

2. Letters as an object
   Example: Let a be the number of apples.

3. Letters as a specific unknown
   Example: 4 is added to $3a$.

4. Letters as a variable
   Example: Which is larger, $2a$ or a^2?

Besides, students may have used letters as labels (e.g. Mr. X or Point A). Some students use letters as a digit holder. For example, they perceive $2x$ as 20-something. Such a student may incorrectly solve the equation $2x + 1 = 25$ as $24 + 1 = 25$ and, hence, $x = 4$.

LEARNING DIFFICULTIES

In this section, learning difficulties associated with the learning of algebra are described. An understanding of students' learning difficulties is helpful in planning instructional strategies to overcome these difficulties and to facilitate learning. Some of the learning difficulties are as follows.

Students are not familiar with the syntax of algebra

The syntax of algebra is not obvious and has to be learned through construction of meaning. Two approaches are suggested to prevent this learning difficulty. First, students should be provided with translation activities where they are required to translate verbal sentences into algebraic expressions/equations and vice-versa. For example:

- An apple cost x cents. An orange costs y cents more than an apple. What is the cost of 8 apples and 12 oranges?
- Make up a word problem that can be solved by solving the equation $2x - 5 = 6$.

Secondly, teachers should read algebraic expressions/equations using verbal language. For example, the equation $2x - 1 = 11$ should be read as "double a number and subtract one from the result give 11".

Translation of verbal language into equations is especially difficult when the language is inconsistent. Koay (1994) described some errors in translation of word problems into equations. She found that students have more difficulty when confronted with inconsistent language (Jack is five times as old as Mark. If Jack is x years old, how old is Mark?) than with consistent language (Jack is five times as old as Mark. If Mark is x years old, how old is Jack?).

Students are confused over the different uses of letters in algebra

Students should be exposed to different uses of algebra. Teachers should alert students when letters are used in ways different from that students already know.

In equations such as $2x - 5 = 6$, the letter is assigned a value that is to be evaluated. Students who use letters in this way tend to have difficulties in tasks where the letters cannot be evaluated. For example, some students tend to "solve" when asked to factorise an expression $x^2 - 9$. These students are likely to proceed to write $x^2 - 9 = 0$ before solving the quadratic equation.

Students also tend to treat letters as objects. Students with this thinking are able to complete tasks such as simplifying $2x + 3x$ but are likely to have difficulty with tasks such as "what is $x + 2$ multiplied by 3?". Students who treat letters as objects are also likely to make an error when asked to write an equation for the situation "for every teacher there are 35 students". They are likely to write $t = 35s$.

Students also may treat letters as a specific but unknown number. Such students have difficulty in understanding that a variable can take different values (e.g., $x + 2 < 10$) and different letters can take the same value (e.g. When is $x + 2a = x + 2b$?).

Students find algebra too abstract

Algebra is dominated by symbols. Teachers should provide more concrete approaches in the early stages of learning algebra. Three examples are given. First, algebra tiles is a standard concrete manipulative available commercially (see Appendix 2A). Secondly, the "area" model provides a concrete way to visualise some of the identities (see Worksheet 4 in this chapter). Thirdly, simple balance can be used to reinforce the idea of equality in solution of linear equations.

TEACHING APPROACHES

Use arithmetic as a bridge to algebra

By using arithmetic, students can explore sufficient specific cases to prepare them for the generalisation that algebra requires. Students in early stages of learning algebra should be given sufficient opportunities to explore and work on specific cases before making generalisations (see Worksheet 1).

Emphasise on making generalisations

In getting students to write algebraic expressions and equations, there are two categories of activities that teachers can do. One is to provide students with verbal information and require them to translate it into expressions and equations. This is common in Singapore textbooks. Another is to provide students with situations that require pattern observation (see Worksheet 2 and Worksheet 3 in this chapter). Observing a pattern is central to early algebra learning. Exploring patterns also help students develop general mathematical competence and an appreciation of the aesthetic qualities of mathematics. The typical structure of such activities include (1) students working on several specific case, (2) students using verbal language to suggest a generalisation, and (3) students using formal algebraic language to summarise the generalisation.

Emphasise understanding

Sometimes the focus of algebra is on the procedural manipulation at the expense of students understanding what they are doing. Worksheet 5 shows how students are encouraged to make sense when they solve algebraic equations.

Use concrete materials

In trying to help students understand, sometimes concrete or pictorial representations are necessary. Worksheet 4 shows how a paper-folding activity is used to help students see the reason behind common identities. Another common concrete material for algebra lessons is algebra tiles. Algebra tiles are simple squares and rectangles. An outline of the algebra tiles is included in Appendix 2A.

Emphasise links to the model method

When teaching students how to use algebraic equations to solve problems, show the use of the model method and algebraic equations as well as the links between the two.

Provide variety in drill-and-practice

Teachers should ensure variations in practice. Two variations are described here. Games can be used to provide students with practice. An example involving factorisation is included in Appendix 2B. Also, practice can be incorporated into open-ended tasks (see Worksheet 6 in this chapter). The advantage of open-ended tasks is that students are encouraged to be creative in generating multiple responses, generating responses in different categories and generating unusual responses.

Sample Activities for Students

WORKSHEET 1

Andy says that $(a + b)^2$ is the same value as $a^2 + b^2$.
Basri says that $(a + b)^2$ is more than $a^2 + b^2$.
Cherry says that $(a + b)^2$ is less than $a^2 + b^2$.

a. By trying out a few examples, decide who is most likely to be correct.

a	b	a^2	b^2	$a^2 + b^2$	$a + b$	$(a + b)^2$

b. Complete these sentences.

$(1 + 7)^2 = 1^2 + 7^2 + 2$ (____)

$(8 + 2)^2 = 8^2 + 2^2 + 2$ (____)

$(4 + 3)^2 = 4^2 + 3^2 + 2$ (____)

$(5 + 6)^2 = 5^2 + 6^2 + 2$ (____)

$(a + b)^2 = a^2 + b^2 + 2$ (____)

[Note: See also http://illuminations.nctm.org/tools/index.aspx.]

WORKSHEET 2

This is a pattern of a house.

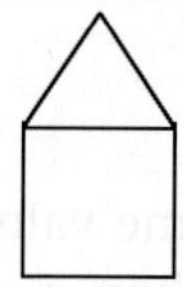

This is a pattern of two houses.

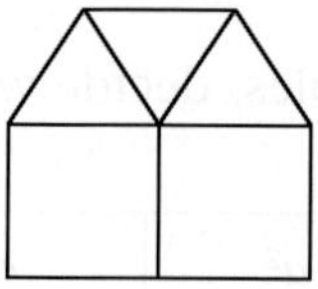

This is a pattern of three houses.

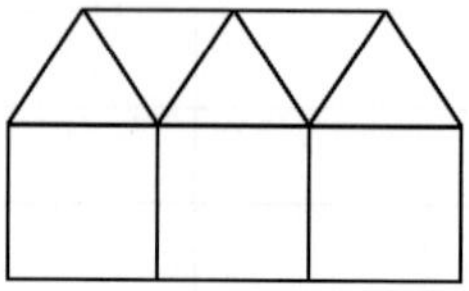

Complete the table.

Number of houses	Number of squares	Number of triangles	Number of pieces
1			
2			
3			
4			
5			
10			
20			
50			

Number of houses	**Number of squares**	**Number of triangles**	**Number of pieces**
a			
	b		
		c	
			d

WORKSHEET 3

Coins are arranged such that each row has one more coin than the previous row.

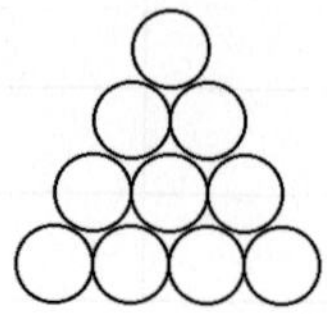

Complete the table.

Number of rows	Number of coins
1	
2	
3	
4	
5	
10	
n	

Explain what you would do to get the number of coins.

WORKSHEET 4

1. Use a piece of coloured paper.

Draw two lines such that you get two squares and two rectangles. The actual measurement does not matter.

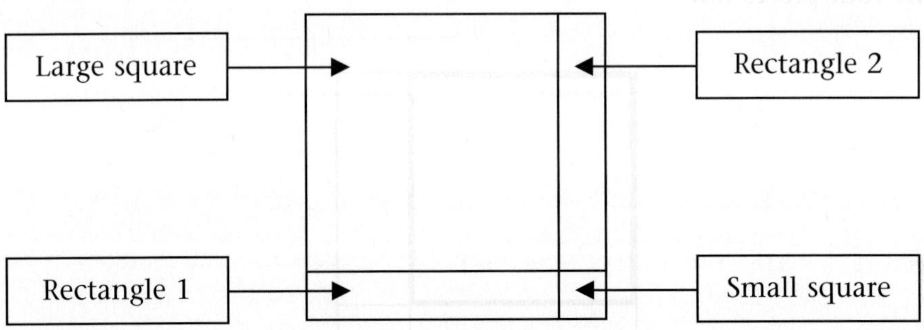

Let the large square have sides of length a units.

Let the small square have sides of length b units.

Label on your paper the length of all the sides of each of the four pieces.

Write down the length of the original square. ________________

Hence, write down its area. ________________

Complete the table.

Piece	Length of sides	Area
Whole square		
Large square		
Small square		
Rectangle 1		
Rectangle 2		

Bee Leng says that $a^2 + b^2$ is the same as $(a + b)^2$. Chelvi disagrees.

Use the squares and rectangles to explain whether Bee Leng or Chelvi is correct.

2. Cut the four pieces out.

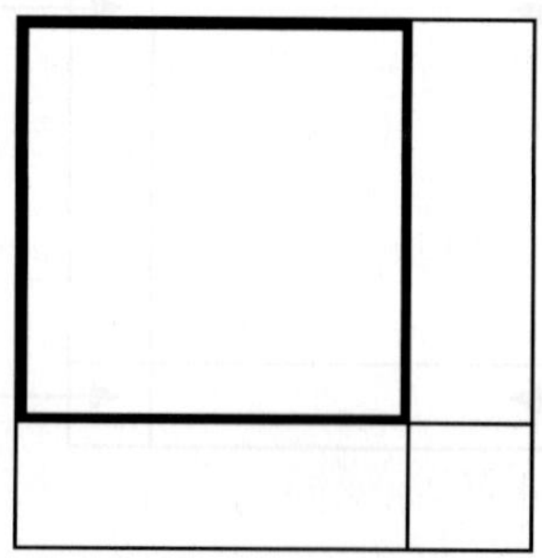

Place the small square over the large square.

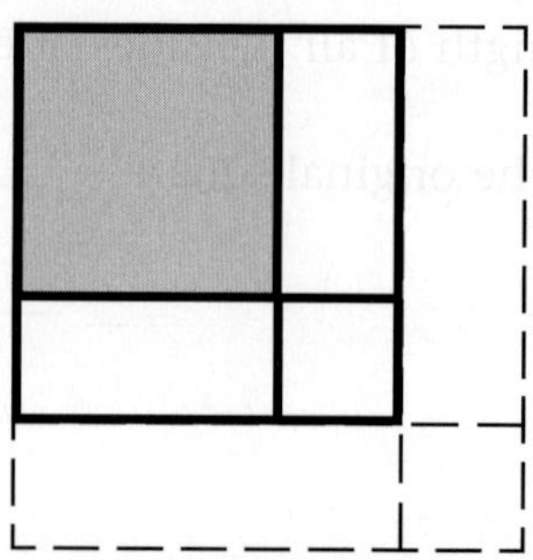

Mark out the square that is shaded.

What is the length of its sides? ________________

What is its area? ________________

Find this area in a different way.

First, find the area (A) of the square with sides a. ________________

Then, find the area (B) of the square with sides b. ________________

Finally, find the area (C) of the rectangle with sides a and b. ________________

David says that the area of the shaded square can be found by A – B.

Edward disagrees. He thinks that it is A – 2B.

Faridah thinks they are both wrong.

Who is probably correct? Show the correct method, giving your answers in terms of a and b.

3. Place the small square over the large square.

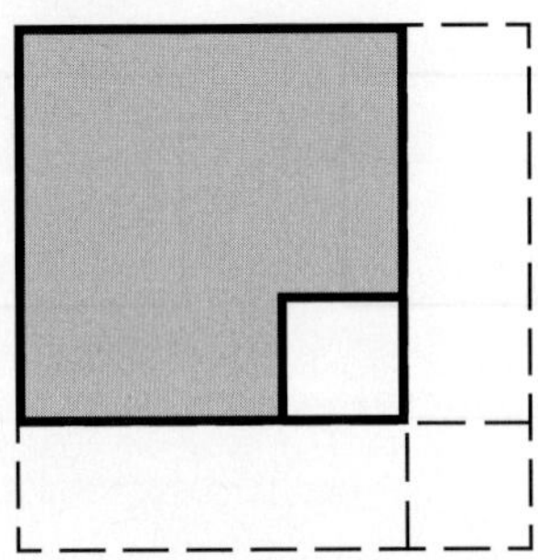

What is the area of the shaded region?

Area of the large square = ________________

Area of the small square = ________________

Area of shaded region = ________________

Cut and rearrange so that the shaded region forms a rectangle. Show how this is done on the sketch.

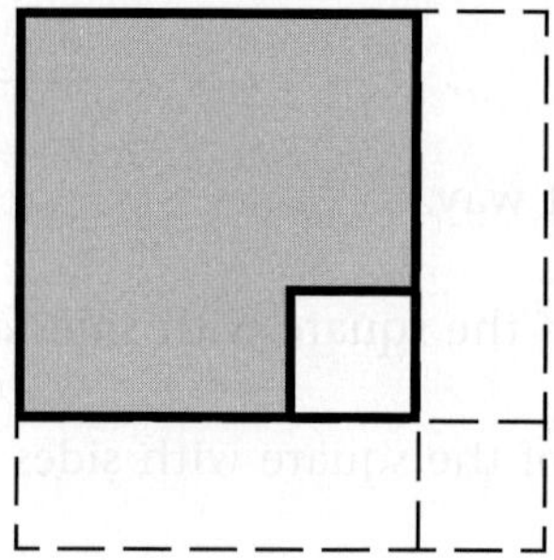

What is the length of this rectangle? ____________

What is the width of this rectangle? ____________

What is the area of this rectangle? ____________

Hence, show that $a^2 - b^2 = (a + b)(a - b)$.

In this lesson, you use what you already know – area of squares and rectangles – to convince yourself about the three important identities in algebra. What are these three identities? Write them here.

WORKSHEET 5

Solve $14 - \frac{15}{7 - x} = 9$.

1. What does it mean to "solve" an equation?

____.

2. What is the value of $\frac{15}{7 - x}$? ☐

3. What is the value of $7 - x$? ☐

4. What is the value of x? ☐

WORKSHEET 6

Write ten different equations where a solution is $x = 3$.

APPENDIX 2A: ALGEBRA TILES

APPENDIX 2B: GAME FOR FACTORISATION OF QUADRATIC FUNCTIONS

Row	Column	Top	Right	Bottom	Left
1	1	$x^2 - 6x + 9$	$(2x + 1)^2$	$(2x - 1)(3x + 1)$	$x^2 - x - 6$
1	2	$x^2 + x - 6$	$(x - 3)(x + 3)$	$(2x - 1)(x - 3)$	$x^2 - 4$
1	3	$x^2 + 5x + 6$		$x^2 + 9$	$4x^2 - 4x + 1$
1	4	$3x^2 + 2x - 1$	$(2x + 1)(2x - 1)$	$9x^2 + 1$	
2	1	$x^2 - 4x + 4$	$(x + 2)(x - 2)$	$(x - 3)^2$	$6x^2 + 5x + 1$
2	2		$(2x + 1)(x + 3)$	$(x - 2)(x + 3)$	$6x^2 - 5x + 1$
2	3	$3x^2 - 5x - 2$	$(2x - 1)^2$		$x^2 + 6x + 9$
2	4	$2x^2 - 7x + 3$	$(2x + 1)(3x - 1)$	$(x - 2)(3x + 1)$	$4x^2 + 4x + 1$
3	1	$x^2 + 4$	$(x + 2)^2$	$(x - 2)(x - 3)$	
3	2	$3x^2 - 7x + 2$		$(2x - 1)(x + 3)$	$x^2 - 9$
3	3	$2x^2 - 5x - 3$	$(x + 2)(x - 3)$	$(x + 1)(3x - 1)$	
3	4		$(2x - 1)(3x - 1)$	$(x - 2)^2$	$x^2 + 4x + 4$
4	1	$2x^2 + 5x - 3$		$(x + 2)(x + 3)$	$6x^2 + x - 1$
4	2	$4x^2 + 1$		$(x - 2)(3x - 1)$	$2x^2 + 7x + 3$
4	3	$6x^2 - x - 1$	$(x + 3)^2$		$4x^2 - 1$
4	4	$x^2 - 5x + 6$	$(2x + 1)(3x + 1)$	$(2x + 1)(x - 3)$	

Directions:

1. Cut out the squares.
2. Fit them together again so that the edges with quadratic functions touch the edges with corresponding factorisation.

FURTHER READING

Further readings on the model method and its links to algebra include:

Carter, J.A., Ferrucci, B.J., & Yeap, B.H. (2002). Developing algebraic thinking. *Mathematics Teaching, 178*, 39–41.

Ferrucci, B.J., Yeap, B.H., & Carter, J.A. (2003). A modeling approach for enhancing problem solving in the middle grades. *Mathematics Teaching in the Middle Grades, 8*(9), 470–475.

Fong, H.K. (1994). Bridging the gap between secondary and primary mathematics. *Teaching and Learning, 14*(2), 73–84.

Kho, T.H. (1987). Mathematical models for solving arithmetic problems. Proceedings of the Fourth Southeast Asian Conference on Mathematics Education, 345–351. Singapore: Institute of Education.

Yan, K.C. (2002). The model method in Singapore. *The Mathematics Educator, 6*(2), 47–64.

REFERENCES

Kieran, C. (1992). The learning and teaching of school algebra. In D.A. Grouws (Ed.), *Handbook of research on mathematics teaching and learning* (pp. 390–419). NY: Macmillan.

Koay, P.L. (1994). *Translation of word problems in algebra.* Paper presented at the Eighth Annual Conference of Educational Research Association, Singapore.

Lee, N.H., & Yeap, B.H. (2002). *Helping children develop algebraic thinking through word problems*. Workshop conducted at the 80th National Council of Teachers of Mathematics Annual Conference in Las Vegas, USA.

Martinez, J.G.R. (1988). Helping students understand factors and terms. *Mathematics Teacher, 81*(9), 747–751.

Mason, J., Graham, A, & Johnston-Wilder, S. (2005). *Developing thinking in algebra.* London: The Open University.

National Council of Teachers of Mathematics. (2002). *Principles and standards for school mathematics*. Reston, VA: National Council of Teachers of Mathematics.

Peck, D.M., & Jencks, S.M. (1988). Reality, arithmetic, algebra. *Journal of Mathematical Behaviour, 7*(1), 85–91.

Singapore Examinations and Assessment Board. (2006). PSLE examination questions 2001–2005 mathematics. Singapore: Hillview Publications.

Singapore Examinations and Assessment Board. (2007). PSLE examination questions 2002–2006 mathematics. Singapore: Singapore Asian Publications.

Toh, T. L. (2006). *Algebra resources for secondary school teachers.* Singapore: McGraw-Hill.

Usiskin, Z. (1988). Conceptions of school algebra and uses of variables. In A.F. Coxford & A.P. Shulte (Eds.), *The ideas of algebra, K-12* (1988 Yearbook) (pp. 8–19). Reston, VA: National Council of Teachers of Mathematics.

Wagner, S., & Parker, S. (1993). Advancing algebra. In P.S. Wilson (Ed.), *Research ideas for the classroom: High school mathematics*. NY: Macmillan.

Chapter 3

Teaching of Graphs

Chua Boon Liang and Ng Kit Ee Dawn

A graph is a pictorial representation of the relationship between two (or more) variables. The modern graph evolved from the work of the 17th-century French philosopher and scientist René Descartes. Also well versed in law and mathematics, one of Descartes' famous contributions to mathematics was the discovery of the Cartesian coordinates (named after him) which provided a system linking geometry to algebra, thereby allowing geometry problems to be solved by algebraic methods. A new branch of geometry, *analytical geometry*, thus emerged.

KEY CONCEPTS IN THE SINGAPORE MATHEMATICS SYLLABUS

In primary school, pupils learn about graphs mainly in statistics where they are taught how to read, interpret and solve problems involving pictograms, bar graphs, line graphs and pie charts. The Cartesian coordinates system is introduced in Secondary 1 for the Special and Express streams and in Secondary 2 for the Normal (Academic) and the Normal (Technical) streams, and students are shown the relationships between the equation of a graph and its pictorial representation.

Graphs of the following types of functions are included in the syllabus: linear, quadratic, cubic, reciprocal, inverse-square and exponential functions. Table 3–1 provides an overview of the Singapore mathematics syllabus on graphs (Ministry of Education, 2006). The fundamental concept of graphs must be firmly established because it will lead to a better understanding of processes such as solving equations by graphical method, as well as other advanced concepts, such as the relationships between the graphs of $y = f(x)$, $y^2 = f(x)$, and $y = |f(x)|$ which are covered in the GCE A-level syllabus.

Table 3-1 Mathematics syllabus for graph topics in Singapore secondary schools

Topics	Special/ Express	Normal (Academic)	Normal (Technical)
Cartesian coordinates in 2D	Sec 1	Sec 2	Sec 2
Graph of a set of ordered pairs	Sec 1	Sec 2	Sec 2
Linear relationships between two variables (linear functions)	Sec 1	Sec 2	Sec 2
Gradient of a linear graph as the ratio of the vertical change to the horizontal change (positive and negative gradients)	Sec 1	Sec 2	Sec 2
Graphs of linear equations in two unknowns	Sec 2	Sec 2	Sec 3/4
Solving simultaneous linear equations in two unknowns by graphical method	Sec 2	Sec 2	Sec 3/4
Graphs of quadratic functions and their properties	Sec 2	Sec 3/4	Sec 3/4
Sketching of graphs of quadratic functions given in the form $y = \pm(x - p)^2 + q$ $y = \pm(x - a)(x - b)$	Sec 3/4	Sec 3/4	
Solving quadratic equations in one unknown by graphical methods	Sec 3/4	Sec 3/4	
Graphs of functions of the form $y = ax^n$ ($n = -2, -1, 0, 1, 2, 3$) and simple sums of not more than three of these	Sec 3/4	Sec 3/4	
Graphs of exponential functions $y = ka^x$, a is a positive integer	Sec 3/4	Sec 3/4	
Estimation of gradients of curves by drawing tangents	Sec 3/4	Sec 3/4	
Interpretation and use of graphs in practical situations	Sec 3/4	Sec 3/4	
Drawing graphs from given data	Sec 3/4	Sec 3/4	
Distance-time and speed-time graphs	Sec 3/4	Sec 3/4	

COMMON ERRORS AND LEARNING DIFFICULTIES

Cartesian coordinates system

1. Plotting points with fractional and decimal coordinates such as $(1\frac{1}{2}, 3)$ and (3.5, 6.2) may be a challenge for some students. The position of a point may be plotted wrongly because some students cannot read off the scales of the axes.

2. Some students do not know how to *choose* appropriate scales for plotting graphs. They make poor estimations of the positions of the axes on the graph paper before actual plotting, resulting in a waste of time redrawing the graph when some of the points cannot fit onto the graph paper.

3. Some students have the following misconceptions about the choice of *axes* and *scales*:
   - The scales for *x*- and *y*-axes must be the same.
   - The axes must always intersect at (0, 0).
   - The intervals on each axis need not be equal.
   - Graphs showing the same data but using different scales are different.
   - Every graph must start from (0, 0) and is a straight line.

   They may also overlook the effect of different scales on the accuracy of data reading.

Graphs of functions of the form $y = ax^n$ ($n = -2, -1, 0, 1, 2, 3$)

1. The concept of *continuity* is not well understood. Kerslake (1981), in her research on children's understanding of graphs, found that many students have difficulty grasping the idea that there are many more points on the line other than those they had plotted. Students usually draw the graph of an algebraic equation after completing a table of values that shows the relationship between variables *x* and *y*. They may think that the points on the graph are the only ones given in the table, unaware that the graph can be extended continuously and that there is an infinite number of points lying on the graph, not only the ones they have plotted.

2. Some students have a poor grasp of the concept of gradient, which is a *ratio* of the vertical distance to the horizontal distance. They do not understand the effect of a change in one of the distances on the gradient. In addition, many also fail to realise that the gradient of a straight line is constant throughout the line – a crucial difference between a straight line and a curve.

3. Many students do not seem to know how to find the *x*- and *y*-intercepts from a given equation. They have difficulty understanding that the *y*-intercept of a graph can be determined by substituting $x = 0$ into the equation, and that, similarly, the *x*-intercept is the point where the *y*-coordinate = 0.

4. Some are unable to visualise graphs from given equations. Others have problems deriving equations from given graphs. As Kerslake discovered in her research, "there appears to be a large gap between the relatively simple reading of information from a graph and the appreciation of an *algebraic relationship*". A distinction between graphs with purposes of disseminating information (i.e. statistical diagrams) and algebraic graphs should be made clear because "while many children will be able to read information from a graph or to plot given data, it seems that only a few will be able to understand the connection between an equation and a graph" (Kerslake, 1981, p. 135).

5. When asked to draw curves, some students produce poor quality graphs – graphs that are thickly shaded or disjointed. Some even simply join the plotted points with straight line segments, creating curves that are not smooth.

6. For quadratic graphs with two values of *x* for every value of *y*, except at the origin, some students often miss out one of the values when reading from graphs.

7. Many students have difficulties drawing the tangent to a curve at a given point.

Graphs in practical situations

1. The first assumption made by students when *visualising* a graph representing a given scenario is to think of straight line segments (Bell, Brekke, and Swan, 1987a, p. 58). *When they do think about curves, many have problems deciding if it should be concave upwards or downwards.*

   The following graphs, relating the height (*H*) and volume (*V*) of water in a container as water is poured into it, testify to this fact.

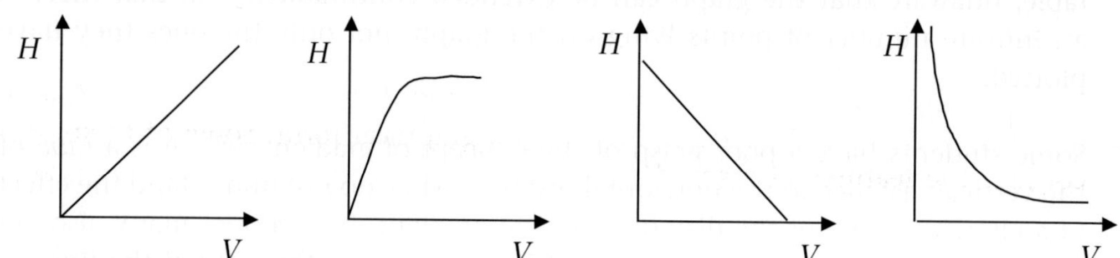

(i) (ii) (iii) (iv)

Get students to work on the following two tasks to get a sense of the learning difficulties they may face.

a. Sketch the two containers best described by (i) and (ii) if water is poured in at a constant rate.
b. Describe the scenarios represented by (iii) and (iv).

2. When interpreting graphs, certain students have poor ability in *coordinating information* relating the two variables on the axes. A good example is given by Bell, Brekke, and Swan (1987b, p. 50).

3. Some students see travel graphs as *a picture of a situation* (Bell et al., 1987a, p. 56). Such a perception may lead to poor interpretation of the context presented by the graph. For instance, students interpret a line slanting upwards from left to right in a distance-time graph as an object going up a slope, and a horizontal line as the object moving on level ground when in fact the object is travelling at a constant speed in the first situation and is stationary in the latter.

4. The visual appearance of certain graphs can be misleading to students. For instance, the following distance-time graph of an object thrown vertically upwards may be interpreted as throwing the object from one person to another.

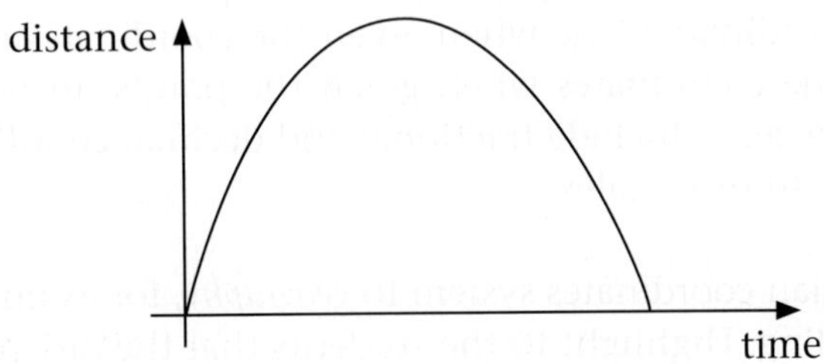

5. Some students are unable to recognise whether the distance in a distance-time graph is referring to the distance from a starting point (that is, displacement) or the total distance travelled. Some even think that the distance travelled is indicated by the horizontal spread of the graph or the length of the graph. Many students also find distance-time graphs confusing when they involve two or more objects travelling from different starting points.

6. Students find it difficult to draw speed-time graphs because they cannot visualise the speed at which they are travelling in a graphical form. Some of them also confuse the features of a speed-time graph with that of a distance-time graph. For instance, an upward slope in a speed-time graph indicates that an object is accelerating (that is, speed is increasing), whereas a similar slope in a distance-time graph shows the object moving at a constant speed.

TEACHING APPROACHES

Cartesian coordinates system

1. Introduce and explain the common terminology used in the topic of graphs. For instance, the word "axes" refers to the horizontal and vertical number lines (rather than the plural form of the tool used for chopping wood).

2. Use the idea of locating objects in daily life to introduce the notion of ordered pairs. For instance, (a) using a class seating plan arranged in rows and columns, get students to locate the position of a fellow classmate, and (b) using a map taken from the street directory, get students to state the location of a building on it. Thereafter, relate this concrete experience to a 2-D representation on graph paper, using the Cartesian coordinates system.

3. Use the *geoboard* to demonstrate how the Cartesian coordinates system works. For instance, use rubber bands to form the horizontal and vertical axes, and then mark the point of origin. Select points on the *geoboard* and get students to write down their coordinates. *Conversely*, have students identify the points when given the coordinates. To relate this concrete experience to the coordinates system represented on a piece of graph paper, provide opportunities for students to locate points on the coordinate plane when given the coordinates (p, q), and similarly, to write down the coordinates when given the points, in particular, the origin and points on the axes. Include fractional and decimal coordinates to check that students are able to read scales.

4. Relate the Cartesian coordinates system to *geography*, for example, map, longitude and latitude reading. Highlight to the students that the ordered pair in Cartesian coordinates represents the intersection point between a vertical line extended from the x-axis and a horizontal line extended from the y-axis. This shows that the point is x units away from the y-axis and y units up or down from the x-axis.

5. Emphasise the importance of the order in which the coordinates are written. For instance, ask students to explain whether (3, 5) and (5, 3) refer to the same point on the coordinate plane.

Drawing a graph

1. Demonstrate the procedures of drawing a graph step-by-step. Provide sufficient time for students to follow each step.

2. Get students to interpret and then state that the pairs of corresponding numbers in the table of values are solutions of the equation of the graph to be drawn. For instance, since the pair of numbers, $x = 1$ and $y = 0$, satisfies the equation $y = x - 1$, it is called a solution of the equation. Also, show them that the solutions can be written as ordered pairs [e.g. (1, 0)].

3. Stress the continuous nature of graphs (i.e. the line or curve represents an infinite set of points although in practice we only plot some points, then join them up to get the graph). To convince students about the legitimacy of connecting some points to produce the graph, teachers can justify the procedure by getting them to plot as many intermediate points as is necessary.

4. Emphasise the following points when getting students to draw graphs:
   - Use a sharp pencil.
   - Label both axes clearly.
   - Use the prescribed scale given in the question, or else choose an appropriate scale if it is not given. In the latter case, the graph should be big enough to cover at least two-thirds of the graph paper.
   - Indicate the scale for both axes clearly.
   - Mark the points neatly with small crosses.
   - Use a curve rule (also known as the *flexicurve*) or French curve to draw a smooth graph (not disjointed, frayed or jagged) through all the plotted points. Discourage free-hand drawing.
   - Highlight that the lowest or highest point plotted may not necessarily be the minimum or maximum turning point of the graph.
   - Label the graph by writing its equation next to it.

Graphs of functions of the form $y = ax^n$ ($n = -2, -1, 0, 1, 2, 3$)

1. Introduce the concept of gradient of a linear graph through practical activities. Anderson and Nelson (1994) suggested getting students to calculate the steepness of steps, handrails and ramps by finding the ratio of the vertical distance to the horizontal distance. Also, get them to predict the effect of changing the vertical distance while retaining the horizontal distance on the gradient, and vice-versa.

2. Guide students to realise that the gradient of a linear graph is the amount of change in y for every 1 unit change in x.

3. Use an investigative approach to help students explore the nature of gradients. For instance, allow them to use an appropriate graphing software to examine the gradients of lines slanting from (a) bottom-left to top-right, and (b) top-left to

bottom-right of the coordinate plane. Include parallel lines for them to realise that they have the same gradients. Also, encourage them to predict the gradients of horizontal and vertical lines.

4. Teach students how to draw, as accurately as possible, the tangent to a curve at a point when they are asked to calculate the gradient of the curve at that point.

5. Get students to compare the difference between the gradient of a line and that of a curve. Let them find out that the gradient of a curve, unlike that of a line, is not constant throughout the curve. It actually varies from point to point.

6. Discuss the key features of the different graphs with students. For instance, the graph of a quadratic function is symmetrical and the graph of $y = \frac{a}{x}$ comprises two identical portions that do not touch the x- and y-axes.

7. Sketching graphs of quadratic functions given in the form $y = \pm(x - p)^2 + q$ or $y = \pm(x - a)(x - b)$ was previously covered in Additional Mathematics, but is now included in the Mathematics syllabus at the GCE O-level. Explain to students that sketching a graph is not the same as drawing a graph. Outline the following steps when getting students to sketch these quadratic graphs:
   - Determine the shape of the graph from the coefficient of x^2.
   - Find the coordinates of the turning point.
   - Find the coordinates of the points where the graph cuts the x-axis and y-axis.

8. Help students to develop a relational understanding of solving equations by graphical method, rather than by just teaching the procedures mechanically.

Graphs in practical situations

1. Highlight the importance of graphs in real life by getting students to perform simple experiments to collect and portray data using graphs. For instance, students can be asked to fill a beaker with boiling water and then record its temperature in °C every 20 seconds. Plot a graph showing temperature of water in °C against time in seconds.

   A motion detector such as CBR-TI can also be used to plot the graph depicting the motion of an object. (You may need to install the ranger program into a TI calculator.)

2. Relate graphs to students' daily lives. For instance, students can be asked to draw a graph to show the relation between the amount of water consumed and the water charges based on the information given in the table below:

	Amount of water consumed (in cubic metres)	Water charges (in cents per cubic metres)
For domestic consumption	1 to 40	117
	Above 40	140

Source: http://www.pub.gov.sg, 14 February 2007.

This activity also allows teachers to integrate National Education into the lesson to discuss about the importance of water conservation in Singapore.

3. Provide opportunities for students to read and interpret graphs. For instance, ask them to tell a story from a distance-time graph or sketch the graph of a given scenario. A useful resource for interpreting graphs is "The Language of Functions and Graphs", a box of teaching materials developed in 1985 by the Shell Centre for Mathematical Education, University of Nottingham.

4. When teaching travel graphs, use a graph whose shape conflicts with the motion to emphasise the point that graphs are not pictures of situation. In fact, they show the relationship between variables given a particular situation. For instance, Figure 3-1(a) shows the actual movement of a jogger running at a constant speed along a track and Figure 3-1(b) is the jogger's speed-time graph.

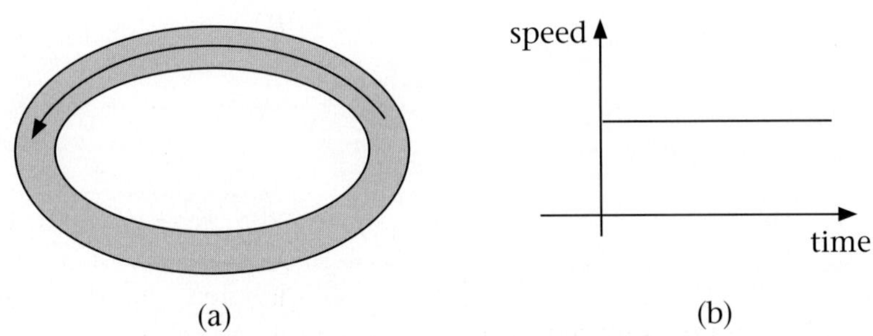

Figure 3-1 Movement and graph of a jogger

5. Distinguish the two types of distance-time graph. One type is where distance refers to the total distance travelled while the other refers to displacement (that is, distance measured from a starting point).

6. Have students to compare and contrast the features of a distance-time graph and a speed-time graph (see Table 3-2). For instance, a horizontal line in a distance-time graph signifies a stationary object whereas a similar line in a speed-time graph shows the object travelling at a constant speed. In addition, the area under a speed-time graph indicates the distance travelled but that of a distance-time graph is of no significant meaning.

Table 3-2 Comparison between distance-time graph and speed-time graph

	Distance-time graph	**Speed-time graph**
Gradient	speed	acceleration
Positive		
Zero	No speed. Object is stationary	Object is travelling at constant speed
Negative		
Area under graph	No significant meaning	Distance travelled

Sample Activities for Teachers

1. The word "graph" appears twice in the question below. What does it refer to in each case?

   The diagram shows the *graph* of $y = x - 1$.

   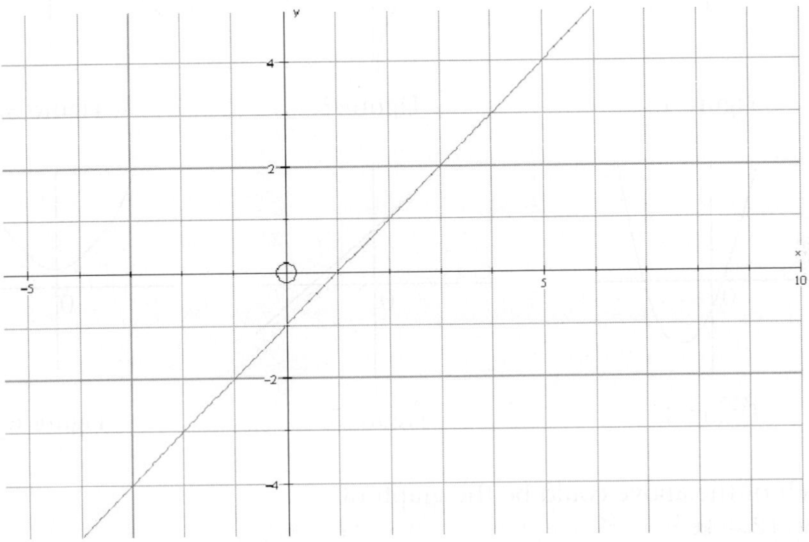

   Solve the following simultaneous equations by drawing another line on the *graph*.

$$y = x - 1$$
$$2x - y = 2$$

2. Describe how you will draw the following lines on graph paper without having to find their equations:
   a. a line with gradient 3 and passing through (–1, 2),
   b. a line with gradient –2 and passing through (3, 1),
   c. a line with gradient 2 and y-intercept 1.

3. Illustrating with examples, explain the difference between *sketching* a graph and *drawing* a graph by discussing the expectations in each case.

4. Describe how you will teach students to handle the following question on matching graphs with their equations.

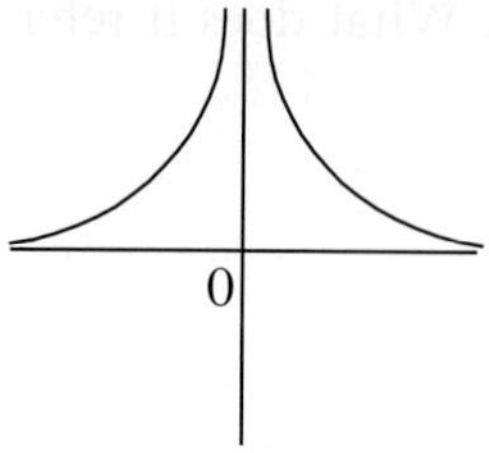

Figure 1

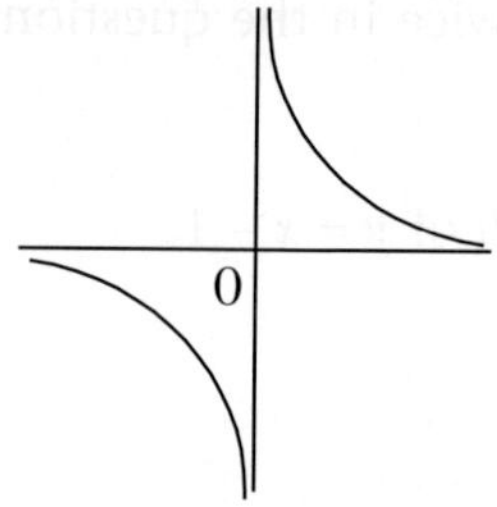

Figure 2

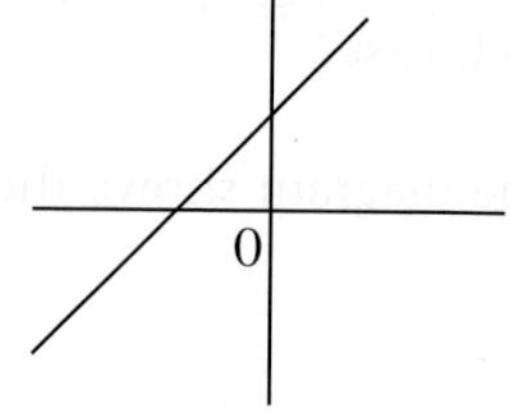

Figure 3

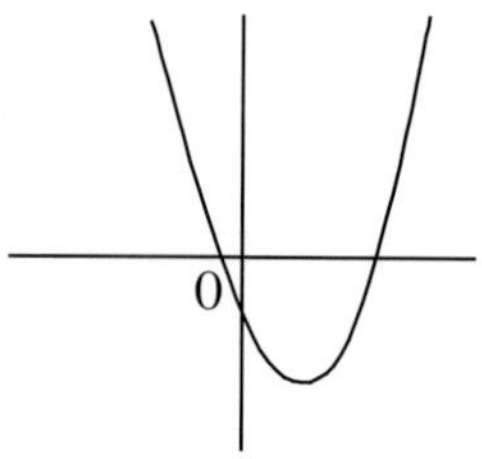

Figure 4

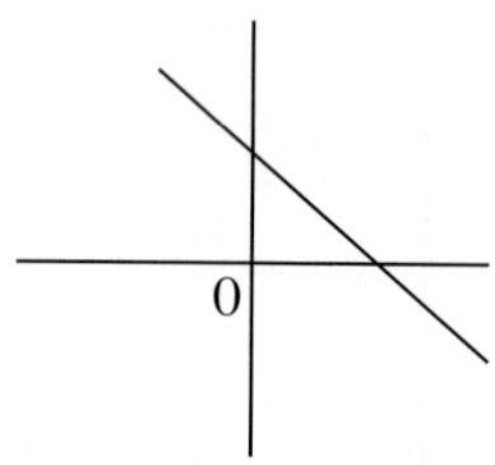

Figure 5

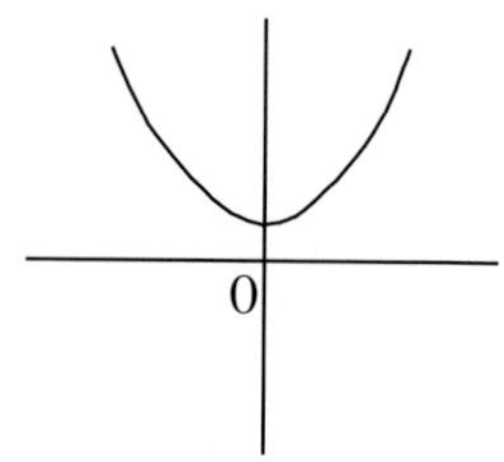

Figure 6

Which of the above could be the graph of

a. $y = 2 - 3x$

b. $y = \dfrac{1}{x^2}$

c. $y = x^2 - 2x - 3$?

5. Describe how you will teach students the technique of drawing, as accurately as possible, the tangent to a curve at a given point.

6. Design a task to hone students' ability to coordinate information relating any two variables on the two axes. You may refer to the article by Bell et al. (1987b) for some examples.

7. Design an activity that allows students to gain physical experience of collecting data and then plotting the distance-time graph. What problems do you think students will encounter in such an activity? How would you help them overcome these problems?

8. Discuss how realistic the following graphs are in representing the motion of vehicles. Diagram (a) is the speed-time graph of a car which starts from rest. Diagram (b) is the speed-time graph of a train over a period of 90 seconds, at the end of which it comes to rest.

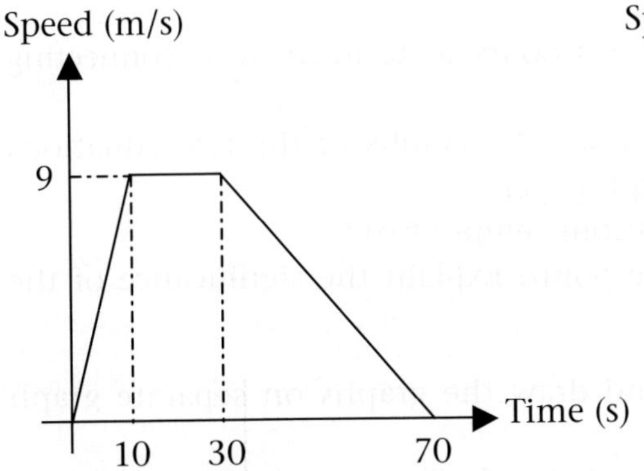

(a)

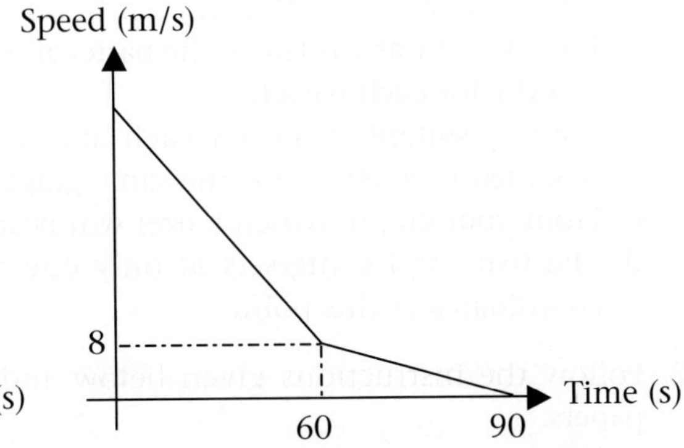

(b)

Sample Activities for Students

1. Barrel A contains 180 litres of water. Water leaks from a small hole at a rate of 15 litres per hour. Barrel B contains 165 litres of water, which also leaks from a small hole at a rate of 10 litres per hour.
   a. If y litres of water is left in the barrel after x hours, write an equation connecting x and y for each barrel.
   b. Using a suitable scale for each axis, draw the graphs of the two equations obtained in a. above on the same graph paper.
   c. From your graph, which barrel will become empty first?
   d. The two graphs intersect at only one point. Explain the significance of the coordinates of this point.

2. Follow the instructions given below and draw the graphs on separate graph papers.
   a. Using a scale of 2 cm to represent 1 unit for the horizontal axis and a scale of 1 cm to represent 1 unit for the vertical axis, draw the axes for –2 ″ x ″ 3 and –6 ″ y ″ 6 on a piece of graph paper. Mark the point (0, –1) with a cross. Starting at this point, move 1 unit to the right, then 2 units up and mark the point with a cross. Next, move 1 unit to the right of the second point, then 2 units up and mark the third point. Repeat this process another time to mark the fourth point. Now go back to the starting point and repeat this process by moving 1 unit to the left, then 2 units down and mark the fifth point. Repeat another time to locate the sixth point. Draw a graph through all the six points.
      i. What is the special name for this type of graph?
      ii. Find its equation.

   b. Using a scale of 2 cm to represent 1 unit for the horizontal axis and a scale of 1 cm to represent 1 unit for the vertical axis, draw the axes for –4 ″ x ″ 4 and 0 ″ y ″ 18 on a piece of graph paper. Mark the origin with a cross. Starting at the origin, move 1 unit each time to the right, then 1 unit up and mark the point with a cross, then 3 units up and mark the third point, then 5 units up and mark the fourth point, then 7 units up and mark the fifth point. Now go back to the starting point and repeat this process by moving 1 unit at a time to the left this time round to obtain four more points. Draw a graph through all the nine points.
      i. What is the special name for this type of graph?
      ii. Find its equation.
      [Part 2b. is adapted from Sobel M.A. and Maletsky E.M. (1999) *Teaching Mathematics, A Sourcebook of Aids, Activities and Strategies*. (3rd ed.). Boston: Allyn & Bacon.]

3. a. Sketch the graphs of the following equations on separate axes:

   i. $y = x$, ii. $y = \frac{1}{x}$, iii. $y = x^2$, iv. $y = \frac{1}{x^2}$

   b. By comparing graphs, state the differences between i. $y = x$ and $y = \frac{1}{x}$, and ii. $y = x^2$ and $y = \frac{1}{x^2}$

   c. Using the graphs you sketched in a., state the number of real solutions for each of the following equations:

   i. $x = \frac{1}{x}$, ii. $\frac{1}{x} - x^2 = 0$, iii. $x^2 - \frac{1}{x^2} = 0$

   [Part c. is not in the syllabus, but it is included here as a higher-order thinking question to challenge the more able pupils.]

4. a. Match each of the graphs below with one of the following equations.

   $y = -x$ $\quad$ $y = a^x$ $\quad$ $y = bx^{-1}$ $\quad$ $y = -x^2 + cx - 3$

   $y = d - (x + 1)^2$

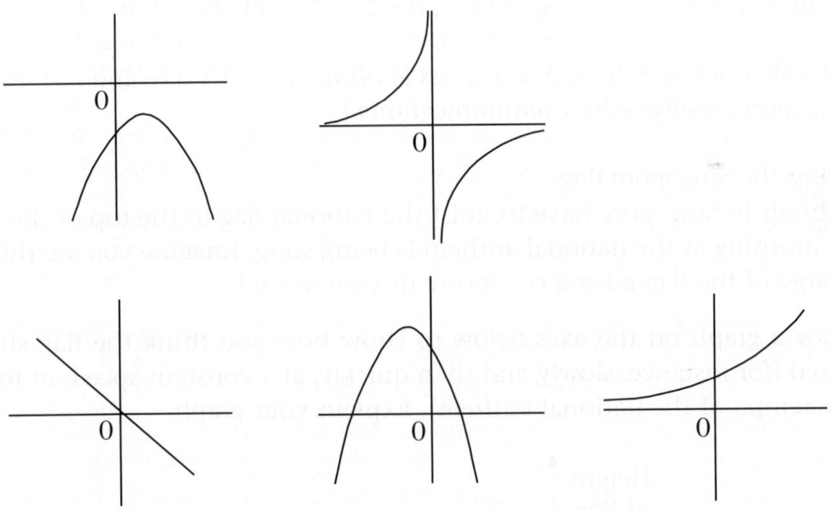

   b. State a possible value for each a, b, c and d.

5. a. Draw the distance-time graph of Yew Meng based on the scenario given below.

   Yew Meng walks at a steady speed of 4 m/s along a level road for 20 seconds. Continuing at the same walking speed, he then walks up a slope for 25 seconds, takes a rest for 10 seconds before walking down another slope for 15 seconds.

   b. Compare and discuss your graph with your friend's.
   [A note for teachers: Look out for common errors and discuss them with students.]

6. a. Using a suitable graphing software, explore the graphs of $y = ka^x$, where k is a non-zero constant, and
   i. $a > 1$, ii. $a = 1$, iii. $0 < a < 1$.

   b. Using a suitable graphing software, explore the graphs of the form $y = \frac{a}{x^m} + bx^n$, where m and n are positive integers, and a and b are non-zero constants. Sketch the graphs of this form when
   i. $m = 1, n = 1$ ii. $m = 1, n = 2$ iii. $m = 2, n = 1$
   iv. $m = 2, n = 2$ v. $m = 3, n = 1$ vi. $m = 2, n = 3$
   [Part 6b. is adapted from *New Express Mathematics 3*, P.Y. Lee and L.H. Fan (Eds.). Singapore: Multimedia Communications.]

7. Hoisting the Singapore flag
   All schools in Singapore have to hoist the national flag to the top of the flagpole every morning as the national anthem is being sung. Imagine you are the prefect in charge of the flag-raising ceremony in your school.

   a. Draw a graph on the axes below to show how you think the flag should be raised (for instance, slowly and then quickly, at a constant speed, or following the tempo of the national anthem). Explain your graph.

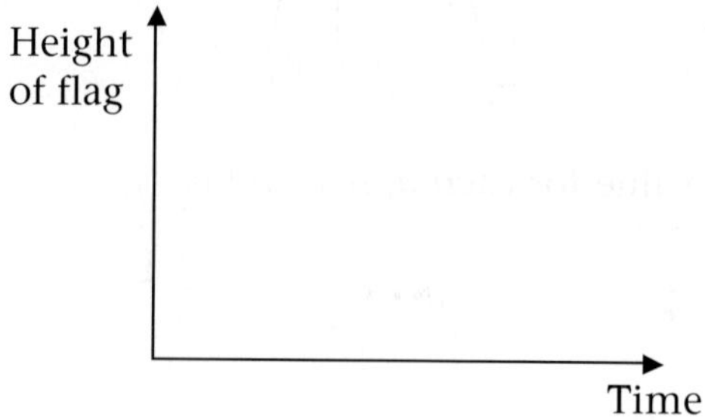

b. Discuss some of the flag-raising procedures and the significance of the flag-raising ceremony with your teacher.

c. Look at the graphs of your friends. Copy three different graphs on the axes below:

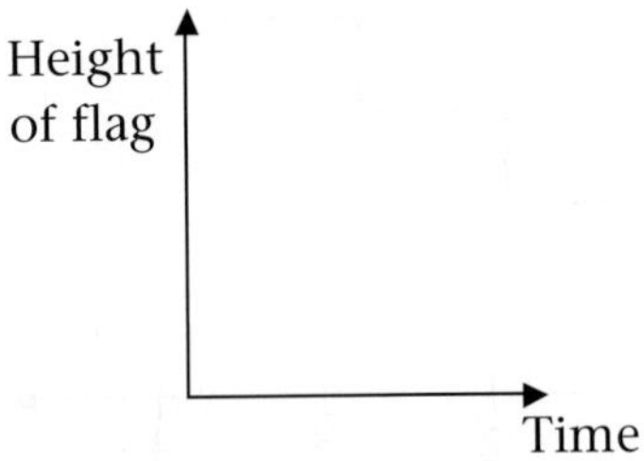

Graph of friend A

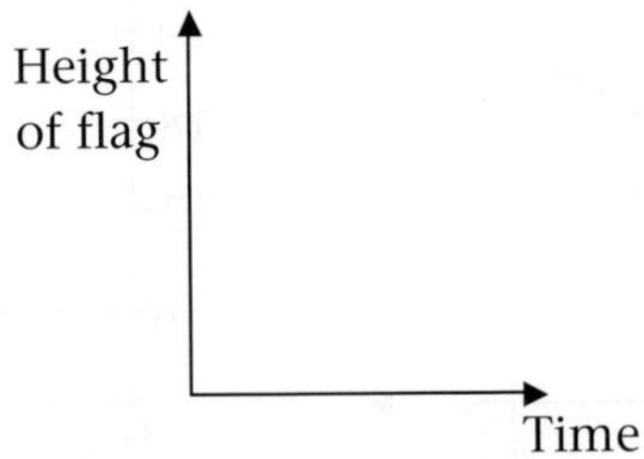

Graph of friend B

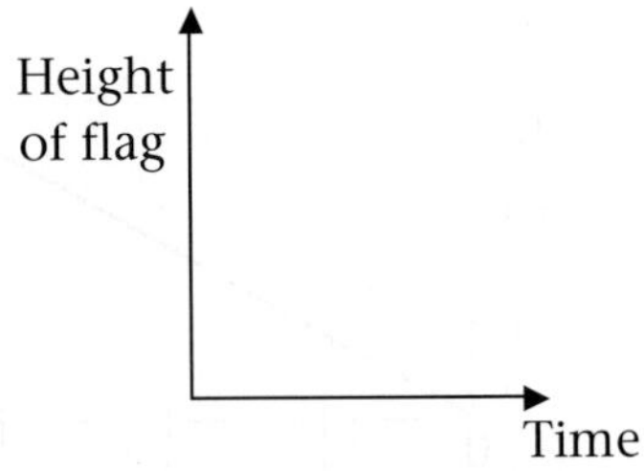

Graph of friend C

How do your three friends propose they raise their flags? Write down what you think they have in mind just by looking at their graphs.

d. Discuss whether the graphs are realistic in showing the motion of the flag when it is being raised.

8. Having fun at East Coast Park
Class 4B went for an outing at the East Coast Park after their GCE O-levels. They saw the following advertisements.

a. Match the graphs below with each advertisement.

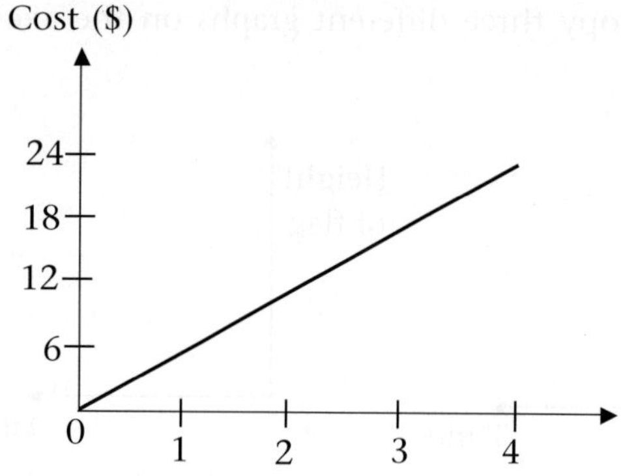

i.

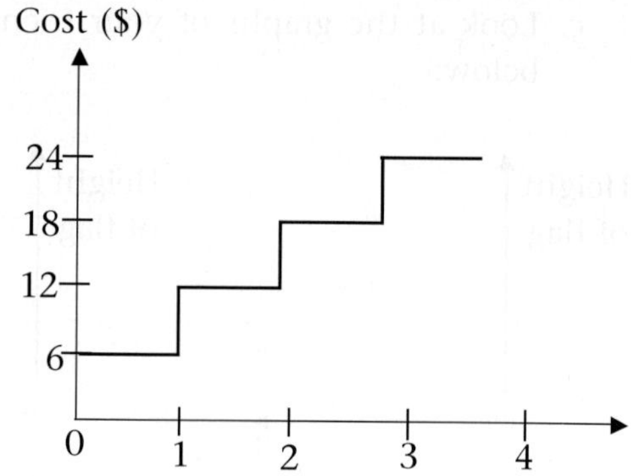

ii.

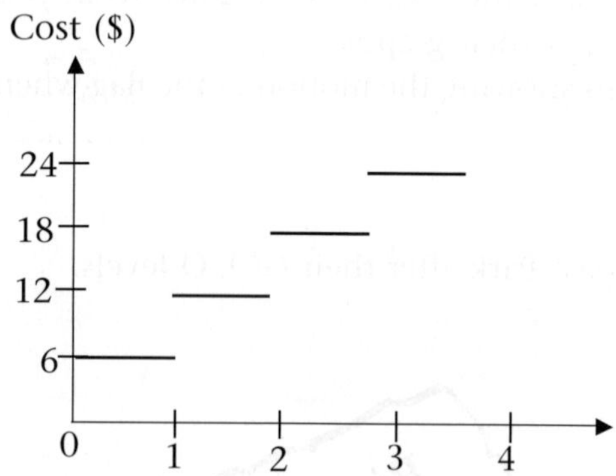

iii.

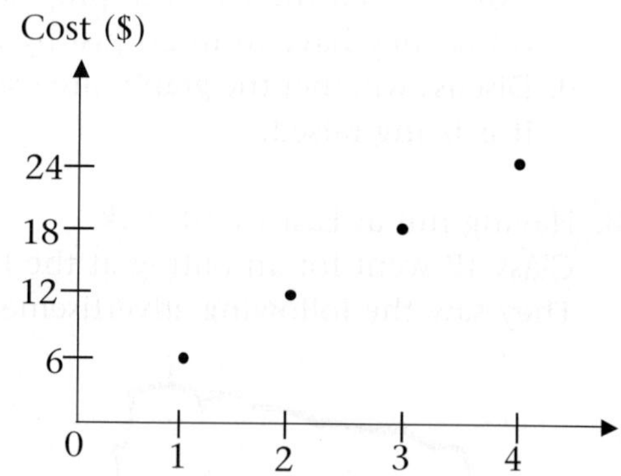

iv.

b. Why do you think the fourth graph is unaccounted for?
Can you think of a suitable story for the graph?

9. Below are nine speed-time graphs of different objects moving over a period of time.
   a. Which of the nine graphs shows each of the following two situations? Explain how you reached your decision.
      i. A car moved at a constant speed, then suddenly crashed into a tree and came to a stop.
      ii. John climbed up the stairs of a building at a constant speed, slowed down, rested for a while and then took a lift down the building.

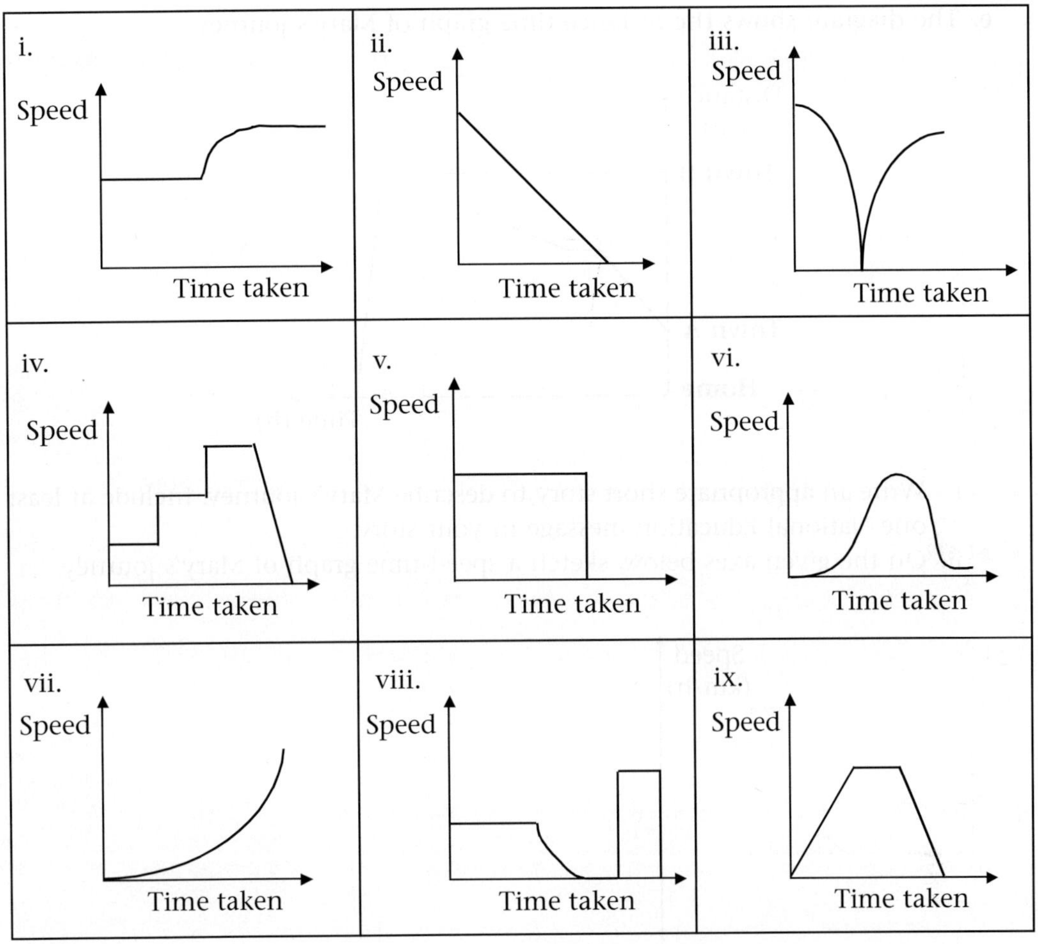

b. If you think that none of the graphs represents any of the two situations, draw your own graphs to depict the situations described in a. above.
c. Write appropriate scenarios for the remaining graphs.
d. How should the speed-time graph of a person on a roller coaster ride look like? Draw it in the axes below. Also, provide a sketch of your roller coaster next to the graph.

e. The diagram shows the distance-time graph of Mary's journey.

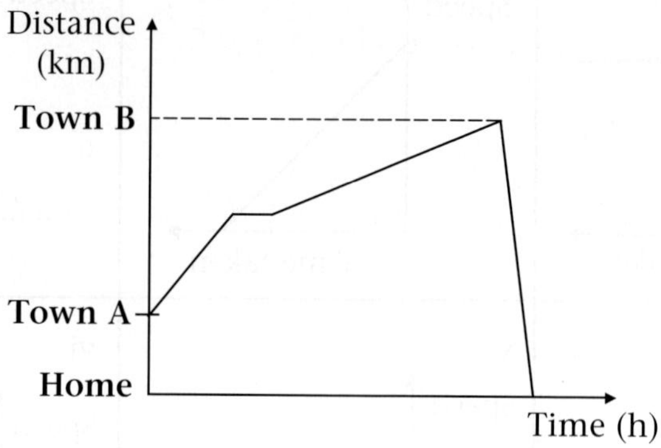

i. Write an appropriate short story to describe Mary's journey. Include at least one National Education message in your story.
ii. On the given axes below, sketch a speed-time graph of Mary's journey.

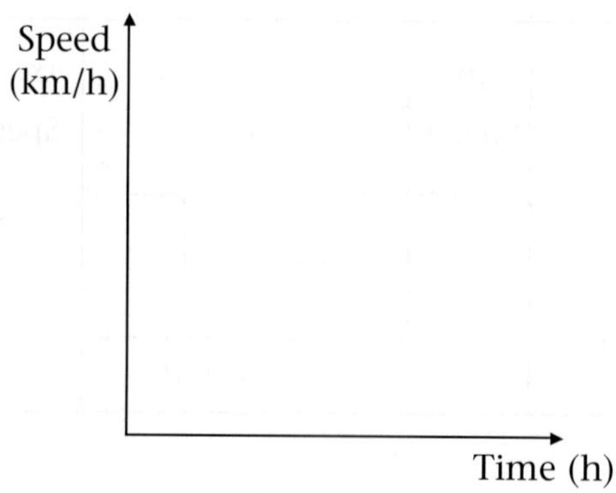

GRAPHMATIC WORKSHEET ON EQUATION OF A STRAIGHT LINE

Objectives:
By the end of the lesson, students should be able to:

1. *compare* the slopes of straight line graphs;
2. *state* the equations of straight line graphs given the gradient and y-intercept;
3. *state* the equations of lines parallel to a given straight line graph; and
4. *sketch* straight line graphs given equations in the form: $y = mx + c$.

Prerequisite concepts:

1. Slope
2. Parallel lines
3. Equation of straight line graphs in the form: $y = mx + c$.

Basic instructions for use of Graphmatica program:

1. Click on the *Graphmatica* icon. Maximise the screen.
2. To `change colour of graph paper` to white — click `options > graph paper > colors > background > white`.
3. To `draw graphs` — type in equations of graphs and then click `enter`.
4. To `change the colours of graphs` on the same piece of graph paper — click `options > graph paper > colors > graph 1`, choose corresponding colour, then `graph 2`, choose corresponding colour, and so on. Press `OK` when you are satisfied.
5. To `change grid range` (i.e. scale) of graph — click `view`, `grid range` and then adjust the desired range of values for your axes.
6. To `label graphs` — click on `edit > annotations`. Type in the equation of the graph and place it next to your graph. To delete your label, click on `edit > annotations`, select the equation of the graph to delete, and then choose `delete`.
7. To `clear screen` — go to `view`, then select `clear screen`.

Part I: Comparing positive slopes

On the *same piece of graph paper*, draw and label the graphs of:

- $y = \frac{1}{4}x + 3$
- $y = \frac{1}{3}x + 3$
- $y = \frac{1}{2}x + 3$
- $y = x + 3$
- $y = 2x + 3$
- $y = 3x + 3$
- $y = 4x + 3$
- $y = 5x + 3$

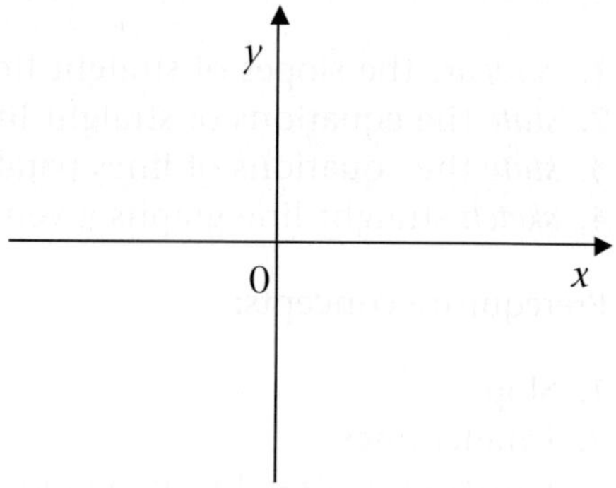

You may wish to adjust the grid range and the colours of your graphs so that everything can be seen within your screen. Copy the screen output in the grid provided.

a. All the equations listed above produce graphs which are sloping upwards/downwards *(delete accordingly)* from left to right.

b. Compare and contrast the graphs:

What are the similarities you have noticed about all the graphs? List as many as you can.	What are the differences you have noticed about some of the graphs?

c. Which graph has the steepest slope? m = ____________________
How do you know?

____

____

d. Without drawing the graph of $y = 8x + 3$, decide if this graph will be steeper or gentler (*delete accordingly*) than your chosen graph in part c.
Why?

____

____

e. Explore three other graphs of $y = mx + c$ by substituting different positive values of m. Try fractions and decimals. Keep the value of c fixed.

- Take m to be from ________ to ________ and c to be fixed at ________.
- Sketch the graphs on the grid provided and write down what you have noticed about the graphs.

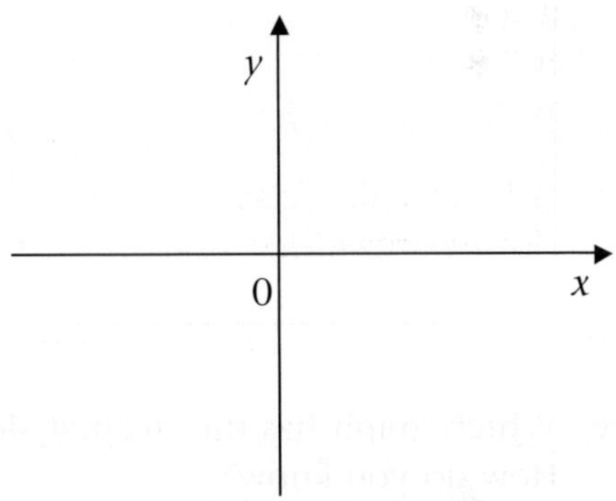

Part II: Comparing negative slopes

Clear the screen. On the *same piece of graph paper,* draw and label the graphs of:

- $y = -\frac{1}{4}x + 3$
- $y = -\frac{1}{3}x + 3$
- $y = -\frac{1}{2}x + 3$
- $y = -x + 3$
- $y = -2x + 3$
- $y = -3x + 3$
- $y = -4x + 3$
- $y = -5x + 3$

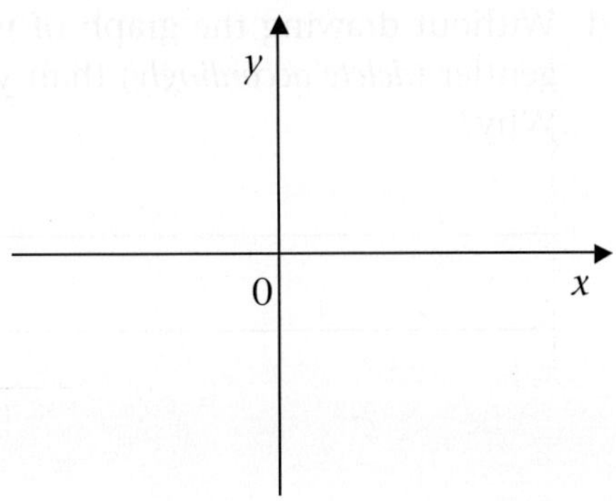

Copy the screen output in the grid provided.

a. All the equations listed above produce graphs which are sloping upwards/downwards (*delete accordingly*) from left to right.

b. Compare and contrast the graphs:

What are the similarities you have noticed about all the graphs? List as many as you can.	What are the differences you have noticed about some of the graphs?

c. Which graph has the steepest slope? $m =$ ____________
How do you know?

____

____

d. Without drawing the graph of $y = -10x + 3$, decide if this graph will be steeper/gentler (*delete accordingly*) than your chosen graph in part c.
Why?

____

____

e. Can you guess what the graphs of $y = mx + c$ will look like when $m = 0$? Why? Try plotting the graphs using Graphmatica for different values of c, keeping $m = 0$.

____

____

Graphs of equation $y = mx + c$ with $m = 0$ are expressed as $y = c$ where c is a constant term. These graphs are ________________ straight lines.

Go through Parts I and II with your teacher.

Part III: Parallel lines and y-intercepts

Clear the screen. On the *same piece of graph paper,* draw and label the graphs of:

- $y = 2x + \frac{1}{4}$
- $y = 2x + \frac{1}{3}$
- $y = 2x + \frac{1}{2}$
- $y = 2x$
- $y = 2x + 1$
- $y = 2x + 2$
- $y = 2x + 3$
- $y = 2x + 4$

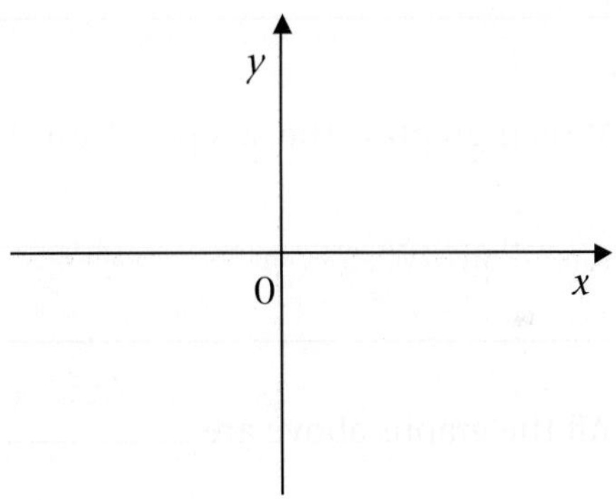

Copy the screen output in the grid provided.

a. Compare and contrast the graphs:

What are the similarities you have noticed about all the graphs? List as many as you can.	What are the similarities you have noticed about some of the graphs?

b. Which graph is the steepest from left to right? Can you tell? Why?

____

____

c. All the graphs above are __________. They share the same value of $\boldsymbol{m}$ = __________.

d. Without drawing the graph of $y = 2x - 7$, decide if this graph will be

i. higher or lower than the graph of $y = 2x$. Why?

____

____

ii. parallel to the graph of $2y = 4x + 10$. Why?

____

Verify your answer using Graphmatica. Add the graph of $y = 2x - 7$ to the grid above.

e. Clear the screen. On the *same piece of graph paper,* draw and label the graphs of:

- $y = -3x + 2$
- $y = -2x + 2$
- $y = -x + 2$
- $y = -\frac{1}{2}x + 2$
- $y = 3x + 2$
- $y = 2x + 2$
- $y = x + 2$
- $y = \frac{1}{2}x + 2$

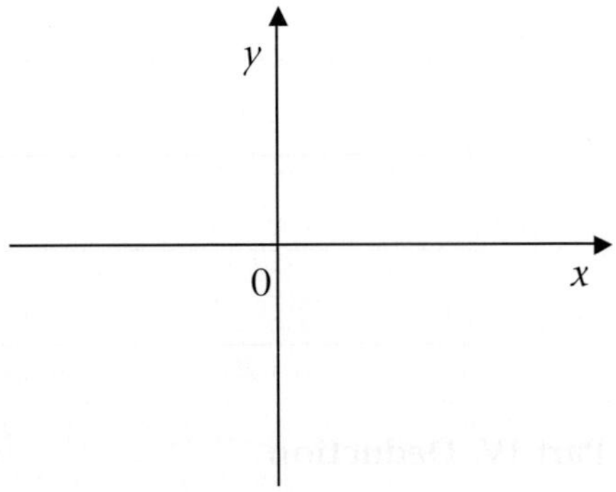

Copy the screen output in the grid provided.

f. Observe the equations of given graphs. What can you say about them? They have the ______ values of ______ but ______ values of ______.

g. Look at how your observations in e. are shown on the screen. All the graphs cut the y-axis at (,) and they are not ______________. Therefore, the value of c determines where the graphs ______ the *y-axis.*

h. Summarise what you have learned about the parameters m and c of the equation of a straight line.

i. m

____

____

____

____

____

____

ii. *c*

____

____

____

____

____

____

Part IV: Deduction

A screenshot from Graphmatica is shown below. Use it to answer the questions that follow.

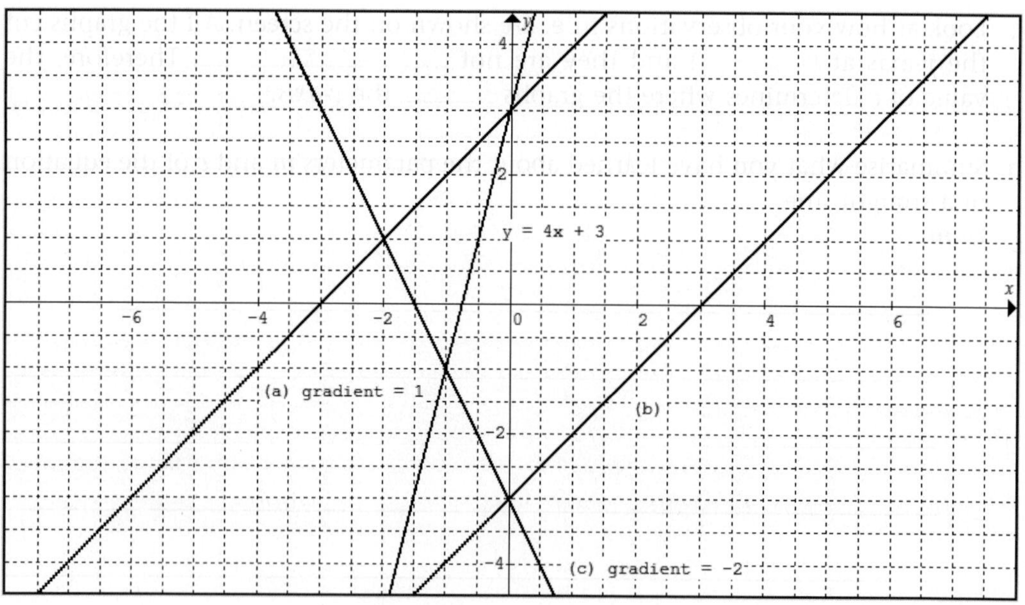

1. State the equation of line (a) ____________. Explain.

2. State the equation of line (b) ____________. Explain.

3. State the equation of line (c) ____________. Explain.

4. On the same axes, label the graph of $y = 4x + 2$, with x-intercept = –0.5.

GEOMETER'S SKETCHPAD ACTIVITY ON QUADRATIC FUNCTIONS

Objectives:
By the end of the lesson, students should be able to

i. state the effects of p and q in the quadratic function $y = (x - p)^2 + q$ on $y = x^2$,
ii. state the coordinates of the turning point from $y = (x - p)^2 + q$,
iii. state the equation of the line of symmetry of $y = (x - p)^2 + q$,
iv. sketch the graph of the quadratic function $y = (x - p)^2 + q$.

Part 1: Investigating the effect of p in $y = (x - p)^2$ on $y = x^2$

1. Plot $y = x^2$ using *Plot New Function* under *Graph.*

2. Create a slider for varying the values of p in $y = (x - p)^2$ as follows:
   Draw a horizontal line, followed by adding a point on it. Label the point as P. Select the point P and measure its x-coordinate value by using *Abscissa (x)* under *Measure.*

3. Plot $y = (x - p)^2$ by linking p to the x-coordinate of P when the equation is entered under *Plot New Function.* Use a different colour to distinguish this graph from $y = x^2$.

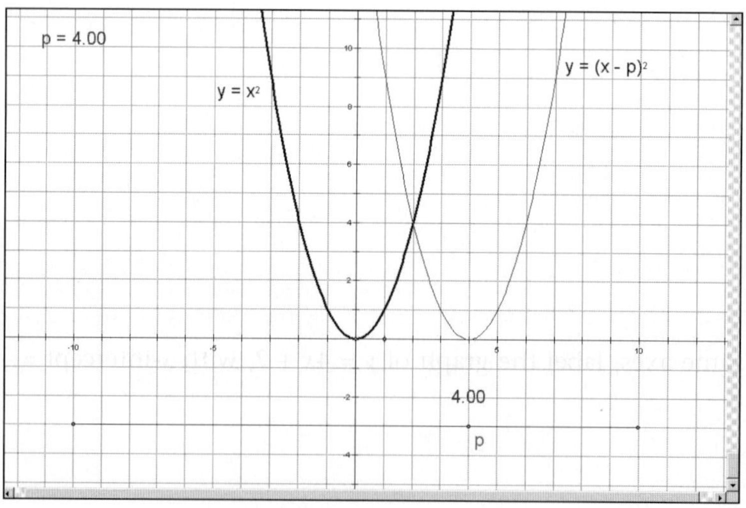

4. By dragging the free point along the slider to vary the value of p, complete the table below.

Equations of the graph $y = (x - p)^2$	Value of p	Coordinates of the turning point	Equation of the line of symmetry
$y = x^2$	0	(0, 0)	$x = 0$
$y = (x - 1)^2$			
$y = (x - 3)^2$			
$y = (x - 7)^2$			
$y = (x + 2)^2$			
$y = (x + 5)^2$			
$y = (x + 8)^2$			

Conclusion 1:

a. What do you think is the effect of the value of p on $y = x^2$?
b. Write down the coordinates of the turning point, in terms of p, of the graph of $y = (x - p)^2$.
c. Write down the equation of the line of symmetry, in terms of p, of $y = (x - p)^2$.

Part 2: Investigating the effect of q in $y = x^2 + q$ on $y = x^2$

1. Starting with a new sketch, plot $y = x^2$.

2. Create a slider for varying the value of q in $y = x^2 + q$.

3. Plot $y = x^2 + q$ by linking q to the x-coordinate of the point on the slider when the equation is entered under *Plot New Function*. Use a different colour to distinguish this graph from $y = x^2$.

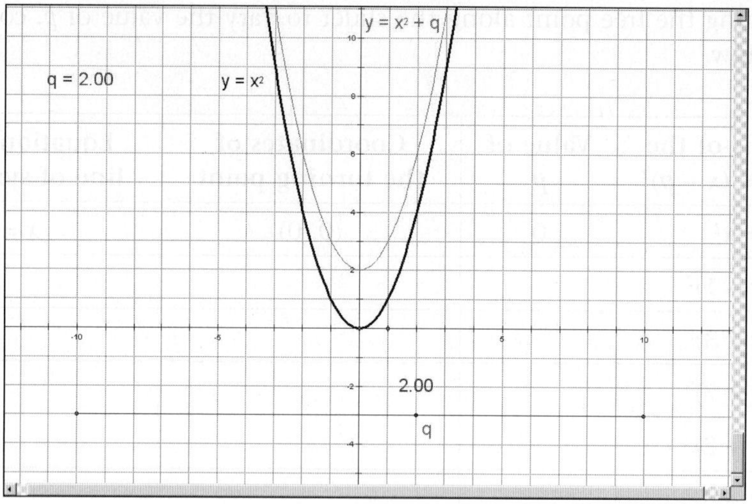

4. By dragging the free point along the slider to vary the value of q, complete the table below.

Equations of the graph $y = x^2 + q$	Value of q	Coordinates of the turning point	Equation of the line of symmetry
$y = x^2$	0	(0, 0)	$x = 0$
$y = x^2 + 2$			
$y = x^2 + 5$			
$y = x^2 + 8$			
$y = x^2 - 1$			
$y = x^2 - 3$			
$y = x^2 - 6$			

Conclusion 2:

a. What do you think is the effect of the value of q on $y = x^2$?
b. Write down the coordinates of the turning point, in terms of q, of the graph of $y = x^2 + q$.
c. Write down the equation of the line of symmetry of $y = x^2 + q$.

Consolidation:

1. a. Using your answers in Conclusions 1 and 2 above, sketch, on separate diagrams, the graph of each of the following quadratic equations.
   i. $y = (x - 2)^2$,
   ii. $y = x^2 + 1$.
   Write down the coordinates of the turning point and the equation of the line of symmetry for each graph.

   b. Hence, predict the coordinates of the turning point and the equation of the line of symmetry for the graph of $y = (x - 2)^2 + 1$. Explain your answer.
   Sketch the graph of $y = (x - 2)^2 + 1$.
   Now, verify your answer by plotting $y = (x - 2)^2 + 1$ with the aid of Geometer's Sketchpad.

   c. Complete the following table by predicting the coordinates of the turning point and the equation of the line of symmetry for each of the quadratic equations.

Equations of the graph $y = (x - p)^2 + q$	**Value of** p	**Value of** q	**Coordinates of the turning point**	**Equation of the line of symmetry**
$y = (x - 2)^2 + 1$				
$y = (x - 2)^2 + 3$				
$y = (x - 2)^2 - 5$				
$y = (x - 2)^2 - 2$				
$y = (x + 1)^2 - 2$				
$y = (x + 3)^2 - 2$				
$y = (x + 2)^2 + 1$				
$y = (x + 4)^2 + 1$				

   Verify your answers by using the Geometer's Sketchpad.

   d. For the quadratic graph of $y = (x - p)^2 + q$, the coordinates of the turning point are __________ and the graph is symmetrical about the line __________.

   e. Sketch the graphs of the following quadratic functions:
   i. $y = (x - 1)^2 + 1$
   ii. $y = (x + 2)^2 - 1$

APPENDIX 3A: GRAPHING SOFTWARE

Software/ website	Source	Features and suggested activities
Geometer's Sketchpad (GSP)	Download evaluation package from http://www.keypress.com/sketchpad/. Developed by Key Curriculum Press (2003), USA.	Dynamic software for exploring geometry. Represents the 2-D Cartesian plane; can be used to plot points, find distance between two points, find midpoint and draw graphs.
MS Excel	Found in most computers using Microsoft products. Developed by Microsoft Inc., USA.	Quick calculations using *f(x)* functions. Allows for tabulation of data and subsequent plotting of graphs (linear and quadratic). Students see the relationship between the algebraic formula they key in and the graph produced.
Graphmatica	Download from http://www8.pair.com/ksoft/. Developed by Keith Hertzer (2003) of kSoft, Inc., USA.	Powerful, easy-to-use, equation plotter with numerical and calculus features. Graphs Cartesian functions – relations and inequalities, polar, parametric and ordinary differential equations.
Autograph	Information about this software can be accessed from http://www.autograph-math.com/. Conceived by Douglas Butler and programmed by Mark Hatsell.	Graphing software for teaching graphs, coordinate geometry, calculus, statistics and probability.

FURTHER READING

Bell, A., Brekke, G., & Swan, M. (1987c) Diagnostic teaching 6: Can the same material be used with classes of different ability? *Mathematics Teaching,* 60–62.

Crawford, A.R., & Scott, W.E. (2000). Making sense of slope. *The Mathematics Teacher, 93*(2), 114–118.

Curcio, F.R. (1989). *Developing graph comprehension: Elementary and middle school activities*. Reston, VA: National Council of Teachers of Mathematics.

Illingworth, M. (1995). *A graphing matter: Activities for easing into algebra.* Emeryville, CA: Key Curriculum Press.

Knuth, E.J. (2000). Understanding connections between equations and graphs. *The Mathematics Teacher, 93*(1), 48–53.

Thomas, D.A., & Thomas, R.A. (1999). Discovery algebra: Graphing linear equations. *The Mathematics Teacher, 92*(7), 569–572.

Winter, M.J., & Carlson, R.J. (1993). *Exploring linear functions.* Menlo Park, CA: Addison-Wesley.

REFERENCES

Anderson, E.D., & Nelson, J. (1994). An introduction to the concept of slope. *The Mathematics Teacher, 87*(1), 27–28.

Bell, A., Brekke, G., & Swan, M. (1987a). Diagnostic teaching 4: Graphical representation. *Mathematics Teaching,* 56–60.

Bell, A., Brekke, G., & Swan, M. (1987b). Diagnostic teaching 5: Graphical representation, teaching styles and their effects. *Mathematics Teaching,* 50–57.

Kerslake, D. (1981). Graphs. In K.M. Hart (Ed.), *Children's understanding of mathematics: 11–16* (pp. 120–136). Northampton, UK: Alden Press.

Ministry of Education. (2006). *Secondary mathematics syllabuses.* Singapore: Ministry of Education.

Shell Centre for Mathematical Education. (1985). *The language of functions and graphs.* Cambridge, UK: Shell Centre for Mathematical Education.

SMP 11–16. (1984). *Graphs 1: 2(b) graphs.* Cambridge, UK: Cambridge University Press.

Chapter 4

Teaching of Statistics

Yap Sook Fwe

Statistics is the science of collecting, organising, displaying and interpreting numerical facts, which we call "data". The term "statistics" has its roots in the Latin word *status*, which means "the state". It was coined by the German scholar Gottfried Achenwall about the middle of the 18th century to mean "collection, processing and use of data by the state".

Pioneer effort in statistical analysis was made by John Graunt (1620–1674) who worked on birth and death records to make predictions about the number of persons who would die from various diseases and the proportion of male and female births that could be expected. Other early work on statistical analysis includes Adolph Quetelet (1796–1874) who worked on crime and mortality rates and Florence Nightingale (1820–1910) who worked with mortality tables during the Crimean War to get British hospitals to improve patient care.

During the 19th century, statistics began to acquire a new meaning as the interpretation of data or methods of extracting information from data for making decisions under uncertainty. Karl Pearson (1857–1936) was the first to use the insight provided by the descriptive analysis based on moments and histograms to draw inference on the underlying family of distributions.

In the 20th century, Sir Ronald Fisher (1890–1962) introduced a systematic methodology of data collection through the design of experiments as well as some basic ideas in the theory of estimation. Jerzy Neyman (1894–1981) and Egon Pearson (1895–1980) developed the theory of formal hypothesis testing. John Tukey (1915–2000) invented a variety of techniques for looking more effectively at data. In his book entitled *Exploratory Data Analysis*, he suggested many of the current graphical representations used to depict statistics, including stem-and-leaf plots and boxplots.

KEY CONCEPTS

At the primary level, students have been taught to read, interpret and solve problems involving picture graphs, bar graphs, line graphs and pie graphs, as well as calculate the average (mean) of a set of data. At the secondary level, the school syllabus (Ministry of Education, 2006) on Statistics involves data handling and data analysis. *At the lower secondary level*, students learn to:

- collect, classify and tabulate data – include practical activities;
- construct and interpret tables, bar graphs, pictograms, line graphs, pie charts, pictograms and histograms with equal intervals – include awareness of their purposes and uses, their advantages and disadvantages;
- interpret and analyse dot diagrams and stem-and-leaf diagrams;
- draw simple inference from statistical diagrams;
- find mean, mode and median – distinguish between the purposes for which they are used;
- calculate the mean for grouped data.

At the upper secondary level, students learn to:

- interpret and analyse cumulative frequency diagrams and box-and-whisker plots;
- estimate quartiles and percentiles;
- use range, interquartile range and standard deviation as measures of spread for a set of data;
- calculate the standard deviation for a set of data (grouped or ungrouped);
- use the mean and standard deviation to compare two sets of data.

Formal statistical inference is only included in the A-level syllabus. However, secondary school students can develop ideas of informal statistical inference through statistical investigations.

TEACHING APPROACHES

1. Wherever possible, use real data in the classroom. Local data that incorporate National Education messages are preferred. The various ways of collecting real data include:

   a. surveys or observational studies;
   b. simple experiments, for example, throwing dice, measurement activities; and
   c. newspapers and published documents, for example, yearbooks, census reports.

2. It is important that students learn how to display data clearly and unambiguously. They should be able to recognise such misleading features as:

    a. absence of, or an inadequate title;
    b. suppressed scale, exaggerated scale;
    c. absence of scale and/or units and/or labels on axes;
    d. size distortion; and
    e. comparison being made between two graphs with different scales.

3. In interpreting graphs, the following points should be noted:

    a. In examining the distribution of a set of data as depicted by a graph, important characteristics, such as shape, location, variability and unusual values should be detected. From careful observations of patterns in data, one can make conjectures about relationships among the variables.
    b. Intermediate values may not have any meaning for line graphs.
    c. The vertical axis of bar charts should always start from zero since the frequency of each category is represented by the height of the bar.
    d. A histogram is used for numerical data. There should be no gaps between classes (unlike bar charts).
    e. The term "histogram" was coined by Karl Pearson to refer to a common form of graphical representation where the area of each column represents the frequency corresponding to the range of its base. For a large sample, a histogram, which is standardised so that its total area is one, can be used to approximate the probability density function of a random variable.

4. Discuss the appropriateness of different measures of central tendency in different situations. Depending on the type of questions asked and the nature of the data being summarised, three different measures of central tendency or averages can be considered as typical or representative of a set of data:

    a. The *mean* is sensitive to extreme values. Physically, the mean of a set of data is the centre of gravity of its distribution.
    b. The *median* provides a better measure of location than the mean when there are some extremely large or small observations. For a set of n observations, the median is the value in the $\frac{n+1}{2}$th position when the data are ordered.
    c. The most frequently occurring value in a set of observations is called the *mode*. There may be zero, one or more modes in a data set.

5. Emphasise the importance of measures of variability in interpreting data.

    a. Statistical measures of variation or dispersion are numerical values that indicate the variability inherent in a set of data measurements. Common measures of dispersion are range, interquartile range, variance and standard deviation.

b. Averages and measures of dispersion are both important when we want to compare the distributions of two or more sets of data.
c. Often, students are confused between the formulas for the variance of a population and its unbiased estimate based on a sample.
d. A larger sample is needed if the data to be collected are more variable.

6. The manipulations and skills involved at the secondary level are usually straightforward and mechanical. However, to develop good data sense, students need to appreciate how these skills fit into the bigger picture of statistical investigation. (Refer to the popular model suggested by Graham (1987); see Figure 4-1.) It is essential to involve students in real-life situations where the collection of data can help in analysing the situation and making decisions or predictions. In the process, students will learn to decide on the type of graphs and statistics appropriate for communicating their findings and conclusions.

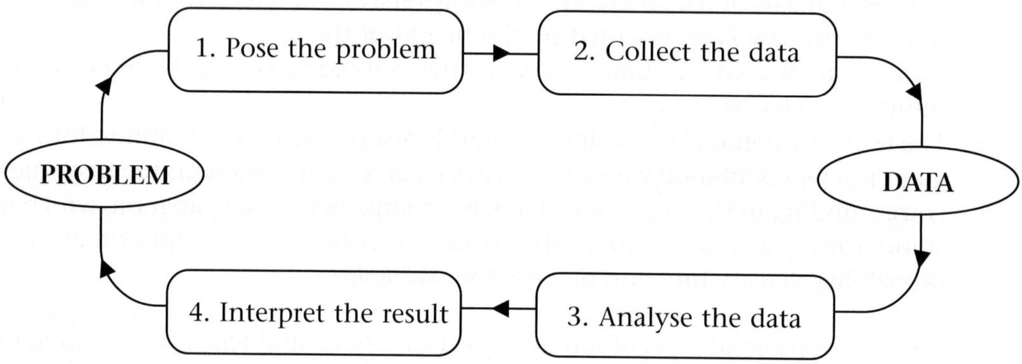

Figure 4-1 Stages of statistical investigation

7. Provide guidance for statistical project work and data analysis:

a. Define the population of interest.
b. Choose appropriate sampling procedure so that the sample collected is representative (not biased). It may not, however, always be possible to collect a random sample which ensures that every sub-set of fixed size in the population has the same chance of being included in the sample.
c. Design a survey or experiment, considering factors and variables to be measured.
d. Screen the data for outliers and possible errors in measurements.
e. Analyse the data and graph them in different ways to gain insights and reveal any relationship(s).
f. Interpret data and communicate results with supporting evidence using graphs and summary statistics.

8. Provide opportunities for students to appraise statistical information from newspapers and other sources. For example:

> **Primary pressure**
> In competitive Singapore the average child of 11 now has less than two hours of free time a day. The rest is all work, work, work.
> *The Guardian*
> (http://education.guardian.co.uk/egweekly/story/0,5500,780944,00.html)

A useful set of guidelines for critically appraising statistical information is given by Huff (1993):

- Who says so? – Source of the data? Any bias? Data reliable?
- How does he know? – Sample size?
- What is missing? – Any information intentionally suppressed?
- Did somebody change the subject? – Conclusion valid? Comparisons fair?
- Does it make sense? – Inference reasonable? Cause and effect mixed up?

SAMPLE ACTIVITIES FOR TEACHERS

1. a. The stem-and-leaf display, dotplot and boxplot are relatively new graphical techniques for displaying or summarising data. Design a classroom activity for students to learn and use these techniques for analysing data generated in the classroom.
   b. Compare and contrast the use of (i) mean, median and mode as an average of a set of data; (ii) range, interquartile range, variance and standard deviation as a measure of dispersion of a set of data.
   c. Discuss some of the properties of mean and standard deviation.
   [Read Aliaga and Gunderson (2006), de Lange (1992) and Watkins, Scheaffer, and Cobb (2004).]

2. Discuss with concrete examples some uses of statistics in everyday life – how and why data are collected. Give a few concrete examples (from different subject areas) in which students can be asked to collect practical data by doing experiments and/or making measurements/observations. [Read Peck (2006); Landwehr and Watkins (1996); and Moore (2001).]

3. Newspapers and local data sources/documents provide good sources for teaching statistics. Examples of local data sources are *Yearbook of Statistics Singapore*, *Monthly Statistical Digest* and the *Singapore Census* conducted every ten years. A convenient reference is the Singapore Department of Statistics website: http://www.singstat.gov.sg/.

a. Create a classroom activity for your students based on data obtained from one or more of these sources. Try to incorporate a National Education message in your activity.

b. Some reports based on data may involve some form of misuse and/or abuse of statistics where the conclusions do not follow the data presented. Critically examine some newspaper items or other local data sources, create an activity for students to help them learn about real-life statistics or understand how data may be misused or abused.

[Read Campbell (2004, Chapter 12); and Huff (1993, Chapter 10).]

4. Teachers need to go through statistical investigations themselves to appreciate the processes involved. In groups of four or five, carry out a statistical investigation.

a. You are guided through your investigation by the following steps:

- pose a problem
- collect the data
- analyse the data
- interpret the result

b. You must represent your data in as many appropriate graphical forms as possible. Try to bring out the importance or usefulness of choosing appropriate graphical representations according to the type of data and purpose.

c. Use measures of central tendency and measures of dispersion to discuss your findings.

d. Present your findings to your class.

[Read Graham (1987) and Baker (1989).]

SAMPLE ACTIVITIES FOR STUDENTS

1. The average monthly temperatures of two cities A and B for a period of eight months (January to August) are shown below:

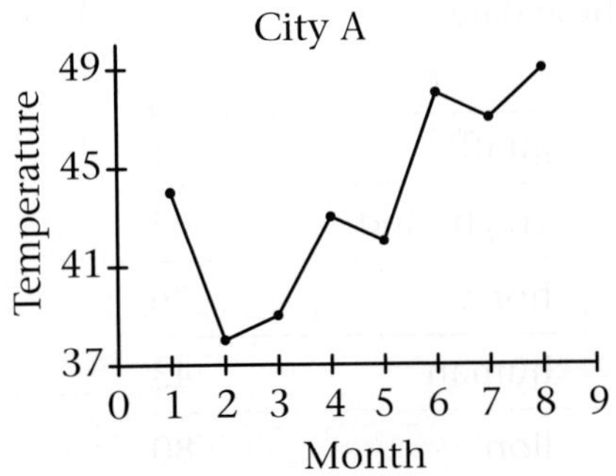

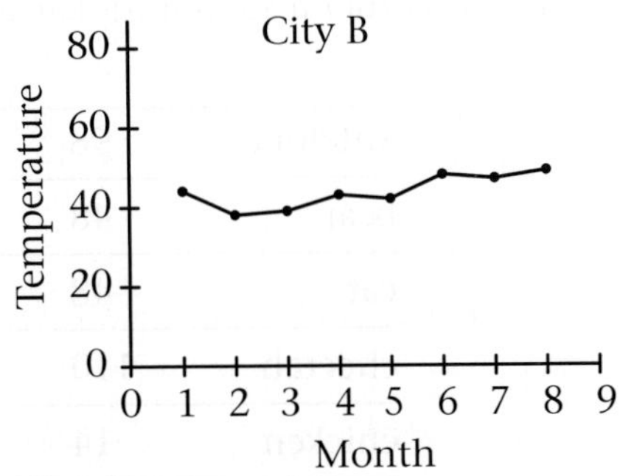

a. Compare the temperature pattern of the two cities.
b. Can you estimate the temperature on 15 March for City A?

2. A physical education teacher conducted a survey to find out which outdoor games are popular among the students in his class.

Game	Basketball	Soccer	Hockey	Volleyball	Tennis
No. of pupils	18	23	6	12	9

Comment on the following bar chart drawn based on the above data.

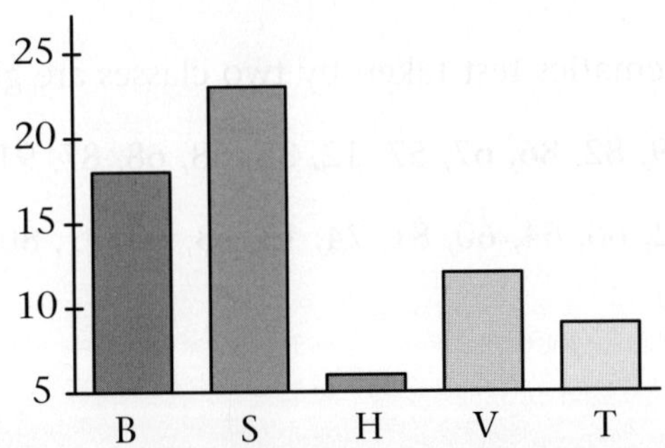

Explain whether each of the following can provide an appropriate display of the data: a pictogram, a pie chart, a dot diagram, a histogram, a line graph.

3. Make a dot diagram of the number of siblings that each student in the class has. Summarise the data by a description of the distribution and appropriate measures of central tendency and dispersion. Note if there is any cluster, gap or outlier(s).

4. The following table gives the speed of animals in km per hour.
   a. Construct a stem-and-leaf display of these data.

antelope	98	giraffe	51
bear	48	greyhound	62
cat	48	horse	76
cheetah	110	human	43
chicken	14	lion	80
coyote	68	pig	18
deer	56	rabbit	56
elephant	40	turkey	24
elk	72	warthog	49
fox	51	zebra	64
jackal	56		

   b. Calculate the quartiles and the interquartile range. [Note that there are different ways of calculating the quartiles of a discrete data set.] Hence, construct a boxplot for these data.
   c. Write a paragraph about the speed of animals.

5. The scores of a mathematics test taken by two classes are given as follows:

Class A: 29, 78, 85, 99, 49, 82, 86, 67, 57, 12, 38, 58, 68, 87, 91, 80, 79, 83, 82, 81

Class B: 72, 78, 83, 12, 62, 66, 64, 60, 81, 74, 13, 63, 60, 71, 80, 62, 89, 61, 70, 74

a. Complete the following back-to-back stem-and-leaf display of these data:

Class A		Class B
	1	
	2	
	3	
	4	
	5	
	6	
	7	
	8	
	9	

b. Compute the quartiles and construct parallel boxplots for these data.
c. Compute the mean and standard deviation for the data of each class.
d. How would you decide which class has done better?

6. In a company, the salaries of ten employees are (in dollars):

   2000, 750, 750, 700, 700, 650, 650, 600, 600, 600

   Find the mean, the mode and the median of the salaries. Which average gives the best picture of how much money employees in the company earn? Why?

7. a. A set of four odd numbers has a mean of 8, a median of 11 and a mode of 13. What are these numbers?
   b. Design a set of data such that the median and the mode are equal and the mean is 7 more than either of them.
   c. Design a set of data such that the mode is 5, the median is larger than the mode and the mean is the largest in value.

8. The table below gives the weight (in grams) of apples in three crates of 100 apples each.

Crate	**Mean weight (g)**	**Median weight (g)**	**Interquartile range**
A	101	103	16
B	104	105	14
C	105	103	15

On the basis of this information, state which crate you would choose to satisfy the following conditions. Give your reasons.

a. the heaviest crate;
b. the crate with at least 50 apples of more than 104 g; and
c. the crate with the apples most exactly matched in weight.

9. The frequency table below shows the snout-vent length (SVL: length from snout to cloacal opening) in millimetres of 111 male and 109 female water monitor lizards from samples taken from Sungei Buloh by a biology researcher (courtesy of Diong, C.H., National Institute of Education).

Class interval SVL (mm)	Frequency	
	Male	**Female**
$20 < x \le 30$	0	2
$30 < x \le 40$	3	20
$40 < x \le 50$	20	40
$50 < x \le 60$	25	25
$60 < x \le 70$	18	19
$70 < x \le 80$	19	3
$80 < x \le 90$	17	0
$90 < x \le 100$	9	0
Total	111	109

a. Estimate the mean and standard deviation of the snout-vent length of each group of lizards.
b. Draw on the same diagram two cumulative frequency curves for the snout-vent length of these two groups of lizards. Estimate the quartiles and hence, the interquartile range.
c. Compare the snout-vent length of the two groups of lizards based on a. and b.
d. A randomly selected lizard has a snout-vent length of 78 mm. Is it likely to be a male or a female?

10. Statistics show that most car accidents occur when cars travel at moderate speeds. Very few accidents occur at speeds more than 100 km per hour. Does it mean that it is safer to drive at higher speeds?

Statistics Worksheet

WHOSE CHILD IS TOP?

Three Singaporean parents are comparing the results of their children who go to the same kindergarten. The following table gives the marks obtained by the children in five graded subjects:

Parent	English	Chinese	Maths	Music	PE
Mrs. Ambitious	75	60	55	65	75
Mrs. Kiasu	70	59	70	77	60
Mrs. Pushy	60	55	94	58	65

1. Determine whose child comes up top by adding up the marks and taking the average for the five subjects.

2. Mrs. Ambitious says that ranking should be used. As her child is top in three subjects, surely he should be the top pupil. For each subject, rank the children 1, 2 and 3 and then add up the ranks. Determine if Mrs. Ambitious' son is the child with the lowest (best) ranking. Use the table below:

Parent	English	Chinese	Maths	Music	PE	Rank total
Mrs. Ambitious						
Mrs. Kiasu						
Mrs. Pushy						

3. However, English, Chinese and Maths are more "important" as they are crucial subjects in Primary 1. Should they be given double weightage? Copy the table below but give the three subjects double weightage (compute on a maximum of 200 marks). Add up the total for each child. Who is top now?

Parent	English	Chinese	Maths	Music	PE	Total
Mrs. Ambitious						
Mrs. Kiasu						
Mrs. Pushy						

The moral of this exercise is that statistics can be manipulated to tell different stories.

(This worksheet was contributed by Lim-Teo Suet Khoh, National Institute of Education.)

Excel Activity

YUMMY M&M'S!

1. Take a packet of M&M's (50 g).

   Guess and record:
   - How many M&M's are there? ________________
   - How many different colours of M&M's are there? ________________

2. Open your package of M&M's, sort them by colour.
   How many of each colour are there? *(Fill in the second column of the table below.)*

Colour	Your guess	Actual number
Total		

3. Use Excel to draw and print two bar graphs: one for your guess, and one for your actual data. Compare the graphs. Explain the similarities and differences between the graphs.

   Similarities:

   ____

   ____

Differences:

____

____

4. How do you calculate the percentage? Fill in the blanks.

$$\text{Percentage of red M\&M's} = \frac{\boxed{}}{\boxed{}}$$

Complete the following table, using your data and the data from the class.
Use Excel to find the percentage of each colour.
Round to the nearest whole number.

Colour	Your packet (%)	Your class (%)
Total		

Draw two pie charts, one for your data and one for your class data.

Compare the graphs.

Explain the similarities and differences between the two graphs.

Similarities:

____

____

____

Differences:

____

____

____

5. If the entire grade level conducts the same activity on M&M's, what results would you expect? Why is this so?

____

____

____

____

____

____

____

(This activity was contributed by Koay Phong Lee, National Institute of Education.)

DATA ANALYSIS ACTIVITY USING EXCEL

In real-life data collection, we often encounter big data sets with many variables of different types. An electronic spreadsheet, such as Excel, provides a convenient tool for data exploration and analysis.

In this lab activity, students are required to handle a data set of moderate size using information technology (IT) skills and to present the results with appropriate graphics and summary. Before the lab activity, the following variables are collected from their own class and entered into a spreadsheet:

a. gender
b. blood type
c. number of siblings
d. height (in centimetres)
e. span (in centimetres)
f. navel height (in centimetres)

1. For the data on blood type, draw a (standard) bar chart, a (standard) pie chart and a pictograph. Interpret the data using the graph(s). Do the different graphs display the data equally well?

2. For the data on number of siblings, draw a histogram. Compute the three different averages – mean, mode and median. Write a short summary about the sibling data.

3. For the height data, construct the following:
   a. a histogram for the males and females;
   b. separate histograms for the males and females.
   Describe the distribution(s) in each case. Compare the distributions of the height of the males and females. Include summary statistics if appropriate.
   [The height data for males and females can also be compared based on stem-and-leaf diagram(s) and boxplots using the freeware WINSTATS from http://math.exeter.edu/rparris/winstats.html.]

4. Are the height and span of a person the same? What is the relationship between these two variables?

   a. Calculate the difference *height – span* and the ratio *span/height*. What can you infer from the summary statistics of these variables?
   b. Draw a scatter diagram (XY scatter) of span versus height. Do you observe any relationship between span and height? You may wish to add a trend line. (Chart > Add Trendline > Linear > Options > Display equation on chart.)

5. Divide height by navel height to obtain a ratio.
   a. Obtain the descriptive statistics of this ratio.
   [To compute averages and spread in Excel – use Tools, Data Analysis, Descriptive Statistics, Summary statistics.]
   b. Construct a cumulative frequency diagram of this ratio.
   c. Read off the quartiles from the cumulative frequency diagram. Are they the same as those in a.?
   d. Decide whether, as a class, the ratio of height to navel height is close to the golden ratio, $\phi = \dfrac{1 + \sqrt{5}}{2}$.

6. For this data set, consider one other way of looking at any of the variable(s) that has not been considered above. Perform an analysis and report your findings.

7. Can the findings based on this set of data be used to make inferences about a bigger population? Explain.

REFERENCES

Aliaga, M., & Gunderson, B. (2003). *Interactive statistics.* Upper Saddle River, NJ: Prentice-Hall/Pearson Education.

Baker, D. (1989). *Facts and figures: A practical approach to statistics.* Cheltenham, England: Stanley Thornes (Publishers) Ltd.

Campbell, S.K. (2004). *Flaws and fallacies in statistical thinking.* Mineola, N.Y.: Dover Publications.

de Lange, J. (1992). *Data visualization.* Scotts Valley, CA: Wings for Learning.

Graham, A.T. (1987). *Statistical investigations in the secondary school.* Cambridge, UK: Cambridge University Press.

Huff, D. (1993). *How to lie with statistics.* NY: Norton.

Koay, P.L., Lim, S.K., & Yap, S.F. (1998). *Secondary mathematics: Enrichment worksheets.* Singapore Hillview Publications.

Landwehr, J.M., & Watkins, A.E. (1996). *Exploring data.* Palo Alto, CA: Dale Seymour Publications.

Ministry of Education (2006). *Secondary mathematics syllabus.* Singapore: Ministry of Education.

Moore, D.S. (2001). *Statistics: Concepts and controversies.* (5th ed.). NY: W.H. Freeman.

Peck, R. (2006). *Statistics: A guide to the unknown.* (4th ed.). Belmont, California: Thomson, Brooks/Cole.

Tukey, J.W. (1977). *Exploratory data analysis*. Reading, MA: Addison-Wesley.

Watkins, A.E., Scheaffer, R.L., & Cobb, G.W. (2004). *Statistics in action*. Emeryville, CA: Key Curriculum Press.

Chapter 5

Teaching of Mensuration

Lim-Teo Suat Khoh and Ng Wee Leng

A measurable attribute is a characteristic of an object that can be quantified. For instance, line segments have length, plane regions have area, and solids have mass and volume that can be measured.

Mensuration is about the measurement of space and is a topic subsumed under the study of measurement. Length, area and volume are measurements of space in 1-, 2- and 3-dimensions respectively.

KEY CONCEPTS

In the lower secondary mathematics syllabus, the topic mensuration, building on concepts already covered in the primary mathematics syllabus, covers largely the various formulae for computing areas and volumes. Following is a summary of the syllabus.

Level	Topic	Remarks
Sec 1	Perimeter and area of ▪ square ▪ rectangle ▪ triangle ▪ circle ▪ parallelogram ▪ trapezium	Perimeter and area of square, rectangle, triangle, circle, semicircle, quadrant and related figures are covered in the primary syllabus Properties, though not formulae for area and perimeter, of parallelogram and trapezium are covered in the primary syllabus

Level	Topic	Remarks
	Volume and surface area of ■ cube ■ cuboid ■ prism ■ cylinder	Volume of cube, cuboid and related solids are covered in the primary syllabus
Sec 2	Volume and surface area of ■ sphere ■ pyramid ■ cone	Not covered in the primary syllabus Cone is introduced in the primary syllabus but not sphere and pyramid
	Arc length and sector area	Not covered in the primary syllabus Taught in the lower secondary syllabus using proportional approach

The key concepts are therefore:

i. Space in 1-dimension: Length, perimeter
ii. Space in 2-dimensions: Area, surface area
iii. Space in 3-dimensions: Volume

TEACHING APPROACHES

1. This topic can be taught in a very procedural manner – give the formula and apply to find areas, volumes of particular figures. Such an approach neither promotes relational understanding nor mathematical thinking.

2. Areas of triangles, parallelograms and trapeziums are related to the area of a rectangle. These relationships form the reasoning for the formulae for the areas. For example, an acute-angled triangle, as well as a right-angled triangle, can be enclosed in a rectangle twice its area. For an obtuse-angled triangle, it is easier to relate it to a parallelogram twice its area. As is seen in the diagram on p. 107, this parallelogram has the same area as a related rectangle.

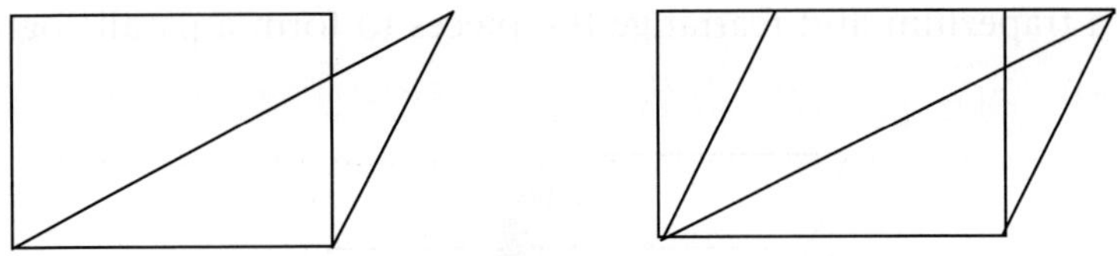

3. Paper models can be used to help visualisation and to establish relations:

   - Cut an obtuse-angled triangle and rearrange the pieces to form a parallelogram with the same base as and half the height of the triangle.

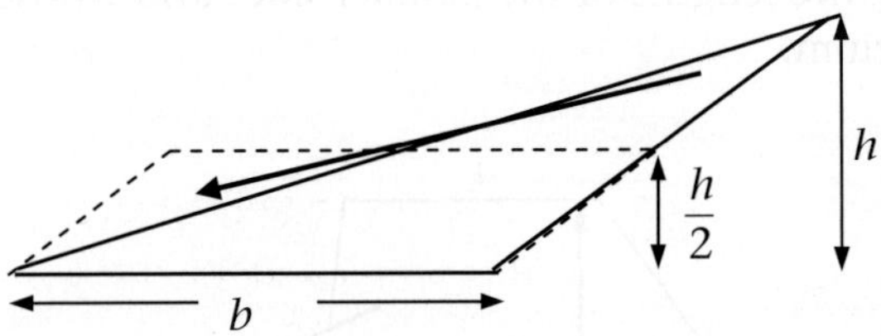

   - Cut a parallelogram and rearrange the pieces to form a rectangle.

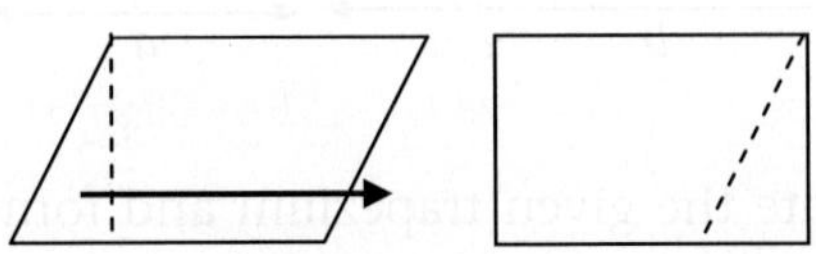

For a parallelogram with a very short base, we can first cut it into smaller parallelograms and then rearrange them as shown below:

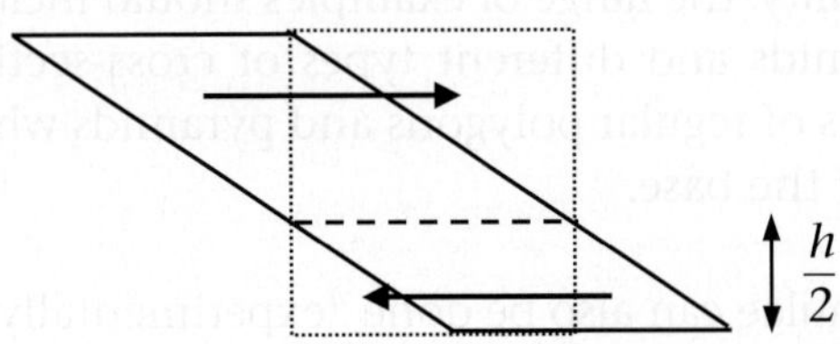

- Cut a trapezium and rearrange the pieces to form a parallelogram.

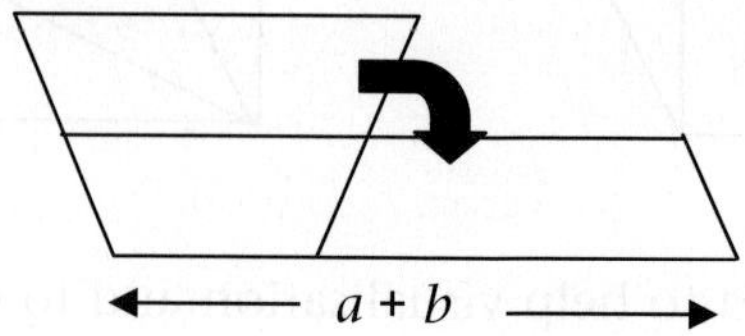

- Cut a trapezium along the line joining the midpoints of the pair of non-parallel opposite sides and rotate one of the pieces to form a parallelogram whose base is the sum of the lengths of the parallel sides and whose height is half of that of the trapezium.

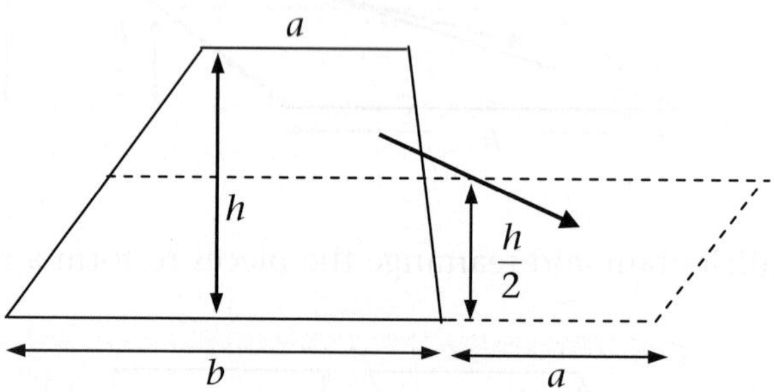

Alternatively, duplicate the given trapezium and form a parallelogram using the two identical trapezia.

- Cut open a paper cone to show a sector.

4. Students must be taught to recognise the various 3-D figures. According to Dienes' principle of variability, the range of examples should include many different types of bases for pyramids and different types of cross-sections for prisms. Do not give only examples of regular polygons and pyramids where the vertex is directly over the centre of the base.

5. Derivation of formulae can also be done "experimentally", for example, compare the volume of a cone/pyramid to that of a related cylinder/prism (same base and height) through pouring sand, beans, etc into differently shaped containers.

6. Students should be encouraged to explore the concepts, to establish formulae and results or to solve problems where visualisation is difficult, by using teaching aids such as

- vanguard paper models,
- polydrons,
- straw with connectors or strings,
- zome or googolplex or other construction toys,
- everyday objects such as candy/chocolates/biscuits/tea containers,
- paper cut-outs with magnets for whiteboard or transparency cut-outs for overhead projector,
- geoboards,
- tangrams,
- Geometer's Sketchpad, and
- simple PowerPoint animation to show transformation of parallelogram into rectangle.

7. To stimulate interest and motivate students, use real-life examples. Get them to make boxes of various shapes and given volumes.

8. Aim to develop students' sense of size, for example: What is the area of a Housing Development Board's 5-room flat? How much water can an Olympic-sized pool hold?

9. Thinking skills which can be promoted within this topic include comparing similarity in formulae (cone versus pyramid), the dimensionality of the formulae and real-life problem solving such as in the design of containers given conditions on volumes and surface areas.

10. Enrichment activities such as those given in the next section can be used to stimulate interest and further applications of the results.

SAMPLE ACTIVITIES FOR TEACHERS

1. What is a prism? What is a pyramid? Must the cross-section/base be regular polygons? Must the vertex of a pyramid be directly over the centre of the base? What is the relationship between a cylinder and a prism? Between a pyramid and a cone? Ensure that you clearly understood the concepts and can explain them well.

2. A mathematics teacher should know the derivation of the formulae for surface area of a sphere, volumes of pyramids, cones and spheres using calculus even though these are beyond the lower secondary syllabus.

3. Derivation of formulae can also be done informally using approximation, by comparing similarity in and/or dimensionality of formulae, and by applying Cavalieri's principle, which states that two solids each with a base in the same plane have equal volumes if every plane parallel to the bases intersects the solids in cross-sections of equal area. For instance, the formula for area of a circle can be determined using that for the circumference of a circle. (Do you know how?) Discuss how you can determine the formula for the
   - surface area of a cone using that for the surface area of a pyramid,
   - surface area of a cone by applying Cavalieri's principle,
   - volume of a sphere using that for the volume of a cone,
   - volume of a sphere using Cavalieri's principle, and
   - surface area of a sphere using that for the volume of a sphere.

SAMPLE ACTIVITIES FOR STUDENTS

1. Tangram explorations
   A tangram is a puzzle made up of seven pieces. You can cut one out of cardboard. A good size is made by cutting up a 10 cm by 10 cm square according to the diagram drawn here. Taking the square to be one square unit, pupils can be asked to form various figures using all or some of the seven pieces:

   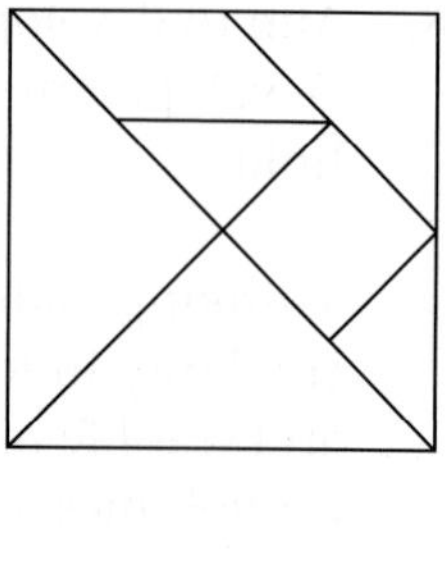

   - triangles of 2, 4, 8 square units,
   - squares of 2, 4, 8 square units,
   - rectangles (not squares) of 2, 3, 6 square units, and
   - parallelograms (not rectangles or squares) of 2, 4, 6 or 8 square units.

2. The value of π
   Primary pupils have often been asked to take π as $\frac{22}{7}$. They need to understand that this is only a rational approximation of π. They also need to understand that π is the ratio of the circumference to the diameter of a circle and is an irrational number. Encourage them to undertake some reading into the various values of π used in history (see Apostol, 1989).

   It is worth mentioning that Zu Chong Zhi 祖冲之 (429–500), a famous Chinese astronomer, mathematician and engineer, was able to determine the value of π accurate to the sixth decimal place. More precisely, he proved that $3.141\,592\,6 < \pi < 3.141\,592\,7$ and recommended the use of $\frac{355}{113}$ for close approximation and $\frac{22}{7}$ for rough approximation of π.

3. The Egyptian historical method of computing area of circle
The method inscribes a circle within a square and subdivides the square into nine smaller squares. Cutting off the corners, the area of the resultant octagon is taken as the approximate area of the circle.

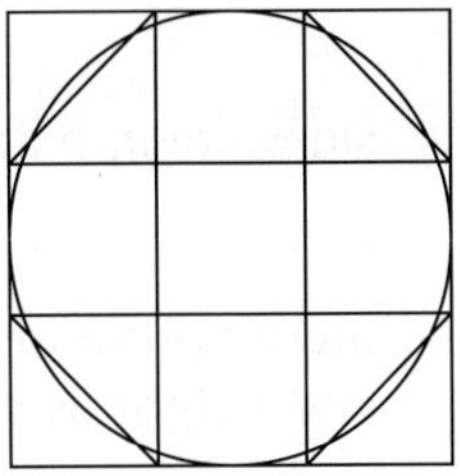

Length of square = $2r$

Area of square = $4r^2$

Area of circle = $\frac{7}{9}(4r^2)$

Comparing with πr^2, an approximate value of π is $\frac{28}{9} \approx 3.111$.

4. Archimedes' computation of π
Archimedes' method of using inscribed and circumscribing regular polygons to approximate the circumference of a circle and repeatedly doubling the number of sides for closer approximations is an interesting and stimulating topic. Students who have done trigonometry can attempt to calculate π using Archimedes' method. Those who know programming can write a simple program to do the repeated calculations.

5. Archimedes' computation of volume of sphere
Archimedes also discovered that the volume of a sphere is two-thirds of the volume of a cylinder which can just contain the sphere. Teachers can lead students to derive the formula for the volume of a sphere.

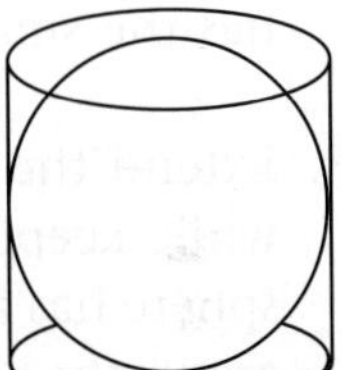

6. Euclid's *Elements*, Book XII, Proposition 7
Euclid proved that any prism with a triangular base can be divided into three pyramids which are equal to one another. Students can prove this result by constructing a model using the idea of Euclid's proof. In fact, students can construct a model to prove that a cube can be cut into three equal pyramids and determine the formula for the volume of a pyramid using that for the volume of a prism.

7. Qin Jiu Shao's formula for area of a triangle
One of the most famous and accomplished mathematicians during the Song dynasty (960–1279), Qin Jiu Shao 秦九韶 stated in the classic *Shu Shu Jiu Zhang* 数书九章 (*Mathematical Treatise in Nine Sections*) that the area of a triangle whose

sides are a, b and c is given by $\frac{1}{2}\sqrt{a^2c^2 - \left(\frac{a^2 + c^2 - b^2}{2}\right)^2}$ which is equivalent to Heron's formula. Students can prove that this formula holds using a geometric proof or by relating it to the formula for area of a triangle in terms of base and height as well as to Heron's formula.

FURTHER MENSURATION INVESTIGATIONS

Areas and perimeters

The first two are enrichment activities which average ability students can handle but the third may require higher ability.

1. Investigate different figures with fixed perimeters but different areas. First, begin with rectangular shapes. Once the students have discovered that the square has the largest area, move on to other shapes, for example, regular hexagon, circle, etc.

2. Investigate different figures with fixed areas and varying perimeters. Which shape has the smallest perimeter?

3. Extend the above to 3-dimensions, for example, for cuboids, maximise volume while keeping surface area constant. Students should be able to discover that a sphere has an even larger volume. Now, fix the volume and minimise the surface area – the sphere too has the minimum surface area. (One learns in physics that soap bubbles are spherical in shape due to surface tension.)

Areas and volumes of similar figures

The problems/investigations below all deal with the concept that the enlargement factor for areas is the square of the linear enlargement factor and that of volumes is the cube of the linear factor.

Problems 1 and 2 should be within the capabilities of average ability students. For the rest, unless the students are of high ability or are used to such investigations, some guiding worksheets may have to be prepared by the teacher.

1. Some friends go to Mario's for pizza.

   Huirong: "A large pizza costs twice as much as a regular pizza."
   Salma: "But the diameter of the large pizza only looks one-and-a-half times as long as that of the regular one."
   Huirong: "Why don't we order two regular ones instead?"

   Does one get more by buying two regular pizzas or one large pizza?

   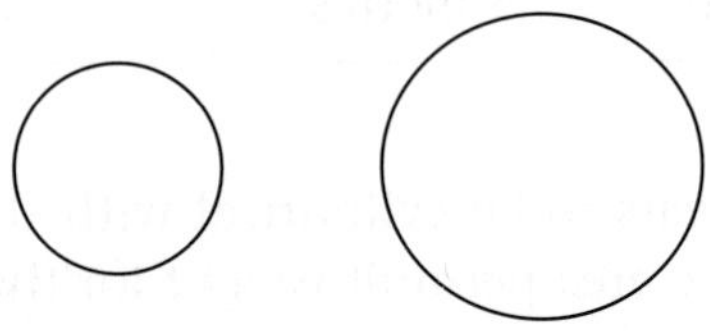

   \$12.50 \$25.00

2. Minghui: "Do you know that there is a place in Katong that sells fabulous dumplings?"

   Sara: "Are they very expensive?"
   Minghui: "Well, the small ones cost \$1 each and the big ones \$2."
   Sara: "\$2? How big are they?"

   Assume that the big dumplings are exactly proportional to the small ones (in ingredients as well as shape) and that the small dumplings are tetrahedra with sides 10 cm in length. How long should the side of the big dumplings be for them to be better buys?

3. Consider a person who is double your linear dimensions. What will the pressure on his feet be, relative to yours? Does this prove that giants cannot exist?

4. Consider the sun bear and the polar bear. Some data are given below:

	Polar bear	Sun bear
Height	3 metres	1.2 metres
Weight	800 kg	50 kg
Waist circumference	3 metres	1.2 metres

Taking the shapes of the bears to be cylindrical with the waist as circular cross-section, work out the surface area per unit weight for the two bears. How quickly an animal loses heat depends on this ratio. Compare the ratio for the two bears.

5. In enlargements of plane figures, the ratio of the areas is the square of the scale factor ratio. Let triangle ABC have sides twice as long as those of triangle PQR.

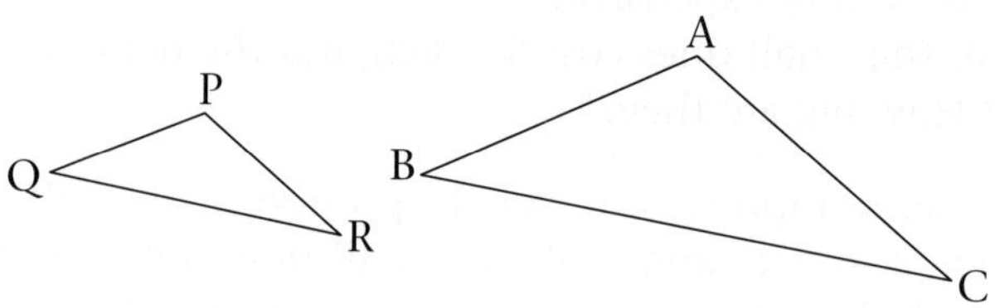

Show by drawing or otherwise that the area of triangle ABC is four times that of triangle PQR.

Now consider two tetrahedra, one of which has linear dimensions double the other. The volume of the large tetrahedron is $8 = 2^3$ times the volume of the smaller cone.

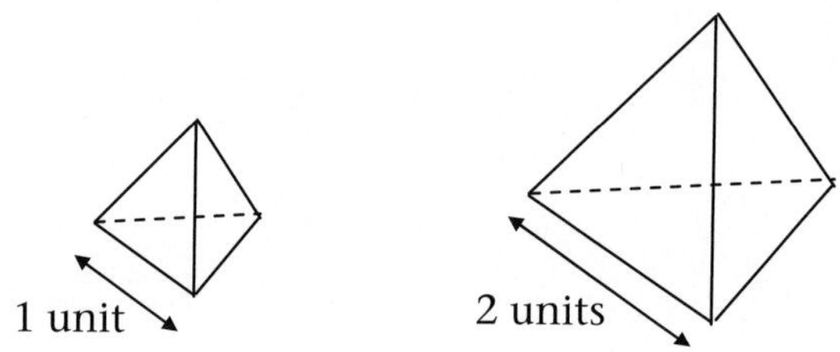

Using a polydron, make the large tetrahedron mentioned above and eight of the small ones. Can you fit the eight small tetrahedra into the large one?

We can fit four of the small ones into the corners of the large tetrahedron. What is the shape of the solid (call it X) needed to fit the four small tetrahedra to form the large tetrahedron? Use the polydron to make X and try to fit the four small tetrahedra into X to form the large tetrahedron. What is X's volume relative to the small tetrahedron? Can you prove it with geometry or trigonometry?

FURTHER READING

Geddes, D. (1994). *Measurement in the middle grades.* Reston, VA: National Council of Teachers of Mathematics.

Lang, S. (1985). *Math!: Encounters with high school students.* NY: Springer-Verlag.

Wills, H. (1985). *Leonardo's dessert, no pi.* Reston, VA: National Council of Teachers of Mathematics.

REFERENCE

Apostol, T.M. (1989). *The story of pi.* Project Mathematics. San Francisco, CA: California Institute of Technology.

Chapter

6

Teaching of Geometry

Leong Yew Hoong and Lim-Teo Suat Khoh

Geometry comes from two Greek root words, "geo" meaning "earth" and "metria" for "to measure". Translated literally, geometry means "earth measuring". It is thus the study of space and a systematisation of the way we view the space around us. Geometry started its practical beginnings in ancient Egypt in the calculation of land measure for taxation. It was the Greeks who first set out to devise rules of measuring areas with proofs. Most elementary geometry topics covered in our schools are part of "Euclidean geometry", named after Euclid, a Greek mathematician (circa 300 B.C.). The development of Euclidean geometry spans a long period; from 10 000 B.C. to the 21st century. More details about Euclidean geometry are available from many websites, such as http://babbage.clarku.edu/~djoyce/java/elements/elements.html.

GEOMETRY CURRICULUM

We can look at the geometry curriculum (topics and teaching approaches) from the following main aspects:

1. Views of geometry
    a. Geometry in the physical world
    b. Geometry as a mathematical system
    c. Geometry as a formal axiomatic structure
    d. Aesthetic and recreational geometry
2. Aims of teaching geometry
    a. To develop spatial intuitions and understanding
    b. To develop logical thinking abilities
    c. To acquire knowledge for other areas of mathematics

3. Basic concepts covered in the syllabus (See Map of geometry topics on p. 119)

    a. Point, line, plane, surface, space, dimension
    b. Angle, parallel lines, perpendicular lines, bisectors
    c. Geometrical figures and properties (regularity, symmetry, congruency, similarity, classification)
    d. Orientation, direction, bearing
    e. Transformations (motion geometry)

4. Relationships between spatial concepts covered
   These include properties of geometrical figures and relationships between various concepts. They can be classified under the following.

    a. Angle properties
    b. Symmetry properties

5. Construction skills in geometry

    a. Practical skills for designs, maps, plans, etc.
    b. Straight edge and compass constructions
    c. Making 3-D models

6. Development of deductive thinking

    a. Geometry is an excellent vehicle for developing reasoning skills in the spirit of the Greek mathematicians. It is close to philosophy in this aspect
    b. Giving reasons, drawing inferences
    c. Constructing proofs – a chain of inferences

7. Understanding the real world

    a. The real-world approach provides motivation, bringing mathematics beyond the classroom
    b. Through practical mensuration and surveying
    c. Through utilitarian value of geometry

8. Investigation and problem solving

    a. Due to the many results that are obtainable in geometry, the topics are particularly suitable for investigations. The spirit of enquiry can be harnessed in looking for results rather than proving given properties. Linked with (7) above, practical problem solving using geometrical concepts shows how mathematics is applied to real-life situations.
    b. Searching for patterns (geometric results)
    c. Putting knowledge of geometry to practical uses (e.g. planning a room, box constructions, designs, etc.)

Map of geometry topics in Singapore secondary schools

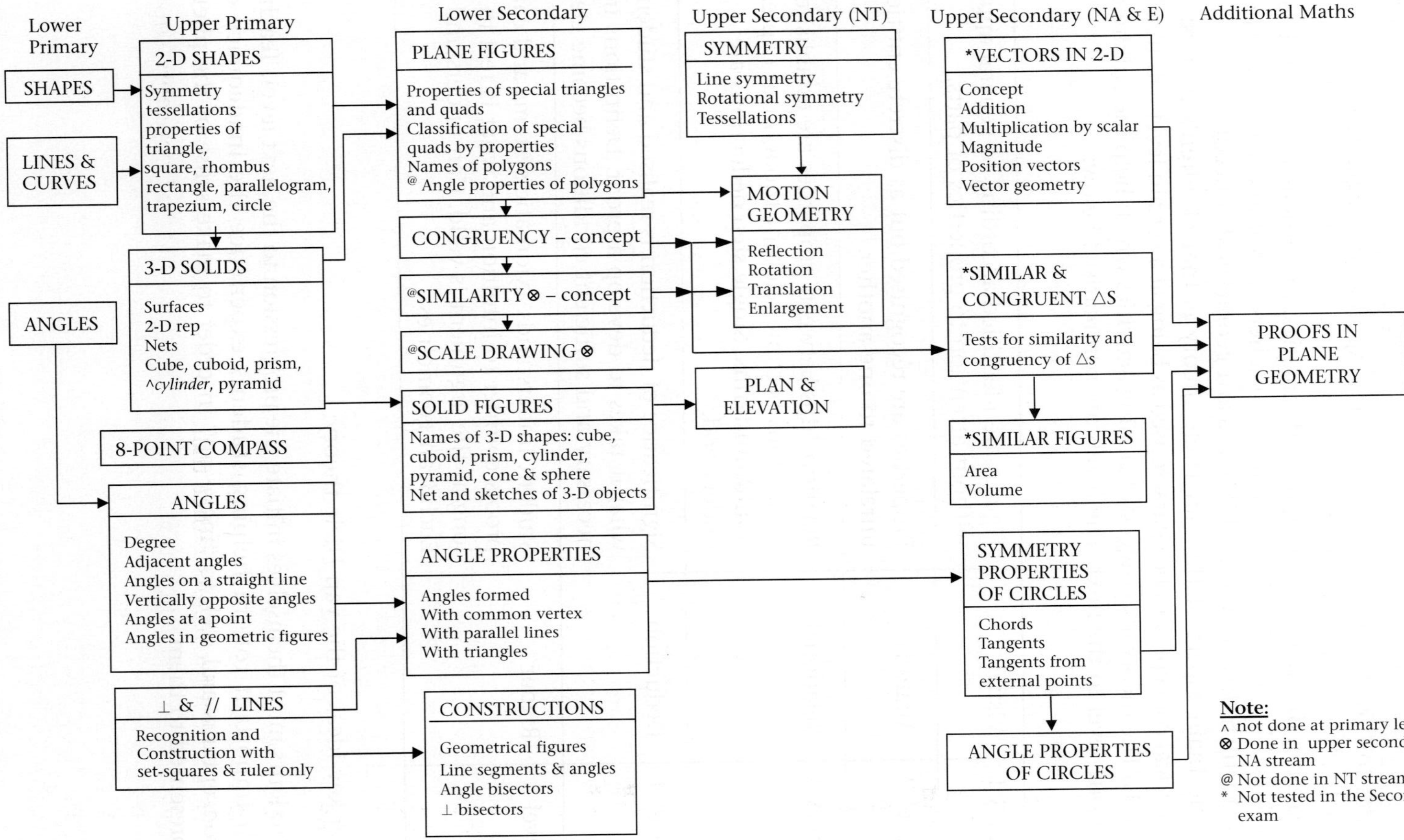

Note:
^ not done at primary level
⊗ Done in upper secondary for NA stream
@ Not done in NT stream
* Not tested in the Secondary 4NA exam

VAN HIELE THEORY

In addition to the curriculum topics and approaches suggested by the nature of geometry, the teaching/learning activities chosen by the teacher should also be guided by learning theories pertaining to mathematics, in particular, the van Hiele theory (developed by two Dutch mathematics teachers, Pierre and Dina van Hiele in the 1960s) which describes how children learn geometrical concepts.

The main aspect of the van Hiele theory is that children's understanding of geometrical concepts can be characterised as being at a certain level within a hierarchy of levels. The theory also suggests teaching activities which help the children progress from one level to the next. The levels are summarised below:

Level 1	Visual	Figures are identified according to general appearance, without attention to properties of parts.
Level 2	Analysis	Properties are recognised but as discrete entities and unrelated to one another.
Level 3	Relational	Relationships between properties are established. Definitions become relevant though not expressed in minimum terms. Single step deductions are understood.
Level 4	Deduction	Significance of deduction is realised and student knows what it takes to develop a proof. Definitions involving necessary and sufficient conditions become clear.
Level 5	Rigour	Student understands axiomatic systems and can accept proofs counter to intuition and what is real to him as long as the argument is valid. Can understand non-Euclidean geometries.

Other key ideas of the van Hiele theory:

1. Students must themselves initiate the progression to the next level. Teachers play an important role in helping students experience the inadequacy of their conceptions and seek to "move up" in order to make sense of the phenomena presented to them.

2. No understanding takes place when teachers and students interact at different levels. Teachers need to start teaching at their students' level of understanding and help them make progress gradually.

3. Each level is characterised by the language used. Language thus plays an important role in teachers' instruction.

Some implications for teaching geometry:

1. A significant number of students enter Secondary 1 at van Hiele level 1. The teacher's challenge is to shift these students' view of geometrical objects from a purely visually-driven mode to one that focuses on their geometrical properties.

   Example: Moving from "real-life" kite to geometric kite.

   Some recommendations:

   a. Start with a "real-life" kite. If possible, bring some of these kites into the classroom for students to see and feel.
   b. Make explicit that the focus of the lesson will be on "geometric kites" and that they will find some differences between a "real-life" kite and the geometric one.
   c. Show drawings of a range of kites of different areas, orientations and sizes of interior angles, such as the ones below:

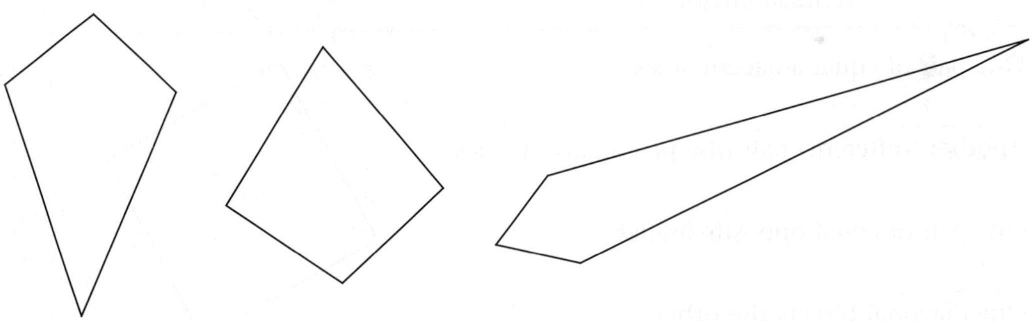

   d. Show some drawings of non-kites as well, such as these:

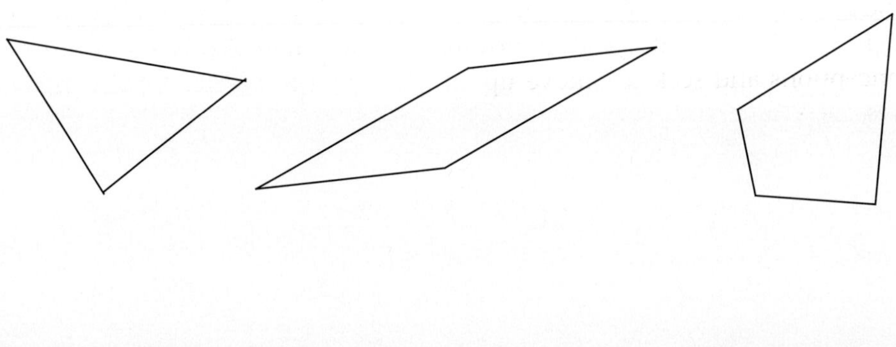

e. Ask students to suggest common properties – such as a pair of equal opposite angles, composed of two isosceles triangles – among these kites.
f. Students are likely to use natural language to describe the common features. Help rephrase their descriptions into more formal language and write them on the board for the students' reference.

2. The next significant challenge may emerge when students need to work towards the idea of definition of geometric objects (i.e. operation at level 3).

   Example: Towards a definition of a kite.

   Some recommendations:

   a. Draw a square and write down the question, "Is a square a kite?" Open the question for (either whole-class or group) discussion. Discussion contents should be recorded and shared with the class.
   b. If there is a need to direct the discussion onto a more productive track, you can start by asking students to help revise the properties of kites – list them.
   c. To answer the question whether a square is a kite, all that is needed is to check the square against the list of kite properties:

A kite must have ... (critical attributes)	**A square has ...**	✔
One pair of equal adjacent sides	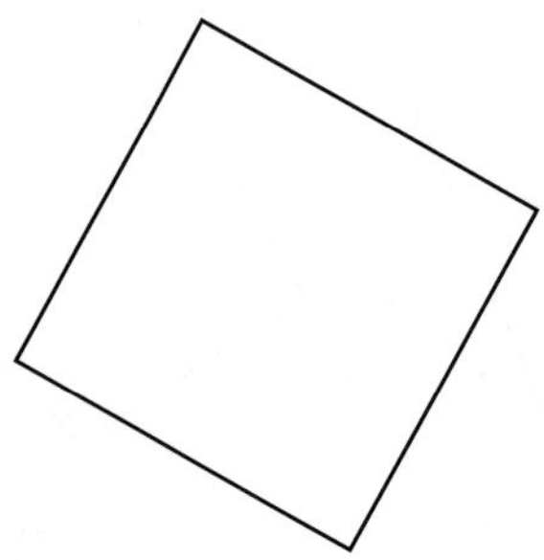	☐
Another (different) pair of equal adjacent sides		☐
One pair of equal opposite angles		☐
One diagonal bisects the other		☐
The diagonals are perpendicular		☐

d. Show by marking equality (of relevant sides, angles and diagonals) on the square and on the checklist, item-by-item, that the square satisfies all the criteria and so answers the question.
e. Lead to the next question, "What then is a kite? Use as few words as possible to describe it". Discuss alternative "definitions" students may offer.

3. Proofs (level 4 activity) can be expected to pose a challenge to many students.

Example: Prove that, for a kite, at least one pair of opposite interior angles are equal.

Some recommendations:

a. Formal written proofs can be rather "abstract". Effort can be made to help students visualise proofs and view them as written explanations of ideas that are intuitively correct.
b. Start with a diagrammatic overview of "proof":

Given conditions (step 1)	**Process/working (step 3)**	**Conclusion (step 2)**
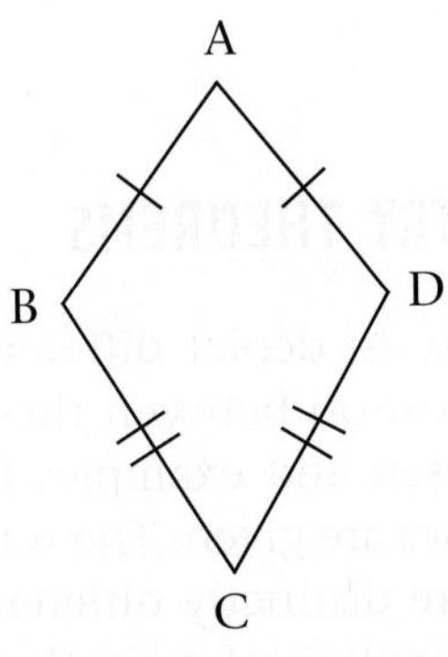	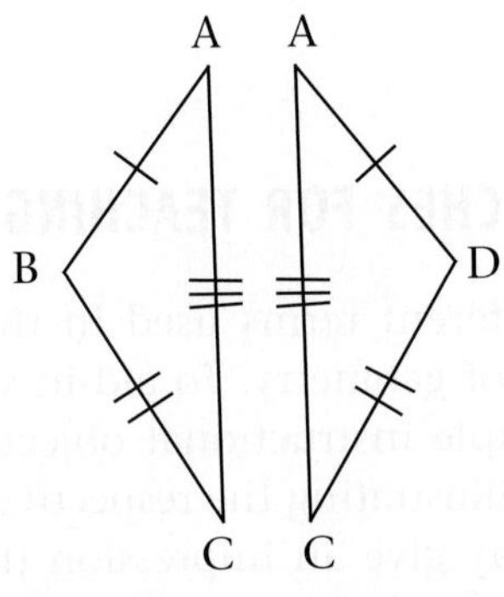	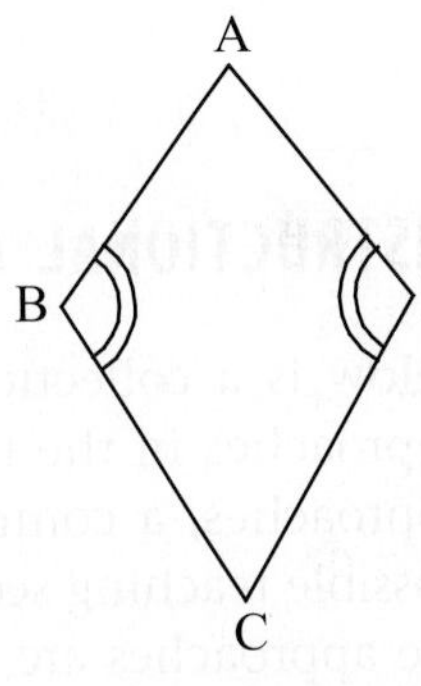
AB = AD, and CB = DC	ΔABC ≡ ΔADC (SSS)	∠B = ∠D

c. Translate the diagrammatic argument into textual form:

Given conditions (step 1)	Process/working (step 3)	Conclusion (step 2)
AB = AD, and CB = DC	Consider △ABC and △ADC AB = AD BC = DC AC = AC So, △ABC ≡ △ADC (SSS) Therefore, ∠B = ∠D	∠B = ∠D

d. Insert the reasoning (shown in italics) to complete the proof.

Consider △ABC and △ADC.
AB = AD (*given condition*)
BC = DC (*given condition*)
AC = AC (*same diagonal*)
So, △ABC ≡ △ADC (SSS)
Therefore, ∠B = ∠D (all corresponding angles are equal in congruent triangles)

INSTRUCTIONAL APPROACHES FOR TEACHING GEOMETRY THEOREMS

Below is a collection of different terms used in the literature to depict different approaches in the teaching of geometry. To aid in your comparison between these approaches, a common sample instructional objective is chosen and examples of possible teaching sequences illustrating the respective approaches are given. The way the approaches are listed may give an impression that they are distinctly different ways of teaching. But in an actual classroom situation, a combination of more than one approach may be in play. They are presented as separate approaches here so that the reader can see the distinct features of each approach.

Sample instructional objective

To explain that the sum of measures of interior angles of an n-sided polygon is $(n - 2) \times 180°$.

Approach 0: Direct teaching

A method of "direct transfer" of knowledge from the teacher to the students.

A procedure a teacher may adopt in this approach involves:

- writing on the board "the sum of measures of interior angles of an n-sided polygon is $(n - 2) \times 180°$" as a formula for students to remember,
- demonstrating how the formula can be applied in some standard exercise questions, and
- getting students to try to work on similar exercises.

Approach 1: Deductive reasoning

Utilise previously known theorem(s) and widely accepted logic and rules to derive a resulting intended proposition.

A procedure a teacher may adopt in this approach involves:

- revising the theorem that the interior angles of a triangle are supplementary,
- stating the theorem "the sum of measures of interior angles of an n-sided polygon is $(n - 2) \times 180°$",
- eliciting from the class a "general" polygon, say, a heptagon (7-sided),
- showing the drawing, and
- proposing that for any n-sided convest polygon $(n - 2)$ of such interior triangles can be formed.

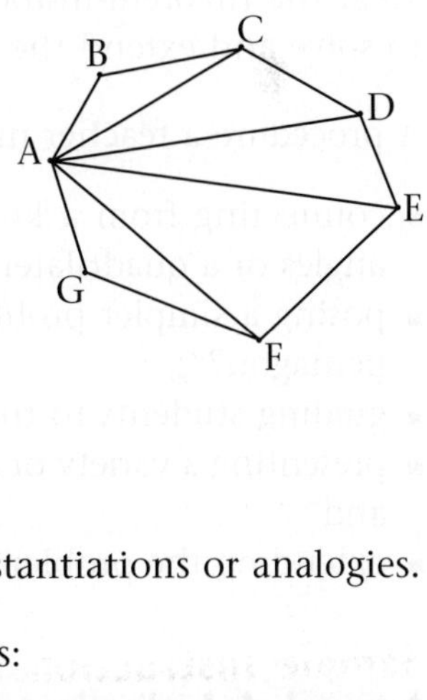

Sum of measures of the interior angles of polygon
= sum of measures of interior angles of all the triangles
= number of triangles $\times$ sum of interior angles of one triangle
= $(n - 2) \times 180°$.

Approach 2: Plausible (inductive) reasoning and conjecturing

Make conscious guesses of generalisations by observing instantiations or analogies.

A procedure a teacher may adopt in this approach involves:

- asking each student to draw a polygon of his choice on his notepad. Students measure the interior angles using a protractor,
- inviting the students to make guesses from observing the data they have collected,
- guiding the students to find the sum of the measures of interior angles, possibly providing a "graphic organiser" such as

# Sides	$\angle 1$	$\angle 2$	$\angle 3$	$\angle 4$	$\angle 5$	$\angle 6$	$\angle 7$	$\angle 8$	. . .	Sum
3										
4										
5										
6										
7										
⋮										
n										

- inviting students to conjecture a formula for the sum of the measures of interior angles of an n-sided polygon.

Approach 3: Problem-based

Treat the theorem-in-focus as a problem. Apply generic problem-solving heuristics to solve and extend the problem.

A procedure a teacher may adopt in this approach involves:

- connecting from a known related problem (e.g. "Remember the sum of interior angles of a quadrilateral?"),
- posing a simpler problem (e.g. "Can you find the sum of the interior angles of a pentagon?"),
- guiding students to the use of problem-solving strategies,
- presenting a variety of approaches used by students – successful and non-successful, and
- extending the problem to deal with n-sided polygons.

Approach 4: Applications to real world

Provide real-world context as a motivation or application of the theorem.

A procedure a teacher may adopt in this approach involves:

- setting a "real" context (e.g. "Floor tiles are usually squares. Must they be squares? Can we use other regular polygons such as equilateral triangles, regular pentagons, and so on, to tile our floors?"),
- inviting suggestions based on students' own experiences, possibly providing them manipulatives to work on (e.g. polydrons, pattern tiles),
- leading students to reason that tiling by the same regular polygon is possible if and only if the measure of the interior angle (in degrees) of the polygon is a factor of 360, and
- directing to the next natural question (e.g. "How do we know the measure of an interior angle of a regular polygon? Well, the next theorem we work on will help …").

Approach 5: Dynamic Geometry (DG) software

Harness the features (not inherent in traditional static media) of DG tools in visual reasoning.

A procedure a teacher may adopt in this approach involves:

- providing a flexible template in DG (e.g. Geometer's Sketchpad) for students to explore, such as the one below,

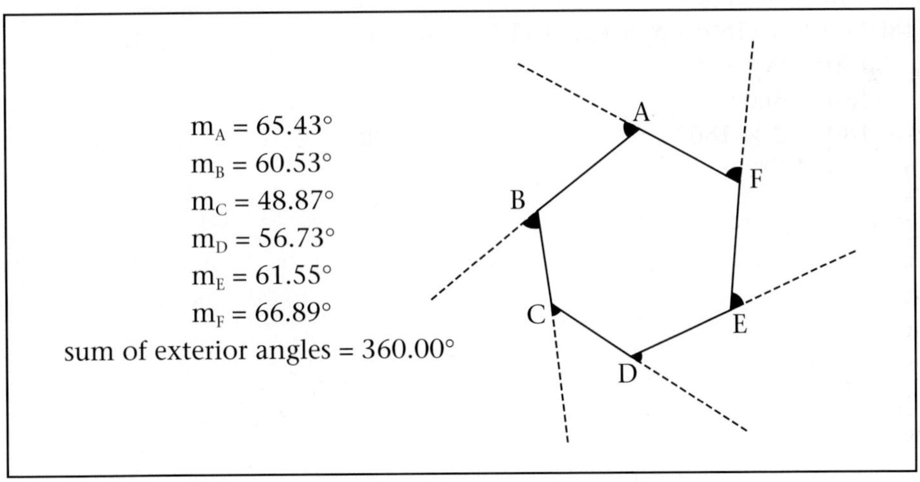

- asking the students if they are convinced that the sum of exterior angles of any hexagon is 360°,
- checking their (visual) reasoning – a possible one being that the vertices A, B, and so on, can be dragged close to one another while conserving the sum, approaching the angle sum at a point, as shown below.

$m_A = 65.43°$
$m_B = 60.53°$
$m_C = 48.87°$
$m_D = 56.73°$
$m_E = 61.55°$
$m_F = 66.89°$
sum of exterior angles = 360.00°

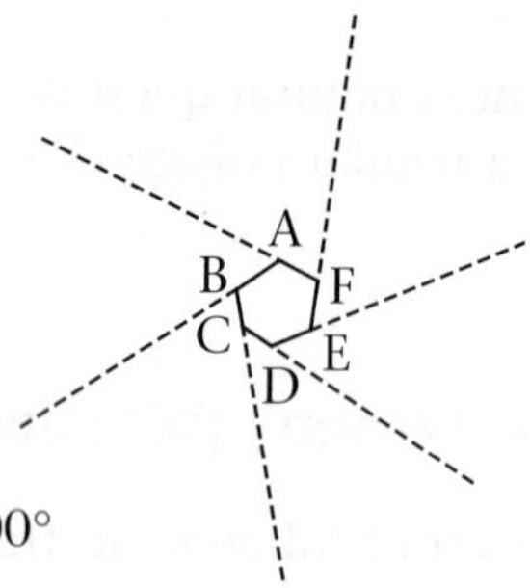

- leading the students to realise, using similar reasoning, that the "sum of exterior angles equal 360°" is true for *all* polygons, and
- showing that for an n-sided polygon with exterior angles $x_1°, x_2°, \ldots, x_n°$,

sum of interior angles
$= (180° - x_1°) + (180° - x_2°) + \ldots + (180° - x_n°)$
$= n \times 180° - (x_1° + x_2° + \ldots + x_n°)$
$= n \times 180° - 360°$
$= n \times 180° - 2 \times 180°$
$= (n - 2) \times 180°.$

SAMPLE ACTIVITIES FOR TEACHERS

1. Proposition: The interior angles of a triangle are supplementary.
   Work on a *deductive "proof"* of this proposition using the results available in school geometry. Think also of other alternative proofs. Be prepared to present the proof(s) to the class as you would to a class in school.

2. Conjecture: Every cyclic trapezium is isosceles.
   Suggest an activity that can potentially lead students via *plausible reasoning* to make the above conjecture. Include graphic organisers that you may use in the activity process.

3. Problem: Draw two tangents to a circle both intersecting at a point P. Suppose each tangent touches the circle at M and N respectively. What is the relationship between PM and PN?

   Devise a simpler/related *problem-of-the-day* that can potentially be extended to the problem above. State how you intend to explicitly link the problem-of-the day to the above problem.

4. Topic: Similarity.
   Discuss some possible *"real-life"* motivations or applications of "similarity". State at which junctures in the development of the topic you would likely introduce the respective "real-life" examples.

5. For each of the lesson foci below, plan a two-period lesson that uses the approaches (or a combination of the approaches) mentioned above. Indicate the key instructional moves that signal the use of the approach(es).

   - Relate "adjacent angles on a straight line", "vertically opposite angles" and "angles at a point".
   - Relate "corresponding angles", "alternate angles" and "interior angles" in the parallel lines setting.
   - Show that all rectangles are parallelograms.
   - Construct the perpendicular bisector of a line segment using only compasses and straight edge.
   - Show that SSS (three sides) is a test for the congruence of two triangles.

ACTIVITY: "WHO AM I?"

Properties of special quadrilaterals

Objective: To classify special quadrilaterals on the basis of their properties

Procedure:

1. Teacher demonstrates how the "game" is played.

   Example:
   - Students have ready paper and pencil for drawing or writing.
   - Teacher reads out the left column line by line (see table below), allowing time for students to figure out alternatives. Repeat when necessary.
   - Pause before the last line to ensure students are ready.
   - Read the last line and await students' answers.
   - Use the table below for discussions.

"Clues"	Possible answers at this juncture
I have four sides ... I have one pair of equal sides ...	Any quadrilateral
I have a pair of parallel sides ...	Square, rectangle, parallelogram, rhombus, trapezium
I have one interior right angle ...	Square, rectangle, trapezium
My diagonals are NOT equal. Draw and name me.	Trapezium 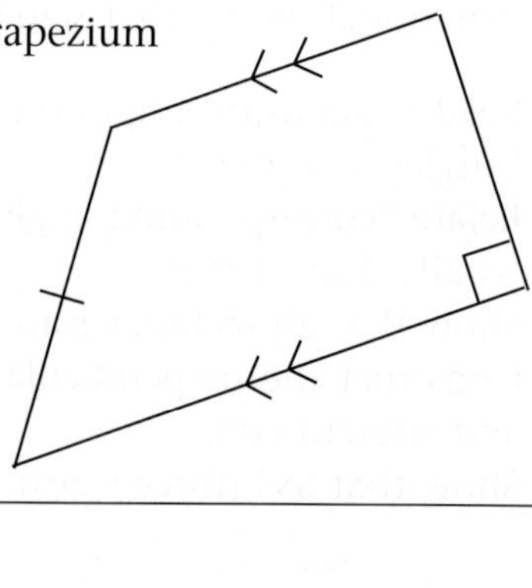

2. In pairs, students can take turn to test one another on other "who am I" items that you create. Other examples:

"I am a quadrilateral ...	"I have two diagonals ...
Some people call me a rhombus ...	They are equal in length ...
Some other people call me a rectangle ...	They are not perpendicular to one another ...
But I have a better name ...	They do not bisect one another ...
Who am I?"	But I have two pairs of equal angles ... Who am I?"

Geometry activities using Geometer's Sketchpad

1. Create a sketch to explore each of the following properties:

   a. Straight lines
      i. vertically opposite angles,
      ii. adjacent angles on a straight line, and
      iii. corresponding, interior and alternate angles of parallel lines.

   b. Triangles
      i. sum of interior angles,
      ii. base angles of isosceles triangles, and
      iii. angles of equilateral triangles.

2. Explore different ways of constructing a drag-resistant

   a. parallelogram,
   b. square,
   c. rectangle,
   d. rhombus,
   e. kite, and
   f. trapezium.

   Investigate the properties of the angles, sides and diagonals of these quadrilaterals and determine the relationship among them.

3. Draw a quadrilateral X and locate the midpoints of its sides. Join these midpoints to form another quadrilateral Y. What can you say about Y? Draw the diagonals of the original quadrilateral X. How are the sides of Y related to these diagonals?

4. Create a template to enable students to explore each of the following:

   a. Regular polygons
      i. sum of interior angles of n-sided regular polygons,
      ii. sum of exterior angles of a regular polygon, and
      iii. line and rotational symmetry of regular polygons.

   b. Arc length and sector area
      i. relationship between arc length and circumference of a circle, and
      ii. relationship between sector area and area of a circle.

   c. Pythagoras' theorem

   d. Motion geometry – investigate the properties of the following transformations:
      i. translation,
      ii. reflection,
      iii. rotation, and
      iv. enlargement.

Worksheet

CIRCLES AND TANGENTS

1. Start with an arbitrary circle with centre O.
   Construct three points A, C and B (in that order), on the circumference of the circle.

   Measure and compare ∠ACB and ∠AOB.

   ___

   Drag point C and/or point B.

   What do you observe?

   ___

2. Construct another point D on the circumference of the circle in step 1.
   Is there a relationship between ∠ACB and ∠ADB?

   ___

   Drag point D and/or point B.

   What do you observe?

   ___

   [Note that C and D can be on the same side or opposite sides of the chord AB.]

3. Draw an arbitrary circle.
   Construct a diameter AB and a point C on the circumference of the circle.

   Measure ∠ACB.

   ___

   Drag point C.

What do you observe?

---

4. Draw an arbitrary circle and three points A, B and C on the circle.
   Construct the tangent line to the circle at point A.

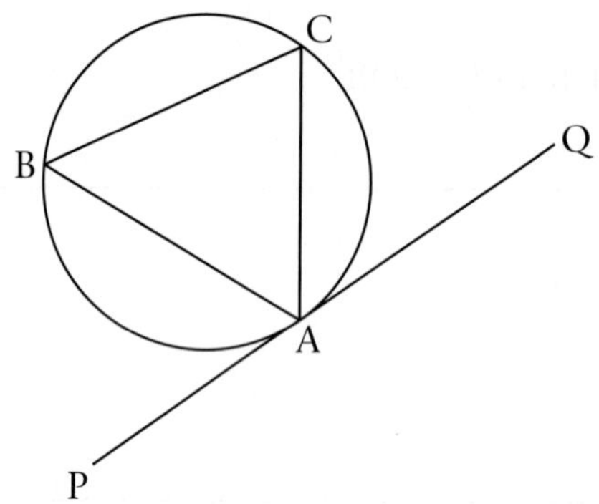

Measure and compare ∠ABC and ∠CAQ.

Drag point A and/or point B (or C).

What do you observe?

---

5. Establish the results of your observations in steps 1 to 4 by formal proofs.
6. Draw a circle and a point not on the circle.
   Construct the tangent line to the circle passing through the point.

For the teachers:

1. For what purpose can the activities in this worksheet be used?
2. How will you modify the worksheet for different groups of students?

Worksheet

CENTRES OF TRIANGLES

Use Geometer's Sketchpad to perform the following tasks. Record your construction steps, observations and diagrams on separate sheets of paper. In this worksheet, geometrical terms are in *italics* when mentioned for the first time.

1. Draw an arbitrary triangle. Make sure it is a closed figure.
   a. Construct the three *perpendicular bisectors* of the sides using the `Construct` menu. Verify that the three perpendicular bisectors are concurrent.
   b. Drag one of the vertices of the triangle. Are the perpendicular bisectors still concurrent?
   c. The point of concurrency is called the *circumcentre* of the triangle. Using the `Construct` menu, construct the circle with this point as centre and suitable radius such that the circle circumscribes the triangle. This is called the *circumcircle* of the triangle. Again drag one of the vertices of the triangle and observe what happens.

2. Start with an arbitrary triangle.

   Construct an *altitude* (i.e. the perpendicular from one vertex to the opposite side). Construct another altitude and the point of intersection of the two altitudes. How would you verify that the three altitudes are concurrent? This point of concurrency is called the *orthocentre* of the triangle.

3. Start with an arbitrary triangle.
   a. A *median* of a triangle is the line joining a vertex to the midpoint on the opposite side. Verify that the three medians of a triangle are concurrent. The point of concurrency is called the *centroid* of the triangle.
   b. The centroid divides each median into two segments. Choose one median and figure out how to use the `Measure` menu to find the ratio of the lengths of these two segments. (There are two ways of doing this in the `Measure` menu: using the `Ratio` command or the `Calculate` command. Explore both ways.) Drag one of the vertices of the triangle and observe whether the ratio varies or remains the same.
   c. Now do the same for the other two medians. Is this ratio the same for all three medians?

4. How would you verify that the three angle bisectors of a triangle are concurrent using GSP?
   This point of concurrency is called the *incentre* of the triangle. The incentre is the centre of the inscribed circle of the triangle. Construct the inscribed circle of the triangle. Drag one of the vertices. Are the sides of the triangle still tangents to the circle? If not, check your construction steps.

5. Draw a large triangle and construct appropriate lines to obtain the centroid, circumcentre and orthocentre. What do you observe about these three points? Drag one of the vertices and observe the relative position of the three points. Is there any constant in the ratio of distances between the three points?

More geometry activities using Geometer's Sketchpad

Activity 1: Midpoints in a quadrilateral. In this activity, you will investigate the quadrilateral formed by joining the midpoints of another quadrilateral.

Sketch:

1. Use the straightedge tool to construct a quadrilateral ABCD.

2. Select AB and click Point at Midpoint in the `Construct` menu to construct midpoint E. Similarly, construct the midpoints of the other three sides: F, G and H.

3. Connect these midpoints to form quadrilateral EFGH. (Select, in order, the four midpoints E, F, G and H and join them by line segments using the `Construct` menu.)

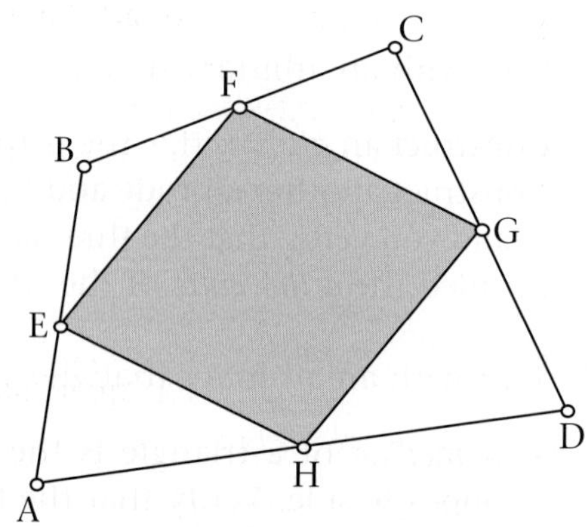

Investigate:
Drag the vertices or sides of the outer quadrilateral. Make sure to drag them to form a variety of sizes and shapes, including concave quadrilaterals.

What do you notice about the midpoint quadrilateral? What can you measure to confirm this conjecture? Write your conjecture below.

____

____

____

____

____

Explore more:

1. Draw diagonal BD. What can you say about the lengths and directions of FG and BD? EH and BD? Can you explain why your conjecture about midpoint quadrilaterals is true?

2. What is the midpoint quadrilateral of a midpoint quadrilateral?

3. What is the midpoint quadrilateral of a trapezium? A parallelogram? A kite? A rhombus? A rectangle? A square?

4. Construct the polygon interior of the original quadrilateral. Select the four vertices A, B, C and D, then choose `Polygon Interior` from the `Construct` menu. Similarly, construct the polygon interior of the midpoint quadrilateral. Select a different colour for each quadrilateral using the `Display` menu. Measure their areas. What can you conjecture about these areas?

5. Under what conditions is a midpoint quadrilateral a rectangle? A rhombus? A square? See if you can construct the most general quadrilateral whose midpoint quadrilateral is one of these.

Activity 2: Shortest journey.
In this activity, two points A and B lie on the same side of a straight line PQ. Find a point X on PQ so that AX + XB is a minimum.

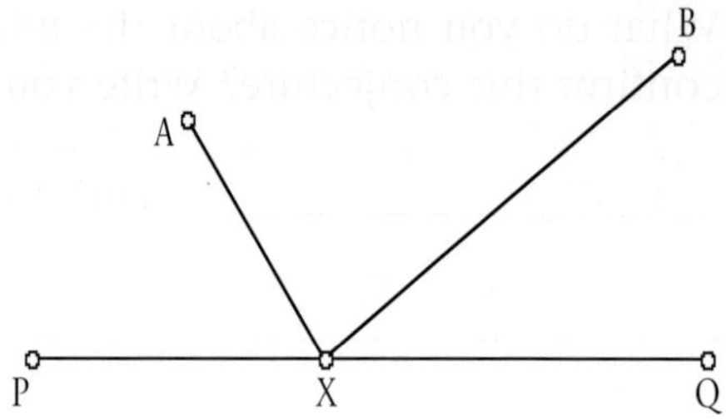

Sketch:

1. Construct points A, B and line segment PQ.

2. Construct any point X on PQ. Construct AX and XB.

3. Measure AX and XB by selecting the segments and clicking `Length` in the `Measure` menu.

4. Calculate their sum by selecting the two measures and clicking `Calculate` in the `Measure` menu.

   ____

5. Move point X on PQ until AX + XB is a minimum. Can you see any relationship between ∠AXP and ∠BXQ? Measure these angles.

   ____

6. Move A and B to different locations and minimise AX + XB again. Does the angle relationship hold?

   ____

7. State your conjectures below. Try to verify it.

   ____

   ____

   ____

   ____

8. Investigate what happens if there are three points A, B and C and you wish to find two points X and Y on PQ so that AX + XB + BY + YC is minimised.

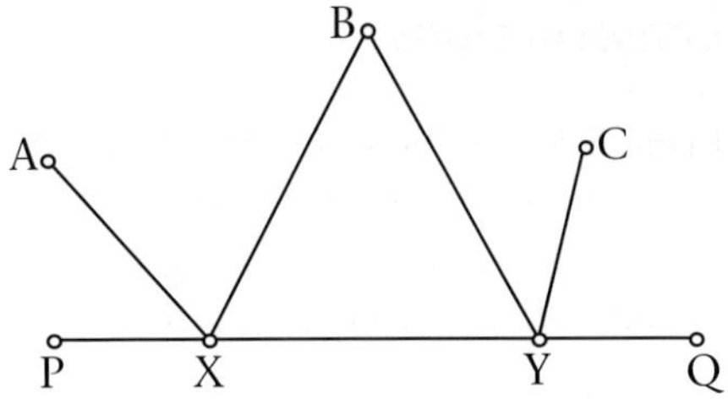

State your conjectures below. Try to verify it.

____

____

FURTHER READING

Activities

Gay, D. (1998). *Geometry by discovery.* NY: John Wiley & Sons, Inc.

Jones, R. (1999). *Paper folding: A fun way and effective method for learning mathematics.* St. Louis, MO: LWCD Inc.

Kenney, M.J., Bezuszka S.J., & Martin J.D. (1992). *Informal geometry explorations: An activity-based approach.* Palo Alto, CA: Dale Seymour Publications.

Kinsey, L.C., & Moore. T.E. (2001). *Symmetry, shape and space: An introduction to mathematics through geometry.* NY: Key College Publishing.

Lund, C.H. (1980). *Dot paper geometry: With or without a geoboard.* New Rochelle, NY: Cuisenaire Co. of America.

Muschla, J.A., & Muschla, G.R. (2000). *Geometry teacher's activities kit: Ready-to-use lessons & worksheets for grades 6–12.* NY: The Center for Applied Research in Education.

Serra, M. (1997). *Discovering geometry: An inductive approach.* Berkeley, CA: Key Curriculum Press.

Silvester, J.R. (2001). *Geometry ancient and modern.* Oxford, UK: Oxford University Press.

Sobel, M.A., & Maletsky, E.M. (1999). *Teaching mathematics: A sourcebook of aids, activities and strategies.* (3rd ed.). Boston, MA: Allyn & Bacon.

Usiskin, Z., Hirschhorn, D., Coxford, A., Highstone, V., Lewellen, H., Oppong, N., DiBianca, R., & Maeir, M. (2002). *Geometry.* Glenview, Ill: Prentice-Hall.

Constructions

Lim, S.K. (1997). Compass constructions: A vehicle for promoting relational understanding and higher order thinking skills. *The Mathematics Educator, 2*(2).

Pegg, J. (1987). Developing basic geometric constructions with understanding. *The Australian Mathematics Teacher, 43*(2).

Van Hiele Theory

Davey, G., & Holliday, J. (1992). van Hiele guidelines for geometry. *The Australian Mathematics Teacher, 48*(2).

Lim, S.K. (1992). Applying the van Hiele Theory to the teaching of secondary school geometry. *Teaching and Learning, 13*(1).

Geometer's Sketchpad Resources

Bennett, D. (2002). *Exploring geometry with the Geometer's Sketchpad: Revised for use with version 4.* Emeryville, CA: Key Curriculum Press.

De Villiers, Michael D. (1999). *Rethinking proof: With the Geometer's Sketchpad.* Emeryville, CA: Key Curriculum Press.

Kimberling, C. (2003). *Geometry in action : A discovery approach using the Geometer's Sketchpad.* Emeryville, CA: Key College Pub.

Serra, M. (1997). *Discovering geometry with the Geometer's Sketchpad.* Berkeley, CA: Key Curriculum Press.

Soon, Y.P., & Yap, S.F. (1999). *Geometric transformations with the Geometer's Sketchpad – "O" level mathematics.* Oxford, UK: Oxford University Press.

Others

Geddes, D. (1992). *Geometry in the middle grades.* Reston, VA: National Council of Teachers of Mathematics.

Jacobs, H.R. (2003). Geometry: Seeing, doing, understanding. (3rd ed.). NY: W.H. Freeman.

Lumpkin, B. (1997). *Geometry activities from many cultures.* Portland, ME: Weston Walch Pub.

O'Daffer P.G., & Clemens, S.R. (1991). *Geometry: An investigative approach.* Reading, MA: Addison-Wesley.

REFERENCES

Bass, L.E., Charles, R.I., Johnson, A., & Kennedy, D. (2004). *Geometry*. Prentice Hall Mathematics Series. NJ: Pearson Education.

Isaacs, I.M. (1998). *Geometry for college students*. London: Thomson Learning.

Lehrer, R., & Chazan, D. (1998). *Designing learning environment for developing understanding of geometry and space*. Mahwah, NJ: Erlbaum.

Chapter 7

Teaching of Trigonometry

Wong Khoon Yoong

Trigonometry is a branch of mathematics that deals with the properties of triangles (planar and spherical) and the trigonometric functions. Historically, it was developed to measure heights of objects (trees, cliffs, etc.) and distances (width of river, etc.) for surveying, navigation and astronomy. Such applications are still found in current practices, which can provide the motivation for students to learn this topic.

The word "trigonometry" is derived from Greek, meaning three (TRI), angle (GONON) and measure (METRON). It deals primarily with the relations between the sides and angles of a triangle and provides efficient methods of performing calculations on triangles. In the past, calculations were done with the use of trigonometric tables which have now been replaced by calculators and computers. Trigonometric tables were constructed by ancient Greek mathematicians to solve problems in mathematical astronomy. These tables were later refined by Muslim mathematicians during the Middle Ages as a tool to calculate the precise times of various religious activities at different locations (such as praying times) and the Islamic calendar.

According to the MacTutor History of Mathematics Archive (http://www-history.mcs.st-andrews.ac.uk/history/index.html), the word "sine" was the Latin translation (*sinus*) of the Arabic word *jaib*, which came from the Hindu word *jya*, the original meaning being a "fold".

Regiomontanus (circa 1463) used the expression *sinus rectus complementi* to designate *cosine*. In 1620, Edmund Gunter abbreviated this to *co.sinus*. Newton first used the term "cosine" in 1658.

The Pythagoras' theorem has a tortuous history. Pythagoras (circa 569–475 B.C.) was an important ancient Greek mathematician but none of his writings has survived. The theorem in various forms, such as the 3-4-5 triangle, was known to the Babylonians (circa 1600 B.C.) and Chinese (Chou Pei, circa 1000 B.C.; Swetz and Kao, 1977). Its formal proof appeared in Euclid's *Elements* as Book I Proposition 47 and its converse as Book I Proposition 48 (323–285 B.C.; Artmann, 1999). Mathematicians from other cultures had provided different proofs of this famous theorem.

The purpose of these historical notes is to encourage students to appreciate that mathematics results from the contributions of people from various cultures and races. In the multi-racial Singapore society, such appreciation is an important aspect of National Education.

KEY CONCEPTS

There are six standard trigonometric ratios: sine, cosine, tangent, cotangent, cosecant and secant. The first three are covered in the N-level and O-level syllabuses, and the last three in Additional Mathematics only.

The key concept underlying these ratios is that the trigonometric ratio of a given angle is independent of the size of the right-angled triangle drawn. This invariant property should be explored by the students using knowledge of similar triangles.

The definitions of these trigonometric ratios are first based on the right-angled triangles. The terms "opposite" and "adjacent" sides refer to the named/mentioned angle, excluding the right angle (the side opposite the right angle is the hypotenuse). Hence, it is important to point out to students that a given side may be "opposite" or "adjacent" depending on which the referenced angle is.

These definitions are later extended to angles of any magnitude using the "unit circle" approach. Up to O-level, angles are expressed in degrees (up to one decimal place). Radian measure is introduced in Additional Mathematics. As an introduction to the calculus of trigonometric functions, approximations for small angles will be needed.

The links among these concepts are shown in the topic map on p. 145.

LEARNING DIFFICULTIES

Several common errors and learning problems are discussed below. To find out more, talk to your students after you have marked their exercises and tests. Most of these errors arise from misconceptions students develop due to various reasons other than carelessness. The common errors are:

1. Not knowing which trigonometric ratio to use for a given right-angled triangle. This arises from recalling the wrong definition or not recognising the angles when the triangle is in "non-standard" orientations. For the first difficulty, mnemonics such as TOASOHCAH may be used. For the second, let students work with triangles in various orientations, especially when the sides are neither horizontal nor vertical.

Map of trigonometry topics in secondary schools

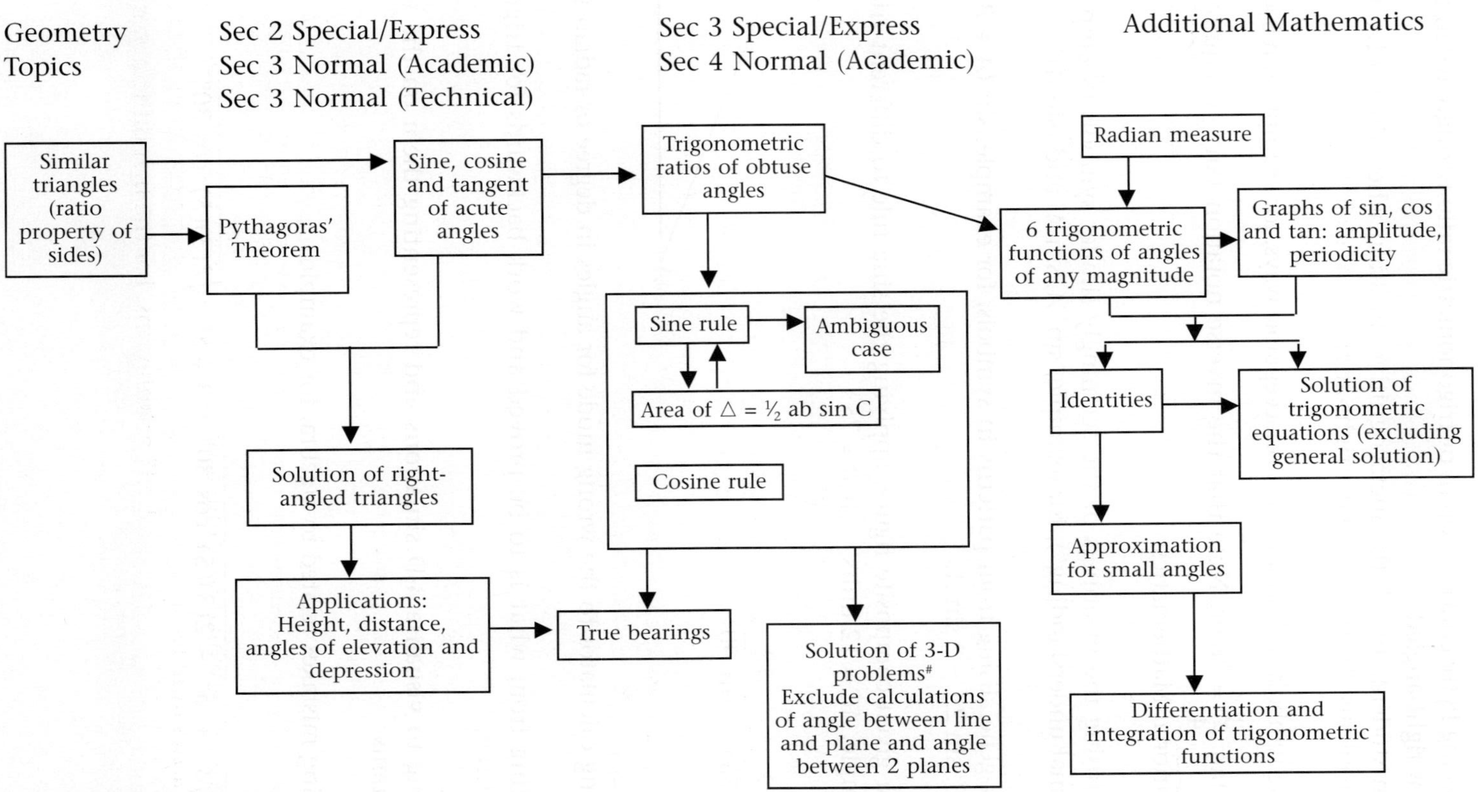

Not for Normal streams

2. Applying Pythagoras' theorem or trigonometric ratio wrongly when the triangle is not right-angled.
   Train students to ask the metacognitive question when they solve these types of problems: "Is the triangle a right-angled triangle?".

3. Using symbols and notations in unacceptable ways, for example, $\tan \theta = \frac{3}{4} = 36.9°$, $\theta = \tan \frac{3}{4} = 36.9°$. Note that the inverse notation $\tan^{-1}$ is required only for Additional Mathematics.

4. Confusing the meanings of the seemingly similar symbols (Skemp called this "formal understanding"), for example, $\sin^2 A$, $\sin A^2$ and $(\sin A)^2$.

5. Over-generalising from patterns in symbols, for example, $\sin (A + B) = \sin A + \sin B$, $\sin 2A = 2 \sin A$.

6. For a given composite figure, applying the sine rule to different triangles, for example, $AC = 12$ units, $\angle ACB = 75°$.

$$\frac{BD}{\sin 75°} = \frac{12}{\sin 90°}$$

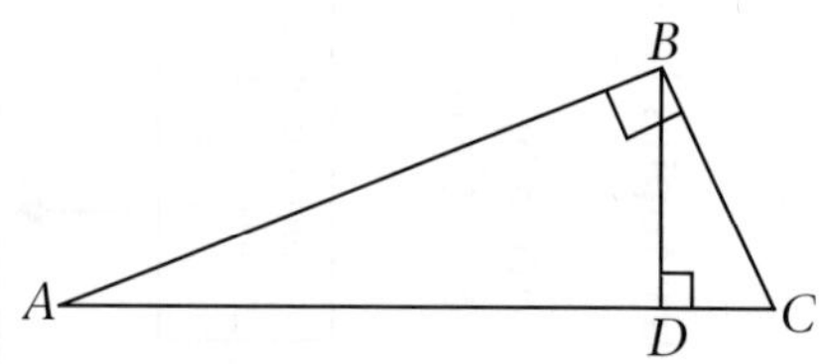

7. Setting calculator to the wrong mode for angles in degree or radian measure.

8. Starting from what is to be proved and work backwards for trigonometric identities.

9. Failing to visualise 3-D situations and representing them on the wrong 2-D diagrams.

10. Making mistakes related to algebra, for example,

$$a = \sqrt{3^2 + 5^2 - 2(3)(5) \cos 30°} = 3 + 5 - \sqrt{2(3)(5) \cos 30°}$$

PYTHAGORAS' THEOREM

Teaching approaches

1. Proving of the Pythagoras' theorem is not required. However, it will promote mathematical reasoning to expose students to proofs that use formal argument (Euclid), algebra (Garfield), manipulatives (Chinese; Kolpas, 1992), ICT (Bennett, 1995) and transformations (Greenbury, 1995). The objective is to help students realise that a given mathematical result can be proved in many different ways. This will promote thinking skills. Note that students are not required to remember these proofs. Decide how many proofs to work through for your class.

2. Students should understand the difference between the Pythagoras' theorem and its converse. However, the proof of the converse may be puzzling to many students and hence may be left out.

3. Give problems that students can solve using the theorem and check the answers using measurement. This makes the problems more concrete and will help them make sense of what they are doing.

Sample activities

Two types of activities are described: one for trainees to understand the pedagogy and one for school students to understand the mathematics. During tutorial sessions, trainees may have to work through both types of activities.

1. (Pedagogy) Examine the textbooks and workbooks. What types of activities will you choose for your lessons on this topic? In what sequence will you carry them out? What modifications and additional materials will you use?

2. (Mathematics) Ask students to draw any right-angled triangle as accurately as possible. Measure the three sides and compute their squares. Ask them to spot patterns. It may be useful to discuss how the students would tabulate the measurements obtained. This is an example of inductive thinking.

3. (Mathematics) Wallis' similarity proof (1616–1703)
   Find two pairs of similar triangles in the diagram shown (*ABC*). Use proportions.

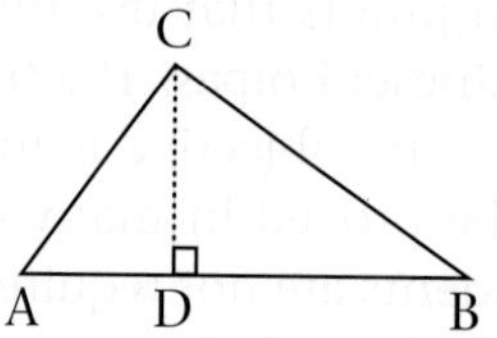

Wallis' similarity proof

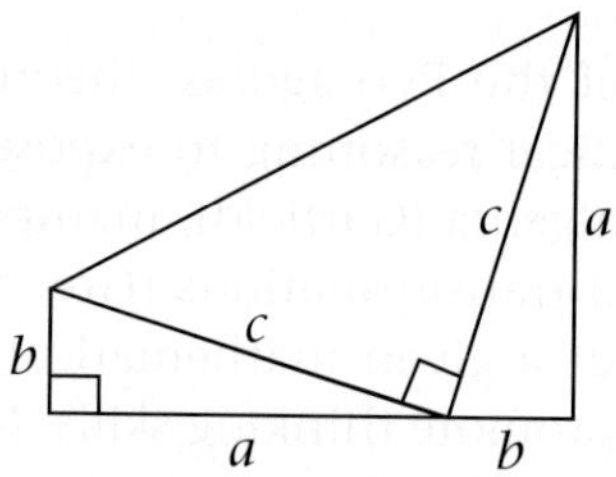

Garfield's trapezium proof

4. (Mathematics) Garfield's trapezium proof (1876)
   To make the proof more meaningful to the students, ask them to construct the shapes and assemble them. [Garfield was the 20th president of the United States. He was a mathematics teacher before he joined the army. He was elected president in March 1881, but four months later was shot dead by a disappointed office seeker.]

5. (Mathematics) Work through the four proofs in *Pythagoras.gsp* from the Geometer's Sketchpad package. Pay attention to differences between a static and a dynamic proof.

6. (Mathematics) Euclidean congruence proof (323–285 B.C.). This is the classical proof and may be too difficult for some students. However, trainees should know this proof.

   The diagram on the right is a very well-known diagram and has been called "the bride's chair", "the peacock's tail" and "the windmill". It has appeared in company logos, T-shirts, book covers, etc.

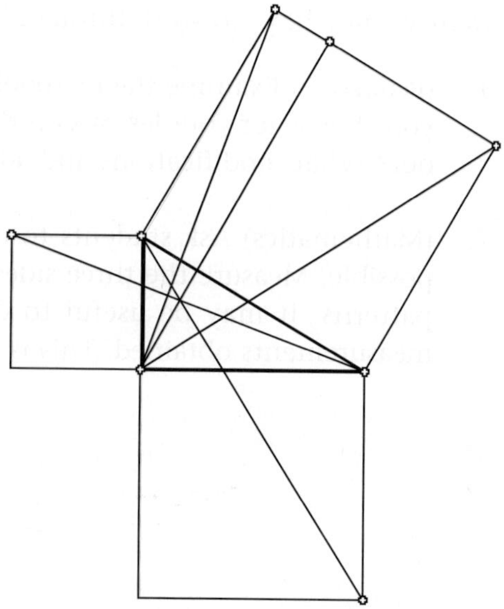

7. (Pedagogy) Design a worksheet for one of the mentioned proofs.

8. (Mathematics) State the converse of the Pythagoras' theorem. For a formal proof using SSS, see Artmann (1999), pp. 44–45.

9. (Mathematics) Try these two challenging problems:
   a. Determine the area of an annulus using one measurement only.
   b. A water lily is 10 cm above the water surface. It is blown 50 cm sideways by a strong wind so that it just touches the water surface. How deep is the pond?

   (Pedagogy) Use b. to illustrate a teaching technique about oral mathematics communication. The teacher reads the question slowly, then asks a few students to explain the question in their own words. Follow up with diagrams. This technique can be applied to any word problem.

10. (Pedagogy) Solve a few difficult problems involving the Pythagoras' theorem and note how you feel about tackling them. Recall your past experiences of learning this theorem in school and university. Consider these reflections when you plan your lessons.

11. (Pedagogy) Get the students to share anecdotes of mathematicians who had made contributions to trigonometry.

12. (Pedagogy) Begin this topic by posing this problem: Given two squares, find a square whose area is the sum of the areas of these two squares (Wittmann, 1996). Alternatively, pose this at the end of the topic. Replace the square with semi-circles or equilateral triangles.

Worksheet

PYTHAGORAS' THEOREM

Objective: To establish a relationship between the areas of squares on the sides of a right-angled triangle

Materials: Vanguard sheet (two colours), set squares, pencil, scissors, sticky tape

Procedure:

1. Draw any right-angled triangle (preferably non-isosceles) on a vanguard sheet and cut it out. Label the hypotenuse c and the other two sides a and b.

2. Using the triangle you have drawn, measure and cut out two squares of sides a and b respectively, using the vanguard of another colour. See Figure 1.

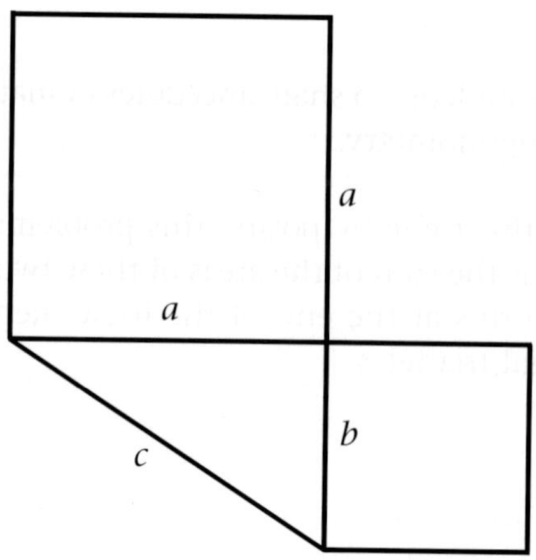

Figure 1

3. Put one square against the other as shown in Figure 2, and draw the dotted line as shown.

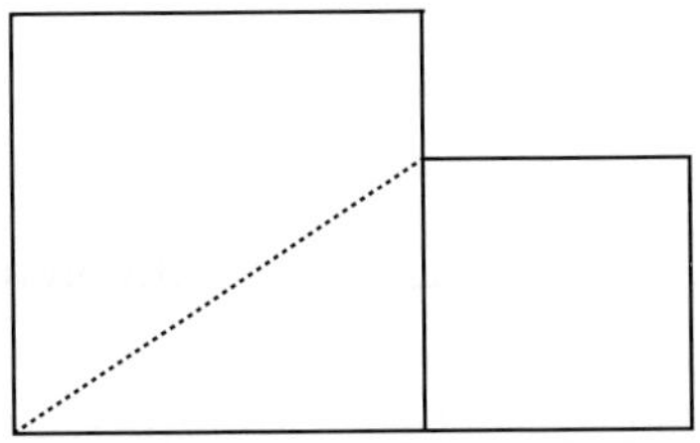

Figure 2

4. Keeping the smaller square in place, rotate the larger square of Figure 2 through 90° clockwise, placing it against the smaller square. Tape the two squares together as in Figure 3. Then draw in the second line as shown in Figure 3.

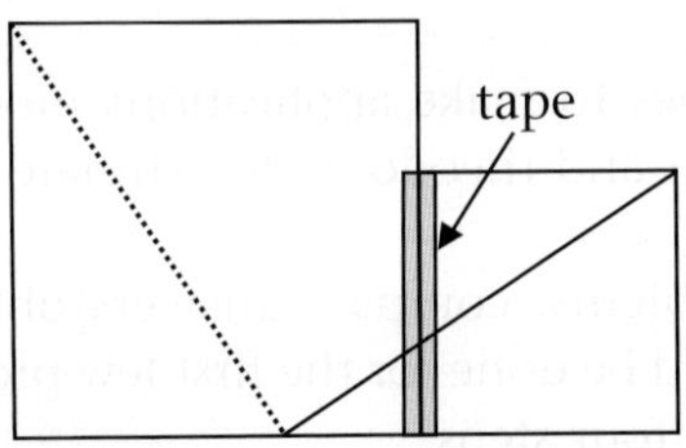

Figure 3

5. Write down the area of the composite figure in Figure 3 in terms of a and b. Cut the composite figure of Figure 3 along the two lines to get three pieces: a jagged pentagon and two triangles.

6. Rearrange these three pieces to form a large square.

7. Check the side of this square against your original right-angled triangle. What is the area of this square?

8. What is the relationship between the areas of the squares of sides a, b and c?

Conclusion:
In a right-angled triangle, the *area* of the square on the ________________ is equal to the sum of the ________________ of the squares on the other two sides. Write this algebraically:

This result is known as ________________ theorem.

TRIGONOMETRIC RATIOS, SINE RULE, COSINE RULE

Teaching approaches:

1. Some trainees ask the students to *prove* that the sine of an angle is opposite divided by hypotenuse. This is a misconception that *definition* can be proved!

2. Use hands-on activities and applets to develop concepts.

3. Conduct practical activities to make applications more real to the students, for example, use a clinometer and theodolite to estimate height of objects.

4. When solving word problems, compare answers obtained by calculation and measurements. This should be done for the first few problems. When solving such problems, refer to Polya's four steps.

5. Use teaching aids to help students visualise 3-D trigonometry problems.

6. Use visual mnemonics such as the following figure, to help students remember trigonometric identities, for examples, $\sin^2 \theta + \cos^2 \theta = 1$ and $\frac{1}{\sin \theta} = \text{cosec } \theta$.

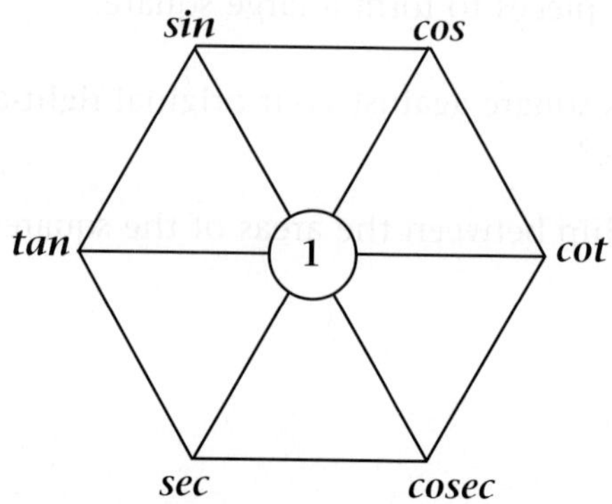

Sample activities

1. (Pedagogy) Study the topic map on p. 145 and discuss the sequences shown on the map. Write specific instructional objectives for a selected topic.

2. (Pedagogy) Examine the textbooks and workbooks. What types of activities will you choose for your lessons on these topics? In what sequence will you carry them out? What modifications and additional materials will you use?

3. (Mathematics) Ask students to draw a 30° right-angled triangle of any size. Measure its opposite and hypotenuse and compute (opposite ÷ hypotenuse). Share the values. Explain to the class that irrespective of the size of the triangle drawn, this value is constant (0.5). Hence, it is appropriate to give it a name, that is, sin 30°. Reinforce this idea using the Geometer's Sketchpad.

4. (Pedagogy) Construct a clinometer or use a commercial one.

Making a clinometer:

a. Cut out a copy of the "protractor" given and paste it on a board, leaving a margin all around.
b. Tie a short piece of string to a weighted bead to make a plumbline.
c. Using some sticky tape, attach the plumbline to the board on the right-hand corner of the "quarter protractor" so that it swings freely from the point of attachment.
d. Attach a straw to the board parallel to the line marking 90°.
e. In the diagram below, angle of elevation = 90° – (90° – θ) = θ.
f. To construct a hypsometer, see Geddes (1992).

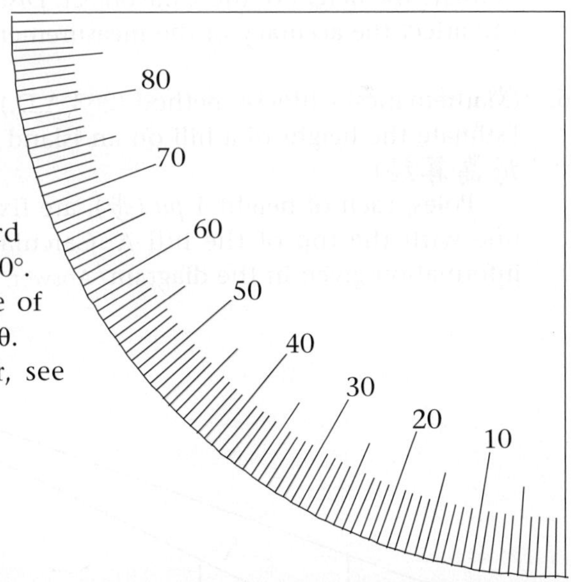

Working principle

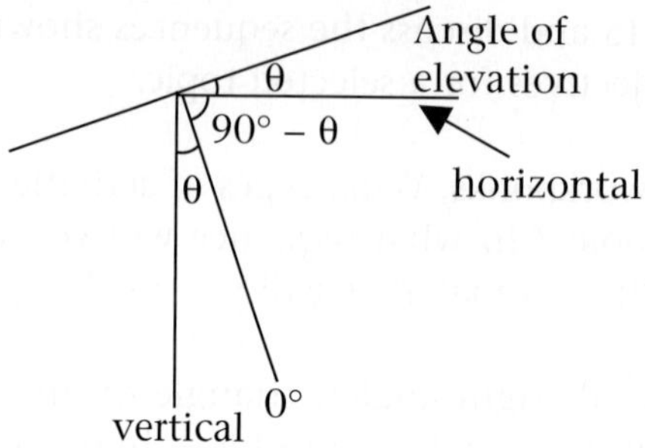

Clinometer in use

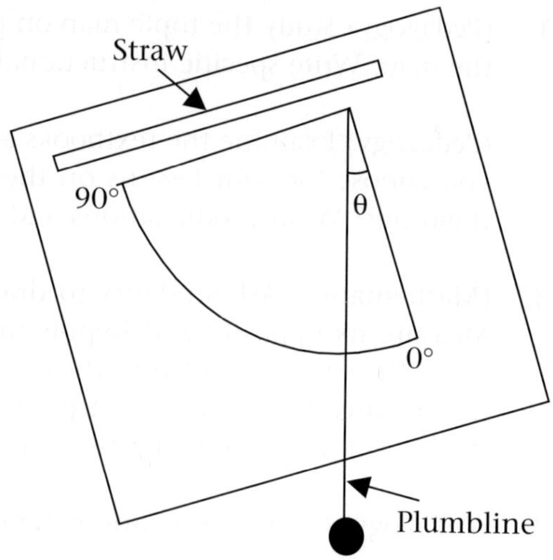

5. (Pedagogy) Estimate the height of objects around the campus using two different methods, one whereby the base of the object can be determined and the other whereby the base of the object cannot be located. Get three or four groups to estimate the height of the same object. Discuss the values obtained. What factors will affect the accuracy of the measurement?

6. (Mathematics) Chinese method (263 A.D.)
   Estimate the height of a hill on an island using two poles (*Hai-Tao Suan-Ching* 海島算经)

   Poles, each of height 1 *pu* (步), are fixed at E and F so that the tips are in line with the top of the hill A. Calculate the height of the hill from the information given in the diagram. Answer: 251 *pu*.

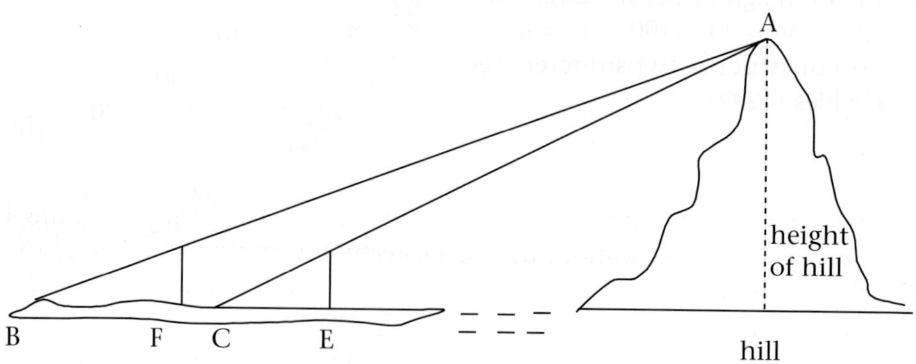

BF = 127 *pu*, CE = 123 *pu*, FE = 1000 *pu*

Another example: Use the following diagram to estimate the height of a cliff when it is not possible to measure the distance from A or B to the foot of the cliff.

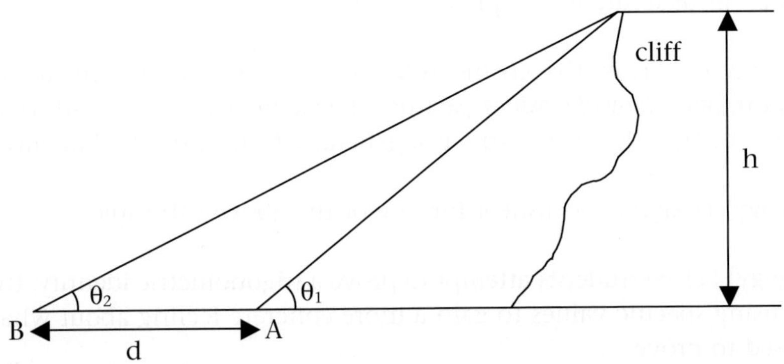

7. (Pedagogy) Some geometry questions found in tests and examinations are mathematically wrong. Identify the mistake in this question: "*TP* and *TQ* are tangents to the circle with centre *O*, radius 5 cm. *TP* = 12 cm, ∠*PTO* = 37°".

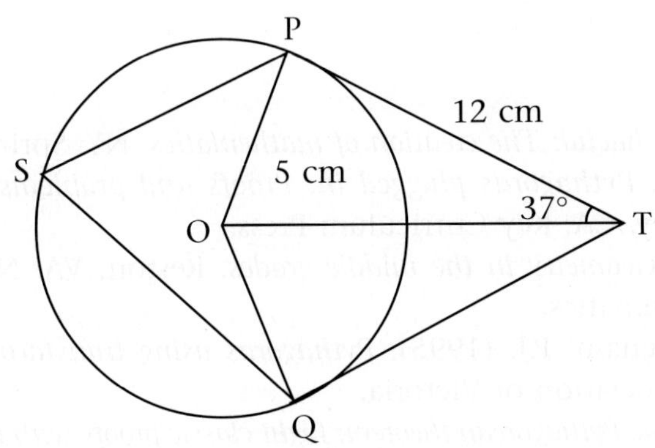

Test setters should check such geometry questions using correct knowledge of trigonometry.

8. (Pedagogy) The "unit circle" is used to define trigonometric ratios for angles of any size. For a demonstration, use *Trigonometry tracers.gsp* from the Geometer's Sketchpad package. This leads up to the functional aspect and graphs of trigonometric functions.

9. (Mathematics) Justify the sine rule by induction (using measurements, tabulation and pattern seeking) and deduction (proof). For the more able class, explore the meaning of the constant $\frac{a}{\sin A}$, that is, the diameter of the circumscribed circle. Check by measurement and justify by proof.

10. (Mathematics) Prove the cosine rule. For an optional activity using Dintzl's dissection, open *Law of Cosines.gsp* from the Geometer's Sketchpad package. Help students see that the cosine rule is a generalisation of the Pythagoras' theorem.

11. (Pedagogy) Design a worksheet for one of the above sub-topics.

12. (Pedagogy) Before students attempt to prove a trigonometric identity, they should check using specific values to gain a more concrete feeling about what they are supposed to prove.

13. (Pedagogy) Prepare some interview questions you might ask to find out how students work out trigonometry problems, for example, "How do you know that?", "What does this figure tell you about ...?". Try out with a few students and report your findings to the class.

REFERENCES

Artmann, B. (1999). *Euclid: The creation of mathematics*. NY: Springer-Verlag.

Bennett, D. (1995). *Pythagoras plugged in: Proofs and problems for the Geometer's Sketchpad*. Berkeley, CA: Key Curriculum Press.

Geddes, D. (1992). *Geometry in the middle grades*. Reston, VA: National Council of Teachers of Mathematics.

Greenbury, G.J. Barcham, P.J. (1995). *Pythagoras using transformations*. Brunswick: Mathematical Association of Victoria.

Kolpas, S.J. (1992). *The Pythagorean theorem: Eight classic proofs with manipulative masters for hands-on understanding*. Palo Alto, CA: Dale Seymour.

Swetz, R., & Kao, T.I. (1977). *Was Pythagoras Chinese? An examination of right triangle theory in ancient China*. University Park, PA: Pennsylvania University Press.

Wittmann, E.C. (1996). Designing teaching: The Pythagorean Theorem. In T.J. Cooney, S.I. Brown, J.A. Dossey, G. Schrage, & E.C. Wittmann (Eds.), *Mathematics, pedagogy, and secondary teacher education* (pp. 97–165). Portsmouth, NH: Heinemann.

Chapter 8

Teaching of Sets

Soon Yu Tiong Spario and Yeo Kai Kow Joseph

The concept of sets does not only help us to classify things but also helps us to count. Long before numbers were invented, numerical records were kept by means of tallies. Keeping a tally involves matching sets of objects and marks and was the beginning of the idea of counting. The importance of counting to sets was first recognised by the 19th-century German mathematician George Cantor (1845–1918). The mathematical theory of sets grew out of his study of infinite sets of real numbers. The language of sets has become an important tool for all branches of mathematics – as a basis for precise definition of higher concepts, and for mathematical reasoning.

KEY CONCEPTS

1. Basic notations and definitions

ε	universal set
$\varnothing$ or $\{\ \}$	empty set
$\in$	is an element of
$\notin$	is not an element of
$\subseteq$	is a sub-set of
$\subset$	is a proper sub-set of
$\cap$	intersection
$\cup$	union

A power set is the set of all sub-sets of a given set, containing the empty set and the original set.

2. Algebra of sets

	Union	**Intersection**
Commutative Laws	$A \cup B = B \cup A$	$A \cap B = B \cap A$
Idempotent Laws	$A \cup A = A$	$A \cap A = A$
Associative Laws	$A \cup (B \cup C) = (A \cup B) \cup C$	$A \cap (B \cap C) = (A \cap B) \cap C$
Existence of Identities	$A \cup \varnothing = A$	$A \cap \xi = A$
Distributive Laws	$A \cup (B \cap C) = (A \cup B) \cap (A \cup C)$	$A \cap (B \cup C) = (A \cap B) \cup (A \cap C)$
De Morgan's Laws	$(A \cup B)' = A' \cap B'$	$(A \cap B)' = A' \cup B'$

3. Venn diagrams
   A Venn diagram has the universal set usually represented by a rectangle which includes circles depicting the sub-sets. The first to systematically use diagrams to represent statements of logic reasoning was the German mathematician and philosopher G.W. von Leibniz (1646–1716). The diagrams used today are sometimes referred to as Euler diagrams after the Swiss mathematician Leonhard Euler (1707–1783), who devised them, but are usually called "Venn diagrams" after the English logician John Venn, who, in 1880, greatly improved the diagrams and popularised their use. A Venn diagram can be employed for any number of sub-sets, but having more than three sub-sets would defeat the purpose of gaining increased clarity.

4. Two principles of counting sets

   a. The inclusion/exclusion principle
      For any sets A and B, $n(A \cup B) = n(A) + n(B) - n(A \cap B)$.
      If A and B are disjoint or mutually exclusive sets, then $n(A \cup B) = n(A) + n(B)$.
   b. Complement principle
      For any set, $n(A') = n(\varepsilon) - n(A)$.

LEARNING DIFFICULTIES

To find out more, discuss with your students after you have corrected their exercises and tests. Most of the errors students make may be explained by the misconceptions they have due to various reasons other than carelessness. Several common errors and learning difficulties are discussed below:

1. As long as sets of physical objects are observed and manipulated, the concept remains a simple one. Difficulties begin when symbols are adopted to communicate the idea of sets and their elements. For example, are the following sets equivalent (i.e. does there exist a 1–1 correspondence between the two sets)? {□, □, □} and {○, ○}

2. Unable to distinguish between:
   - the element "a" in a set and the sub-set {a};
   - the symbols $\in$ and $\subset$;
   - $\varnothing$, 0 and the set {0} which is a set with 0 as its only member;
   - $n(A)$ and the actual elements of A;
   - $\cup$ and $\cap$;
   - statements involving sets. For instance, look at the following examples involving sets P and Q:
     a. There are ten elements in P (maybe also in Q).
     b. There are ten elements in P only (definitely not in Q).

3. Quite often, students get confused over union and intersection of sets when the notation of complement is involved. This creates difficulty particularly when students are asked to shade the regions in a Venn diagram corresponding to some given expressions of sets. Some students also find it hard to solve word problems that involve counting and Venn diagrams.

4. When set notation is used to express certain statements, students have difficulty in translating set notation into statements and vice-versa.

TEACHING APPROACHES

1. Coloured chalks, buttons and attribute blocks may be useful as teaching aids.

2. It is important to stress that a set must be clearly defined. We should be able to identify it if an object is a member of a clearly defined set. Provide some examples of sets not clearly defined. For example: T is a set of TV actors admired by my classmates.

3. In order to reinforce the concepts of set, element, number of elements, intersection and union, discuss everyday examples with the class.

4. Many examples of empty sets may be introduced to arouse interest. Ask the students to name some of the empty sets that they know and you may be amazed with the many strange and funny examples that they can come up with.

5. You may wish to have a class discussion to clarify the use of the terms "and" and "or" in set language as compared to their use in ordinary language.

6. Use words like "common places" for intersection, "patch" for union and "outside" for complement when the Venn diagram is taught.

7. Logic and deductive reasoning should be linked to sets and Venn diagrams to show the usefulness of learning sets. Note that for Venn diagrams, complex representation which combines several characteristics does not aid learning or memory.

8. To enhance logical thinking and to motivate students' interest, the idea that classification can be done in different ways depending on criteria could be included in the teaching of sets, for example, classifying a group of famous people.

SAMPLE ACTIVITIES FOR TEACHERS

1. Classify the following using a Venn diagram:

   a. triangles;
   b. quadrilaterals.

2. True or false:

   a. For any set X, $\varnothing \subseteq X$.
   b. $\varnothing \in \{\varnothing\}$
   c. $\varnothing \subseteq \{\varnothing\}$
   d. $\varnothing \subseteq \{\ \}$
   e. $2 \in \{\{2\}\}$
   f. $\{3, 4\} \subseteq \{\{3, 4\}, \{3\}, 4\}$

3. a. How many sub-sets can you form from {1, 2, 3}?
   b. How many elements are there in the set: {1, 2, 1, 3, 1}?

4. a. For any two sets, A and B, write down the possible relationships between them using set notations. Depict each case using a Venn diagram.
   b. Consider the two sets, A and B, in the following Venn diagram.

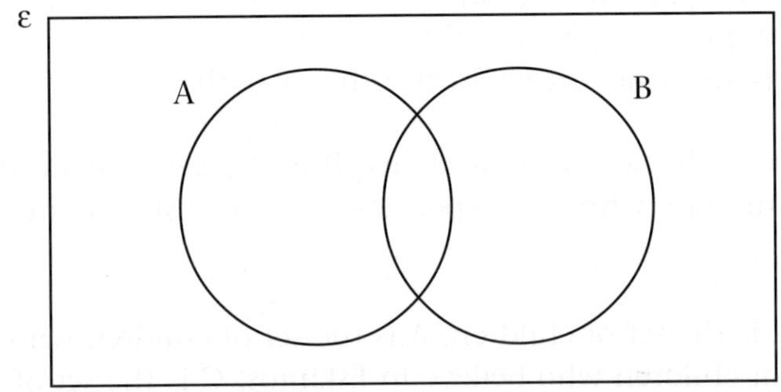

There are four distinct regions in the diagram. How many ways can you shade one or more of these region(s)? Express each possible case using set notations.

5. Establish a one-one correspondence between

   a. the set of natural numbers and the set of integers;
   b. the set of integers and the set of rational numbers.

SAMPLE ACTIVITIES FOR STUDENTS

1. State using appropriate set notations:

   a. 4 is not a member of set P;
   b. set Q is completely contained in set R;
   d. the number of elements not in S is 5;
   d. sets T, U and V have no element common in all of them;
   e. the set W is made up of elements in X or Y.

2. Given that ε is the set of people in Singapore, P the set of people who are over 18 years of age, Q is the set of people who have passed a driving test, R is the set of people who are allowed to drive a car, express in set language the following statements:

   a. People in Singapore who are allowed to drive a car are those who are over 18 and have passed a driving test;
   b. People in Singapore who are not over 18 or have not passed a driving test are among those who are not allowed to drive a car.

3. Given that ε is the set of pigs, A is the set of greedy pigs, B is the set of healthy pigs, C is the set of fat pigs, express in set language the following statements:

   a. All healthy pigs are greedy;
   b. Some healthy pigs are not fat;
   c. All healthy pigs are greedy and fat;
   d. All fat pigs are either greedy or healthy or both.

4. Given that ε is the set of all students, P is the set of male students and Q is the set of students who wear spectacles, write a statement corresponding to $P \cap Q' \neq \varnothing$.

5. Given that ε is the set of children, A is the set of children who believe in fairies, B is the set of children who believe in Eskimos, C is the set of children who are in school. Write a statement corresponding to each of the following:

   a. $A \not\subset B$. b. $C \cap B = \varnothing$.

   Express in set language the following statements:

   c. All children in school believe in fairies;
   d. Some children believe in both fairies and Eskimos.

6. Three sets, A, B and C, satisfy the following conditions:

   $n(A \cap B) \neq 0$, $C \subseteq B$ and $A \cap C = \varnothing$.

   Draw and label a Venn diagram to illustrate these sets.

7. Some people were interviewed to find out whether they spoke Mandarin, English, Mandarin and English, or neither Mandarin nor English.
   In the Venn diagram below,

   ε is the set of people who were interviewed.
   F is the set of people who spoke Mandarin.
   S is the set of people who spoke English.

The letters w, x, y and z represent the number of people in each of the sub-sets shown. Given that $n(\varepsilon) = 250$, $n(F) = 80$ and $n(S) = 220$,

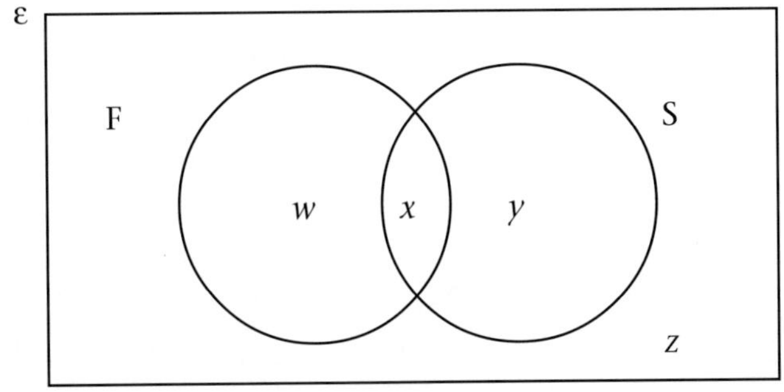

Find

a. the maximum possible value of w;
b. the maximum possible value of z;
c. the maximum possible number of people who spoke both Mandarin and English.

FURTHER READING

Cyril, E. (1974). *Sets and relations.* London: Macdonald Educational.

Gullberg, J. (1997). *Mathematics from the birth of numbers.* NY: W.W. Norton & Company.

Lee, P.Y., Teh, K.S., & Looi, C.K. (1995). *New syllabus D mathematics 4 – Teacher's resource manual.* Singapore: Shing Lee.

School Mathematics Project. (1991). *16–19 mathematics: Mathematical structure* (Chapter 2). Cambridge, UK: Cambridge University Press.

Schoen, H.L. (1974). Some difficulty in the language of sets. *Arithmetic Teacher*, March, 236–237.

Scott, P. (1999). Sets & counting. *Australian Mathematics Teacher,* 55(3), 17–20.

Chapter 9

Teaching of Counting

Tay Eng Guan

Combinatorics is a branch of mathematics dealing with discretely structured problems. Its scope of study includes selections and arrangements of objects with prescribed conditions, configurations involving a set of nodes interconnected by edges (called "graphs"), and designs of experimental schemes according to specified rules. Combinatorial problems and their applications can be found not only in various branches of mathematics, but also in other scientific disciplines such as engineering, computer science, operational research, management sciences and the life sciences. Since computers require discrete formulation of problems, the combinatorial technique has become an essential and powerful tool for engineers and applied scientists, in particular, in the area of designing and analysing algorithms for various problems which range from designing the itineraries for a shipping company to sequencing the human genome in the life sciences.

The *counting problem*, which seeks to find out how many arrangements there are in a particular situation, is one of the basic problems in combinatorics. Counting has been used in the social sciences for measuring the power of a player in a decision-making body (such as a company's board, a parliament or the United Nations Security Council). In chemistry, Cayley used graphs to count the number of isomers of saturated hydrocarbons while Harary and Read counted the number of certain organic compounds built up from benzene rings by representing them as configurations of hexagons joined together along a common edge. Recently, counting has been used in genetics to study the structures of DNA and RNA.

KEY CONCEPTS

The teacher ought to be familiar with the following key concepts.

1. Terminology – commonly used and not so commonly used

   - A *way* of doing something – a completed situation that satisfies the stated requirements.

     Example 1: There are two roads joining Singapore to Johor and five roads joining Johor to Malacca. Find how many different routes there are from Singapore to Malacca using these roads.

     Using the Causeway is one way of going from Singapore to Johor but NOT a way of going from Singapore to Malacca.

   - A *component* of doing something – part of a series of sub-situations that link up to form a completed situation that satisfies the stated requirements.

     Using Example 1 above, going from Singapore to Johor and going from Johor to Malacca are two components of going from Singapore to Malacca.

   - A *case* (or less frequently, a *category*) of doing something – is a collection of similar ways of doing something.

     Example 2: How many numbers between 1 and 100 (both inclusive) are divisible either by 3 or by 5?

     Numbers divisible by 3 will form one case and numbers divisible by 5 but not by 15 will form the other case.

2. Breaking into cases

   - Comprehensiveness – ensure that the cases cover ALL possibilities.

     Example 3: How many numbers greater than 250 can be formed using the digits 1, 2, 3, 4 and 5?

     Case 1: 5-digit number.
     Case 2: 4-digit number.
     Case 3: 3-digit number – Case 3a: Number starting with 2.
     Case 3b: Number starting with 3, 4 or 5.

   - Uniqueness – ensure that there is no double counting.

     In Example 2 above, taking the cases as "divisible by 3" and "divisible by 5" will result in double counting of numbers divisible by 15.

   - "The shorter end of the stick" – when the number of cases seem too many, it is likely that solving the "complementary" problem will be faster.

Example 4: How many numbers between 2000 and 8999 (both inclusive) do not have four different digits?

Cases would be "one pair, two unique", "two different pairs", "one triple, one unique" and "four same". Instead, consider the complementary problem – how many HAVE four different digits? Subtract this from the total number of numbers between 2000 and 8999 (both inclusive) to get the answer.

3. Components

- There is more than one set of components to achieve the same end result.

  Example 5: How many 3-digit numbers can be formed from the digits 2, 3, 4, 5, 6 and 7?

  Method 1: Three components – choose the first digit, then the second digit and finally the third digit.

  Method 2: One component – direct application of formula ${}^6P_3$.

  Method 3: Two components – choose three digits, and then arrange the three digits.

- Use the multiplication principle carefully. Basically, it works when the tree formed by all the possible ways is "uniform", that is, within each level, every node has the same number of branches. Methods 1 and 3 of Example 5 above both give rise to "uniform" trees. The next example is one where the tree formed is not "uniform".

  Example 6: There is one boat-trip each from Kampong Ulu to Towns A, B and C in Sarawak. There are one, two and three flights to Singapore from Towns A, B and C respectively. How many ways are there to travel from Kampong Ulu to Singapore?

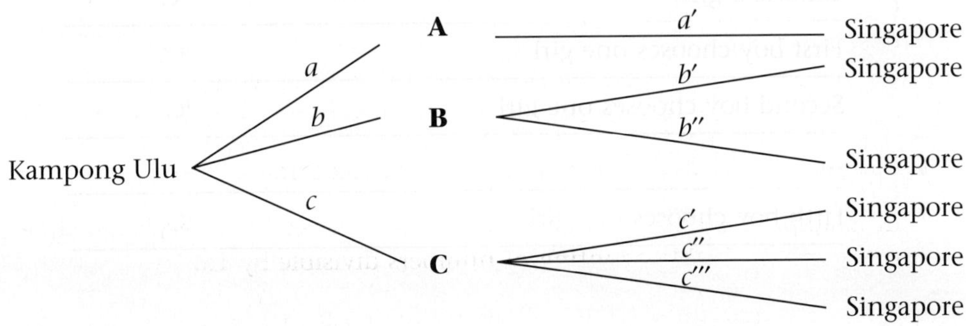

- In a tree diagram, a way is represented by a sequence of branches that *must* begin at the source-node and end on one of the end-nodes. Thus, the total number of ways of doing something is the total number of such sequences of branches. In Example 6 above, taking K to represent Kampong Ulu and S to represent Singapore, the sequences of branches such that each represents one way of travelling from K to S are *aa′*, *bb′*, *bb″*, *cc′*, *cc″* and *cc‴*.

LEARNING DIFFICULTIES AND TEACHING APPROACHES

1. Not knowing how to start

   One way to deal with this problem is to write down one acceptable way, then a few more ways, and then try to list systematically. Also, list some non-examples.

   Example 7: A team consisting of five mixed pairs for badminton is to be selected from 10 boys and 11 girls. Find the total number of different teams which can be formed.

   Suppose the boys are labelled *A* to *J* and the girls *a* to *k*. Then one possible way is {*Aa*, *Bb*, *Cc*, *Dd*, *Ee*}. Continue doing some more examples till the student understands what is required and is able to form some approach to solving the problem. A non-example is {*AB*, *CD*, *EF*, *gh*, *ij*}. Teach students to label efficiently so that the problem can be attempted quickly.

   Next, the problem can be solved by "acting out" the approach. Using Example 7 above, we could have:

Action	Number of ways
Choose 5 boys	${}^{10}C_5$
Choose 5 girls	${}^{11}C_5$
First boy chooses one girl	${}^{5}C_1$
Second boy chooses one girl	${}^{4}C_1$
…	…
Fifth boy chooses one girl	${}^{1}C_1$

Total number of ways = ${}^{10}C_5 \times {}^{11}C_5 \times 5!$
OR we could have:

Action	Number of ways
Choose 5 boys	${}^{10}C_5$
First boy chooses one girl	${}^{11}C_1$
Second boy chooses one girl	${}^{10}C_1$
...	...
Fifth boy chooses one girl	${}^{7}C_1$

Total number of ways = ${}^{10}C_5 \times 11 \times 10 \times 9 \times 8 \times 7$.

2. Is this a permutation problem or a combination problem?
   Clarify that the question is ill defined in the first place. In Example 5 above, the problem can be solved using permutation directly or as a mix of combination and permutation. A mindset that it is either one or the other is debilitating for further work in this area. The more accurate question would be "Is this a permutation *approach* or a combination *approach* or is it something else?", to which the answer would be "Let me see your approach first". If the student does not know what approach to take, go back to the first point in this section.

3. Difficulty in checking reasonableness of answer
   To overcome this difficulty, form upper and/or lower bounds for the answers. In Example 7 above, an upper bound could be the number of possible sets of five unrestricted pairs and a lower bound could be the number of possible sets of five mixed pairs from five boys and five girls.

   If two different methods give two different answers, at least one of them must be wrong. For the larger answer, try to disprove it by looking for cases where there is double counting. For the smaller answer, try to disprove it by looking for missing cases.

Example 8: A school is organising an alumni reunion and would like to play music from the 1970s era during an intermission. The school has a CD with 15 Abba songs, a CD with 17 Bee Gees songs and a CD with 20 Carpenters songs. How many ways are there to play 5 songs (where the order of play does not matter) for the intermission given that there must be at least 1 song from each group and that each song chosen is played exactly once?

One student reasoned that there were ${}^{15}C_1 \times {}^{17}C_1 \times {}^{20}C_1$ ways of getting at least a song from each band and ${}^{49}C_2$ ways of getting the other 2 songs from the remaining 49 songs. Thus, the number of ways is ${}^{15}C_1 \times {}^{17}C_1 \times {}^{20}C_1 \times {}^{49}C_2$ = 5997600.

Another student reasoned on the following cases:
(1, 1, 3), (1, 2, 2), (1, 3, 1), (2, 1, 2), (2, 2, 1), (3, 1, 1)
where a = number of Abba songs, b = number of Bee Gees songs and c = number of Carpenters songs in (a, b, c).

Thus, the number of ways is ${}^{15}C_1 \times {}^{17}C_1 \times {}^{20}C_3 + {}^{15}C_1 \times {}^{17}C_2 \times {}^{20}C_2 + {}^{15}C_1 \times {}^{17}C_3 \times {}^{20}C_1 + {}^{15}C_2 \times {}^{17}C_1 \times {}^{20}C_2 + {}^{15}C_2 \times {}^{17}C_2 \times {}^{20}C_1 + {}^{15}C_3 \times {}^{17}C_1 \times {}^{20}C_1 = 1661750$.

Who is correct?

First, note that 5997600 > 1661750. Thus, if the first student is wrong, then it is likely that he has double counted somewhere and we have to show the double counting; if the second student is wrong, it is likely that he has missed out some cases, and we have to show which cases have been missed out.

As it turns out the first student is wrong as shown in the following double count. Suppose A1, B1 and C1 are chosen first, and then A2 and B2 are chosen from the remaining songs. Thus, the selection is A1, B1, C1, A2, B2. Now, suppose A2, B2 and C1 are chosen first, and then A1 and B1 are chosen from the remaining songs. The selection will be A2, B2, C1, A1, B1 but this selection is the same as the one earlier as the order of the songs is not important. We have illustrated a double count and so clearly shown that the first student's reasoning is wrong.

4. Cannot understand why 0! = 1
In one textbook the explanation is given as follows:

We define 0! = 1 so that the formula ${}^nP_r = \dfrac{n!}{(n-r)!}$ holds true for $r = n$.

Discuss this, in particular about 'definitions' in mathematics, in class.

5. Inability to manipulate the ! symbol
   Force the student to expand the factorial term for manipulation. In other words, write out in full, for example, $5! = 1 \cdot 2 \cdot 3 \cdot 4 \cdot 5$ or $n! = 1 \cdot 2 \cdot 3 \cdots n$.

6. Hard topic to teach
   Teachers ought to know at least 150% of the content. In general, Additional Mathematics teachers ought to know counting at A-level, and A-level maths teachers ought to know more advanced methods and examples of counting.

SAMPLE ACTIVITIES: SOME PROBLEMS INVOLVING COUNTING

1. Find the number of subsets $\{a, b\}$ of distinct numbers from the set $\{1, 2, \ldots, 100\}$ such that

   i. $|a - b| = 7$; and
   ii. $|a - b| \le 7$.

2. There are 14 family members in a photo studio. Five of them are children. In how many ways can these 14 family members be arranged in a row if:

   i. there are no restrictions?
   ii. the 5 children must be together?
   iii. no 2 children are standing next to each other?
   iv. between two particular adults A and B, there are no adults but exactly 3 children?

3. The figure below shows eight distinct points $a_1, a_2, b_1, b_2, b_3, c_1, c_2, c_3$ on the sides of $\triangle ABC$. How many triangles can be formed using these points as vertices?

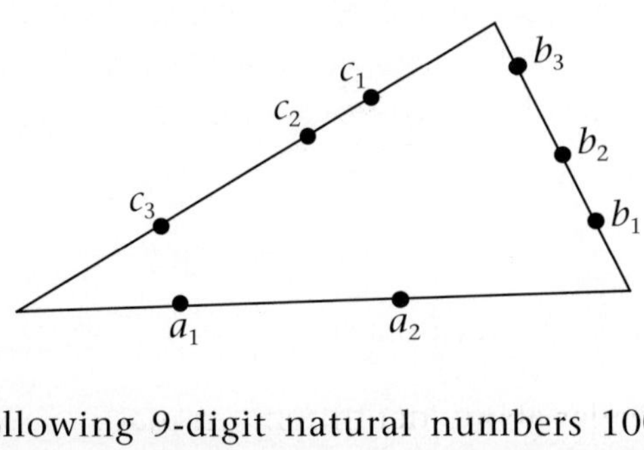

4. In each of the following 9-digit natural numbers 100100011, 666633333, 383838383, 777777777, every digit appears at least four times. Find the number of such 9-digit natural numbers.

FURTHER READING

Teh, K.S., & Looi, C.K. (2001). *New syllabus Additional Mathematics*. (7th ed.). Singapore: Shing Lee.

Chen, C.C., & Koh, K.M. (1992). *Principles and techniques in combinatorics*. Singapore: World Scientific.

Koh, K.M., & Tay, E.G. (2002). *Counting*. Singapore: World Scientific.

Chapter 10

Teaching of Probability

Ho Juan Beng

Probability is the branch of mathematics that seeks to study uncertainty in a systematic way. A probability is a measure, or estimate, of the likelihood of an event happening. It can be expressed in qualitative terms such as "very likely", "certain", "unlikely", "impossible" or on a numerical scale which extends from 0 to 1 with 0 as "impossible" and 1 as "certain". Most possible happenings have intermediate probabilities. For example, the probability that a fair coin lands with heads uppermost is said to be 50%.

PROBABILITY ASSIGNMENT

People think about, and assign the probability of an event in different ways. However, this does not affect the way in which probabilities are manipulated mathematically, since everyone agrees on the algebraic and arithmetical procedures that must be followed to produce consistent results.

1. *Classical approach:* Historically, the concept of sample space was linked to the idea of equal likelihood of all single outcomes of the sample space. The probability of an event is obtained from dividing the number of outcomes favourable to this event by the total number of outcomes in the sample space.

2. *Frequentist approach:* The probability of an event is obtained from the observed relative frequency of that event in repeated trials. Probabilities are not obtained exactly by this procedure but are estimated as the limit towards which the relative frequency tends.

3. *Subjectivist approach:* Probabilities are subjective evaluations of situations. The basic assumption here is that subjects derive their probabilities from their knowledge of the experimental conditions. The probability of an event, therefore, varies from subject to subject.

APPLICATIONS OF PROBABILITY

In the last 200 years, the techniques of probability have been applied in many different fields of study.

1. According to the quantum theory of physics, the fundamental structure of a universe is random. It is best to use probabilities to describe the organisation of sub-atomic particles, atoms in crystals and gas molecules.

2. Probabilistic understanding of how genes are transmitted from parents to children is the basis of modern models of inheritance.

3. Probability has affected modern medical research and influenced medical decision making. For example, the model of the AIDS epidemic is based on probability arguments.

4. In financial sector, actuaries use probability models to evaluate life assurance and annuities, and to set fair levels of premiums and contributions. Banks apply probability to estimate the risk of granting credits to different applicants.

5. The influence of forensic evidence based on probabilities has been increasing in court cases.

KEY CONCEPTS

1. *Experiment:* In probability, an experiment is basically any process of observation or measurement.

2. *Outcome:* A result of an experiment is called an outcome of the experiment. An outcome need not be numerical. An outcome may consist of more than one item of information.

3. *Sample space:* The collection of all possible outcomes is called the sample space for the experiment.

4. *Event:* An event for an experiment is a result satisfying some given condition. An event that consists of a single outcome is called an *elementary event,* and an event that consists of more than one outcome is called a *compound event.*

5. *Mutually exclusive events:* Events are said to be mutually exclusive if one of the events occurs, then the other event or events cannot occur.

6. *Independent events:* When the probability of two events occurring together or in sequence is the product of the probability of each of the individual events, then the individual events are said to be independent events.

7. *Conditional probability:* The conditional probability of E given F, written P(E | F), is the probability of event E occurring on the condition that event F occurs.

8. *Addition rule:* $P(E \cup F) = P(E) + P(F) - P(E \cap F)$.

9. *Multiplication rule:* $P(E \cap F) = P(E \mid F)P(F)$.

10. *Possibility diagram:* Sample spaces of outcomes listed as ordered pairs can be set out in a possibility diagram to facilitate the calculation of the probability of an event.

    Example: Draw a possibility diagram when two ordinary six-sided dices are thrown.

11. *Probability tree diagram:* A probability tree diagram is a useful tool for evaluating the probability of combined events.

    Example: Randomly draw (without replacement) two balls from a box containing three black balls and six white balls.

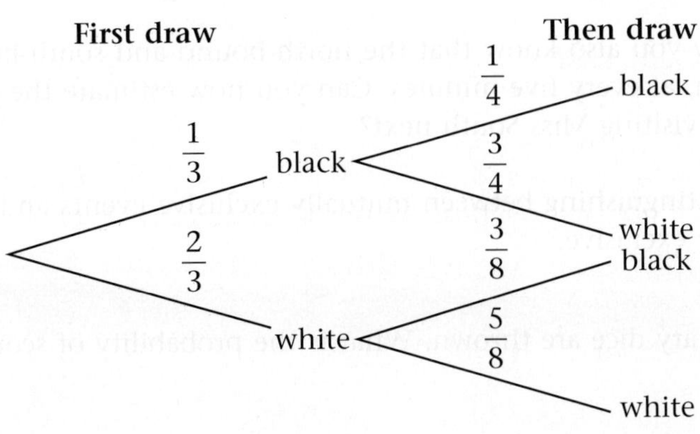

Note that the probabilities on the branches for the second draw are conditional probabilities. For example, P(the second ball is black | first ball is white) = $\frac{3}{8}$.

OBJECTIVES IN GCE O-LEVEL PROBABILITY SYLLABUS

1. Calculate the probability of single events.
2. Calculate the probability of simple combined events, using possibility diagrams and tree diagrams where appropriate.
3. Use addition and multiplication of probabilities under appropriate conditions.
4. Solve problems involving mutually exclusive events or independent events.

LEARNING DIFFICULTIES

1. Students frequently have problems in listing the sample space. They often have the mistaken belief that outcomes are equally likely to happen when they are not.

   Examples:
   a. What is the probability of getting two heads and one tail in three coin tosses?
   b. John Tan has two girl friends. To visit one he takes a north-bound train, to visit the other, a south-bound train. He always lets "chance" decide for him which girl to visit, by taking the first train that comes along, whether it is going north or south.
      What is the probability that his next visit will be to Miss South?

      i. $p = \frac{1}{2}$? ii. $p < \frac{1}{2}$? iii. $p > \frac{1}{2}$?, or iv. We can't tell?

   Suppose now you also know that the north-bound and south-bound trains run equally often, at every five minutes. Can you now estimate the probability that John will be visiting Miss South next?

2. Failure in distinguishing between mutually exclusive events and events that are not mutually exclusive.

   Examples:
   a. Two ordinary dice are thrown. What is the probability of scoring a total of 6 or 11?

b. Two ordinary dice are thrown. What is the probability of scoring a total of 5 or a difference of 1?

3. Failure to distinguish between independent events and events that are not independent.

   Examples:
   a. In a two-child family, one child is a boy. What is the probability that the other child is a girl?
   b. In a two-child family, the older child is a boy. What is the probability that the other child is a girl?

4. Inappropriate handling of combined events: addition and multiplication of probabilities.

   Example:
   A bag contains 100 identical balls; 70 of them are black and the rest white. Two balls are drawn in succession without replacement.
   a. Find the probability that the first ball drawn is black and the second ball drawn is white.
   b. Find the probability that the first ball drawn is black or the second ball drawn is white.

5. Relying on representativeness to estimate the likelihood of events.
   a. The tendency to predict that the outcome which has not appeared for some time will be the next outcome – "negative recency" or "gambler's fallacy".

      Example:
      The probability of a baby being a girl is about $\frac{1}{2}$.
      Mrs. X's first six children are girls. The probability that her seventh child will be a boy is

      i. greater than $\frac{1}{2}$, ii. equal to $\frac{1}{2}$, or iii. less than $\frac{1}{2}$.
   b. The composition of a sample should resemble the composition of the population.

      Example:
      The probability of a baby being a boy is about $\frac{1}{2}$.
      Which of the following sequences is more likely to occur in having six children?

      i. BGGBGB,
      ii. BBBBGB, or
      iii. about the same chance for each of these sequences.

c. Using the probability of an outcome in a single trial for the probability of an outcome in multiple trials.

Example:
What is the probability that among six children three will be girls?

d. Insensitivity to the effects of sample size.

Example:
Which of the following is more likely to occur?
i. 7 white balls in 10 drawn from a population of 1,000 white balls and 1,000 black balls, or
ii. 70 white balls in 100 drawn from the same population.
(Assume that the balls are drawn with replacement.)

e. Unusual events have low probabilities.

Example:
A number is formed by drawing four cards in succession without replacement from a pack of ten cards each printed with a digit 0 to 9. Which event is more likely?

i. 0123, ii. 9876, iii. 1357, or iv. 3856.

6. Relying on availability to estimate the likelihood of events.
People tend to make predictions about the likelihood of an event based on the ease with which instances of that event can be constructed or called to mind.
Example:
To form committees from a group of ten people (a person may serve on more than one committee) will there be more distinct possible committees of eight people or more distinct possible committees of two people?

7. People have no idea how fast partial products can grow or decay in counting problems.

Example:
There are n people in a group. The probability that at least two of the people have the same birthday is more than $\frac{1}{2}$. What is the least value of n?

TEACHING APPROACHES

1. If the concept of probability is taught based on sets, then it is necessary to teach sets first.

2. Most of us have some idea of what probability is about. Begin with events within the students' experiences to illustrate the probabilities of events including those which are *certain* or *impossible.*

3. The students could be provided with a set of events for which they are to place in order from impossible to certain.

4. Introductory probability should be activity-based, experimental probability.

5. Intuition may not agree with reality; what appears to be equally likely outcomes may not be equally likely. Understanding the reasoning behind erroneous thinking and deduction is just as important as obtaining the correct answer. Useful techniques include listing sample space, drawing a possibility diagram or probability tree diagram, simulation, etc.

6. Encourage students to analyse probabilistic statements critically. In particular, draw students' attention to the assumptions that go into the calculations, for example, randomness, independence, mutual exclusiveness.

7. Encourage students to try various approaches and check for consistency. If different answers are obtained, reasons that led to the discrepancies should be examined to identify the correct answer.

SAMPLE ACTIVITIES FOR TEACHERS

1. Chevalier de Mere, a French nobleman of the 17th century reasoned that in a single throw of a fair die, P(getting 1) = $\frac{1}{6}$, so in two throws, P(1 appears at least once) = $\frac{1}{6} + \frac{1}{6} = \frac{1}{3}$. What is wrong with this reasoning?

2. The Monty Hall problem
   Behind one of the three doors is a car; behind the other two are goats. The master of ceremonies knows where the car is. You pick a door and the master of ceremonies opens one of the remaining doors (obviously one with a goat). You are then given the option to switch doors. Should you switch?

3. Bertrand's cabinet
   A cabinet has three boxes, each with two divisions. Three gold and three silver coins are put in the divisions so that one box contains two gold coins, one box two silver coins and one box a gold coin and a silver coin. Choose a box and open one of its divisions. If the division contains a gold coin, what is the probability that the other division also contains a gold coin?

4. The prisoner's dilemma
   Among three prisoners, A, B and C, two are to be released. The prisoners know this, but not the identities of the two. Prisoner A asks the guard to tell him the identity of one prisoner other than himself who is to be released. The guard refuses and explains that he does not want to hurt prisoner A's chances for release. According to the guard, the probability of A to be released is $\frac{2}{3}$. If he discloses the identity of one of the prisoners other than A who is to be released, then only one out of the remaining two including A can be released. So, the probability of A to be released will be reduced from $\frac{2}{3}$ to $\frac{1}{2}$. Is the guard correct in his reasoning?

5. The three spinners below each point to two equally likely numbers. If you compete with another player in a game in which each selects a spinner and the winner is the spinner of the higher number, what strategy would you adopt?

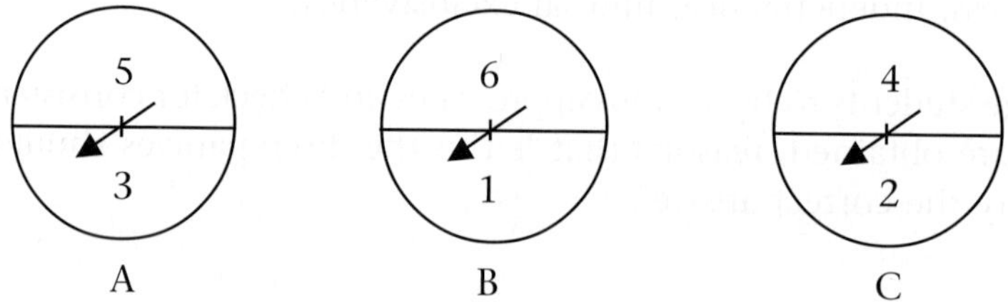

6. What is the probability that among six persons, at least two have their birthday in the same month? State any assumptions that you have made in your calculation.

7. If a chord is chosen at random on a fixed circle, what is the probability that its length exceeds the radius of the circle?

SAMPLE ACTIVITIES FOR STUDENTS

1. Coin flipping

   a. Divide the class into groups of two. One student in each group will flip a coin. The other student will record the number of heads. Repeat the flipping for about 50 times. The data obtained by the class will then be collated by tabulating the cumulative relative frequencies of group 1, groups 1 and 2, groups 1, 2 and 3, and so on. This activity illustrates the frequentist's approach to probability. It also clarifies the meaning of equally likely outcomes.

b. Flip two coins simultaneously as in a. Record the number of two heads, one head and zero head. Tabulate the cumulative relative frequencies. Discuss if the three outcomes are equally likely.

2. Thumbtack flipping
Perform the activity as in 1a. Here, there are only two possible outcomes – either the tack lands with its pin upright or down. Is the probability of each outcome equal to $\frac{1}{2}$?

3. Box A contains 6 white balls and 2 black balls. Box B contains 8 white balls and 4 black balls. All the balls are identical except for their colours. A ball is to be randomly selected from one of the boxes. If the ball drawn is white, you will win a prize. Which box will you select?

4. Consider the following games:
Game 1: Two players A, and B, take turns to spin the two spinners shown below. If the product of the score is even, A wins; otherwise, B wins.

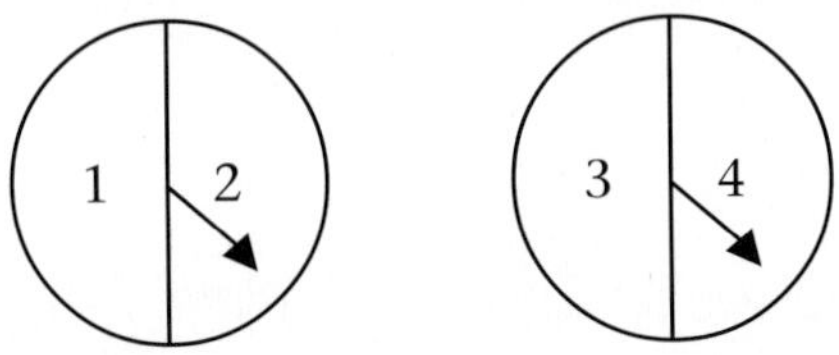

Game 2: Two players, A and B, take turns to throw two ordinary fair dice. If the difference is 0, 1 or 2, A wins; otherwise, B wins.

a. Explain whether each game is fair.
b. Re-design whichever game that is not fair.

5. Two black, one red and one white cards are shuffled and laid on the table face downwards. Two cards are picked at random. What is the chance that they are both black?

6. A box contains 4 red balls, 2 yellow balls and 3 green balls. Suppose two balls are randomly drawn one after another (without replacement).
What is the probability that

a. both balls are green?
b. the second ball is green?

7. 9% of the population in a city is 60 or more in age. 50% of the city's population is female. (See the table below.)

Age	Male	Female	Total
< 60	458	452	910
≥ 60	42	48	90
Total	500	500	1000

Are the following statements true or false? Explain your answer.

a. The probability that a randomly chosen person will be at least 60 and female $= 0.09 \times 0.5$;

b. The probability that a randomly chosen person will be at least 60 or female $= 0.09 + 0.5$.

Worksheet

PROBABILITY

In a game show, a participant, Rama, is invited to walk through a maze, each path leading to one of two rooms, A or B.

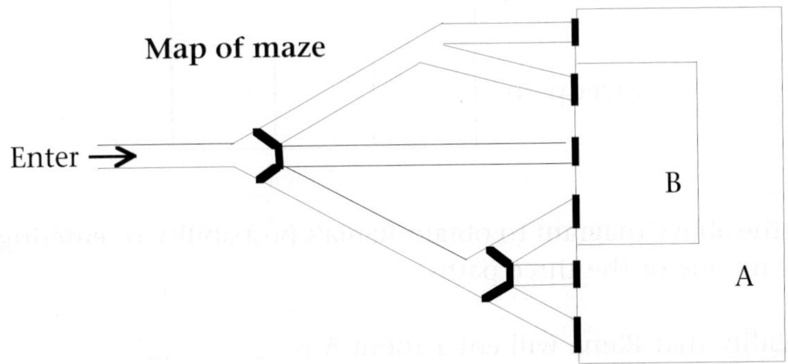

His partner (a home viewer), Mani is shown a map of the maze (see above) and is asked to place the big prize in one of the two rooms. (Rama will not be informed about Mani's choice.)

1. Rama and Mani will win the game if Rama enters the room with the big prize. In which room should Mani place the big prize? Explain your answer.

2. We will try to find the probability that Rama will enter each room by using the unit square below.

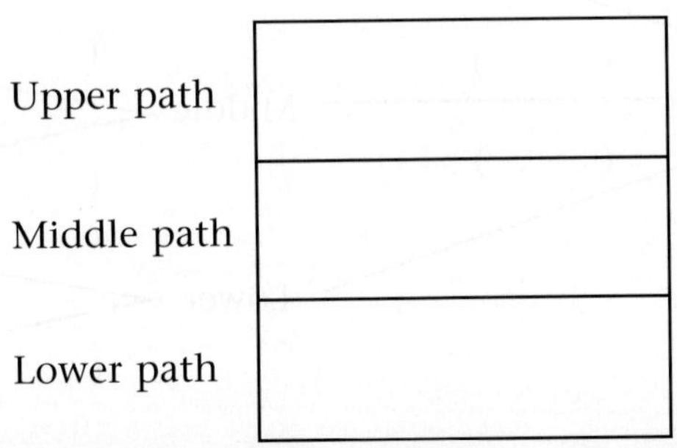

If Rama is equally likely to choose any of the three paths, the probability of selecting each path is ______________.

3. At each junction, Rama makes his choice randomly. For example, if he has chosen the upper path, then he is equally likely to enter room A or room B.

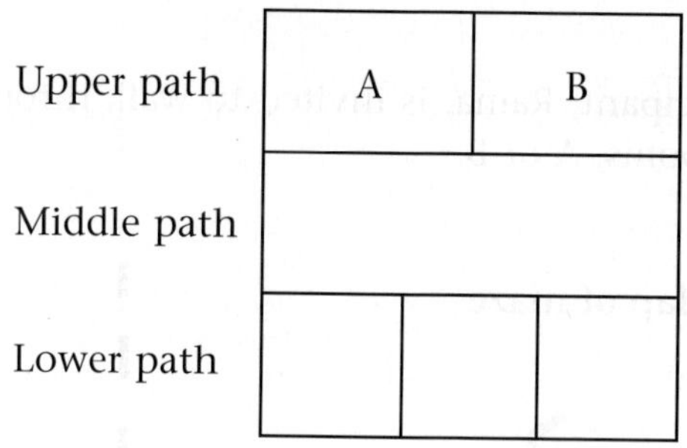

Complete the above diagram to obtain Rama's probability of entering each room after selecting one of the three paths.

The probability that Rama will enter room A is ______________________.

The probability that Rama will enter room B is ______________________.

4. Another way of representing Rama's choices and the associated probabilities is to use the "tree" diagram.

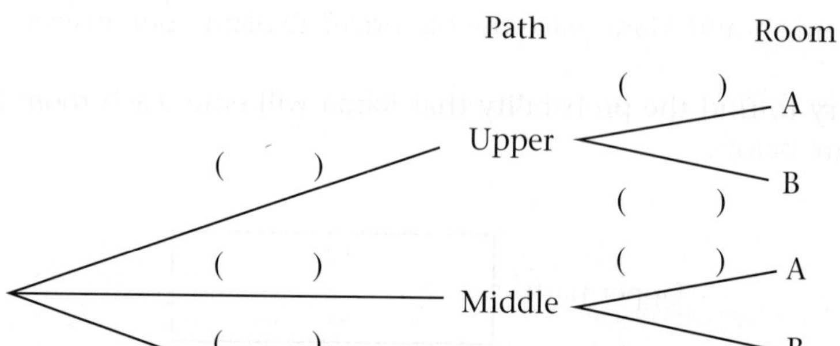

Complete the above diagram by entering the probabilities of Rama's choices into the appropriate brackets.

5. Using the probability tree, the probability that Rama

   a. chooses the upper path and enters room B is ______ × ______ = ______.

   b. chooses the middle path and enters room B is ______ × ______ = ______.

   c. chooses the lower path and enters room B is ______ × ______ = ______.

   d. enters room B is ________________.

   In a. to c., we have used a rule in probability known as the *multiplicative rule.*

FURTHER READING

English, R. (1992). Developing a feel for probability. *Mathematics in School, 21*(2), 14–18.

Ernest, P. (1984). Introducing the concept of probability. *Mathematics Teacher, 77*(7), 524–525.

Green, D.R. (1983). School pupils' probability concepts. *Teaching Statistics, 5*(2), 34–42.

Hope, J.A., & Kelly, I.W. (1983). Common difficulties with probabilistic reasoning. *Mathematics Teacher, 76*, 565–570.

Isaac, R. (1995). *The pleasures of probability.* NY: Springer-Verlag.

Kapadia, R., & Borovcnik, M. (1991). *Chance encounters: Probability in education.* Dordrecht, the Netherlands: Kluwer Academic Publishers.

Koay, P.L., Lim, S.K., & Yap, S.F. (1998). *Secondary mathematics: Enrichment worksheets.* Singapore: Hillview Publications.

Lightner, J.E. (1991). A brief look at the history of probability and statistics. *Mathematics Teacher, 84*(8), 623–630.

Lovitt, C., & Iowe, I. (1993). *Chance and data: Investigations, volume 1.* Carlton, Victoria: Curriculum Corporation.

McColl, J.H. (1995). *Probability*. London: Edward Arnold.

Newman, C.M., Obremski, T.E., & Scheaffer, R.L. (1987). *Exploring probability.* Palo Alto, CA: Dale Seymour Publications.

Rowntree, D. (1984). *Probability without tears.* NY: Charles Scribner's Sons.

Shulte, A.P., & Smart, J.R. (1981). *Teaching statistics and probability*. Reston, VA: National Council of Teachers of Mathematics.

Sobel, M.A., & Maletsky E.M. (1988). *Teaching mathematics: A sourcebook of aids, activities and strategies.* Upper Saddle River, NJ: Prentice-Hall.

Szekely, G.J. (1986). *Paradoxes in probability theory and mathematical statistics.* Dordrecht, the Netherlands: D. Reidel Publishing Company.

Chapter

11

Teaching of Higher Algebra

Fan Lianghuo

In this chapter, we will discuss issues concerning the teaching of the following topics in higher algebra: indices, binomial theorem, functions (including quadratic, exponential and logarithmic functions), remainder theorem, and finally, inequalities. All of these topics have much importance in modern mathematics and can help students develop a better understanding of what mathematics is as a subject.

INDICES

Curriculum and key concepts

In the mathematics curriculum, the content requirement in this topic includes "positive, negative, zero and fractional indices" (GCE O-level), "indices and surd notation and rationalising the denominators" (GCE AO-level). The textbooks usually introduce the contents in Elementary Mathematics (Secondary 3) and Additional Mathematics respectively.

Below are the main concepts and notations:

1. $a^n = \underbrace{a \times a \times a \times \cdots \times a}_{n\ times}$, where **the base** a is a real number; **the index** (plural: **indices**) or **the exponent** n is a positive integer, and a^n is called **the** n**th power of** a and read a to **the** n**th power** or a **to the power** n.
2. $a^{-n} = \dfrac{1}{a^n}$, where $a \neq 0$, and n is a positive integer.
3. $a^{\frac{1}{n}} = \sqrt[n]{a}$, where $a > 0$, n is a positive integer, and the "$\sqrt[n]{\ }$" is a **radical sign** and $\sqrt[n]{a}$ is called a radical expression.

4. $a^{\frac{n}{m}} = (\sqrt[m]{a})^n = (\sqrt[m]{a^n})$, where $a > 0$, and n and m are positive integers.
5. $a^0 = 1$, where $a \neq 0$.

Learning difficulties

Indices are a new notation system for students in their learning. Hence, they often over-use their previous knowledge of numbers, algebraic expressions and base 10 numerical system, thus making the following commonly seen errors.

1. $a^m + a^n = a^{(m+n)}$ (from $am + an = a(m + n)$)
2. $a^m \times b^n = (ab)^{(mn)}$ (from $am \times bn = (ab) \times (mn)$)
3. $a^m + b^m = (a + b)^m$ (from $am + bm = (a + b)m$)
4. $a^3 \times a^2 = a^6$
5. $a^{10} \div a^2 = a^5$
6. $a^{10} \div b^2 = (\frac{a}{b})^5$
7. $a^2 \times a^5 = a^{10}$
8. $a^2b^5 = (ab)^7$
9. $(a^5)^2 = a^7$
10. $a^8 - a^2 = a^6$
11. $a^{-2} = -2a$
12. $a^0 = 0$

For the above (4) to (11), can you explain why students often make the mistakes? In addition, if you are asked by your students to prove $a^0 = 1$, how do you go about it?

A relevant issue here involves the radical sign especially when $n = 2$, that is, the notation of "$\sqrt{\ }$". Are the following expressions correct? Why?

$$\sqrt{9} = \pm 3; \quad \sqrt{a^2} = \pm a$$

Many secondary students have difficulty making the correct judgment about the two expressions and explaining the reason. You might wish to discuss them with your tutor or your fellow trainee teachers.

In expressing numbers using the standard form, $a \times 10^n$, where $1 \le a < 10$, and n is an integer, students often have misconceptions about the range of a; some students think the range is $0 < a < 10$. Some less able students also have difficulty in comparing the following numbers expressed in indices,

$$1.01 \times 10^8 \text{ and } 8.98 \times 10^5;\ 0.01 \times 10^{12} \text{ and } 198 \times 10^8$$

What mistakes do you think they will possibly make and why? Are all of them written in the standard form?

Teaching suggestions

1. Use concrete numbers well enough before proceeding to use variables in index notation, so students can be better prepared to accept the new notation.

2. Provide real-life examples to motivate students and develop their number sense, for example,

   i. Mass of earth: 5.97×10^{34} kg.
   ii. Singapore's population: 4,017,700 in 2000; 4,483,900 in 2006. [Note: All Singapore's national data in this chapter are from the government's official statistics. See the government online resource at: http://www.singstat.gov.sg/.]
   iii. Singapore government debt: 200,005.6 million dollars at the end of 2005.
   iv. Singapore's income tax: $\$2.62 \times 10^9$ in 1997; $\$1.27 \times 10^{10}$ in 2005.
   v. To be a millionaire: $\$100 \times 2^{14}$ (in the TV programme *Who Wants to Be a Millionaire*, the prize starts from \$100, then \$200, \$300, \$500, \$1,000, \$2,000, \$4,000, etc.).

   Examples like the above can help students see the need to introduce the index notation and express large numbers in the standard form, and also enhance their knowledge about the real world and about the nation.

3. Pay attention to the mistakes students make during their learning. Teachers can use "conflicting teaching strategy" to let students correct their mistakes by themselves. For example, if students obtain $a^8 - a^2 = a^6$, then the teacher can ask them to find the result of $a^8 \div a^2$, or that of $10^8 - 10^2$ to force them to realise the mistake they have made and then find the correct answer.

BINOMIAL THEOREM

Curriculum and key concepts

Binomial theorem is introduced in Additional Mathematics. It reveals the pattern of the algebraic expression of a power of a binomial $(a + b)^n$, which is as follows:

$$(a + b)^n = a^n + {}^nC_1a^{n-1}b + {}^nC_2a^{n-2}b^2 + \cdots + {}^nC_ra^{n-r}b^r + \cdots + {}^nC_{n-1}ab^{n-1} + b^n$$

where a and b can be any numbers or algebraic expressions, n is a positive integer, and

$${}^nC_r = \frac{n(n-1)(n-2)\cdots(n-r+1)}{r(r-1)\cdots 3\cdot 2\cdot 1} = \frac{n!}{r!(n-r)!}$$

[Note: We also use $\binom{n}{r}$ to denote ${}^nC_r$.]

Learning difficulties

1. Students have difficulty in understanding why the binomial theorem works, and in remembering the formula in the theorem.
2. Students are confused by the general rth term and mistake ${}^nC_ra^{n-r}b^r$ for the rth term.
3. Students have great difficulty in appreciating how powerful this theorem is and therefore they can only apply the theorem in a very narrow way.

Teaching suggestions

1. To help students understand why there is such a theorem, teachers can begin by letting them observe the following expressions in concrete cases:

$$(a + b)^0 = 1$$

$$(a + b)^1 = 1 \cdot a + 1 \cdot b$$

$$(a + b)^2 = 1 \cdot a^2 + 2 \cdot ab + 1 \cdot b^2$$

$$(a + b)^3 = 1 \cdot a^3 + 3 \cdot a^2b + 3 \cdot ab^2 + 1 \cdot b^3$$

$$(a + b)^4 = 1 \cdot a^4 + 4 \cdot a^3b + 6 \cdot a^2b^2 + 4 \cdot ab^3 + 1 \cdot b^4$$

$$(a + b)^5 = 1 \cdot a^5 + 5 \cdot a^4b + 10 \cdot a^3b^2 + 10 \cdot a^2b^3 + 5 \cdot ab^4 + 1 \cdot b^5$$

Indicate that each expansion of the above is only determined by the power n, therefore, there should exist a formula to write the expansion.

2. Relevant to the above point, teachers can lead students to investigate the so-called Pascal's triangle starting with a few rows of numbers, for example:

```
            1
          1   1
        1   2   1
      1   3   3   1
    1   4   6   4   1
  1   5  10  10   5   1
1   6  15  20  15   6   1
1  7  21  35  35  21  7  1
```

   a. Do any numbers repeat in the whole array? How about in each row?
   b. Is there a pattern to generate each number in the array?
   c. Can you predict the next row and add it to the array?
   d. Is there a pattern in the diagonal numbers?

   After the students have become aware of the relations among the different numbers in the above array, teachers should ask students to further write down the ninth row, tenth row, etc., then accordingly write the expansions of $(a + b)^8$, $(a + b)^9$, and so on.

   [Note: Teachers should know the relevant history of this triangular arrangement of the binomial coefficients. Although it is often attributed to the French mathematician Blaise Pascal who described them in 1653, it was, however, known long before to Chinese mathematicians, Zhu Shijie (1303), Yang Hui (1261) and Jia Xian (circa 11th to 12th century).]

3. Introduce the following formula:

$$(a + b)^n = a^n + {}^nC_1a^{n-1}b + {}^nC_2a^{n-2}b^2 + \cdots + {}^nC_ra^{n-r}b^r + \cdots + {}^nC_{n-1}ab^{n-1} + b^n$$

   Help students observe the features of this formula and point out the following aspects, so the students can establish a clearer understanding of the structure of the formula and remember it more easily.

   a. The expansion contains $n + 1$ terms.
   b. The powers of a decrease by 1 in each successive term.
   c. The powers of b increase by 1 in each successive term.
   d. The sum of the indices in each term of the expansion adds up to n.
   e. ${}^nC_ra^{n-r}b^r$ is the $(r + 1)$th term of the expansion, but not the rth term.

f. With $\binom{n}{0} = \binom{n}{n} = 1$, the expansion can be expressed as the following:

$$(a+b)^n = \binom{n}{0}a^n + \binom{n}{1}a^{n-1}b + \binom{n}{2}a^{n-2}b^2 + \cdots + \binom{n}{r}a^{n-r}b^r + \cdots + \binom{n}{n-1}ab^{n-1} + \binom{n}{n}b^n$$

g. Depending on the students' background, teachers can try to connect the $(r+1)$th term to the combination of $a^{n-r}b^r$, that is, there are $\binom{n}{r}$ different ways of choosing $n-r$ times of a from all $(a+b)$ in $\underbrace{(a+b) \times (a+b) \times (a+b) \times \cdots \times (a+b)}_{n\ times}$.

4. Teachers should create opportunities for students to apply the theorem in a variety of ways so as to help them appreciate the usefulness of the theorem and the aesthetics of mathematics. The following are some commonly used examples in this aspect.

Example 1. Use the binomial theorem to deduce that $\sum_{r=0}^{n} {}^nC_r = 2^n$.

Example 2. Expand $(x^2 + \frac{1}{x^2} - 2)^3$. (Hint: $x^2 + \frac{1}{x^2} - 2 = (x - \frac{1}{x})^2$.)

Example 3. Prove that $1999^{1999} + 2001^{2001}$ is divisible by 2000.

QUADRATIC FUNCTIONS

Curriculum and key concepts

Quadratic functions can be generally expressed as $y = ax^2 + bx + c$, where a, b and c are real numbers and $a \neq 0$. They are a special type of functions. Quadratic functions are closely inter-related to quadratic equations. They play a very important role in students' learning of mathematics. The topic of quadratic functions is introduced in Elementary Mathematics starting from Secondary 2.

Learning difficulties

1. Students get confused about the differences and connections among "quadratic expressions", "quadratic functions" and "quadratic equations".

2. Students are unclear about the differences and connections between "roots of a quadratic equation" and "zeros of a quadratic function", and that between "solving a quadratic equation" and "factorising a quadratic expression".

3. Students memorise the relevant formulas and procedures with respect to completing the square, factorising and using the general formula (the quadratic formula), without a clear understanding of the connection among them.

4. Students often ignore the precondition $a \neq 0$ for $ax^2 + bx + c$ to be a quadratic expression.

5. Students do not see the reason why when the discriminant $b^2 - 4ac = 0$, it should be said that the function $y = ax^2 + bx + c$ $(a \neq 0)$ has two identical zeros. Instead, they often say the function has only one zero.

Teaching suggestions

1. Teachers should explain the concepts involved and see to it that students understand the differences and connections.

2. Teachers should make clear to students that the methods of "completing the square", "factorising" and "using the general formula" (the quadratic formula) in solving quadratic equations (or finding the roots of quadratic functions) are fundamentally the same and thus interchangeable. Mathematically, we can argue that they are all from the same simple principle, that is, if $a \times b = 0$, then either $a = 0$ or $b = 0$.

3. Teachers should also use information technology (e.g. Maple, Graphmatica or a graphing calculator) in teaching this topic, in particular, when teaching the properties of quadratic graphs. Teachers can also use graphs of quadratic functions as a platform to introduce concepts in sketching graphs of $f(x) \pm a$, $f(x \pm a)$, $af(x)$ and $f(ax)$.

4. Use a variety of techniques to determine the maximum and minimum points of quadratic graphs, arithmetically (completing the square), algebraically (applying

the general formula), graphically (observing the symmetry property of quadratic graphs) and analytically (calculus method) when appropriate.

EXPONENTIAL AND LOGARITHMIC FUNCTIONS

Curriculum and key concepts

Exponential functions $y = a^x$ $(a > 0, a \neq 1)$ and logarithmic functions $y = \log_a x$ $(a > 0, a \neq 1)$ are introduced in Additional Mathematics. They are two very important types of functions in mathematics, and one is the inverse function of the other, as can be seen from the following relationship:

$$n = a^b \Leftrightarrow b = \log_a n.$$

Before students are taught exponential and logarithmic functions, they would have learned the topic of indices, surds and logarithms, which is a necessary preparation for this new topic.

Although nowadays school mathematics curriculum usually introduces exponentiation (or exponent operation) first, and then use it to introduce logarithms, in the history of mathematics logarithms were invented before exponentiation. In fact, logarithms were formulated independently by John Napier in 1614 and by Joost Burgi in 1620, but the possibility of defining logarithms as exponents was recognised by John Wallis in 1685 and by Johann Bernoulli in 1694.

Learning difficulties

1. Students have difficulty grasping the concepts of exponents and logarithms. For example, they think that 0.2^{-5} is negative, but lg 0.34 is positive.

2. Students have trouble using the notations correctly. For instance, they write $\log_a mn$ to represent $\log_a(mn)$, and they mistake $\log_a m^n$ for $(\log_a m)^n$.

3. Students over-generalise the laws of basic mathematics operations they have learned when it comes to the operations of exponents and logarithms. For example, they write $\log_a(mn) = \log_a m \times \log_a n$ and $\log_a(m - n) = \log_a m - \log_a n$.

4. Students get confused about the domains and ranges of exponential and logarithmic functions, and this results in mistakes. For example, they write $\log_a x^2 = 2 \log_a x$ without considering if $x > 0$ or not. They also have difficulty interpreting the meaning of a^m, when m is irrational.

5. Students have trouble remembering the scope of the values of the base a. Even if they remember the base a should be positive, they will often forget that it cannot be 1.

6. Students have difficulty applying what they have learned in this topic to solve real-life problems.

Teaching suggestions

1. When teachers introduce the most important relationship, $n = a^b \Leftrightarrow b = \log_a n$, they should provide students with many examples with concrete numbers to familiarise them with it, for example, from $2^3 = 8$, write an equivalent logarithmic expression.

2. Teacher should compare the laws of indices with the laws of logarithms to help students establish explicit connections between them.

3. Teachers should provide students with good questions and activities for them to appreciate the application of logarithmic and exponential functions in real-life situations and develop their problem-solving ability. Note some commonly seen examples can be found from the following scenarios: population growth modelling; gross domestic product growth (rate); calculation of interest; radioactive substance (radioactivity); Richter scale and intensity of earthquake; pH scale in chemistry; decibel scale in physics. The first few scenarios can be linked to National Education.

4. Teachers should pay attention to the connection between graphs and algebraic expressions in teaching this topic.

5. Teachers can explain the meaning of a^m, when m is irrational, by using graphs and in an intuitive way.

REMAINDER THEOREM

Curriculum and key concepts

Remainder theorem and its relevant contents, including long division of polynomials, factor theorem and factorisation of polynomials, are introduced in Additional Mathematics. The theorem says: **If a polynomial $f(x)$ is divided by $(x - a)$, then the remainder is $f(a)$.**

The remainder theorem can be deduced from long division of polynomials and from the fact, $f(x) = (x - a)Q(x) + R$, where $Q(x)$ is the quotient, and R is the remainder.

The factor theorem, which says that $(x - a)$ **is a factor of** $f(x)$ **if and only if** $f(a) = 0$, is a corollary of the remainder theorem. It can be used to factorise polynomials.

Long division, synthetic division and its generalisation

This section contains something new but it is relevant to the topic. For brevity, we shall use concrete examples to explain the main ideas.

1. Long division is a conventional algorithm for performing polynomial divisions. An example is given below.

$$
\begin{array}{r|l}
 & 5x^3 + 3x^2 + 9x - 7 \\
\hline
x^2 + 2x - 3 & 5x^5 + 13x^4 + 0x^3 + 2x^2 - 7x - 10 \\
 & 5x^5 + 10x^4 - 15x^3 \\
\cline{2-2}
 & \quad 3x^4 + 15x^3 - 2x^2 \\
 & \quad 3x^4 + 6x^3 - 9x^2 \\
\cline{2-2}
 & \qquad 9x^3 + 11x^3 - 7x \\
 & \qquad 9x^3 + 18x^3 - 27x \\
\cline{2-2}
 & \qquad\quad -7x^2 + 20x - 10 \\
 & \qquad\quad -7x^2 - 14x + 21 \\
\cline{2-2}
 & \qquad\qquad 34x - 31
\end{array}
$$

In the above, the placement of the quotient is different from that which we often see in mathematics textbooks (e.g. see Teh and Looi, 2001, p. 31). We suggest you place the quotient in the above example, which is $5x^3 + 3x^2 + 9x - 7$, at the top of $5x^5 + 13x^4 + 0x^3 + 2x^2$ instead of $0x^3 + 2x^2 - 7x - 10$, so students can see clearly how the coefficients of the quotient are obtained, and be better prepared for the generalised synthetic division method (Fan, 2003).

2. The classical synthetic division is the short-cut method of doing long division when the divisor is of the form $(x - c)$. The example below is for $(3x^4 - 8x^3 + 4x + 5) \div (x - 2)$.

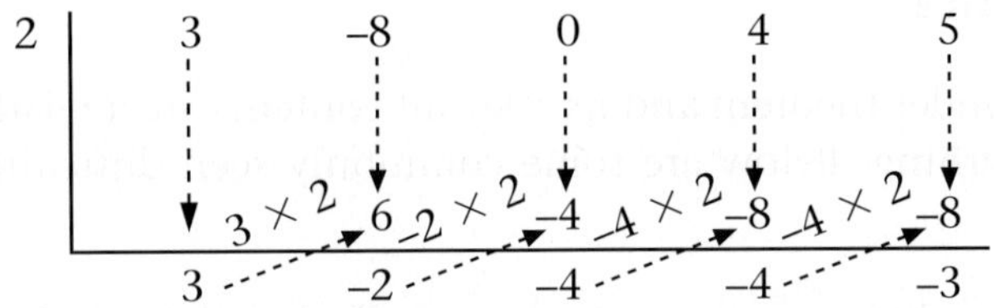

The quotient is $q(x) = 3x^3 - 2x^2 - 4x - 4$, and the remainder is $r = -3$. Notice that the array of numbers above is the typical traditional arrangement for the method. However, we suggest you use the following arrangement, which is more consistent with the generalised synthetic division method.

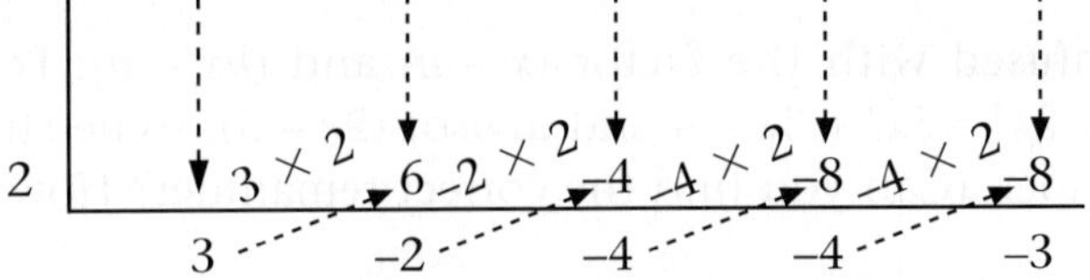

3. One interesting fact is that the generalised synthetic division can be applied to polynomial divisions with the leading coefficient of the divisor being 1. The so-called "synthetic array of numbers" below explains how it can be done in the case of $(5x^5 + 13x^4 + 2x^2 - 7x - 10) \div (x^2 + 2x - 3)$.

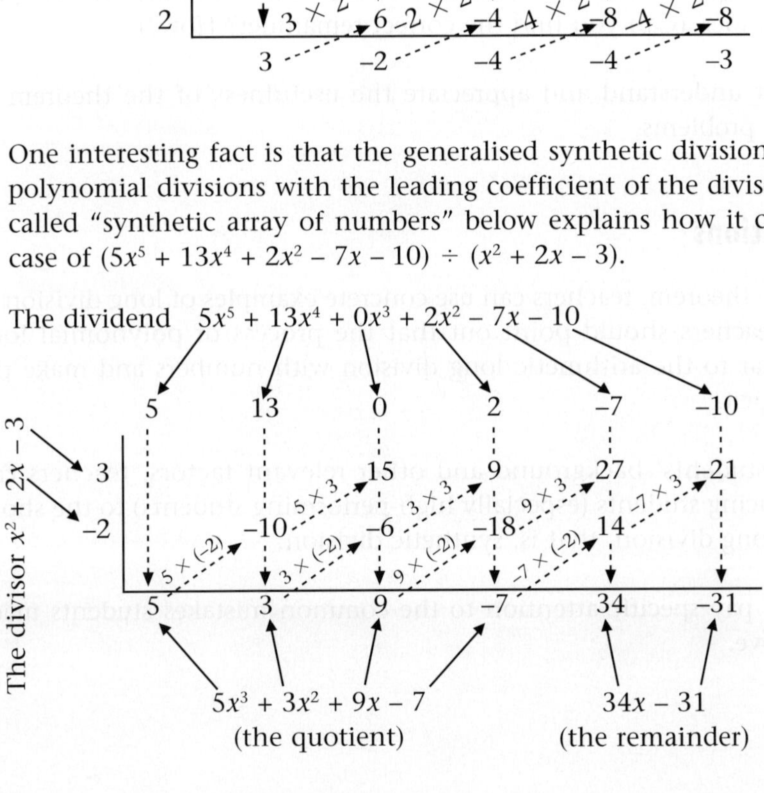

For a more detailed explanation about the generalised synthetic method, see Fan (2003).

Learning difficulties

In general, the remainder theorem and its relevant contents are a relatively easy topic for teaching and learning. Below are some commonly seen difficulties/mistakes in students' learning.

1. When doing long division, students do not display the missing terms in the dividend and/or divisor. For example, when doing $(5x^5 + 13x^4 + 2x^2 - 7x - 10) \div (x^2 + 2x - 3)$, they forget the hidden term "$0x^3$" in the dividend during the process (see the correct working on p. 196).

2. Students get confused with the factor $(x - a)$ and $(x + a)$. For example, for polynomial $f(x) = 3x^3 - 2x^2 + 5$ and divisor $(x + 2)$, some students will give $f(2)$ as the remainder.

3. Students get confused with the factor $(x - a)$ and $(bx - a)$. For example, for polynomial $f(x) = 2x^4 - 5x^2 + 3x - 4$ and divisor $(2x - 5)$, some students will give $f(5)$ as the remainder. (Can you find the correct remainder? How?)

4. Students do not understand and appreciate the usefulness of the theorem in solving relevant problems.

Teaching suggestions

1. To introduce the theorem, teachers can use concrete examples of long division of polynomials. Teachers should point out that the process of polynomial long division is similar to the arithmetic long division with numbers and make the connection explicit.

2. Depending on students' background and other relevant factors, teachers can consider introducing students (especially high-performing students) to the short-cut method of long division, that is, synthetic division.

3. Teachers should pay specific attention to the common mistakes students made as indicated above.

4. Teachers should expose students to a variety of problems that can be solved by applying the remainder theorem and relevant procedures. (See Question 16 at the end of this chapter.)

5. Students should be allowed, whenever appropriate, to use graphing calculators with symbolic computation functions (e.g. TI-92) or computer algebra systems (e.g. Maple) to check (or even obtain in some cases) the relevant answers.

INEQUALITIES

Curriculum and key concepts

Linear inequalities as a topic is introduced in Elementary Mathematics (Secondary 1 and Secondary 3/4)), and inequalities involving other contents are not taught as a single specific topic; instead, they are included in different parts of the secondary school mathematics curriculum, particularly in Additional Mathematics.

There are basically three kinds of issues involving inequalities. The first is to compare two quantities or mathematics expressions to establish the inequalities. The second is to solve mathematics inequalities. The last is to prove given inequalities.

Learning difficulties

Many students have much difficulty dealing with inequalities. Some can repeat the same mistakes, careless or conceptual, throughout their secondary school education. Below are some commonly seen problems or misconceptions in their learning.

1. $2a > a$ (How about $2 + a > a$? Is it true?),

2. $a^2 > 0$ (How about $\dfrac{1}{a^2} > 0$? Is it true?),

3. if $a^2 > b^2$, then $a > b$ (If $a > b$, will we have $a^2 > b^2$? Moreover, if $a^3 > b^3$, will we have $a > b$?),

4. if $a > b$, then $ac > bc$ [Note: Many students have trouble accepting that if $a > b$ and $c < 0$, then $ac < bc$; even if they acknowledge it, they will often forget it again when it comes to application. But will we have $a + c > b + c$, when $a > b$ and $c < 0$?], and

5. if $\frac{a}{b} > \frac{c}{d}$, then $ad > bc$ (Do you know when it holds?).

Many problems arise from the fact that students over-generalise their knowledge of equalities without understanding the concepts of inequalities.

Solving inequalities could also be very difficult especially when students do not have a clear understanding of the properties of inequalities and the functions involved.

Proving given inequalities is a most difficult and intellectually most challenging task for students, and as a matter of fact, for anyone who studies mathematics. [Note: Try to prove the inequality given in Question 8 at the end of this chapter. Can you prove $\frac{1}{1 \times 2} + \frac{1}{2 \times 3} + \cdots + \frac{1}{n \times (n + 1)} < 1$? How about $\frac{a}{b + c} + \frac{b}{c + a} + \frac{c}{a + b} \geq \frac{3}{2}$ (a, b, c are all positive)? Are they easy or difficult to prove? Why?] However, the requirement in Singapore's school mathematics curriculum is quite moderate in this aspect.

Teaching suggestions

1. Teachers must realise that it is not easy for students to learn about inequalities, therefore, they need to pay attention to the difficulties students encounter and maintain a reasonable pace in teaching. Do not underestimate students' difficulty in their learning in this topic.

2. Teachers can use concrete numbers to introduce the concepts and properties involving inequalities, particularly at the initial stage. For example, to explain that it is not true to say "if $a^2 > b^2$, then $a > b$"; teachers can ask students to observe the case of $a = -4$ and $b = -3$.

3. Teachers should emphasise to students that they should not over-use their knowledge of equalities when dealing with inequalities. For this purpose, teachers can compare and contrast the properties of equations and inequalities.

4. In solving inequalities, teachers can use graphs which are an intuitive and powerful tool. In this connection, IT tools can also be used to facilitate students' learning.

SAMPLE QUESTIONS

The following questions have mathematical and/or pedagogical implications. They can be used as individual tasks or group work, and done during tutorial sessions or after.

1. Given the mass of an atom is 3.7×10^{-23} g, can you estimate how many atoms there are in your body? Express your result in the standard form.

2. If your students ask you how to prove $a^0 = 1$, how will you handle the question?

3. When do we use the term "power"? How about "indices"? Are these two terms interchangeable in all cases?

4. Are the following expressions correct?

$$\sqrt{9} = \pm 3; \quad \sqrt{a^2} = \pm a$$

   If a student cannot answer the question, how will you explain it to him or her?

5. Evaluate $\dfrac{3^{x+1} - 3^{x-2}}{3^{x-1} - 3^{x+2}}$.

6. Use Internet search engines (e.g. Yahoo, Google) to find some websites on Pascal triangles (some people call it "Yang Hui triangles"). Recommend to your class three to five such websites that you think will be most helpful. Write a short essay to summarise your findings about the history of the Pascal triangles and its connection with the binomial theorem.

7. Do you know how to judge if a positive integer is divisible by 11? Write a mathematics statement for the rule, and then use the binomial theorem to prove it.

8. Prove $\left(\dfrac{a+b}{2}\right)^n \leq \dfrac{a^n + b^n}{2}$, where a and b are real numbers such that $a + b \geq 0$ and n is a positive integer.

9. Assume that some students in your class argue that some quadratic equations cannot be solved using the method of "completing the square", and some argue that some quadratic equations cannot be solved using the method of "factorisation". How will you respond?

10. Find the range of the values of p for which the function $f(x) = px^2 + 5x + 1$ has two real and distinct zeros. Can you predict what the mistakes are that students might make in solving this question?

11. Explain the rationale when the discriminant $b^2 - 4ac = 0$, it should be said that the function $y = ax^2 + bx + c$ $(a \neq 0)$ has two coincident zeros, and not only one zero.

12. Read some encyclopaedias of mathematics or Internet resources to find out how logarithms were invented and how they are related to exponents. Write a short essay to explain your findings.

13. According to the 2002's *Yearbook of Statistics Singapore*, the total population of Singapore was 4,100,000 in 2001. If the targeted population of Singapore in 2020 is 5,500,000, then what should the yearly population growth rate from 2001 to 2020 be, given that the growth rate will be the same for every year over this period? Moreover, what mistakes do you think students will make in trying to solve this question?

14. Acid rain is a serious environmental issue in many parts of the world. Find the pH levels of acid rain and non-acid rain. Is acid rain a problem in Singapore? Explain your answer.

15. If a polynomial $f(x)$ is divided by $(bx - a)$, then is the remainder still $f(a)$? Why or why not?

16. It has been claimed that there are five different types of questions about the applications of the remainder theorem. Can you write as many different kinds of questions as possible to represent different applications of the remainder theorem?

17. (Optional) Using the generalised synthetic division method introduced in this chapter, find the quotient and remainder of $(4x^6 - 3x^3 + 2x - 1) \div (x^4 - 2x^2 + 3)$.

18. If $\frac{a}{b} > \frac{c}{d}$, list, respectively, all the conditions on a, b, c and d for the two inequalities $ad > bc$ and $ad < bc$ to be true.

19. Can you use a number of different ways to solve the inequality: $x^2 - x + 6 < 0$? Which way(s) will you choose in your teaching? Why?

20. Reflect on your own experience of learning mathematics involving inequalities as a student. What do you think was the most difficult or troubling part (concepts, or properties, or skills, or a particular question, etc.) for you? Why? Write a short essay about your reflection and share your experience with your fellow trainee teachers.

FURTHER READING

Brant, S.A., & Zeidman, E.A. (1996). *Intermediate algebra: A functional approach.* NY: HarperCollins.

Fan, L. (2003). A generalization of synthetic division and a general theorem of division of polynomials. *Mathematical Medley, 30*(1), 30–37.

Gelfand, I.M., & Shea, A. (1993). *Algebra.* Boston, MA: Birkhäuser.

Kluepfel, C. (1981). When are logarithms used? *Mathematics Teacher, 74*(4), 250–253.

Larson, R., Hostetler, R.P., & Heyd, D.E. (2000). *Elementary and intermediate algebra: A combined course.* Boston, MA: Houghton Mifflin.

Lumpkin, B. (1997). *Algebra activities from many cultures.* Portland, ME: J. Weston Walch.

Murdock, J., Kamischke, E., & Kamischke, E. (1998). *Advanced algebra through data exploration: A graphing calculator approach.* Berkeley, CA: Key Curriculum Press.

Stewart, J., Redlin, L., & Watson, S. (2000). *College algebra.* (3rd ed.). Pacific Grove, CA: Brooks/Cole.

Tussy, A.S., & Gustafson, R.D. (1999). *Intermediate algebra.* Pacific Grove, CA: Brooks/Cole.

Teh, K.S., & Looi, C.K. (2001). *Additional mathematics.* Singapore: Shing Lee.

Chapter 12

Teaching of Functions

Eric Fredrick Wood

In mathematics, the concept of the *function* is a major organising principle. Functions are simply sets of ordered pairs which have a special property, namely, that for any x value there is exactly one y value. There can be several x values for one y value however. Functions appear in a number of places in the Singapore mathematics syllabus, so the purpose of this chapter is not to follow along with the order of the syllabus but to provide an overview for the teacher of some of the important aspects of teaching this topic.

KEY CONCEPTS

It is important to make sure that as teachers we use correct and descriptive language so that students do not get the wrong impression or idea. For example, we should not say that $y = x^2$ is a function, because strictly speaking it is not a function as defined. This expression is not a set of ordered pairs – it is an equation. It would be correct to call it an *equation which generates a function* or simply the *equation of a function*. Similarly, we should not say that a parabola is a function, rather, it is the *graph of a function*. The basic definition is the thing that allows us to test if graphs are in fact graphs of functions by using the vertical line test: If a set of ordered pairs has more than one y value for a given x value, there will be multiple points vertically above one another and so a vertical line will cut the graph more than once. The link between the graph of a function and its equation is an important one to make, just as the fact that some graphs do not necessarily have an equation that can generate them (graphs of real-world data, for example); this does not mean that the graph is not the graph of a function!

TEACHING APPROACHES

Despite the fact that this definition seems abstract and formal, one can think about functions in a simple way. When we say that one thing "is a function" of another we mean that the value of one depends on the other. So, what you start with governs what you end up with – many things in the real world and life in general also operate this way! A nice diagrammatic way to put this into practice is to have students think about a "function machine".

This is an old concept but one that can still be used effectively to generate every function that we actually consider in secondary mathematics. The idea is simple enough: we have a "manufacturing" machine which produces an "output" for a given "input". You decide on the "processing instructions" and the input, and then the output is automatically produced. Often a diagram such as Figure 12-1 is used for this purpose. If you put this diagram (or a similar one) on a transparency for the overhead projector then you can change the processing instructions and the input values to produce a wide range of functions from linear through trigonometric.

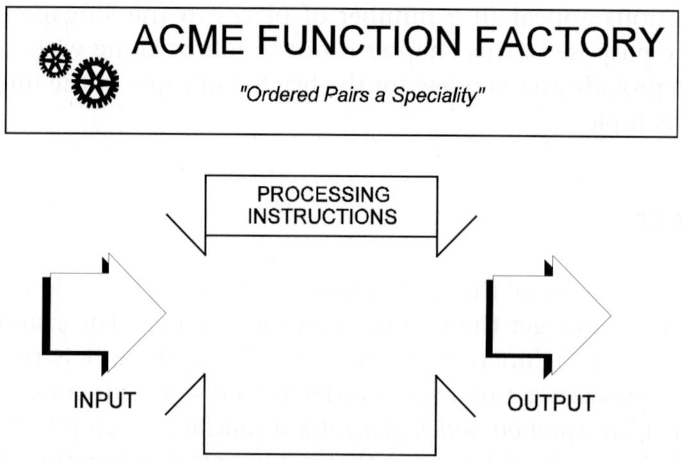

Figure 12-1 A typical function machine

For example, if the processing instructions were "Multiply by 2 and add 3" an input of 4 would result in an output of 11 and generate the ordered pair (4, 11) and so on for other inputs. Later you can establish that the function could also be generated by the equation $y = 2x + 3$. If the processing instructions were "Find the exponent on 10 that will produce the input value" then an input of 10 would produce an output of 1 and an input value of 1,000 would produce an output of 3, generating the ordered pairs (10, 1) and (1,000, 3). Later you can establish that this function could be generated by the equation $y = \log_{10} x$. The trigonometric functions can also be generated by similar means and a set of activities for this purpose is included.

A variety of free applets which use the function machine idea are also available at:

http://matti.usu.edu/nlvm/nav/frames_asid_191_g_3_t_1.html

http://www.ecu.edu/si/cd/interactivate/activities/fm/index.html

http://www.mathsnet.net/algebra/functionmachine.html

http://score.kings.k12.ca.us/lessons/functions/machine.html

Teaching the inverse can be done in a similar fashion. If a function machine has processing instructions "Multiply by 2 and add 3" then to reverse this process we must undo each of these instructions. We would have to "Subtract 3 and divide by 2" to arrive at the inverse function. Using these instructions, an input of 5 would produce an output of 13 for the original function. Using the instructions for the inverse function, an input of 13 would produce an output of 5. So the defining equation of the function is $y = 2x + 3$ and the defining equation for the inverse would be $y = \dfrac{x - 3}{2}$ which can be re-arranged to produce $2y = x - 3$ or $x = 2y + 3$. Now ask the students if they see any relationship between the equation of a function and the equation of its inverse and the familiar idea of interchanging the x and y is clear. It is important, however, that the idea of an inverse as an undoing process is well understood before trying to find quick ways to generate equations which, tends to be done very mechanically and without understanding.

Another point which needs to be emphasised in this discussion is that although an inverse can be created by undoing each of the operations of the original they must also be done in the *reverse* order. Once again, this idea can be approached from a very concrete perspective: think of the steps in wrapping a gift that you wish to send by mail to someone.

Wrapping	**Unwrapping**
Place item in box	Remove ribbon
Put on lid	Unwrap paper
Seal with tape	Remove tape on lid
Wrap box with paper	Remove lid
Attach ribbon	Take item out of box

It is now clear that the undoing operation requires that each individual step be undone but in the reverse order. Discussions such as this one help to make the idea of the inverse of a function a common sense one rather than an abstract mathematical concept. Once students can actually generate an inverse they can then be encouraged to experiment with the graphs of various functions and their inverses to see if they are related. The notion that the inverse is the reflection in the line $y = x$ is important and can be done as an investigation using graphing software. One caution is in order: often the aspect ratio of the screen is such that graphs do not have the same size unit on both axes and so the line $y = x$ is not at 45°. The point about the inverse and the function having graphs that are reflections around the line $y = x$ can be confusing. Make sure that if you give students an investigation to do, you use software which will not present this problem.

Another common investigation with functions is to examine the effect on the graph of changing various parameters. For example, investigate how the graph of the function $y = ax^2 + bx + c$ changes as we vary the values of a, b and c. Appropriate graphing software makes such investigations very efficient and saves quite a lot of classroom time. For example, Geometer's Sketchpad can be programmed to allow for such investigations. An even easier way to do this is to use freely available applets that employ "sliders" to allow the students to change parameter values and to examine the effects on the graph in an animated and dynamic environment. One typical applet can be downloaded from http://illuminations.nctm.org/mathlets/grapher/index.html.

Keep in mind, however, that if you do use technology for these kinds of explorations, you must build into your lesson a way for students to record what they have found out – otherwise they will not remember the results of their investigations. For example, ask them to use the software to investigate a number of graphs and have them sketch the results on a graph grid for their notes.

Particular kinds of functions can be introduced in many other ways such as explorations and investigations (as in the case of circular functions) or through interesting problems. This section provides you with a variety of ideas for teaching about linear, quadratic, cubic, reciprocal, trigonometric, logarithmic and absolute value functions. In some cases, complete lesson handouts are provided and in other cases, problems that could be used as the focus of a lesson are provided. In each case, teaching notes are given to illustrate some of the important points that are embedded in the problems or student investigations.

SAMPLE ACTIVITIES

Linear and quadratic functions

Problem 1

The yearbook committee at Singapore National High School is making plans for the next edition of the yearbook. The treasurer, Chin Wei, has already met with the publisher's representative and gives his report to the rest of the committee. "The representative said that if we order 500 books the total cost will be $17,500; if we order 1,000 books the total cost will be $25,000; and if we order 2,000 books the total cost will be $40,000." Ping Li is the sales manager. She asks, "But what if we don't want to order any one of those numbers of books, how much will it cost for, say, 750?"

1. Draw a graph based on the information given by the publisher's representative using the total cost (y) versus number of yearbooks (x). What appears to be true about the three points?
2. Establish an equation that relates the total cost and the number of yearbooks ordered.
3. The graph appears to indicate that if the school does not order any yearbook, there would still be a total cost of $10,000. Is this correct? Explain.

[Teaching note: The relationship here is linear but the points on the graph should not be joined with a solid line as fractional values of yearbooks have no meaning. This problem leads into the second problem and is required in later discussion so they should both be done.]

Problem 2

Back at the yearbook club meeting, another problem has arisen. Ping Li says, "That's great, we can figure out how much it will cost us for any number of yearbooks. The problem is we don't know how many to order because we aren't sure how many we can sell!" At this point Riduan speaks up, "I have the sales figures from the last ten years and it seems that the number of yearbooks that were sold depended on the price."

1. Riduan presents the figures for the number of yearbooks sold and the corresponding price to the committee. It is reproduced below:

Number sold	1,000	1,020	1,040	990	970	960	1,030	980	920	1,010
Price ($)	30	28	26	31	33	34	27	32	38	29

Graph the number of yearbooks sold (y) versus the price (x).

2. Is the number of yearbooks sold a function of the price? If so, find the equation that relates number sold and price. If not, explain why not.

3. If the price of the yearbook is $40, how many do you think they could sell?

[Teaching note: The graph in this case is linear but with a negative gradient. It is useful to have students calculate the gradient and see its meaning in the context of this problem.]

Riduan has noticed a fundamental law of economics: If the price goes up, sales decrease, and if the price falls, sales increase. In this situation we notice that 1,000 books will sell at a price of $30 and that *every* $1 *price reduction results in the sale of* 10 *more yearbooks. Every* $1 *price increase results in the sale of* 10 *less yearbooks.* Ping Li is really excited now. The profit that the yearbook makes is used by the school to sponsor a needy family in a developing country so she wants to make as much profit as possible. She knows, however, that too high a price will cause sales to suffer, and too low a price will not make much money. She thinks that she can use the data that Riduan has collected to construct a mathematical model that will help her decide how to maximise the profit. She also thinks that at the same time this information may help her to establish how many yearbooks to order and what price to charge.

4. Draw a chart similar to the one shown below and then use the information in the previous discussion to complete it:

Number of yearbooks to be sold	Total printing cost ($)	Selling price ($)	Total sales revenue ($)	Profit ($)*
1,000	1,000 × 15 + 10,000 = 25,000	30	1,000 × 30 = 30,000	30,000 – 25,000 = 5000
1,100		20		
900		40		
800		50		
		60		
		70		
		80		
		85		
		90		

* Sales revenue – printing cost.

5. What do you notice about the points?

6. Estimate at what price the yearbook would make a maximum profit.

7. Would it be a good price for the yearbook? Explain.

8. At what price is the profit zero? How many books sold would this correspond to? In business this is called the *break-even point*.

9. Do the ordered pairs that make up the graph form a function? Explain.

10. What is the domain and range of the profit function?

The interesting thing about the ordered pairs (or function) representing the relationship between profit and price is that unlike many of the other functions that we have studied, they do not form a straight line. As a matter of fact, a smooth curve can be drawn through the points. This curve resembles the path taken if you toss a ball to a friend or the shape of the water jet at the water fountain. In fact, the mathematical equations for the trajectory of a tossed ball and the relationship between profit and price in this example are very similar.

[Teaching note: This is a rich problem which allows for a discussion of both linear and quadratic functions, all based on a realistic and understandable real-world situation. The graph of the data for the second problem should look something like the one below. The problem also uses charts to help students organise their work. Providing students with a chart will often speed up the investigation substantially and ensure that the appropriate calculations are properly recorded.]

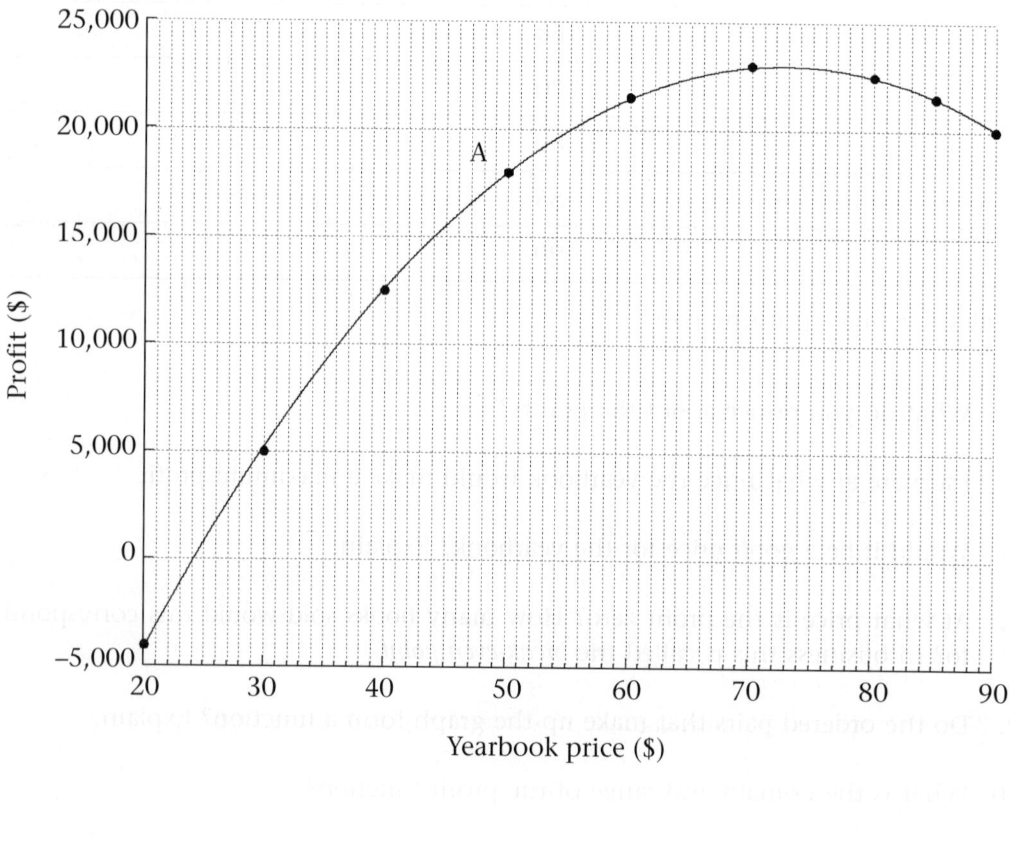

Problem 3

Consider the problem of Joanie and Kamini. They want to build a pen for their pet rabbit. They have exactly 100 metres of fencing material that Kamini's father gave them. They want the pen to have as large an area as possible. What dimensions should they make the pen?

1. They could make it long and narrow, say 49 metres by 1 metre, and that would make an area of 49 square metres. Or they could make it 30 metres by 20 metres and produce an area of 600 square metres. Both use the same amount of fencing material. Make a chart in your notebook similar to the one below and complete it:

Length	Width	Fencing used	Area
45	5	$2 \times 45 + 2 \times 5 = 100$	$45 \times 5 = 225$
40	10		
30			
20			
8			
2			
l			

2. Draw a graph with length on the *x*-axis and area on the *y*-axis. Sketch a smooth curve through these points. Estimate what dimensions would produce the maximum area.

3. Do the ordered pairs of the graph form a function? Explain.

4. What is the domain and range?

5. Are you justified in drawing a solid curve through these points? Explain.

[Teaching note: This problem might look like a calculus problem but it need not be. Students can do this as an independent investigation and be introduced to quadratic functions through the discussion. The resulting graph should look something like the one below.]

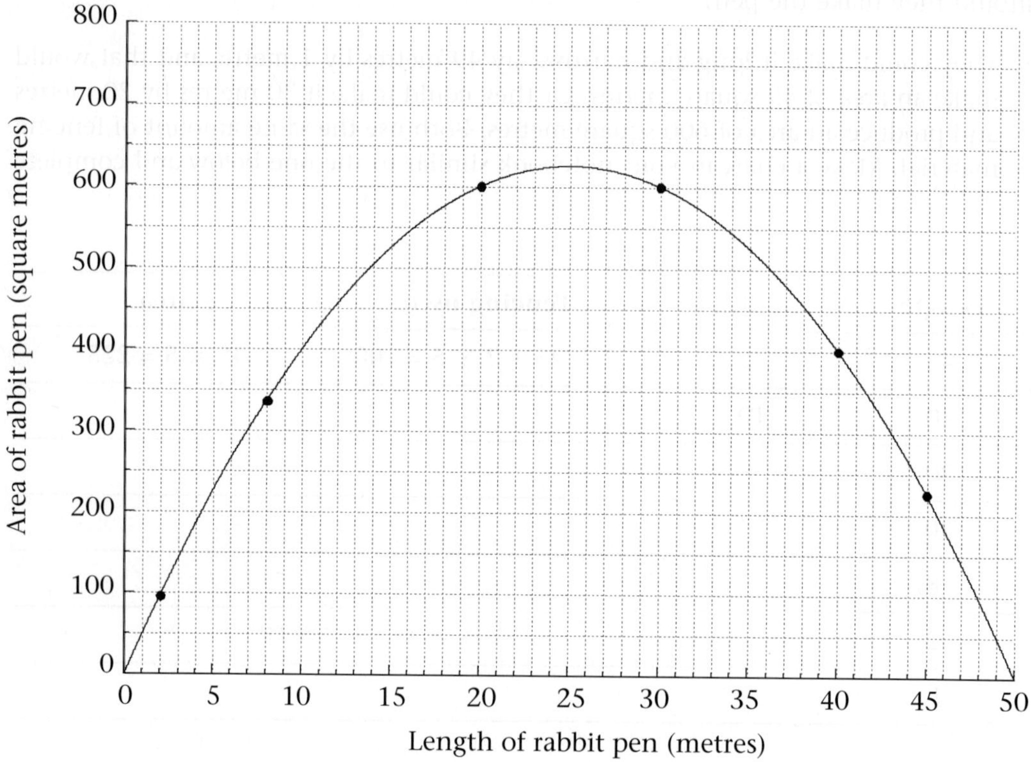

Problem 4

This activity is designed to be a worksheet that can be used as it is. It allows students to investigate an interesting situation and then to use their findings to generate a parabola and a discussion of quadratic functions. It is designed to be used in conjunction with a TI83+ graphing calculator but it also could be modified for use with software such as Excel or other graphing software that allows curves to be fitted to data such as GNUPLOT (freely available). Alternatively, the teacher might just use the problem to generate the idea of a parabolic curve and then proceed in a more traditional fashion.

Getting a driver's licence is an important milestone in everyone's life. Part of becoming a good driver is understanding how long it takes to stop your vehicle and using this information to judge the distance between vehicles safely. But what is the relationship between speed and stopping distance?

Car magazines test the performance of cars and one of the things that they typically report is the braking distance, that is, how far the car travels once the brakes have been fully applied.

This information, for a 1999 Chevrolet Monte Carlo SS based on tests done by *Car and Driver* magazine, is given in the chart below:

Speed (km/hr)	Braking distance (metres)
0	0
10	0.46
20	1.85
30	4.16
40	7.39
50	11.5
60	16.6
70	22.6
80	29.55
90	37.40
100	46.17
110	55.87
120	66.49
130	78.03
140	90.50

1. When the speed doubles does the stopping distance double too? Illustrate your answer with at least two pieces of data from the table.
2. When the speed triples does the braking distance triple? Illustrate your answer with at least two pieces of data from the table.
3. One way to get some idea about how the speed and the braking distance are related is to draw a graph, or try to find an equation that relates the two. You can use your calculator to help find an equation that represents this data.

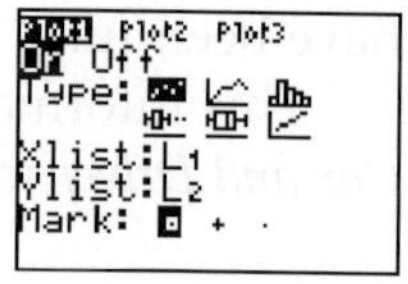

- Press [Y=]. Use [CLEAR] and the scroll buttons to clear all graphs.
- Press [2nd] [Y=] to select STAT PLOT. Then press 1 to select plot 1. Use the scroll buttons and [ENTER] to make sure the settings are as shown.
- Press [STAT] 1 to get the list editor. If there are any numbers in the first two columns they must be cleared. Move the cursor into each column heading and then press [CLEAR] [ENTER].
- Move the cursor to the space below L1. Enter the numbers 0, 10, 20, 30, 40, 50, 60, 70, 80, 90, 100, 110, 120, 130, 140 in List 1. Press 0 [ENTER] 10 [ENTER], and so on.

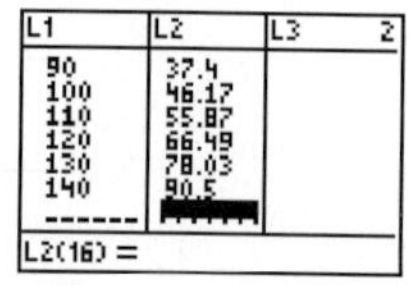

- Move the cursor to the space below L2. Enter the numbers 0, 0.46, 1.85, and so on in List 2. Press 0 [ENTER] .46 [ENTER] 1.85 [ENTER], and so on.
- Press [ZOOM] 9 and the graph appears. When you press these buttons the calculator automatically resets the window to contain all of the data points.

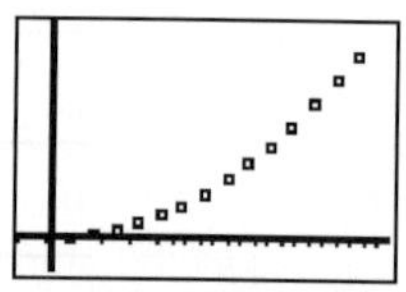

4. It is still not clear what the relationship is between speed and braking distance but the calculator can help us to find the best fitting straight line for this data.

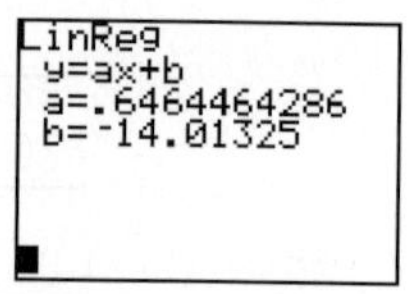

- Press [STAT] and then choose CALC. Press 4 and [ENTER] to find the equation of the best fitting straight line for the data.
- Press [Y=] and make sure the cursor is beside y_1. Press .646 [X,T,Θ,*n*] [−] 14.01 [GRAPH].
- You have entered the equation $y = 0.646x - 14.01$ and graphed it along with the data points entered earlier.

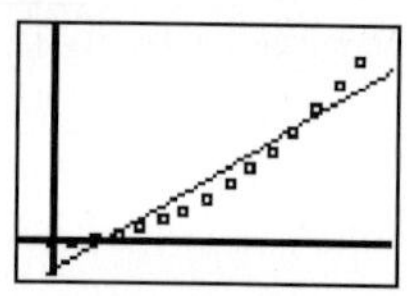

5. But how good is the equation $y = 0.646x - 14.01$ as a mathematical model of braking distance (y) versus speed (x)?
   a. If the speed is 30 km per hour use this equation to find the braking distance. How close is it to the data in the table?
   b. If the speed is 100 km per hour use this equation to find the braking distance. How close is it to the data in the table?
   c. Explain if you think this equation is a good model or a poor model for this situation. Give reasons.

6. We can use our calculator yet again to see if we can find a better model.

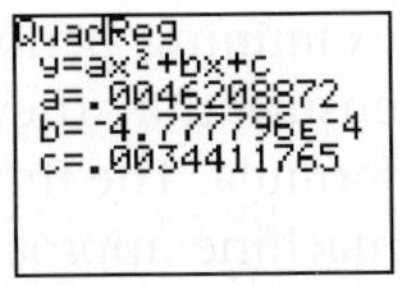

- Press STAT and then choose CALC. Press 5 and ENTER to find the equation of the best fitting quadratic for this data. (Don't worry about what a quadratic is, we will find out soon enough!)
- Press Y= and place the cursor beside y_1. Press CLEAR. Press .00462 X,T,Θ,*n* x^2 − .000478 X,T,Θ,*n* + .003 GRAPH.

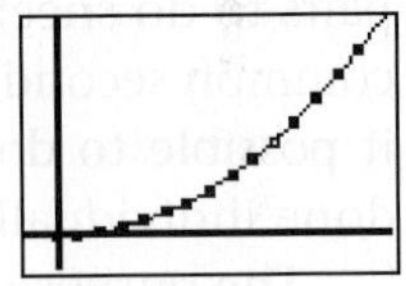

This is the graph of the equation $y = .00462x^2 - .000478x + .003$ and as you can see it is a much better fitting graph than the straight line. Equations like this one that have a squared term in them are called *quadratic equations.* This word comes from the Latin word *quadrus* which means "square". So quadratic equations are equations of the form where $y = ax^2 + bx + c$ where $a \neq 0$.

7. If the speed is 30 km per hour use the equation $y = .00462x^2 - .000478x + .003$ to find the braking distance. How close is it to the data in the table?

8. If the speed is 100 km per hour use this equation to find the braking distance. How close is it to the data in the table?

9. Explain if you think this equation is a good model or a poor model for this situation. Give reasons.

Curves like this one are called parabolas and are found in many applications. We will be studying much more about parabolas in the lessons ahead.

TRIGONOMETRIC FUNCTIONS

The next series of activities and explorations allows students to develop the idea of periodic functions in general and the trigonometric functions in particular through experimental data. They should be done in order as they form a sequenced package. The first activity has students drawing a graph of real-world data that results in a sinusoidal graph. The notions of period and amplitude can be discussed without any mention of trigonometry. The second exercise produces a similar graph but allows for a transition to angles as the variable rather than days of the year. In this exercise students will get different graphs but they will all have the same amplitude and period. Only the vertical shift will be different. The next exercise has students examining periodic functions that cannot be easily specified by equations just to ensure that they have got the functional idea rather than mechanically using a formula. The final three sheets provide a more structured discovery, using a function machine approach, to the three trigonometric functions. Students should work in pairs to do sheet A and sheet B with each student having a different first sheet and common second sheet. They can compare their results after they are done. This makes it possible to do the *sine* and *cosine* functions together quickly. Sheet C should be done individually.

The purpose of this sequence is to help students appreciate the functional nature of trigonometric graphs. When they just press the SIN button on their calculator or think of it as the ratio of two sides of a right-angled triangle, they do not appreciate the trigonometric ratios as generating functions. The key idea is that when an angle is put into the function machine, a number comes out – a different one depending on the processing instructions. Furthermore, the values generated can be for any angle, not just those less than 90°.

An interesting exercise at the end of the section is to have students use their knowledge of the effects of various parameters on the graphs of functions to try to establish an equation that will pass through the points of the graph from the first exercise and then check how good the equation would be for predicting the length of the day in Manila on the date that they do this exercise. The graph on p. 219 shows the original data along with the graph of the equation $y = 0.84 \sin(0.98x - 79.27) + 12.13$ and as you can see the fit is excellent. [Note: Manila is chosen because it is in Southeast Asia but is far enough north that there is a change in the number of daylight hours. Data for Singapore do not yield this kind of graph! Other datasets that will produce a reasonable sinusoid are average monthly temperatures for locations that have different seasons.]

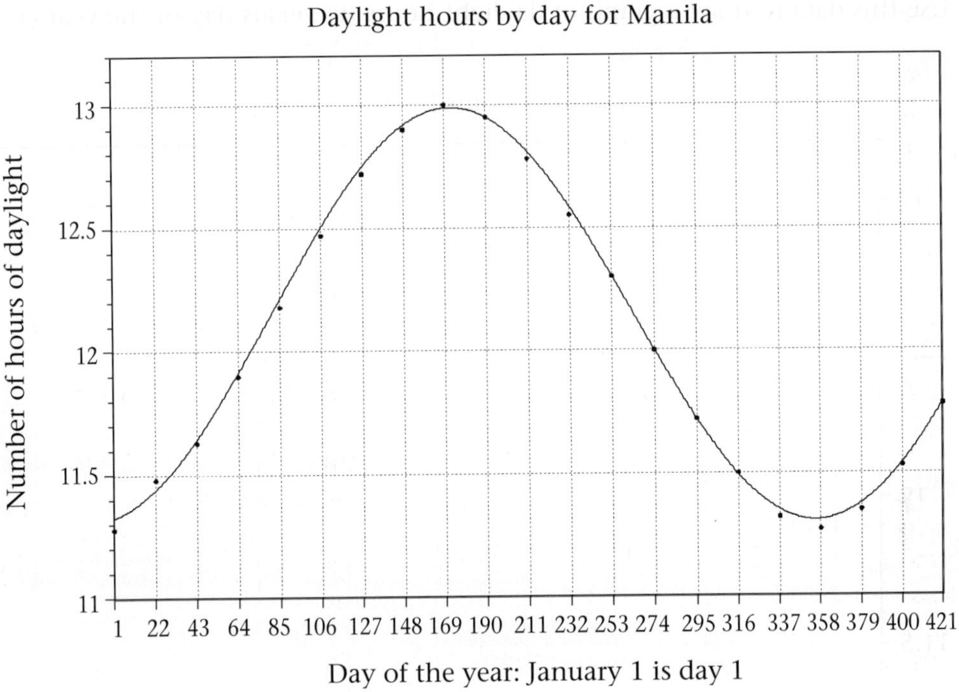

Sunrise, sunset and mathematical functions

Activity 1

The table you are given reports the sunrise and sunset times for Manila in the Philippines for each day of the year. Each day has been assigned a number using January 1 as day 1 and then counting forwards for all other dates. The first few dates for the following year are also included and that is why their values are greater than 365.

1. Convert each time to a 24-hour system using decimal parts of an hour rather than hours and minutes. Subtract the sunrise and sunset times to complete the last column in the table. Work in groups of three with each person doing one-third of the dates and then sharing the information with the rest of the group members.

2. Use this data to draw a graph of daylight hours (y) versus day of the year (x).

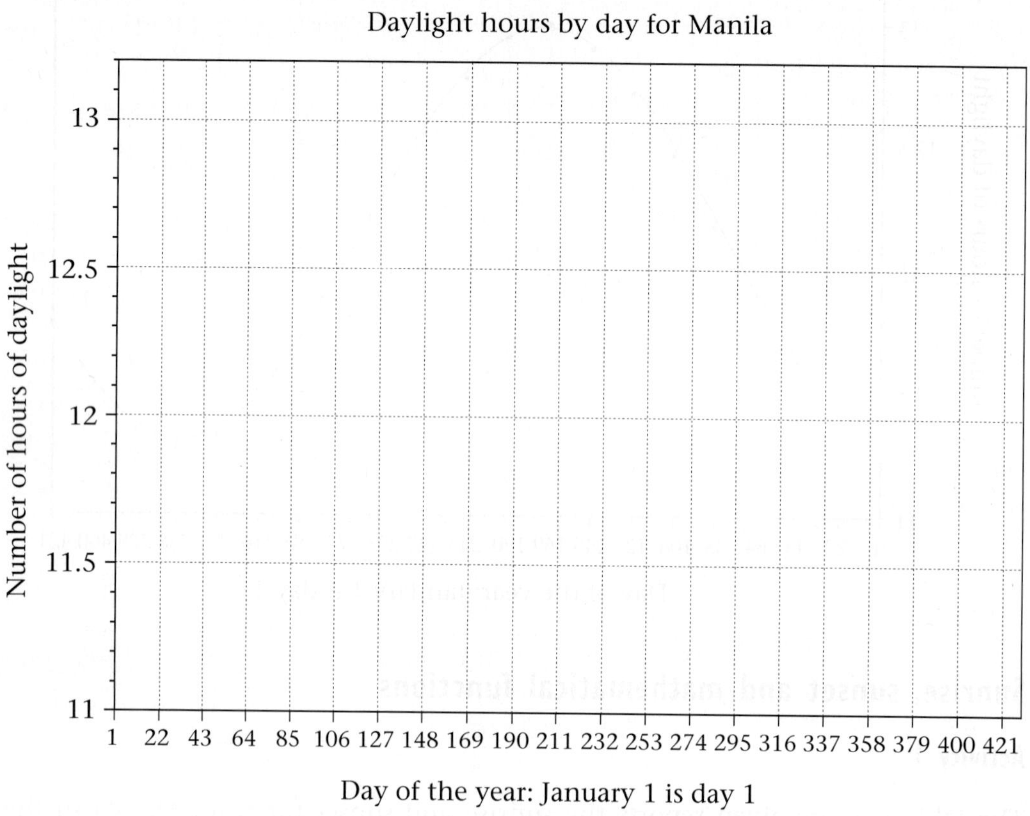

3. Does this set of data form a function? If so why, if not explain.

4. Find December 21 on the graph. What do you notice?

5. Find another day with the same number of hours of daylight as 21 March. What date would this be?

6. What would be true about the number of daylight hours for 21 March 2002 compared to 21 March 2003?

7. Graphs that repeat over and over again in the same pattern are said to be *periodic* and the period refers to how often this repetition occurs. What would be the period of this relation?

Sunrise and sunset times for Manila

Date	Day no.	Sunrise	Sunset	Hours of daylight
Jan 1	1	6:21	17:38	
Jan 22	22	6:25	17:50	
Feb 12	43	6:21	17:59	
Mar 5	64	6:11	18:05	
Mar 26	85	5:56	18:07	
April 16	106	5:42	18:10	
May 7	127	5:31	18:14	
May 28	148	5:26	18:20	
June 18	169	5:27	18:27	
July 9	190	5:33	18:30	
July 30	211	5:39	18:26	
Aug 20	232	5:43	18:16	
Sept 10	253	5:44	18:02	
Oct 1	274	5:46	17:46	
Oct 22	295	5:49	17:32	
Nov 2	316	5:55	17:25	
Dec 3	337	6:06	17:25	
Dec 24	358	6:17	17:33	
Jan 13	379	6:24	17:45	
Feb 3	400	6:24	17:56	
Feb 24	421	6:16	18:03	

Activity 2

There are other activities that can produce interesting mathematical graphs. You are provided with a diagram of the face of a clock with only the hour hand showing. Tape it to your desk anywhere you like as long as the top edge of the paper is between 1 and 10 cm from the top edge of the desk. Make sure that the edges of the paper are parallel to the edges of your desk.

1. Measure the distance (in centimetres) from the tip of the hour hand to the top edge of your desk for each hour, starting at 1 o'clock and ending at 12 o'clock. Remember that the distance must be the straight line distance to the top edge of the desk measured at right angles to this edge.

2. Record your data in the table below.

Hour	1	2	3	4	5	6	7	8	9	10	11	12
Distance												

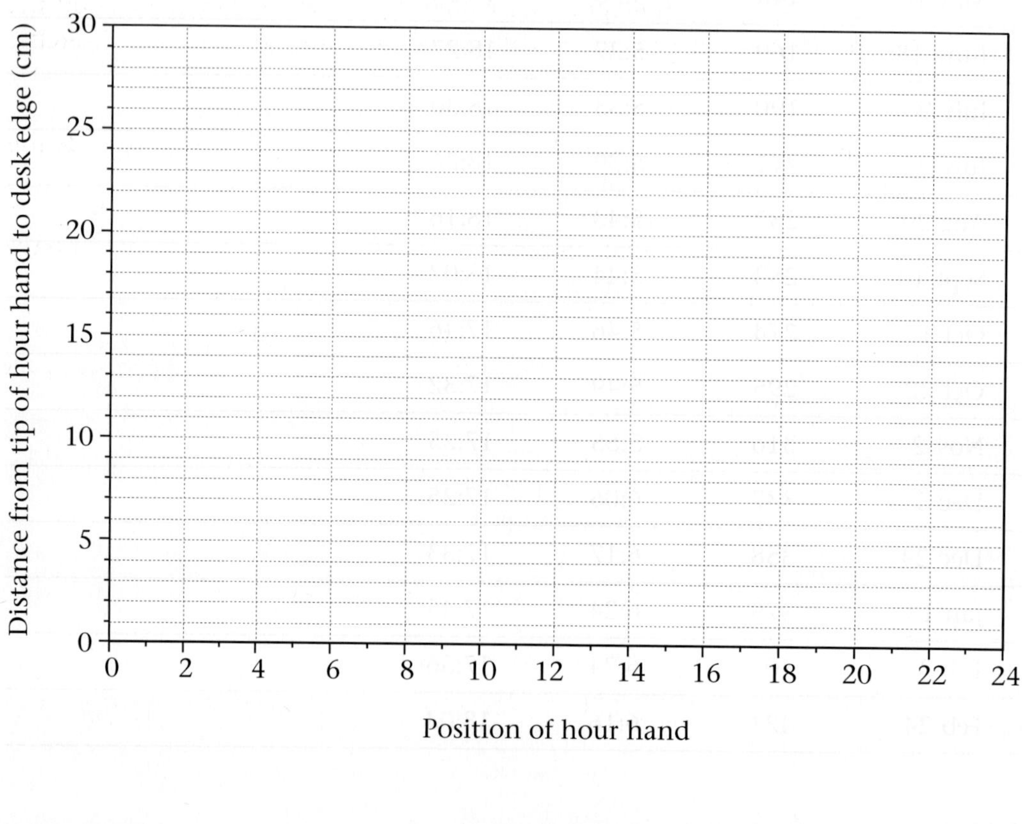

3. Draw a graph of hour (x-axis) versus distance to the top edge of the desk (y-axis).

4. Does this set of points form a function? Why/Why not?

5. Is it periodic? If so, what is the period? If not, why not?

6. Assume that in our experiment, 1 o'clock represents 1 a.m. and that 12 o'clock is noon. If we call 1 p.m. 13:00 hours and continue making measurements all the way up to 24:00 hours, explain why you could fill in another chart without making any measurements.

7. Make up another chart from 13:00 to 24:00 hours and add these points to the graph. What do you notice?

8. If you think of 00:00 (midnight) as an angle of 0°, then what angle could you associate with (a) 1 a.m., (b) 7 a.m., (c) 11 a.m., and (d) 3 p.m.

9. If you draw your graph with the angle on the x-axis and the distance along the y-axis, would the graph change? Establish what angle would be equivalent to each position of the hour hand recorded in your table. Relabel the x-axis below the original labels using the appropriate angles. Now if you graph angle on the x-axis and distance on the y-axis, will the graph look the same or different? Explain.

10. Is there any reason why you could not carry out this experiment to include the distances for the hour hand at 1:30, 2:30, and so on? Explain.

11. In what ways is this last graph similar to or different from the graph you have drawn for the number of daylight hours?

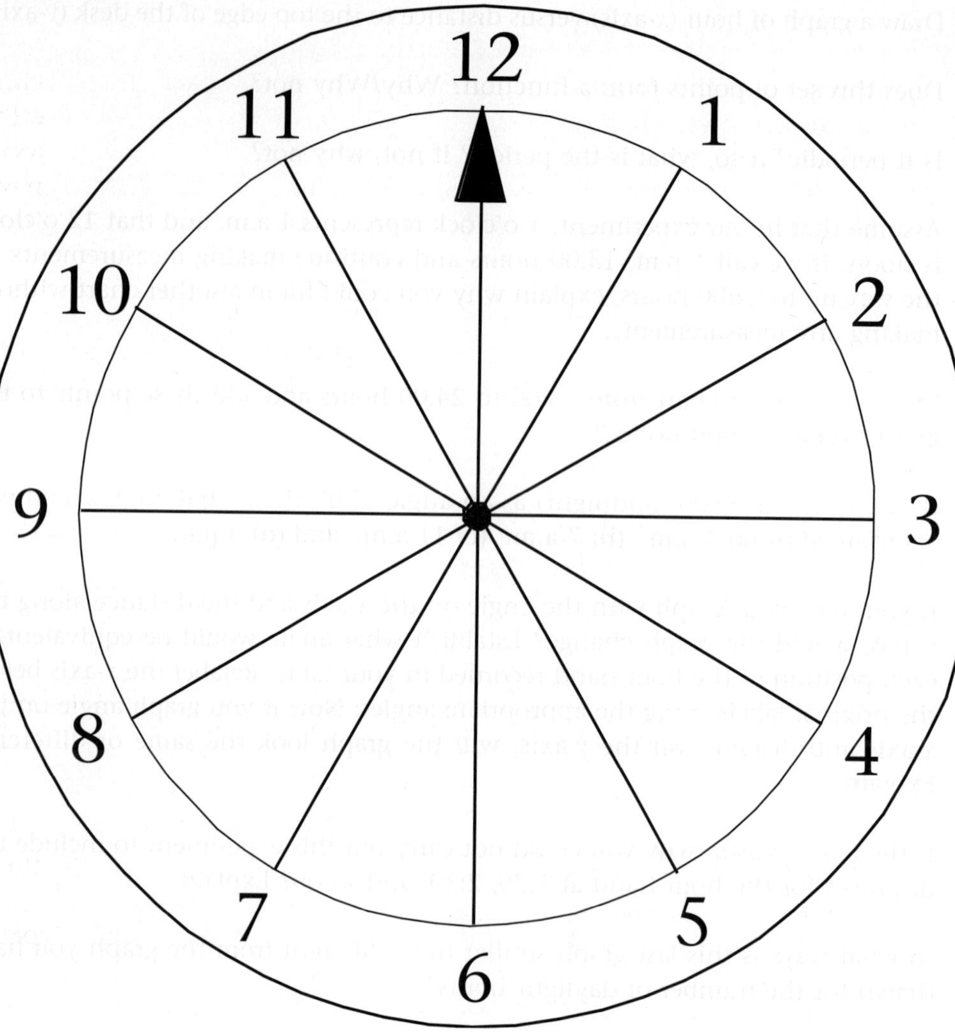
12
1
2
3
4
5
6
7
8
9
10
11

Making connections with periodic functions

1. In 1900, Willem Einthoven invented the electrocardiograph (EKG). This machine measures the electrical impulses that cause the heart to beat. Doctors use this record to help them in diagnosing heart problems; and, many medical shows on TV have video displays of the classic spiked pulse of the heartbeat. Einthoven was awarded the Nobel Prize in 1924 for his invention. Below is a typical tracing from an EKG for a healthy adult.

Typical EKG for normal adult

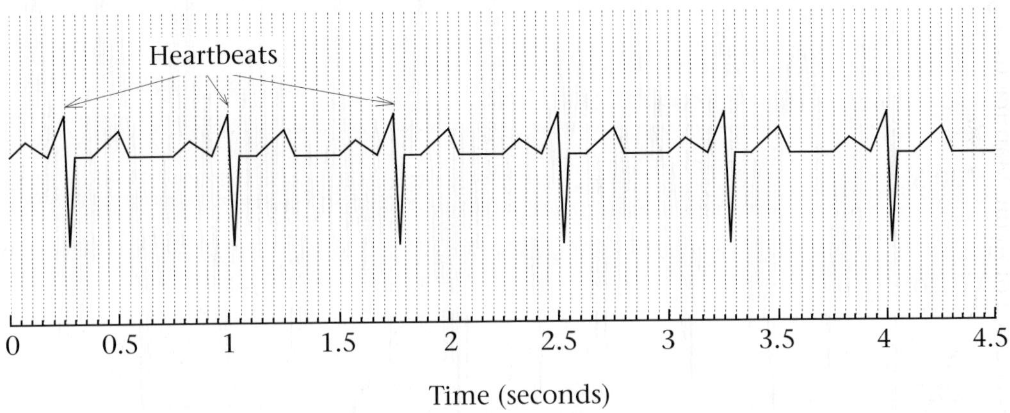

a. Based on the portion of the graph that you can see, would you say that this is a periodic function? Explain.
b. Assume the graph illustrated is represented by $y = f(x)$. Is $f(0.5) = f(2)$? Explain.
c. Find two values of a that make $f(a) = f(3)$ a true statement.
d. How many complete cycles occur between $t = 0.5$ and $t = 3.5$ seconds?
e. What is the period of this graph?
f. Based on your answer to e. what would you say is the heart rate in beats/minute for this person? Is this normal?
g. If the heart rate was 120 beats/minute, what would be the period of the EKG tracing in minutes? In seconds?
h. Animals such as cats and dogs have heart rates quite different to humans. The heart rate for an elephant is 46 beats per minute. What would be the period of the corresponding EKG tracing?
i. A canary's heart beats 1,000 times per minute. What would be the period of the corresponding EKG tracing (if a canary would sit still for such a thing!)?

2. Some stock market analysts believe that stock prices vary in a predictable pattern and that if these patterns could be established it would make decisions about buying and selling stocks much easier. The average weekly stock price for the Acme Manufacturing Company for a five-year period is illustrated below.

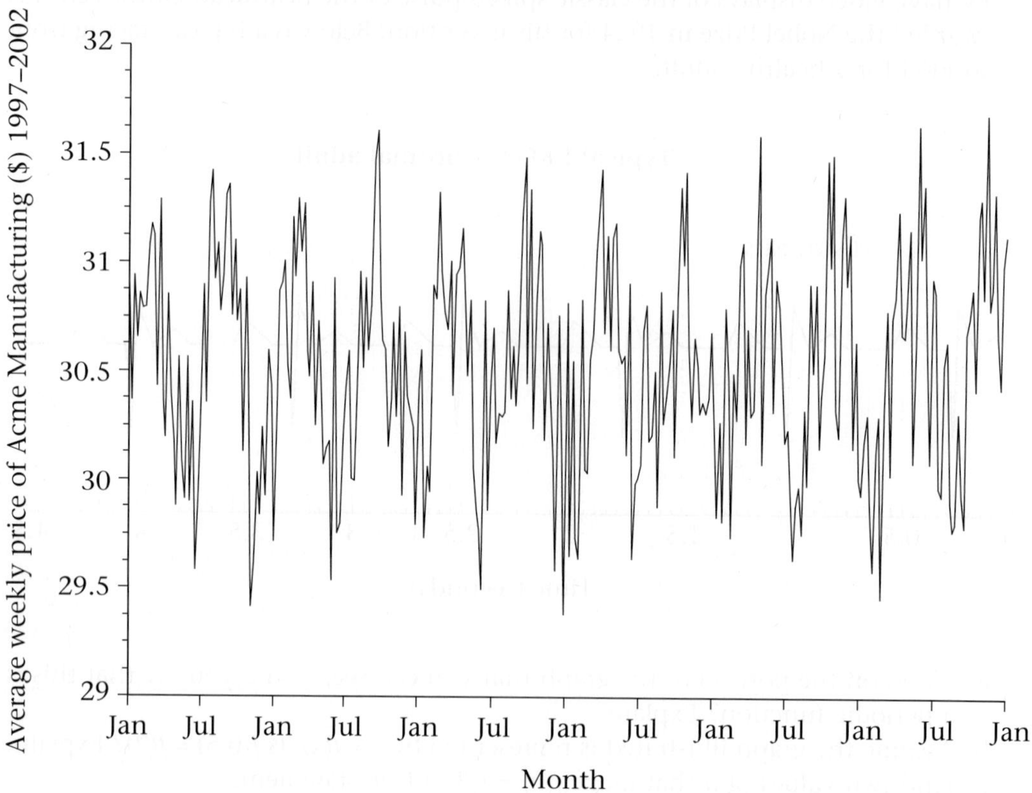

a. Explain why this set of points forms a function.
b. What are the maximum and minimum values for this function?
c. When was the stock at its highest value over the past five years?
d. When was the stock at its lowest value over the past five years?
e. Based on the portion of the graph that you can see, would you say that this function is periodic? Explain.
f. What does the word "cyclic" mean? Would you say that these stock prices are cyclic? Explain.

Exploring circular functions – A

1. Use the function machine below and the circle to fill in the table of values for this function. For example, if you draw a 45° angle, the *y*-coordinate of the point where the angle cuts the circle will be 0.71. This produces the ordered pair (45°, 0.71).

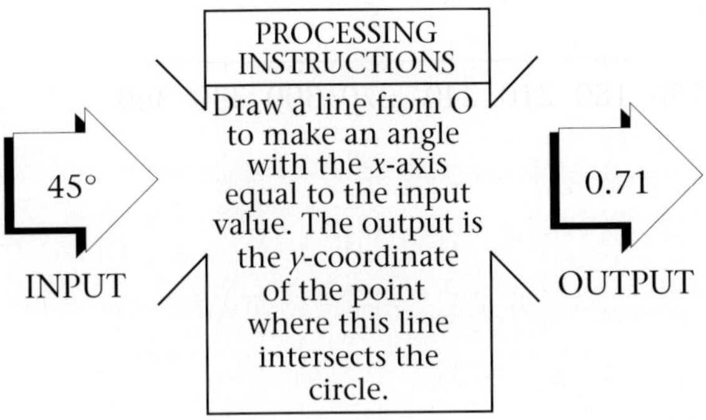

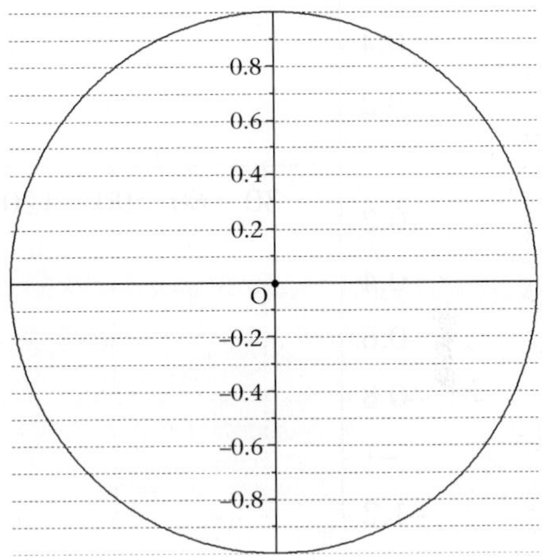

Angle (°)	0	30	60	90	120	150	180	210	240	270	300	330	360
Function value													

2. For every point on the unit circle will there be a corresponding angle?

3. For every angle will there be a corresponding point on the unit circle?

4. Are we justified in joining these points with a smooth continuous curve? Explain.

5. Plot these ordered pairs on the grid below. Comment on your observation.

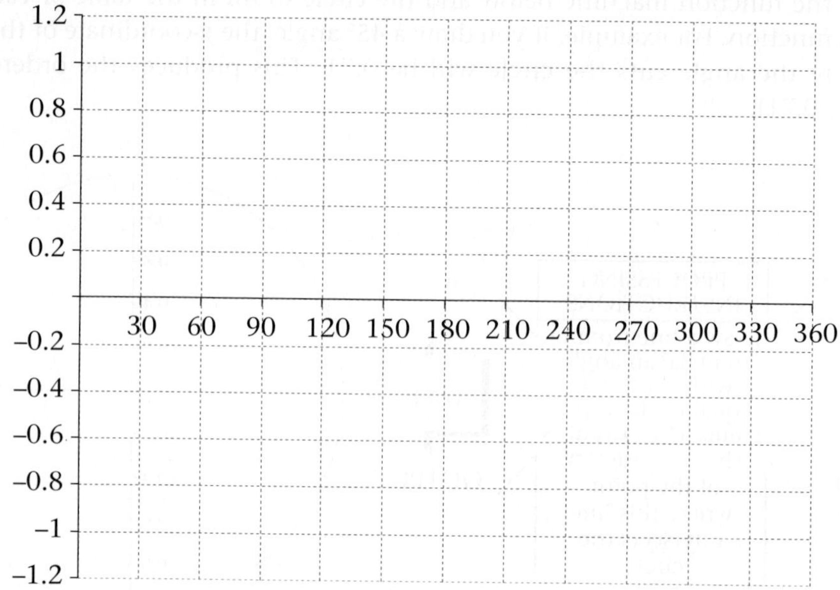

6. Compare your unit circle and function machine with that of your neighbour. In what ways are they the same or different?

7. Compare your graph with that of your neighbour. In what ways are they the same or different?

8. Where have you seen graphs similar to these before?

9. Would you say that the functions defined by these function machines represent periodic functions or not? Explain.

The functions in these two exercises are called the *sine* (Exploration – A) and *cosine* (Exploration – B) functions. The *sine* function is defined by $\sin \theta = \frac{y}{r}$ where r is the radius of the circle used to generate the ordered pairs and θ is the angle. If the radius is 1 (as in this case), we can simply use the y-coordinate as we did here. The *cosine* function is defined by $\cos \theta = \frac{x}{r}$.

10. Sketch the graph of $f(x) = \sin \theta$ and $f(x) = \cos \theta$ in your notebook. Label the axes and state the *domain* and *range* for each function.

Exploring circular functions – B

1. Use the function machine below and the circle to fill in the table of values for this function. For example, if you draw a 60° angle, the *x*-coordinate of the point where the angle cuts the circle will be 0.5. This produces the ordered pair (60°, 0.5).

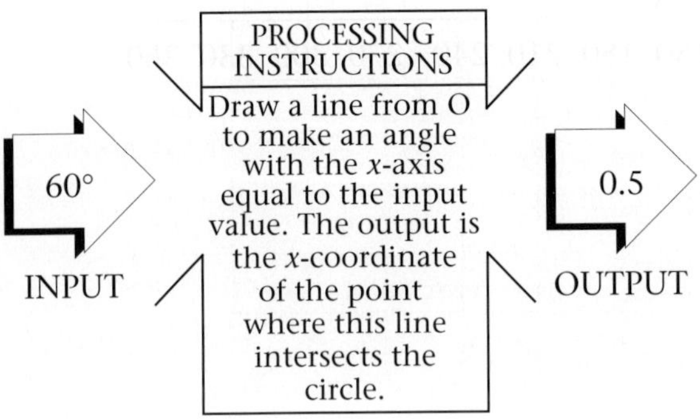

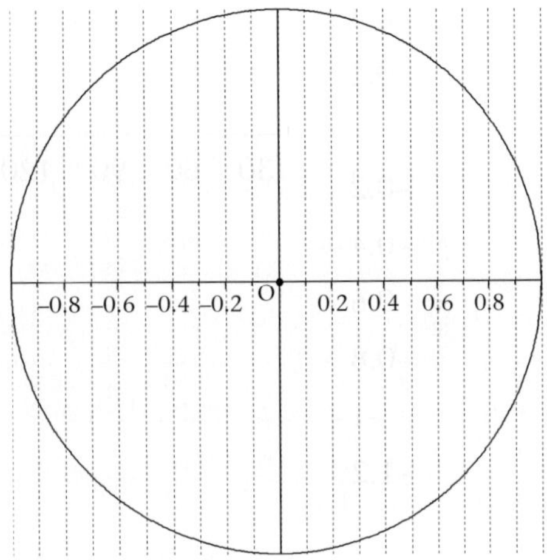

Angle (°)	0	30	60	90	120	150	180	210	240	270	300	330	360
Function value													

2. For every point on the unit circle will there be a corresponding angle?

3. For every angle will there be a corresponding point on the unit circle?

4. Are we justified in joining these points with a smooth continuous curve? Explain.

5. Plot these ordered pairs on the grid below. Comment on your observation.

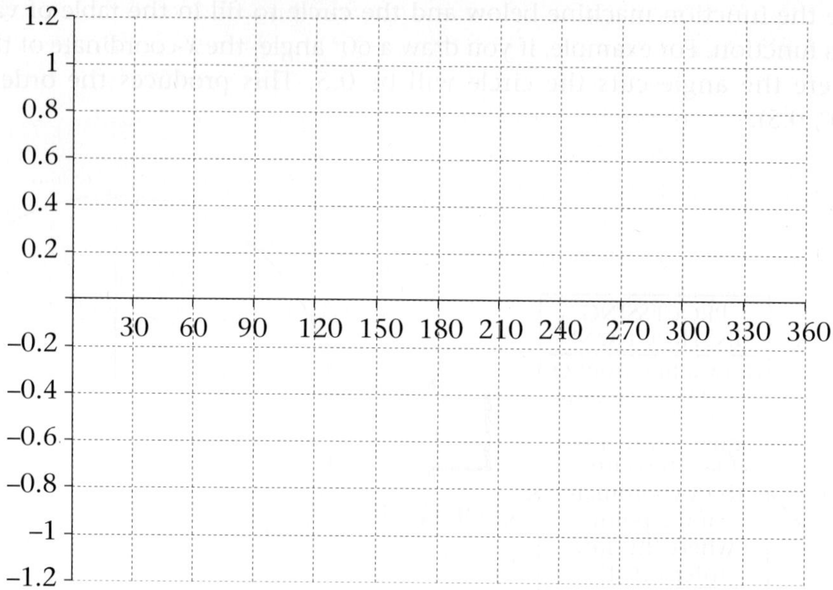

6. Compare your unit circle and function machine with that of your neighbour. In what ways are they the same or different?

7. Compare your graph with that of your neighbour. In what ways are they the same or different?

8. Where have you seen graphs similar to these?

9. Would you say that the functions defined by these function machines represent periodic functions or not? Explain.

The functions in these two exercises are called the *sine* (Exploration – A) and *cosine* (Exploration – B) functions. The *sine* function is defined by $\sin\theta = \frac{y}{r}$ where r is the radius of the circle used to generate the ordered pairs and θ is the angle. If the radius is 1 (as in this case), we can simply use the y-coordinate as we did here. The *cosine* function is defined by $\cos\theta = \frac{x}{r}$.

10. Sketch the graph of $f(x) = \sin\theta$ and $f(x) = \cos\theta$ in your notebook. Label the axes and state the *domain* and *range* for each function.

Exploring circular functions – C

As we have seen in the previous exercises, the function machine can be programmed to produce different functions depending on the procedure that is part of the machine. This last set of processing instructions will produce yet another circular function. The function machine on the left is used in conjunction with the diagram on your handout. This diagram illustrates a circle along with a tangent line. Recall that a tangent is a line that intersects a circle at only one point. Once again, the radius of the circle is exactly one unit and the marks on the tangent line are 0.1 units. Use your own copy of the unit circle and the function machine along with its defined rule to generate a table of values for this function for angles of –60°, –45°, –30°, 0°, 30°, 45°, 60° ... 360°, 390° and 420°. (Hint: If the terminal ray of the angle does not hit the tangent line, just extend the other end until it does). Make up a table similar to this one to help organise your work:

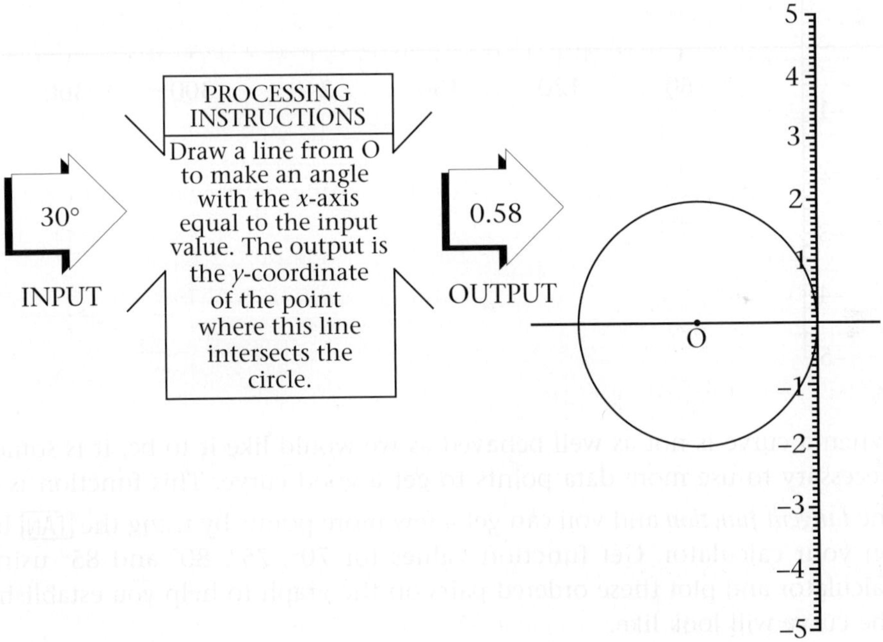

Angle (°)	–60°	–45°	–30°	0°	15°	30°	45°	60°	...	420°
Function value										

1. For every point on the tangent line will there be a corresponding angle?

2. For every angle will there be a corresponding point on the tangent line? Explain. The angles that do not produce values are 90° and 270° (and all coterminal equivalents). It is useful to draw dotted vertical lines at these angle values on the x-axis so that we know the function is undefined at these values.

3. Now plot the ordered pairs in your table of values on a graph.

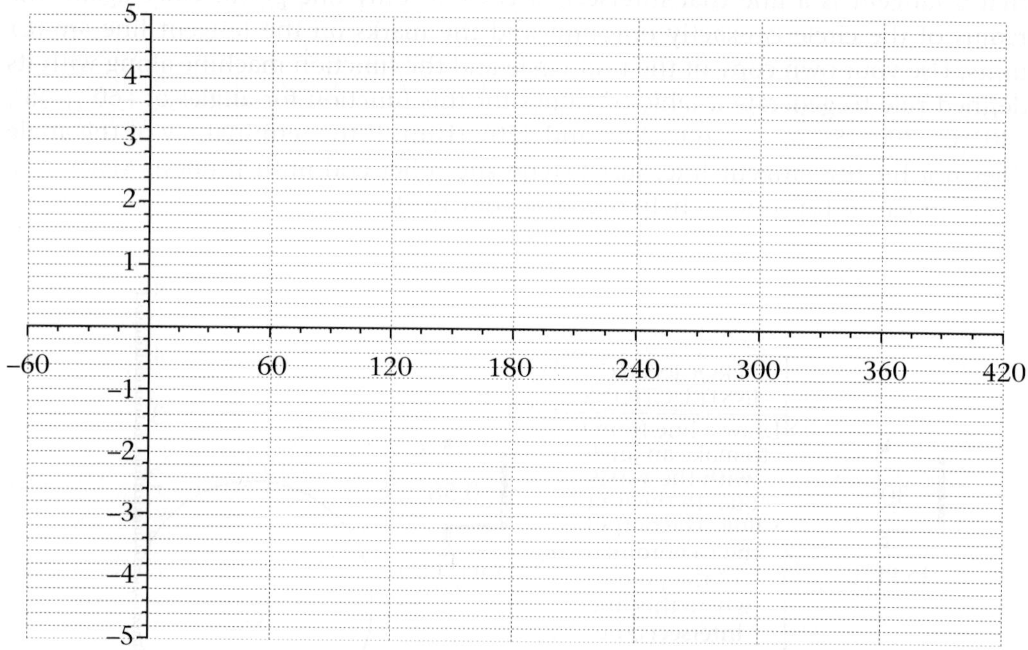

4. When a curve is not as well behaved as we would like it to be, it is sometimes necessary to use more data points to get a good curve. This function is called the *tangent function* and you can get a few more points by using the TAN button on your calculator. Get function values for 70°, 75°, 80° and 85° using the calculator and plot these ordered pairs on the graph to help you establish what the curve will look like.

5. Try to draw a smooth curve through the points. Comment on your observation, particularly the ways this curve is similar to or different from the graphs of the sine and cosine functions.

6. Explain why the ordered pairs in the graph form a function.
7. Explain why the function appears to be periodic.
8. What is the period of this function?
9. What are the maximum and minimum values of this function?
10. For what values of the angle does the value of the function appear to be 0?
11. For what values of the angle does the value of the function appear to be undefined?
12. What are the domain and range of the tangent function?
13. Try to find tan 90° on your calculator. What happens? Explain.

Cubic functions

Problem 1

The Acme Carton Company makes rectangular cardboard boxes. They were able to buy a large shipment of precut pieces of cardboard 20 cm by 10 cm from a company that had gone out of business. They purchased this cardboard at a low cost and now want to make boxes by cutting a square piece out of each corner, folding up the sides and taping them. What dimensions should they make the boxes if they wish to maximise the volume?

1. To get an idea of what might happen to the volume when we use a different sized cutout on each of the corners, copy the chart below into your notebook and then complete it.

Cutout size (cm)	Length (cm)	Width (cm)	Height (cm)	Volume (cm^3)
1	20 – (2)(1) = 18	10 – (2)(1) = 8	1	(18)(8)(1) = 144
0.8				
3.8				
4.5				
0.3				

2. Graph the ordered pairs representing (height, volume) from your chart. Is there any obvious pattern to the points? Explain.

   Although we can be reasonably certain that the points are not in a line, it is not clear what kind of shape they follow and the graph is not helpful in establishing the maximum volume of the container. Let us use a slightly different approach, one that makes use of algebra. If the side of the square cutout is x then the length of the cardboard would be $20 - 2x$ and the width $10 - 2x$. This would give an expression for volume in terms of x, $f(x) = (20 - 2x)(10 - 2x)(x) = 4x^3 - 60x^2 + 200x$, where $f(x)$ is the volume.

3. Graph this function along with the five data points that we have established in the chart.

4. What is the domain of the function *f(x)*?

5. What is the range of the function *f(x)*?

6. What restrictions would you put on the domain if you want the results of this exploration to provide a reasonable model for the relationship between the volume and the size of the cutout square?

7. Estimate the maximum volume of the cardboard container from the graph.

8. Estimate the size of the cutout that would produce a maximum volume.

9. Graph the function *f(x)* on your calculator and use the trace feature to estimate the maximum volume and the cutout size that produces it. Does it agree with the value from the graph above?

[Teaching note: The points that the students plot here are deliberately chosen to have them think initially that the curve might be a parabola. Note that the points do not lie symmetrically around a centre line and so this is not possible. The function is a cubic and so the graph cannot be a parabola (see graph below).]

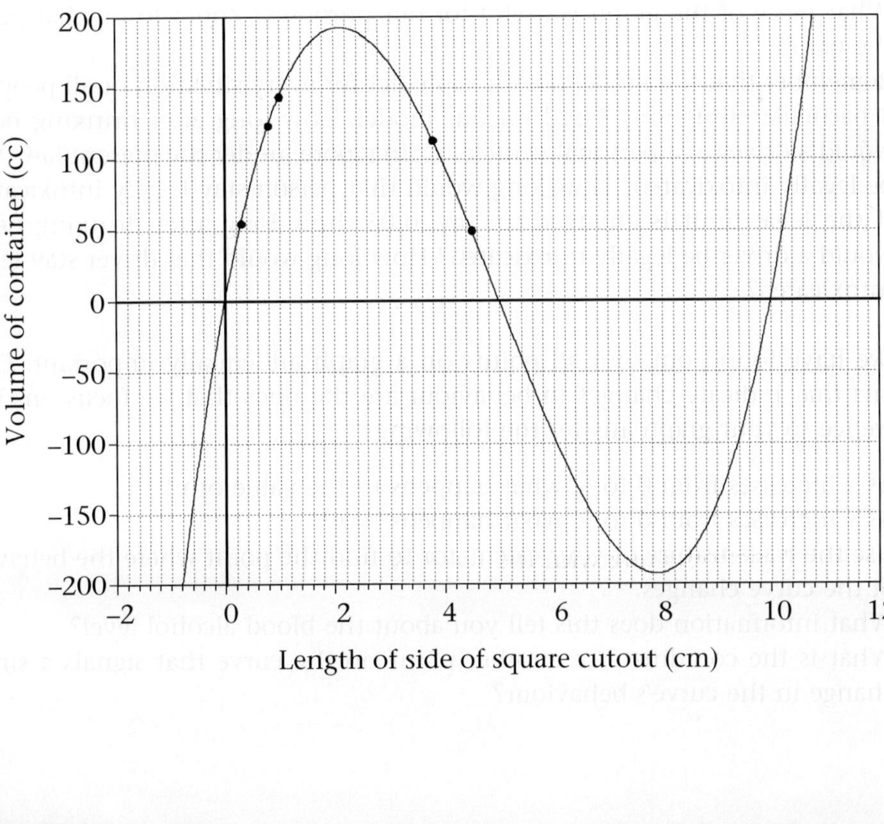

Problem 2

As a society we have become increasingly aware of the problem of drivers who operate motor vehicles while under the influence of alcohol. There are legal limits for alcohol concentration in the bloodstream. If a person is above the legal limit, he or she is considered to be intoxicated. These limits are given in parts of 1 percent so, for example, 0.10 means one-tenth of one percent. No function can exactly model the alcohol concentration in the bloodstream over time; however, one function that is a reasonable approximation is $y = -0.0015x^3 + 0.1058x$. The concentration of alcohol (y) is a function of the number of hours after consuming an alcoholic beverage (x). The value of the function (concentration of alcohol) is measured in tenths of a percent.

1. a. What is the degree of this polynomial?
   b. List the various coefficients starting with a_3.

2. Use your graphing calculator to answer each of the following:

   a. Graph $f(x)$ on the calculator. By examining the graph, state the domain and range of the function.
   b. Now, take into consideration the real-life situation that the function is modelling. State what you believe the restricted domain and range would be. What piece of the graph is useful for our purposes? Zoom in on that part of the graph.
   c. Remember that the model does not predict for every situation or all people in a particular situation. Based on our model, how long after drinking begins would a driver of a personal vehicle in Singapore, under the present law (0.10) be legally intoxicated? How long would that person stay legally intoxicated?
   d. If the legal limit is changed to, say, 0.05, how long after drinking begins would a driver be legally intoxicated? How long would that driver stay legally intoxicated?

3. As we have found out, not all points on a graph are equally important. Often points that indicate changes in behaviour are the ones that we focus on. With reference to your graph answer the following:

   a. As x increases from 0 to 4, what happens to the value of y?
   b. As x increases from 6 to 9, what happens to y?
   c. Use the trace feature of your calculator to find the point where the behaviour of the curve changes.
   d. What information does this tell you about the blood alcohol level?
   e. What is the coordinate of another point on the curve that signals a similar change in the curve's behaviour?

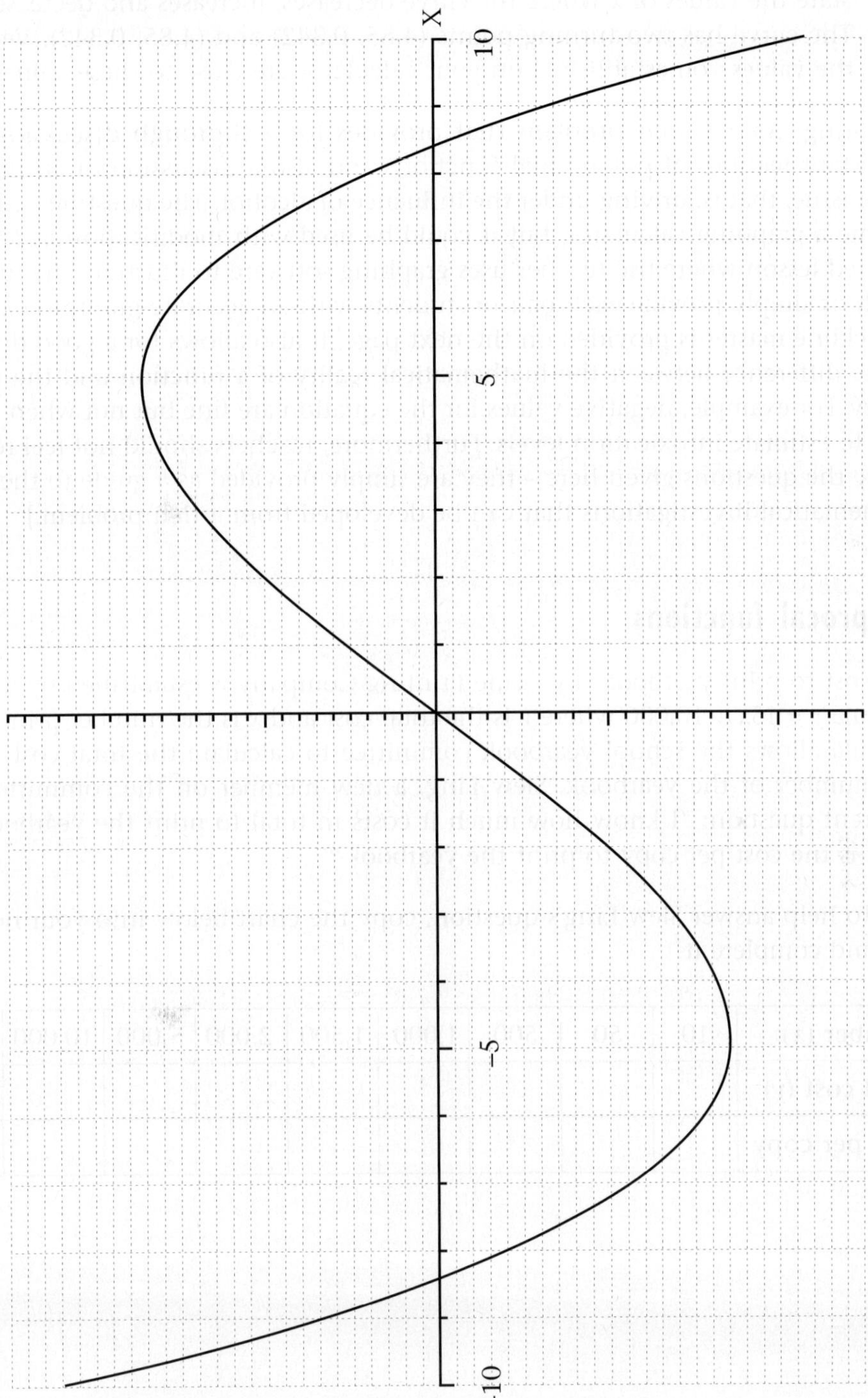
X
Y
10
5
−5
−10

f. State the values of x where the curve decreases, increases and decreases again.
g. The curve has two turning points (4.85, 0.342) and (4.85, 0.342). Verify that the values you established on your calculator are close to these values.

[Teaching note: A rich problem that provides for a thorough discussion of the important features of polynomial functions and also a discussion of an important social issue, that is, driving under the influence of alcohol. The questions asked here assume a graphing calculator, but it could be used with modification as a teacher-directed lesson where the teacher uses graphing software to illustrate the function's graph or simply provide each pair of students with an accurate graph to examine – a Blackline master is provided on the next page. It also allows for a good discussion of the difference between the mathematical reality of a function and the physical reality. For example, negative values for the equation are fine but not when they are used to estimate intoxication levels. Furthermore, teachers should not feel restricted to use the questions given here – they are simply provided as a guide to the kind of mathematical investigations that can be developed from a rich problem.]

Reciprocal functions

The cost to print yearbooks by Acme Printing Company is established by using the formula $y = 15x + 10{,}000$ where y is the total cost and x is the number printed. This formula allows the school yearbook committee to calculate the total cost to print any number of the yearbook. Siew Ling, a new member on the committee has a different question: "I know how much it costs in total to print the yearbooks, but what is the cost per copy to print the yearbook?"

1. To help answer Siew Ling's question, copy the chart below into your notebook and complete it.

Number (x)	10	50	500	1,000	1,500	2,000	5,000	10,000	20,000
Total cost (y)									
Cost per copy									

2. Draw a graph with cost per copy on the y-axis and number of yearbooks printed on the x-axis. Is the graph linear?

3. Is this the graph of a quadratic function? If so, explain why. If not, explain why not.

4. In what way(s) is this graph similar to or different from the graphs that you have seen?

5. Try to draw a smooth curve through the points on your graph. Do the points form a function? Explain.

6. What is the domain and range?

7. Graph the function $y = 15 + \dfrac{10,000}{x}$ for $0 \le x \le 500$ and $0 \le y \le 500$.

8. As the number of yearbooks ordered increases, what happens to the price per copy? Is there any limit to this trend?

9. As the number of yearbooks ordered decreases, what happens to the price per copy? Is there any limit to this trend?

10. Where does the curve intersect the x-axis? Explain.

11. Where does the curve intersect the y-axis? Explain.

12. If we graph this function without any regard for its real-life meaning, we could use x-values that are negative. Graph the function for $-500 \le x \le 500$ and $-500 \le y \le 500$. The graph of the function will never cross the line even though it will approach it very closely as x becomes very large. For example, when $x = 10,00,000$, $y = 15.001$. The line $y = 15$ is called a *horizontal asymptote*. Similarly, the curve will never intersect the y-axis, even though it gets closer and closer as x approaches a value of 0. The y-axis is called a *vertical asymptote*.

[Teaching note: Reciprocal functions which often have asymptotes are quite abstract for students. The original graph which can be drawn from the values in the chart will look like the one below.]

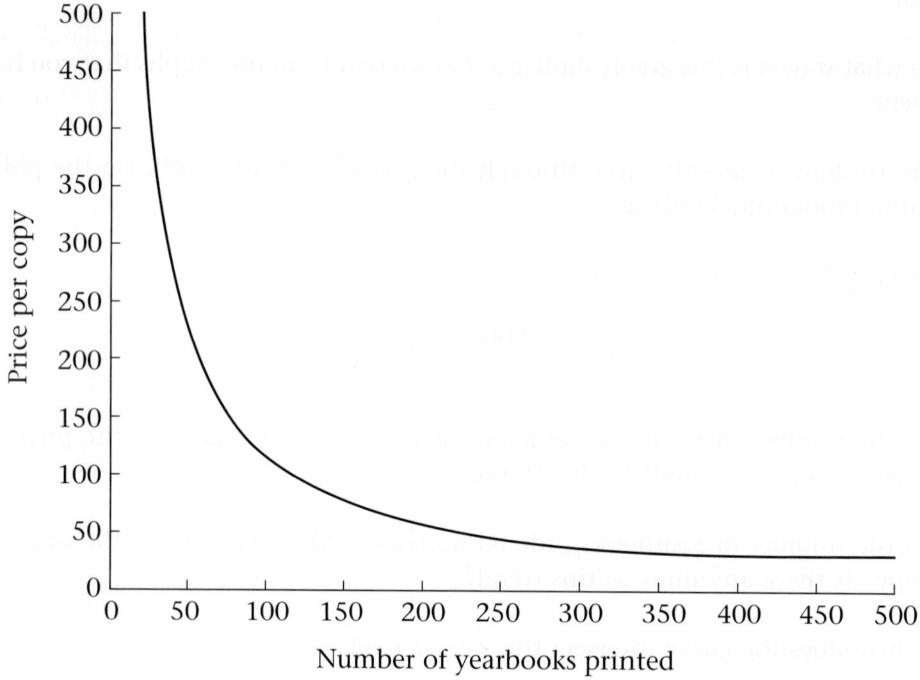

This example is actually quite easy to comprehend and yet has all these abstract features. It is worth having the students examine the situation algebraically. In the chart, we divided the total cost by the number of copies to find the price per copy. This means that the *price per copy*, $p(x)$ is defined by a new functional equation $p(x) = \dfrac{15x + 10{,}000}{x} = 15 + \dfrac{10{,}000}{x}$. Recall that this expression does not define a polynomial function because the exponent on the variable is not a whole number. Functions such as this one, where the variable is the denominator of a fraction are called *reciprocal functions*. It is worth pointing out to students that the features in this graph are ones that they have not seen before in the functions that have been studied, and they may seem a bit unusual; BUT recall that this "unusual" function came about from examining a real-life situation. It is very common in business applications where there is a large start-up cost and then smaller costs per item once production begins. For example, it may cost millions of dollars to develop a computer chip, but once it is developed, it might cost only a few dollars in materials to produce. It is for this reason that prices usually decrease when products are produced in large quantities. Once again, graphing software or graphing calculators can be used to advantage in the discussion of this problem. The more traditional graph of the basic reciprocal function (see below) would evolve quite easily from the "real-life" data in the table that the students created.

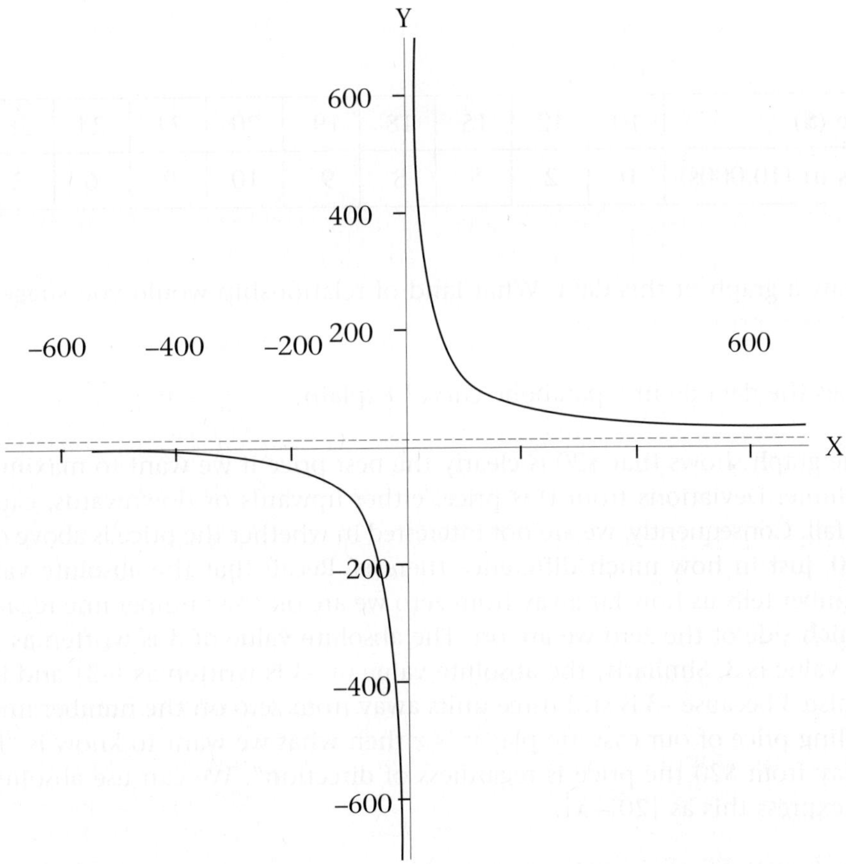

Absolute value functions

Problem 1

Often when selling products, we note that as the price goes up, the sales volume will go down. In many cases this principle is true as consumers stop buying goods they think are too expensive. However, it is also true that consumers will often stop buying something that is inexpensive because they perceive that it is "cheap" and of poor quality! The Santron Electronics Company makes a small portable cassette player. It has found that the number sold (in units of 10,000) varies as the selling price is changed. The data collected by its marketing division is given in the chart below.

Price ($)	10	12	15	18	19	20	21	24	28	30
Sales in (10,000s)	0	2	5	8	9	10	9	6	2	0

1. Draw a graph of this data. What kind of relationship would you suggest exists between price and sales?

2. Does the data lie in a parabolic curve? Explain.

3. The graph shows that $20 is clearly the best price if we want to maximise sales volume. Deviations from this price, either upwards or downwards, cause sales to fall. Consequently, we are not interested in whether the price is above or below $20, just in how much difference there is. Recall that the absolute value of a number tells us how far away from zero we are on the number line regardless of which side of the zero we are on. The absolute value of 3 is written as $|3|$ and its value is 3. Similarly, the absolute value of –3 is written as $|-3|$ and its value is also 3 because –3 is still three units away from zero on the number line. If the selling price of our cassette player is x then what we want to know is "How far away from $20 the price is regardless of direction". We can use absolute value to express this as $|20 - x|$.

4. Evaluate $|20 - x|$ if x (the selling price) is a. 21, b. 12, c. 30, d. 18, e. 19, and f. 32.

5. Looking at the graph, how much did the sales fall when the price changed from $20 to $10?

6. What is the rate of change of sales volume per $1 price change?
The graph clearly illustrates that each $1 change in price results in a drop in sales volume of one unit (10,000). We also know that at $20 per cassette player the sales volume is ten units (100,000). We can now establish an equation that will act as a mathematical model for consumer behaviour with respect to this product. Sales volume in units of 10,000 cassette players (y) is related to price (x) by the equation $y = |20 - x|$.

7. Graph the function $y = |20 - x|$ along with the data from the table above. Does the function pass through all the data points?

8. What is the domain and range of the mathematical function?

9. What restrictions would you want to put on the domain and range if this is to be a reasonable model for the relationship between sales and profit?

10. Graph each of the following on your calculator. Leave all the graphs on the screen.

    a. $y = |x|$.
    b. $y = |x - 20|$.
    c. $y = -|20 - x|$.
    d. $y = -|20 - x| + 10$.
    e. Explain why $|20 - x|$ is the same as $|x - 20|$.
    f. How does the graph in d. compare to the graph in Question 1 above? Explain.

[Teaching note: The way that a teacher would use this problem depends on many factors. It could be set up as a student investigation or a teacher-led discussion or some combination of the two. It does, however, provide a way to introduce the absolute value function (see graph on p. 244) and to tie together some of the work on transformation of graphs to generate an equation that makes sense for the data. Like many mathematical ideas that seem very abstract for students, this one can be discussed in the context of this very realistic and common sense problem.]

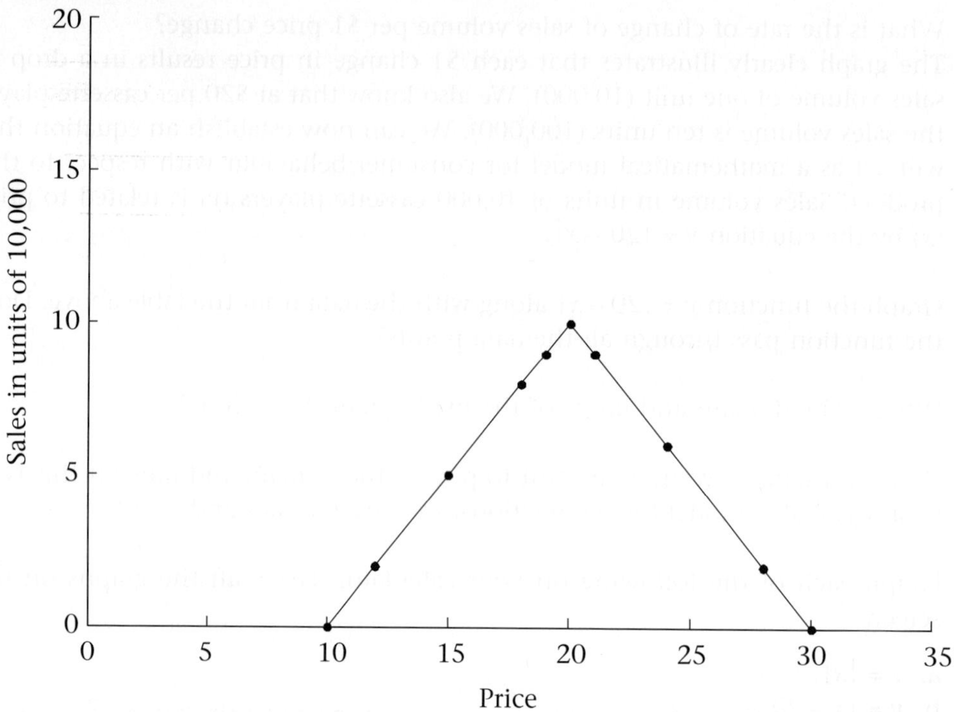

Logarithmic functions

Problem 1

Newborn babies visit the doctor regularly during the first few months of their lives to ensure that they are growing properly. The doctor measures the circumference of the head and then compares this to charts which give average values to see if the child is developing properly. The chart below gives the average head circumference at various ages for boys.

Age (months)	1	2	3	6	9	12	15	18	21	24	33	36
Head circumference (boys – cm)	40.7	42.3	43.6	45.9	47.4	48.5	49.3	50	50.5	51	52	52.2

1. Draw a graph of this data with age on the *x*-axis and head circumference on the *y*-axis.

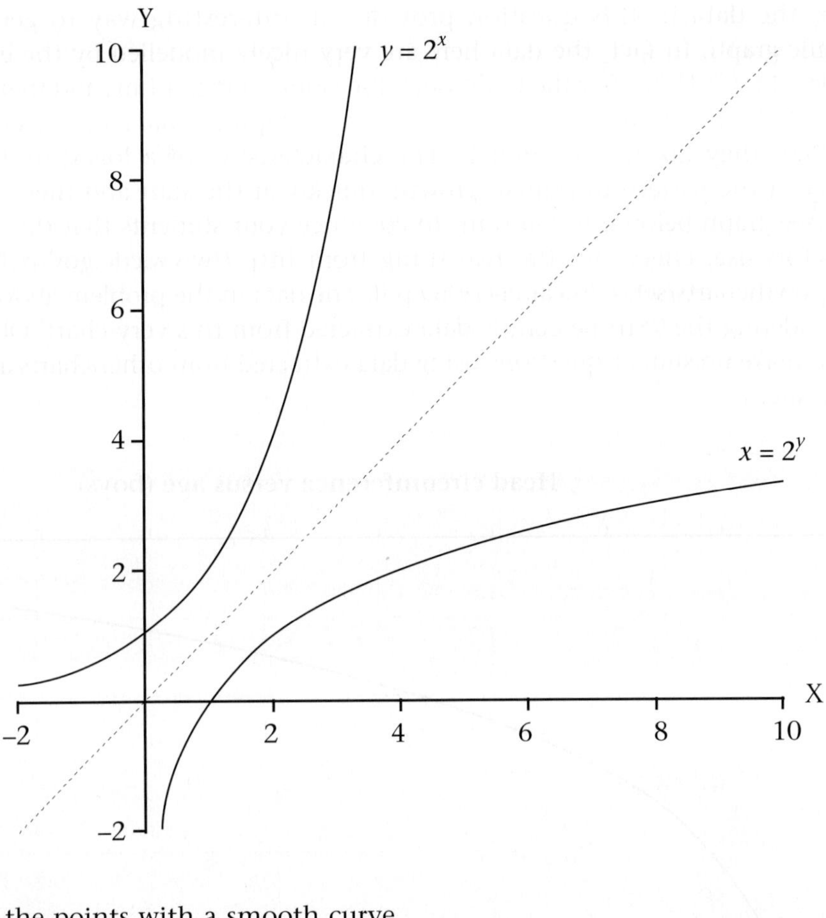

2. Join the points with a smooth curve.

3. Estimate the head circumference of a four-year-old boy. What factors do you think will affect the accuracy of this estimate?

4. Would this graph allow you to estimate the average head size for an adult (say, at age 21)? Why/Why not?

5. What kind of mathematical function could produce this shape of graph?

[Teaching note: The logarithmic function can be introduced as the inverse of the exponential function coupled with the function machine idea; however, it is a fairly abstract idea for students at this level.]

However, the data in this question provides an interesting way to generate a logarithmic graph. In fact, the data here are very nicely modelled by the equation $y = 7.8 \log_{10}(14x) + 31.3$. After the traditional discussion of logarithms and their graphs it is useful to be able to return to this problem and graph the data and this function and see that they do, in fact, match. The characteristics of a logarithmic graph intuitively fit the pattern of human growth: quickly at the start and then levelling off later (see graph below). If you want to convince your students that this is really what doctors use, check out the real thing from http://www.cdc.gov/nchs/data/nhanes/growthcharts/set2clinical/cj41l069.pdf. The data in the problem above comes from considering the 95th percentile data extracted from this very chart! Obviously you could make up similar questions using data extracted from other charts available from this site.

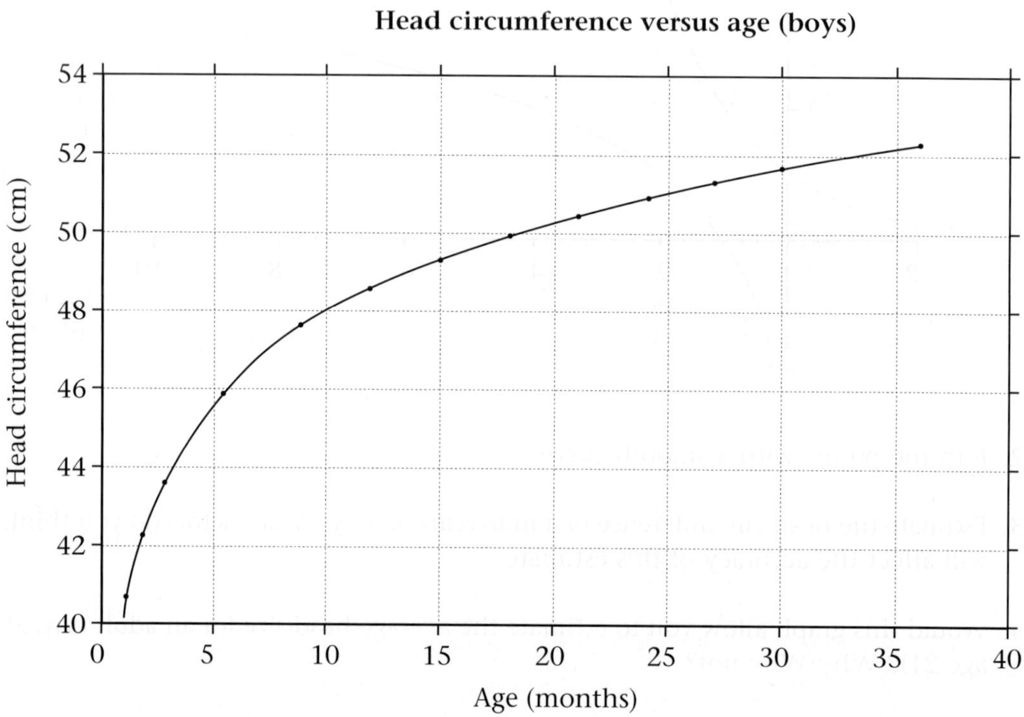

Chapter 13

Teaching of Calculus

Ang Keng Cheng

Calculus was invented in the 17th century as a tool for investigating problems that involve motion. It arose from two fundamental geometric problems that have been discussed for more than 2,000 years: the area problem and the tangent problem.

THE AREA PROBLEM

At least 2,500 years ago, the ancient Greeks found areas of plane surfaces using the "method of exhaustion". It is possible to find the area of any polygon by dividing it into triangles (see Figure 13-1) and adding up the areas.

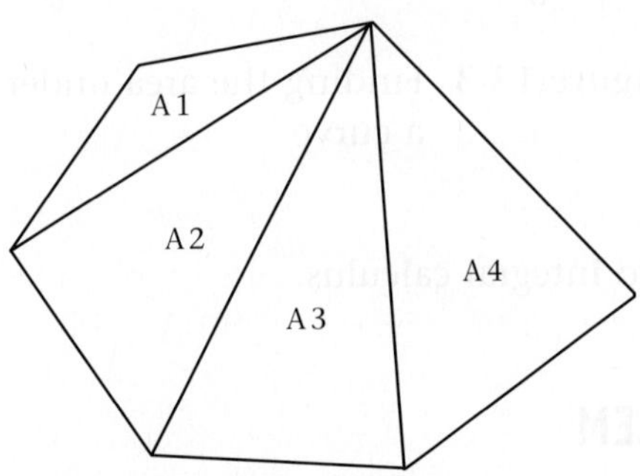

Figure 13-1 Finding the area of polygon

For a curved figure we need to develop a method for finding the area as shown in Figure 13-2, and then apply the same technique to the other portions of the curve. To be more specific, we have to find the area under the curve $y = f(x)$ over an interval $[a, b]$ (Figure 13-3):

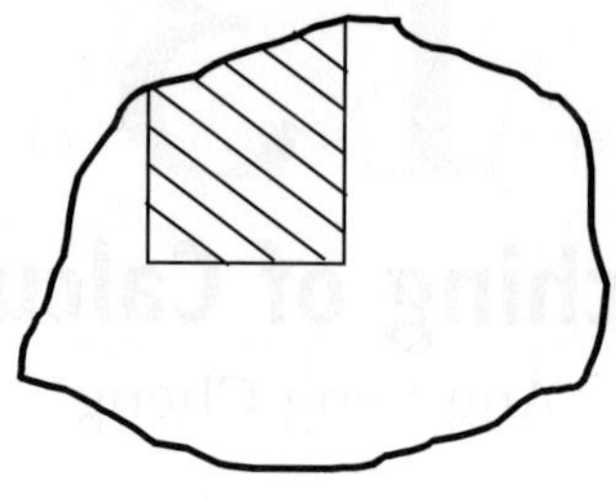

Figure 13-2 Finding the area of a curved figure

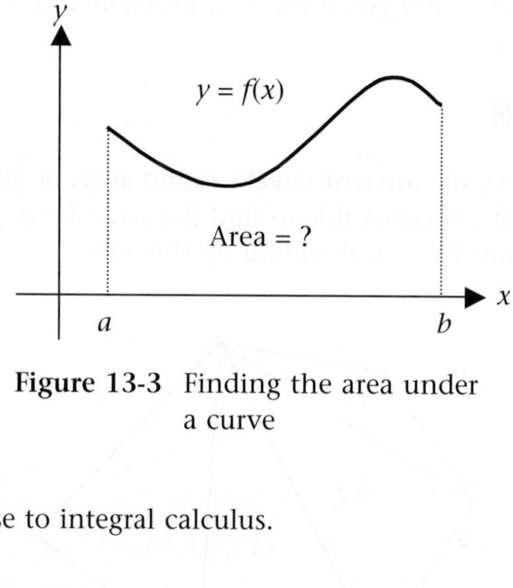

Figure 13-3 Finding the area under a curve

This problem gives rise to integral calculus.

THE TANGENT PROBLEM

The other problem is: What do we mean by the line tangent to the curve $y = f(x)$ and how do we find an equation for this line? The word "tangent" comes from the Latin word *tangens* which means "touching". This question gives rise to the idea of derivatives and *differential calculus*.

Both the area and the tangent problems require the use of the idea of limits to handle. The notion of *limit* is the initial idea which separates calculus from

Elementary Mathematics. Sir Isaac Newton (1642–1727) and Gottfried Wilhelm Leibniz (1646–1716) independently discovered the connection between derivatives and integrals and are both credited with the invention of calculus.

KEY CONCEPTS

The fundamental theorem of calculus

The relationship between derivatives and integrals is described by the *fundamental theorem of calculus*. This theorem connects the two seemingly independent problems.

Consider the case of travelling in a car and taking readings off the speedometer and odometer. The speedometer gives the speed (or velocity) while the odometer measures the distance travelled. Suppose we let the velocity be v and the distance covered be d. Can we find v if we know d and vice-versa? If we know everything about one quantity, we must be able to find the other. In fact, the whole subject of calculus is built upon the relation between quantities such as the two described, and the fundamental theorem of calculus gives us the relationship.

Figure 13-4 is a map linking concepts leading to calculus.

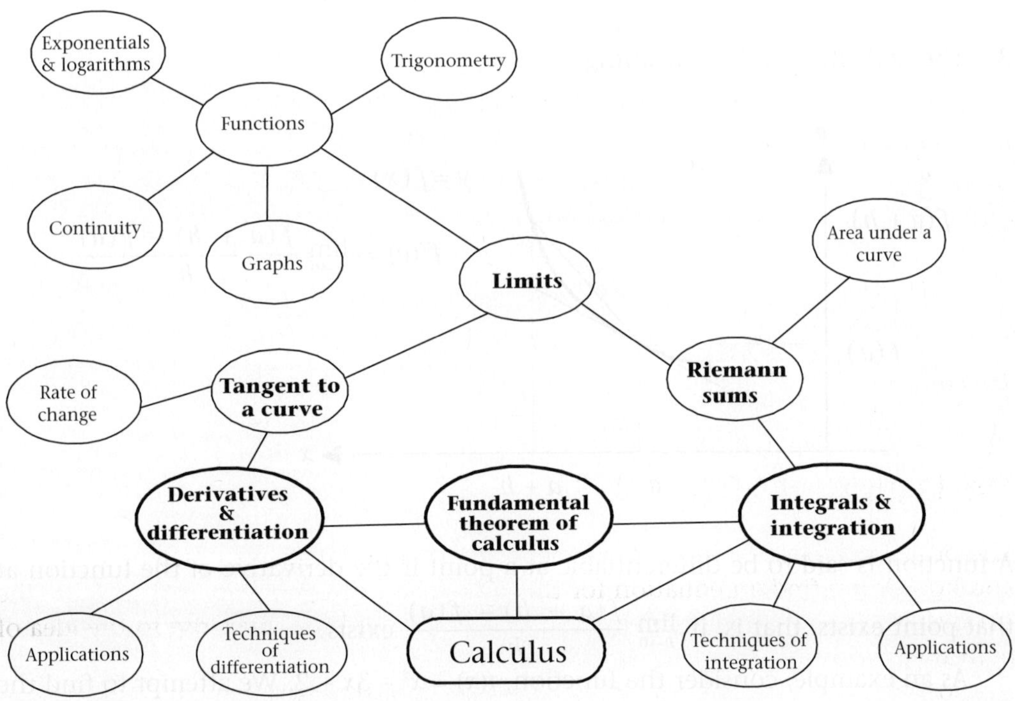

Figure 13-4 A map linking concepts leading to calculus

Some essential basic concepts

1. Functions and limits

   a. Definition of a function. Use of the "vertical line test" to determine whether a graph represents a function.
   b. Meaning of limit of a function at a point. Ideas about limits may be presented either graphically or analytically.

2. Tangents to a curve

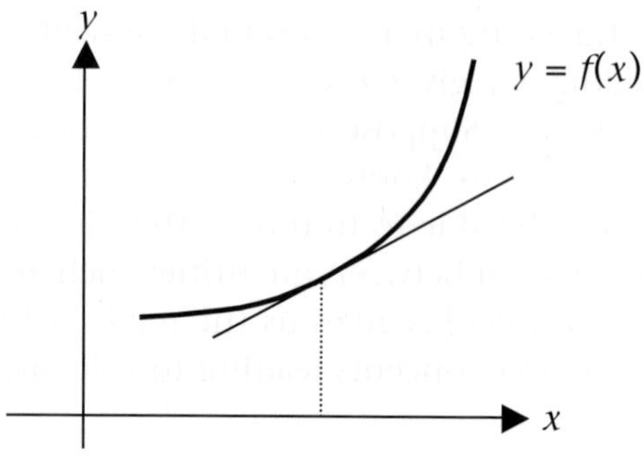

3. The derivative and its meaning

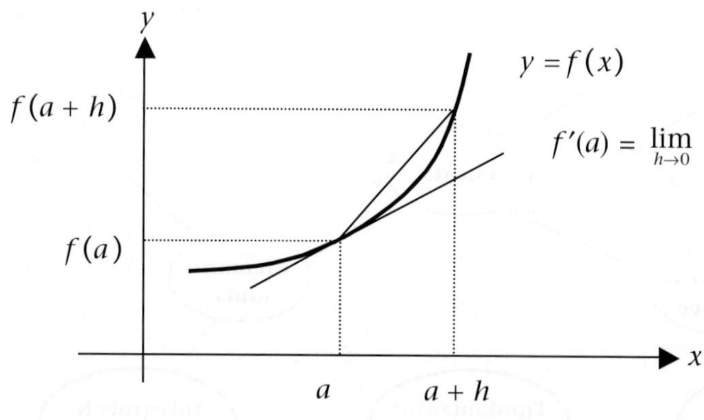

$$f'(a) = \lim_{h \to 0} \frac{f(a + h) - f(a)}{h}$$

A function is said to be differentiable at a point if the derivative of the function at that point exists, that is, if $\lim_{h \to 0} \frac{f(a + h) - f(a)}{h}$ exists.

As an example, consider the function, $f(x) = x^2 - 3x + 2$. We attempt to find the derivative at $x = 2$ by definition. We can construct the following table:

h	$\frac{f(2+h)-f(2)}{h}$
0.5	1.5
0.1	1.1
0.01	1.01
0.001	1.001
	...

h	$\frac{f(2+h)-f(2)}{h}$
–0.5	0.5
–0.1	0.9
–0.01	0.99
–0.001	0.999
	...

The following are three situations where the function described by the graph is not differentiable at point $x = a$:

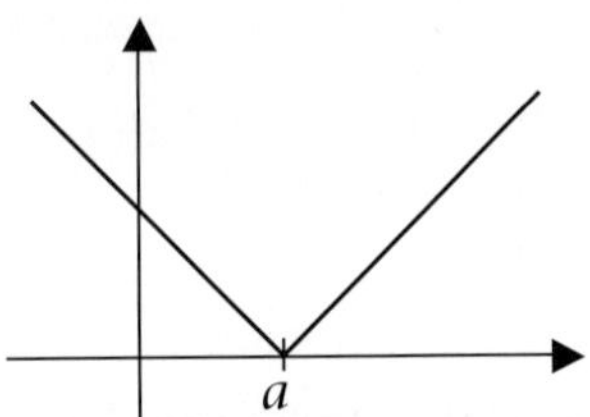

Corner or kink

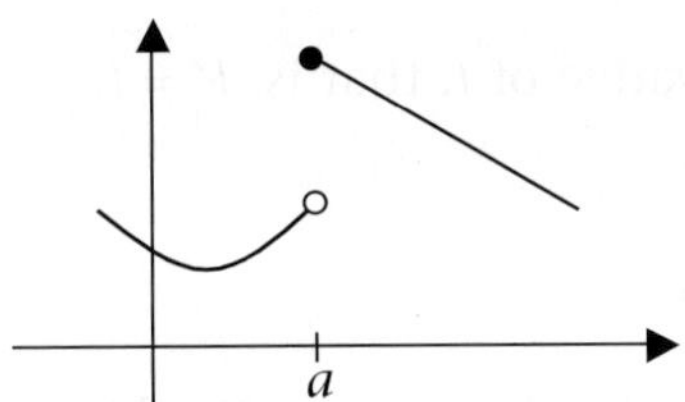

Discontinuity

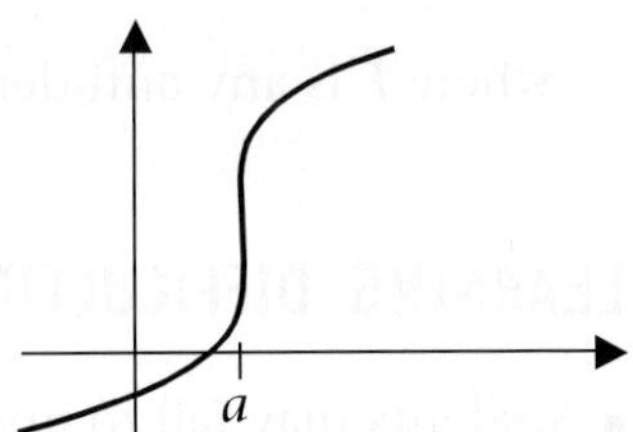

Vertical tangent

4. Integration
   The meaning of integration.
   - Integration as a limiting process of finding area under a curve.

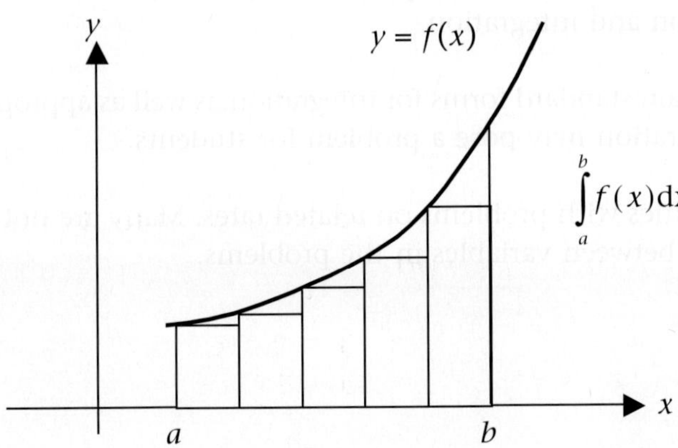

$$\int_a^b f(x)\mathrm{dx} = \lim_{n\to\infty} \sum_{i=1}^{n} f(x_i)\Delta x_i$$

- Integration as a process of anti-differentiation

5. The fundamental theorem of calculus

   Part 1:

   If f is continuous on $[a, b]$, then the function g defined by $g(x) = \int_a^x f(t)dt$, where $a \le x \le b$ is continuous on $[a, b]$ and differentiable on (a, b) and $g'(x) = f(x)$.

   Part 2:

   If f is continuous on $[a, b]$, then

$$\int_a^b f(x)dt = F(b) - F(a)$$

   where F is any anti-derivative of f, that is, $F' = f$.

LEARNING DIFFICULTIES

- Students may fail to understand or appreciate the meaning of the derivative even though they know the rules of differentiation. This will often make the topic appear to be one involving only memorising and mastering certain procedures.

- Formal or rigorous definitions of functions and limits are often not taught or emphasised at the secondary level. As a result, it is hard to explain certain "rules". For instance, why is the first derivative of sin x with respect to x equal to cos x?

- Students may question the usefulness of the topic if all they do is just follow some preset rules of differentiation and integration.

- The ability to recognise certain standard forms for integration as well as appropriate substitution to use in integration may pose a problem for students.

- Students often have difficulties with problems on related rates. Many are not able to see or link relationships between variables in the problems.

TEACHING APPROACHES

1. Ensure that prerequisites such as coordinate geometry, graphs of functions, trigonometry and some topics in algebra are well understood before teaching calculus.

2. Notations should be firmly established and well understood by students. Be aware that it takes time to get used to new notations.

3. Applications of the derivatives should be made real to students who may have problems setting up the models. Teachers need to provide opportunities for students to have experience in defining variables in, say, problems involving rates of change. Students should be encouraged to be systematic in solving such problems. Drawing a diagram, stating the variables and the relationship between them will help.

4. Approach should aim for intuitive but correct understanding. In difficult topics such as limits, numerical approaches using calculators could help students understand the meaning without abstract definitions.

5. Students tend to learn calculus in a mechanical way without true appreciation. This may lead to errors and misconceptions. There should be more emphasis on linking the algebraic or algorithmic approach to the geometric (graphical) meanings.

6. Teachers can make use of graphing tools (such as Graphmatica) or a computer algebra system (such as Maple V) to illustrate concepts. These can also be used to allow students to explore concepts such as gradients and tangents.

7. In addition, one could mention the motivation for learning calculus. For instance:
   - Calculus provides us with the tools to better understand and represent the real physical world, which is not static. The real world consists of things and events which are usually in some form of motion or change.
   - With calculus, we may be able to find a way to optimise our means.
   - Calculus applications provide excellent examples of the utilitarian value of learning mathematics.
   - Calculus also provides opportunities to integrate concepts from other areas of mathematics, such as algebra, geometry, trigonometry, and so on.
   - At a higher level, calculus is applied to other disciplines, thus giving students a glimpse of how mathematics may be applied in the real world.

For further suggestions and ideas on teaching strategies, the reader may wish to refer to Ahuja, Lim-Teo, and Lee (1998).

SAMPLE ACTIVITIES FOR TEACHERS

Discuss the following:

1. What do you understand by the "derivative" of a function. How would you introduce the concept?

2. What is the meaning of integration? Discuss the various approaches to integration that you may adopt to introduce this concept. Why does integration give the area under the curve?

3. Traditionally, differentiation is taught before integration. Can we teach integration first? Discuss the implications in terms of students' understanding of the concepts.

4. Very often, when students are first introduced to derivatives, they are taught the rules of differentiation. Should the idea of limits be taught first? Is differentiation meaningful without the knowledge of limits? At what stage should a student be introduced the idea of limits?

5. How would you explain the following:

   $\frac{d}{dx}e^x = e^x$ and $\int \frac{1}{x}dx = \ln|x| + C$?

6. What are maximum and minimum points? Why do we set $\frac{dy}{dx} = 0$? Will this method or process find all turning points?

7. What are points of inflexion and how do you find them?

   A common misconception is that if $\left.\frac{d^2y}{dx^2}\right|_{x=a} = 0$, then there is a point of inflexion at $x = a$. How would you show that this is incorrect?

SAMPLE ACTIVITIES FOR STUDENTS

1. A stone is thrown into a pond, creating a circular ripple whose radius increases at the rate of 1 m/s. How fast is the area (in sq m/s) of the circular ripple increasing three seconds after the stone hits the water?

2. A rectangular strip of plastic with a width of 20 cm is folded into a length of guttering as shown in the figure on the right. Where should the folds be located to enable the gutter to carry as much water as possible?

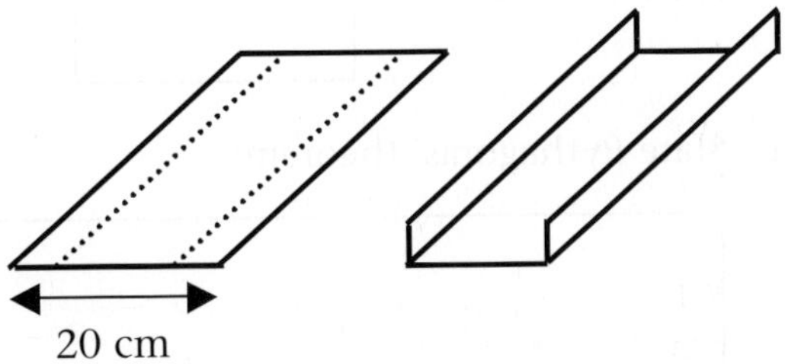

3. Let A and B be the points of intersection of the parabola $y = x^2$ and the line $y = x + 2$, and let C be the point on the parabola where the tangent line is parallel to the graph of $y = x + 2$. Show that the area of the parabolic segment cut from the parabola by the line (see diagram on right) is four-thirds the area of triangle ABC.

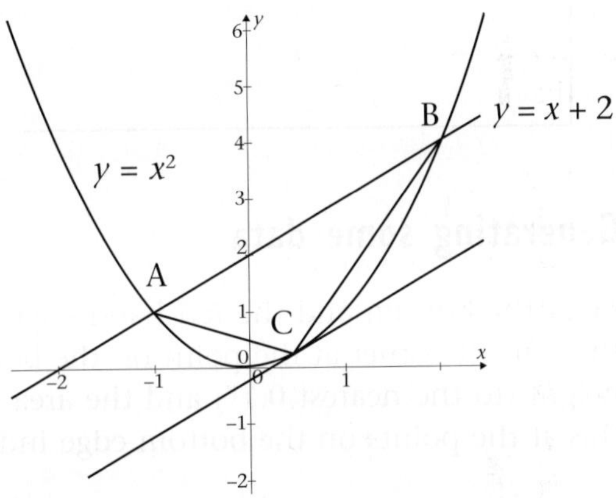

4. The following are activities using the TI-83. Place a sheet of A4 size paper (8.5″ by 11″) in landscape mode (i.e. sideways). Fold the top-left corner down to a point on the bottom edge to form a triangle in the bottom-left corner. Where should you place the top-left corner in order to maximise the area of the triangle?

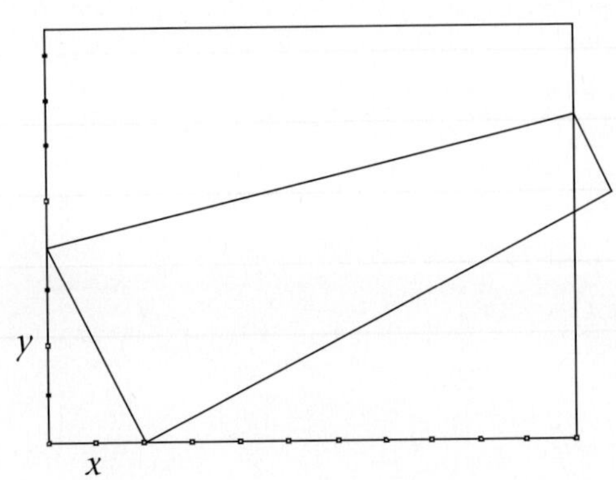

SOME PRELIMINARIES

Triangles

i. Area of a triangle = [ ]

ii. State Pythagoras' theorem:

[ ]

Generating some data

Mark the bottom and the left-hand edge of the piece of paper in 0.5″ units. Place the top-left corner at the point on the bottom edge which measures 1″. Record the height (to the nearest 0.1″) and the area of the triangle in the table below. Repeat this at the points on the bottom edge indicated in the table below.

Base (x)	Height (y)	Area (A)
1		
2		
3		
4		
5		
6		
7		

Base (x)	Height (y)	Area (A)
8		
9		
10		
11		

Relationship between the height and base

i. Plot the points (x, y) in the figure below.
ii. Which function do you think fits your data?
iii. Confirm your answer in (ii) by finding an algebraic relationship between the base x and the height y. Express y in terms of x. (Hint: remember that the hypotenuse of the triangle is part of the left-hand edge.)
iv. Draw the graph of the function $y(x)$ in the figure below. How accurate is your set of data?
v. Find the domain of $y(x)$.
vi. Find the range of $y(x)$. What is the value of $y(x)$ for $x \geq 8.5$?

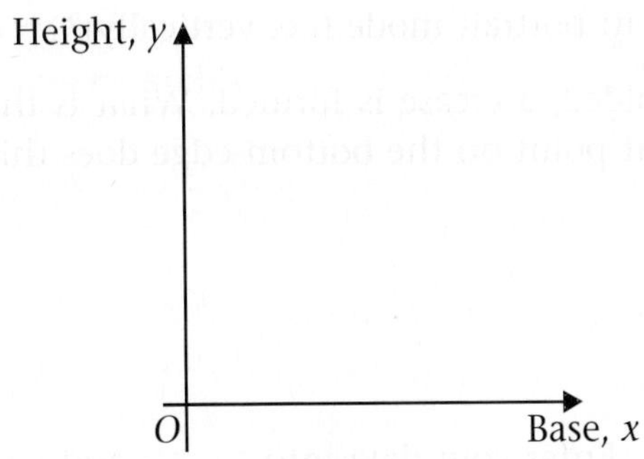

Relationship between the area and base

i. Plot the points (x, A) in the figure below.
ii. From your data, estimate the maximum area and determine the point on the base for which this maximum occurs.
iii. Determine an algebraic relationship between the area A and the base x.
iv. Draw the graph of the function $A(x)$ in the figure. How accurate is your set of data?

v. Determine from the graph, the maximum value of $A(x)$ and the value of x for which it occurs. Compare your result with the result in (ii).
vi. Confirm the answer in (v) using calculus.

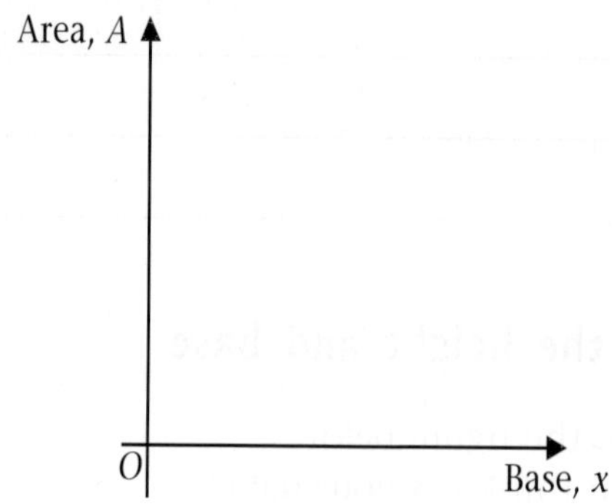

Extensions

i. What are the corresponding results when

- the edge of the paper measuring 11″ is cut to a length of 5.5″ (A5 size)? What if it is further cut to a size of 4″?
- the paper is A3 size (two A4s side by side in portrait mode) and placed in landscape mode?
- the paper is placed in portrait mode (i.e. vertically)?

ii. When the paper is folded, a crease is formed. What is the maximum length of the crease and at what point on the bottom edge does this occur?

TI-83 help

i. To plot data points:

- Press `[STAT],EDIT`. Enter your data into `L1`, `L2` and `L3`.
- Press `[2nd]STAT PLOT`. Select `Plot1` and `Plot2`. `Plot1` plots height versus base, while `Plot2` plots area versus base.
- Use `[ZOOM],ZOOM,9:ZoomStat` to fit all data points in the window.

ii. To plot the graph of a given function:

- Press `[Y=]`. Enter the required function in `Y1`.
- Press `[GRAPH]`.

Other graphing calculator activities may be found at http://www.ti.com/calc/docs/activities.htm.

FURTHER READING

Ang, K.C., & Awyong, P.W. (1999). The use of Maple in first year undergraduate mathematics. *The Mathematics Educator, 4*(1), 87–96.

Bressoud, D.M. (1992). How should we introduce integration? *The College Mathematics Journal, 23*(4), 296–298.

Cipra, B. (1989). MISTEAKS ... *and how to find them before the teacher does ....* (2nd ed.). Boston, MA: Academic Press.

Fulton, S.R. (1994). Can Maple help in teaching calculus with limited time and staff? *Proceedings of the Maple Summer Workshop and Symposium* (pp. 63–70). Boston, MA: Birkhäuser.

Grinstein, L.S. (Ed.). (1977). *Calculus: Readings from the mathematics teacher*. Reston, VA: National Council of Teachers of Mathematics.

Lim, S.K. (1989). Division by zero. *Teaching and Learning, 9*(2), 65–74.

McGivney, R.A. (1990). Forward homework – A motivational tool. *The College Mathematics Journal, 21*(5), 400–402.

Neill, H., & Shuard, H. (1982). *Teaching calculus*. Bishopbriggs, Glasgow: Blackie & Sons.

Orton, A. (1991). Exploring first year calculus. *Mathematics in School*, January, 32–33.

Tall, D. (1985). Understanding the calculus. *Mathematics Teaching, 110*, 48–53.

REFERENCE

Ahuja, O.P., Lim-Teo, S.K., & Lee, P.Y. (1998). Mathematics teachers' perspective of their students' learning in traditional calculus and its teaching strategies. *Journal of the Korea Society of Mathematical Education Series D: Research in Mathematical education, 2*(2), 89–108.

Chapter 14

Teaching of Vectors

Toh Tin Lam

VECTORS

Physical quantities are of two kinds: scalars, which have magnitude but no associated direction, for example, mass, length, volume, temperature, distance, speed, time, work, energy; and vectors, which have both magnitude and an associated direction, for example, displacement, velocity, acceleration, force, momentum, moment.

As a school subject, vectors helps to develop spatial visualisation. It provides alternative ways of proving geometrical results in two and three dimensions. The study of mechanics (especially kinematics, relative velocity, forces and work done) can be seen as an application of vectors. The basic facts learned in vectors also provide the necessary ingredients for understanding vector space and linear algebra, which have useful applications in science, engineering, statistics and navigation.

History

The method of calculating the combined action of two or more mechanical forces by adding them according to the parallelogram law had been known since the time of Aristotle. However, the germinal ideas of modern vector theory date from around 1800 when Caspar Wessel (1745–1818) and Jean Robert Argand (1768–1822) described how a complex number $a + bi$ could be given a geometric interpretation in a coordinate plane.

W.R. Hamilton (1788–1856) showed that complex numbers could be regarded as ordered pairs of real numbers in 1837. He was also the first to use the term "vector" for a directed line segment in his book *Lectures on Quaternions* (1853). In 1844, the German mathematician Hermann Grassmann (1809–1877) introduced his concept of hypernumber. He treated *n*-dimensional geometry and hypercomplex systems in a much more general way than did Hamilton. From the ideas of Grassmann and Hamilton, American mathematician and physicist, J.W. Gibbs developed much of vector analysis as we know it today. For more details, see, for example, Gullberg (1997).

Key concepts

1. Geometrically, a vector is represented by a directed line segment. A vector representing a displacement from a point A to a point B is said to have the initial point or origin A and the terminal point B.

2. Several notations are currently in use for vectors: $\overrightarrow{AB}$, $\vec{a}$, $\underline{a}$ or $\mathbf{a}$.

3. Magnitude of $\mathbf{a}$ is denoted by $|\mathbf{a}|$ or a.

4. Two vectors are said to be equal if they have the same magnitude and the same direction. (This definition of equality is that used in vector geometry where vectors are treated as free vectors. In physics, other definitions may have to be used, for example, two forces are equal if they have the same magnitude and the same direction along the same line of action.)

5. Vectors with unit magnitude are called *unit vectors*.

> Think:
> For any non-zero vector $\mathbf{a}$, $\dfrac{\mathbf{a}}{|\mathbf{a}|}$ is always a unit vector along the direction of $\mathbf{a}$. Can you explain why?

Algebra of vectors

1. *Negative vector:* The negative of a vector $\mathbf{a}$ is written as $-\mathbf{a}$ and defined as a vector with the same magnitude as $\mathbf{a}$ but in the opposite direction.

2. *Zero* or *null vector:* To interpret the meaning of $\mathbf{a}-\mathbf{a}$, it is necessary to introduce a vector with zero magnitude. This is denoted by $\mathbf{0}$ and has no directional property. Alternatively, we say that the zero vector is the only vector whose direction is indeterminate.

3. *Addition of vectors:* Use the parallelogram law or triangle law. The sum of a given set of vectors is called the resultant. Vector addition satisfies the following properties:

   i. Closure: If **a** and **b** are two vectors, then **a** + **b** is also a vector.
   ii. Commutative: For any two vectors **a** and **b**, **a** + **b** = **b** + **a**.
   iii. Associative: For any three vectors **a**, **b** and **c**, **a** + (**b** + **c**) = (**a** + **b**) + **c**.

4. *Subtraction of vectors:* This may be explained in two ways:

   Let $\overrightarrow{OA} = \mathbf{a}$ and $\overrightarrow{OB} = \mathbf{b}$.

   a. Since $\overrightarrow{OA} + \overrightarrow{AB} = \overrightarrow{OB}$, we have $\overrightarrow{OB} - \overrightarrow{OA} = \overrightarrow{AB}$ or $\mathbf{b} - \mathbf{a} = \overrightarrow{AB}$.
   b. $\mathbf{a} - \mathbf{b} = \mathbf{a} + (-\mathbf{b})$

   Subtraction of vectors is important in relative velocity calculations and in such calculations, (a) is more efficient than (b).

5. *Scalar multiple:* Product of a scalar and a vector to produce another vector. If **a** is a vector, then the scalar multiple k**a** is a vector with

   - the same direction of **a** if k is positive
   - the opposite direction of **a** if k is negative
   - $|k\mathbf{a}| = |k||\mathbf{a}|$ [Note that on the right-hand side, the first $|k|$ denotes the absolute value of a scalar, while the modulus in $|\mathbf{a}|$ denotes the magnitude of a vector.]

   Properties of scalar multiples:

   i. $(p + q)\mathbf{u} = p\mathbf{u} + q\mathbf{u}$
   ii. $p(\mathbf{u} + \mathbf{v}) = p\mathbf{u} + p\mathbf{v}$
   iii. $p(q\mathbf{u}) = (pq)\mathbf{u}$
   iv. $1\mathbf{u} = \mathbf{u}$
   v. $(-1)\mathbf{u} = -\mathbf{u}$

Geometry of vectors

1. Linear combination of vectors: Let **a** and **b** be the position vectors of points A and B with respect to some origin O. Then, if m and n are any non-zero scalars,

   a. $m\mathbf{a} + n\mathbf{b}$ is a linear combination of **a** and **b** and it can be represented geometrically using the parallelogram law of addition.

   b. Ratio theorem: $\dfrac{n\mathbf{a} + m\mathbf{b}}{n + m}$ is the position vector of the point dividing AB in the ratio $m{:}n$. Equivalently, for any scalar t, $t\mathbf{a} + (1 - t)\mathbf{b}$ gives the position vector of a point on AB.

2. Try to explain the following:
   a. Let $\lambda\mathbf{a} = \mu\mathbf{b}$, where **a** and **b** are non-zero vectors. If **a** and **b** are not parallel, then $\lambda = \mu = 0$.
   b. For any two non-zero vectors **a** and **b**, $h\mathbf{a} + k\mathbf{b} = m\mathbf{a} + n\mathbf{b}$ implies $h = m$ and $k = n$ provided that **a** and **b** are not parallel vectors.

3. Many geometrical results and theorems can be proved using simple vector method, for example,

   - midpoint theorem (for a triangle)
   - diagonals of a parallelogram bisecting one another
   - midpoints of any quadrilateral forming a parallelogram
   - medians of a triangle are concurrent (point of concurrence is called the centroid)

Learning difficulties

1. Students may not be able to see the applications of vectors to real life.

2. Students often confuse vector arithmetic with scalar arithmetic, for example, a force of 50 N is applied and another force of 20 N is applied. The total force applied is 50 + 20 = 70 N. Students, as this example illustrates, often overlook the importance of the directions of the force applied.

Teaching approaches

1. Introduce vectors through translation. Activities such as treasure hunt, navigation using maps or movement of chessboard (or snake and ladder) pieces may be used for motivation.

2. Addition of vectors by parallelogram law can be demonstrated by applying two or more forces at a point. Addition of vectors by triangle law can be illustrated by successive displacements (compared with the way elephants parade, the trunk of one elephant hooked to the tail of the preceding one).

3. Physical examples of scalar multiples of vectors are **F** = m**a** and Displacement = t**v**. [Extensions: Scalar product of vectors may be related to work done and projections; vector product of vectors may be related to vector moments and vector areas.]

4. Relate vectors on Cartesian plane to coordinate geometry and show the connections. For example, ratio theorem may be viewed as a generalisation of the method of finding the midpoint of a line segment in a coordinate plane.

APPLICATIONS OF VECTORS: KINEMATICS

Kinematics deals with the movement of particles (without focusing on the *why* but on the *how* particles move). Movement involves the description of the position (i.e. the *displacement*), the rate of change of the position (i.e. the *velocity*) and the rate of change of velocity of the moving particles. As displacement, velocity and acceleration are examples of vectors, the theory of vectors can hold for kinematics as well.

The vector **AB** is interpreted as the *position vector of the point B from A*. It is also the *displacement* of the point B from A. Thus, *displacement* describes the position of a point B from A. Most of the time we refer to the position vector of A, denoted as **OA**, as the *displacement* of A (from O).

When an object moves, its position changes with time. The rate of change (with respect to time) of the particle is called its *velocity*. An object is said to move with *constant velocity* if it moves with constant speed and maintains the same direction (see worksheet activities on Understanding Velocity, p. 270). An object can move with constant speed but changing velocity (what about constant velocity but non-constant speed?). The magnitude of the velocity is the speed at which the particle travels. When an object moves with a constant speed, the distance travelled can be computed as the product of the speed and time.

We can generalise the result to vectors. Refer to the following table for comparison.

Scalar quantities	Vector quantities
If an object moves with constant speed, distance travelled = Time × speed	If an object moves with constant velocity, change in displacement = Time × velocity (displacement: the position vector of a point from the origin)

Learning difficulties

1. Students may find difficult the use of vector notation in describing the displacement and velocity of a moving object. For example, what is the difference in meaning between "A car is at the point with position vector 4**i** + 5**j** m" and "A car is moving with velocity 4**i** + 5**j** m/s"?

2. Students may be confused between describing the actual position of a particle moving with constant velocity and the change in displacement. For example, a car starts from the point with position vector **2i** + 3**j** m. It travels with a constant velocity of 4**i** + 5**j** m/s. At any time *t* (in seconds),

the change in displacement = *t* (4**i** + 5**j**) m the actual position of the car (with reference to the origin O) = (2**i** + 3**j**) + *t*(4**i** + 5**j**) m

A teacher needs to have a sound understanding of basic kinematics concepts. Also, the concepts on 1-dimensional and 2-dimensional motion may not be exactly the same. Teacher may run the following TRUE/FALSE questions to test their understanding:

1.	An object travelling at a constant speed does not experience any acceleration.
2.	An object travelling with a constant non-zero acceleration definitely experiences a change in speed.
3.	The magnitude of displacement of a particle is the distance travelled by the particle.
4.	An object travelling at minimum velocity is travelling at minimum speed.
5.	When an object travels with positive acceleration, it travels at an increasing speed.
6.	Acceleration is defined as the rate of increase of velocity with respect to time.
7.	When an object travels at positive velocity, its speed is increasing.
8.	When an object has a positive displacement, its speed is increasing.
9.	The velocity of an object is defined as the rate of change of its displacement with respect to time.

10. The speed of an object is defined as the rate of change of distance travelled with respect to time.

11. The speed of an object equals the magnitude of its velocity.

12. Refer to the speed-time graph below.

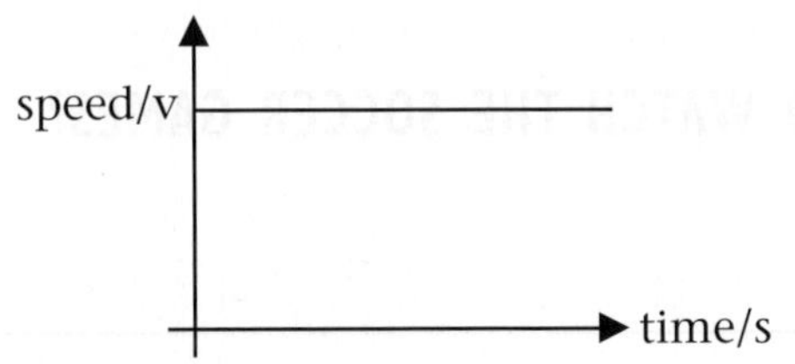

The particle definitely does not experience any acceleration.

13. There is nothing wrong with the statement "The velocity of a car is 2 m/s".

Toh TL, On In-Service Mathematics Teachers' Content Knowledge on Kinematics. Asia-Pacific Forum on Science Learning and Teaching, Vol 6 Issue 2, Article 7 (Dec 2005).

Teaching approach

1. Students need to be familiar with the description of displacement and velocity in Cartesian coordinates system (i.e. in **i**, **j** notation). An object can move with constant speed but not constant velocity but not vice-versa. Let students solve some simple kinematics problems in two dimensions using Cartesian vector notations.

2. Avoid confusing students with unrelated issues (such as conversion of units, etc.), for example, consider the following question:

   "A man travels with velocity 5**i** + 6**j** km/h. What is the change of his displacement after 30 min?"

(A student may get the wrong answer if he forgets to convert the units but this may not reflect his lack of mastery of kinematics. It could just be a slip.)

Worksheet

INTRODUCTION TO VECTORS

WHERE TO WATCH THE SOCCER GAMES?

Ali is a diehard soccer fan from Malaysia. He wants to watch some of the games played in the S-League.

His daughter who lives in Singapore, provides him with a map of the city-state and the names of the eight stadiums where the matches will be played.

B	Bedok Stadium	**N**	National Stadium
J	Jalan Besar Stadium	**T**	Tampines Stadium
P	Toa Payoh Stadium	**U**	Jurong Stadium
Y	Yishun Stadium	**W**	Woodlands Stadium

1. Look at the map on p. 269. Locate **T** and **W** and express $\overrightarrow{OT}$ and $\overrightarrow{OW}$ as column vectors.

2. Given that $\overrightarrow{OB} = \begin{bmatrix} 7 \\ -1.5 \end{bmatrix}$ and $\overrightarrow{OJ} = \begin{bmatrix} 3 \\ -2 \end{bmatrix}$, locate the Bedok Stadium (**B**), and the Jalan Besar Stadium (**J**) on the map.

3. On the first night, Ali travels from the Jalan Besar Stadium (**J**) to the Bedok Stadium (B) and then proceeds to the Tampines Stadium (**T**).

   a. Express $\overrightarrow{JB}$, $\overrightarrow{BT}$ and $\overrightarrow{JT}$ as column vectors.

   b. Find $\overrightarrow{JB} + \overrightarrow{BT}$.

   c. Compare $\overrightarrow{JB} + \overrightarrow{BT}$ with $\overrightarrow{JT}$.

4. On the second night, Ali travels from the Jurong Stadium (**U**) to the National Stadium (**N**) to watch Fandi Ahmad play.

   a. Express $\overrightarrow{OU}$ and $\overrightarrow{ON}$ as column vectors.

   b. Find $\overrightarrow{OU} - \overrightarrow{ON}$ and $\overrightarrow{ON} - \overrightarrow{OU}$.

   Which of the expressions represent $\overrightarrow{UN}$?

5. On the third night, Ali travels from the Jalan Besar Stadium (**J**) to another stadium. His route is represented by the column vector $\begin{bmatrix} -5 \\ 6 \end{bmatrix}$.

   a. Which stadium is his destination?
   b. Given that the scale of the map is 1 unit to 2 km, determine the distance between the two stadiums.

6. Ali is staying with his daughter while he is in Singapore. If **D** represents his daughter's house and $\overrightarrow{OD} = \frac{1}{4}\overrightarrow{OW}$, express $\overrightarrow{OW}$ as a column vector and find $\overrightarrow{OD}$. Locate **D** on the map.

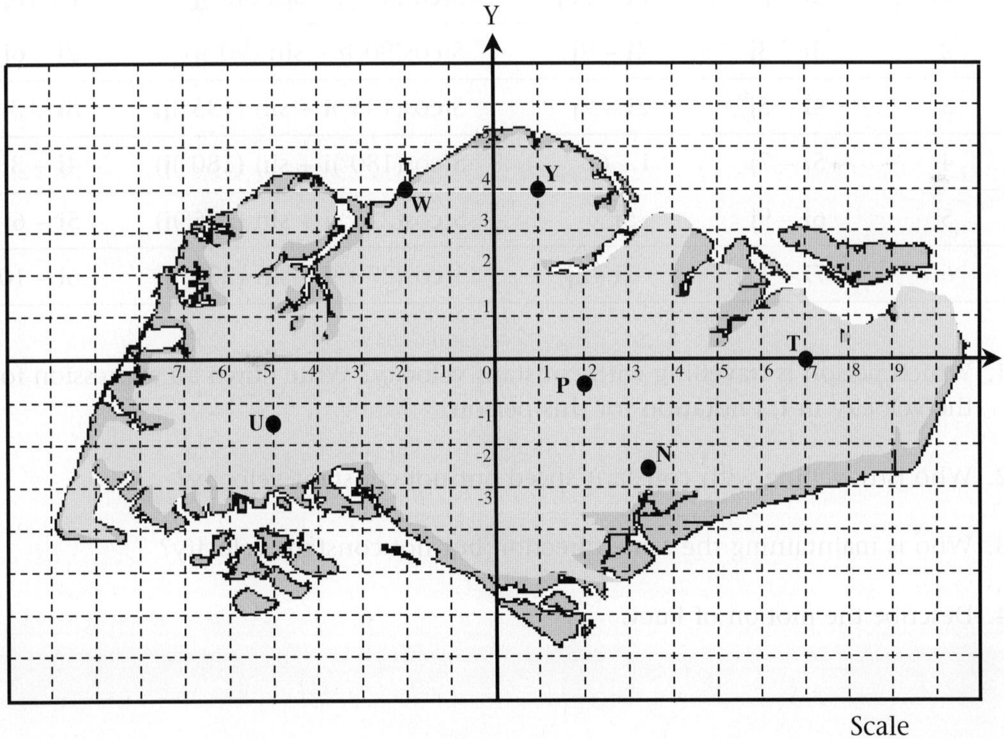

Scale
1 unit : 2 km

UNDERSTANDING VELOCITY

What do you understand by the terms "velocity" and "speed"?

The position vectors of four persons (Beatty, Charmaine, Lucy and Nancy) for the first six seconds are shown in the following table. Assume that the paths they take are smooth. Find out which person is travelling with constant velocity (same magnitude and direction). You may use the graph paper on p. 271 to help you decide.

Time (t=)	Beatty	Charmaine	Lucy	Nancy
0	**i** + **j**	6**i** – 11**j**	5**i**	–11**j**
1	2**i** – **j**	5**i** – 10**j**	5(cos(45°)**i** + sin (45°)**j**)	**i** – 10**j**
2	3**i** – 3**j**	4**i** – 9**j**	5(cos(90°)**i** + sin (90°)**j**)	2**i** – 6**j**
3	4**i** – 5**j**	2**i** – 7**j**	5(cos(135°)**i** + sin (135°)**j**)	3**i** + 3**j**
4	5**i** – 7**j**	**i** – 6**j**	5(cos(180°)**i** + sin (180°)**j**)	4**i** + 3**j**
5	6**i** – 9**j**	–5**j**	5(cos(225°)**i** + sin (225°)**j**)	5**i** – 6**j**
6	7**i** – 11**j**	–2**i** +2**j**	5(cos(270°)**i** + sin (270°)**j**)	6**i** – 10**j**

1. Which person is travelling with constant velocity? Write down an expression for the velocity in **i**, **j** notation for this person.

2. Who is travelling with constant speed but not constant velocity?

3. Who is maintaining the same direction but not constant velocity?

4. Describe the motion of Lucy.

FURTHER READING

de Lange, J. (1991). *Flying through mathematics – Trigonometry, vectors & flying*. Scotts Valley, CA: Wings for Learning.

Porter, R.I. (1970). *A school course in vectors*. London: G. Bells & Sons, Ltd.

Perkins, M.P. (1993). *Advanced mathematics: An applied course*. London: Collins Educational.

REFERENCES

Gullberg, J. (1997). *Mathematics from the birth of numbers*. NY: W.W. Norton & Company.

Koay, P.L., Lim, S.K., & Yap, S.F. (1998). *Secondary mathematics – Enrichment worksheets with solutions & teaching notes*. Singapore: Hillview Publications.

Toh T.L. (2005), On in-service mathematics teachers' content knowledge on kinematics. Asia-Pacific Forum on Science Learning and Teaching, *6*(2), Article 7 (Dec 2005). http://www.ied.edu.hk/apfslt/v6-issue2/tohtl/.

Chapter 15

Teaching of Matrices

Martyn Quigley and Yeo Boon Wooi Joseph

Although matrices have been around for a long time, the topic appeared in the Singapore school curriculum only in the last 40 years or so. Matrices have been found to be an excellent tool in practically every modern numerate discipline, from acoustics to zymurgy[1]. They are one of the great unifying topics in modern mathematical thinking.

HISTORY

The earliest known use of a matrix to solve linear equations was in the ancient Chinese mathematical classic *Jiuzhang Suanshu* (九章算术, *Nine Chapters on the Mathematical Art,* see Li Yan and Du Shiran, 1987, pp. 46–48) in about 200 B.C. However, it was not until the 19th century that matrices were used to solve mathematical problems in the West. Most likely it is the fact that the Chinese used a counting board that took the form of a grid which made it easier for them to use matrices.

Three mathematicians played important roles in the development of matrix theory in the late 19th century. They were James Sylvester (1814–1897), William Rowan Hamilton (1805–1865) and Arthur Cayley (1821–1895). Sylvester and Cayley were good friends, and although they did not work together, they cooperated in developing matrix theory. Sylvester was the first to use the term "matrix". Hamilton, a noted physicist, astronomer and mathematician, also used what was essentially the algebra of matrices under the name of *linear and vector functions*. The mathematical concept of *vector space* grew out of Hamilton's work on the algebra of vectors.

---

[1] Zymurgy: the branch of chemistry that deals with fermentation processes, as in brewing or distilling or making wine.

KEY CONCEPTS

In Elementary Mathematics, students are expected to be able to use matrices to:

- display and interpret information in matrix form of any size,
- find sums and products of matrices and use them to solve problems,
- calculate and use the product of a scalar with a matrix.

In Additional Mathematics, students are expected to be able to use matrices to:

- find the determinants and the inverses of 2×2 matrices,
- express a pair of simultaneous linear equations in two variables in the matrix form and use it to solve the equations.

It is important therefore to develop students' flexibility of thinking about matrices and not to confine them to computational procedures.

Terminology

Students will come across a number of new terms in the study of this topic and it is important to explain them carefully including giving guidance on pronunciation and usage. In the following list, the stressed syllable is in capitals.

Matrix	(MAY-tricks)
Matrices	(MAY-tree-seas)
Element	(ELLy-ment)
Determinant	(dee-TER-min-ant)
Singular	(SING-gyou-lah)

LEARNING DIFFICULTIES

Most of the difficulties with matrices arise from faulty learning of the multiplicative properties of matrices. It is necessary therefore to take special care when dealing with multiplication of matrices, and in particular, when showing why "multiplication" of matrices is so awkward. Another source of misconception is the illegal operation of dividing by a matrix.

TEACHING APPROACHES

The trick – insofar as there is a trick – in teaching matrices lies in selecting good metaphors. Students have to learn how to use matrices in several settings. Because the topic is new, if it is introduced in isolation, the students have nothing to connect to and are reduced to the instrumental learning of a few computational routines. This inevitably leads to many students performing poorly, and greatly adds to their dislike of and frustration with matrices. Ideally, the same metaphor should be used for the whole topic. Although this can be done (through incidence matrices), it may become somewhat strained and it is probably better to use different metaphors at different stages.

Metaphor 1: Table of values

The simplest way to introduce matrices is by means of a table of values. Choose a type of table which is of interest to students. Football league tables are often quite fun and they provide a natural way to introduce addition of matrices. Here for instance is a pair of tables representing home and away matches for the five soccer teams in the UK's Premier League in February 2007.

H: Home

Team	Played	Won	Drawn	Lost	For[2]	Against[2]	Points
Arsenal	13	8	5	0	32	10	29
Aston Villa	13	6	4	3	15	11	22
Blackburn	13	6	2	5	16	16	20
Bolton	14	8	3	3	20	12	27
Charlton	13	4	3	6	11	17	15

[2] The "For" column shows the number of goals scored by the respective team and the "Against" column shows the number of goals conceded by the team.

A: Away

Team	Played	Won	Drawn	Lost	For	Against	Points
Arsenal	13	6	2	5	16	12	20
Aston Villa	14	1	7	6	13	22	10
Blackburn	14	4	2	8	14	22	14
Bolton	13	6	2	5	12	16	20
Charlton	14	1	2	11	9	30	5

From the tables, we simply extract the numbers in the same rectangular patterns and call them matrices. One great advantage of this metaphor is that we can easily able attach meanings to the rows (information about each team) and columns (number of games and points). We can also introduce the terms "row", "column", "size", "dimension", etc. Further, we can see from the tables that the teams have different home and away records, so to find which team is leading the championship race, we need to combine the tables by adding numbers in corresponding positions. This is a very natural way to show how we find H + A, and it is readily understood because it has meaning for the students.

Note that this metaphor works well to show matrices as tables of values for addition but it is not so useful when we multiply one matrix by another. In the example, it is not at all obvious what multiplying one league table, H, by another, A, would mean. About the best we can do is to show how to calculate the points earned by a team,[3] something like this:

$$\begin{pmatrix} 8 & 5 & 0 \\ 6 & 4 & 3 \\ 6 & 2 & 5 \\ 8 & 3 & 3 \\ 4 & 3 & 6 \end{pmatrix} \times \begin{pmatrix} 3 \\ 1 \\ 0 \end{pmatrix} = \begin{pmatrix} 29 \\ 22 \\ 20 \\ 27 \\ 15 \end{pmatrix}$$

The trouble comes when you try to justify writing the points earned for a win, draw and loss as a 3×1 matrix.

[3] A win scores 3 points; a draw scores 1 point; a loss scores no points.

All in all, it is probably better to introduce another metaphor when you reach the topic of multiplication of one matrix by another.

Another type of table might better suit your students; it is up to you to decide. Failing all else, you could use a table of values such as one you might construct to draw a graph.

Metaphor 2: Sweet shop arithmetic

Mrs. Sim goes shopping. Suppose she buys five oranges at 20¢ each and three grapefruits at 60¢ each. We can write the numbers of fruit as an ordered pair – in this case (5 3) – and the prices as another ordered pair – (20 60). The total cost is the *scalar product* of the two ordered pairs. So the bill for Mrs. Sim is (in cents)

$$(5\ 3) \cdot (20\ 60) = (5 \times 20 + 3 \times 60) = (280).$$

We can also write the second ordered pair as a column $\begin{pmatrix} 20 \\ 60 \end{pmatrix}$ and then form the scalar product by making the row (5 3) "dive down" the column like this:

$$(5 \quad 3)\begin{pmatrix} 20 \\ 60 \end{pmatrix} = (5 \times 20 + 3 \times 60) = 280.$$

Last week, oranges were 15¢ each and grapefruits were 65¢ each. Mrs. Sim's bill then was:

$$(5 \quad 3)\begin{pmatrix} 15 \\ 65 \end{pmatrix} = (5 \times 15 + 3 \times 65) = 270.$$

There is no reason why we should not do both calculations together by making the row numbers "dive down" each of the price columns in turn:

$$(5 \quad 3)\begin{pmatrix} 20 & 15 \\ 60 & 65 \end{pmatrix} = \begin{pmatrix} 5 \times 20 + 3 \times 60 \\ 5 \times 15 + 3 \times 65 \end{pmatrix} = \begin{pmatrix} 280 \\ 270 \end{pmatrix}.$$

This is a pretty feeble explanation of why we multiply matrices this way, and notice that it is purely arbitrary – there is no reason for writing calculations out like this.

Nevertheless, this – or a variant – is probably the most common metaphor used to introduce matrices. It probably explains why so many students have little relational understanding of the topic.

Metaphor 3: Incidence matrices

Singa Airlines has flights connecting four cities. Their flights can be represented by the following network:

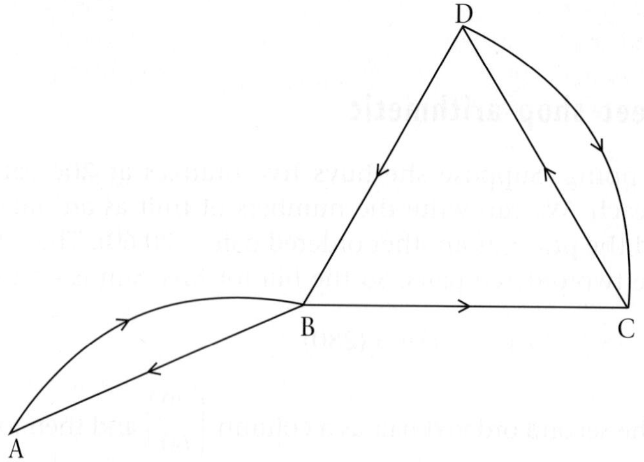

This network holds important information for the airline traveller about the possible connections between the different cities. The arrow indicates the direction of the flight. For example, there is no direct flight between A and C, and to go from B to D one must pass through C. The incidence matrix, M (below), shows whether it is possible to travel directly from one city to another: a 1 indicates there is one direct flight and a 0 indicates that there is none.

$$\begin{array}{c} \\ A \\ B \\ C \\ D \end{array}\begin{array}{c} \begin{array}{cccc} A & B & C & D \end{array} \\ \begin{bmatrix} 0 & 1 & 0 & 0 \\ 1 & 0 & 1 & 0 \\ 0 & 0 & 0 & 1 \\ 0 & 1 & 1 & 0 \end{bmatrix} \end{array}$$

1. Calculate M^2. What does M^2 mean? Why?

2. Calculate M^3 and M^4 and interpret their meaning.

3. What would M^0 have to be? Why?

4. Calculate $M^3 + M^2 + M + M^0$. What is the meaning of the absence of 0 in this sum matrix?

This metaphor can be made quite realistic with a bit of effort to make it reflect local cities, but care is needed, for if you choose cities such as Singapore, Hong Kong, Jakarta and Manila you will find that the number of flights is quite large.

Basic properties of matrices are easy to extract provided you stress that the rows have a meaning (number of ways to leave a city) and the columns have meanings (number of ways to arrive at a city). To introduce addition of matrices you need to use two networks connecting the same cities. For instance, SIA and RBA both fly between Singapore (SIN) and Bandar Seri Begawan (BWN). You can draw one network in red and superimpose the other in blue.

This is not as weird as it seems and is quite natural in practice. What is a little harder to explain is how multiplication works. You need to ask the question: "How many ways can you leave BWN for SIN by SIA and return by RBA?" Again, this question is not quite so bizarre as it seems. For instance, you take a 3D/2N free and easy holiday from BWN to SIN using SIA. The outward trip arrives in SIN on day one at 1415, but the return flight on day three leaves SIN at 0915 and arrives back in BWN at 1115 – so the morning of the third day of your holiday is spent travelling home (BWN), and the afternoon *at* home (BWN). If, on the other hand, you take the RBA on the return flight, you can travel at 2115, so you get to spend the whole of the third day and the early evening in Singapore. For this reason, many Bruneians choose exactly this arrangement for their holiday, that is, outwards by SIA but home by RBA.

Partial answers for the above questions:

1. M^2 represents the number of ways to travel from one city to another using exactly two flights.

2. Similar meaning for M^3 and M^4. Notice that the (2, 3) element of M^3 is 2. Therefore, there are two ways to travel from B to C using exactly three flights.

3. $M^0 = I$ because the only city you can travel to using 0 flight is the city itself.

4. Absence of 0 means you can travel from any one city to any other city using at most three flights.

Metaphor 4: James Bond

007 is in deep trouble and has run out of cash. He needs to petition his boss for extra money to keep up his extravagant lifestyle, and of course being a secret agent he needs to send his message in code. He composes his message "SEND MONEY NOW" using the following procedure.

1. First, he replaces each letter in the message by a number according to the obvious code.

A	B	C	D	E	F	G	H	I	…	X	Y	Z
1	2	3	4	5	6	7	8	9	…	24	25	26

His message is translated as follows:

S	E	N	D	M	O	N	E	Y	N	O	W
19	5	14	4	13	15	14	5	25	14	15	23

2. This is a pretty feeble code and the average eight-year-old would crack it without any trouble. So 007 is a bit more devious. He chooses a super encoder to camouflage his message in a special way. The encoder he chooses is written like this:

$$\begin{pmatrix} 3 & 2 \\ 1 & 1 \end{pmatrix}$$

and he rewrites his encoded message in groups of four numbers like this:

$$\begin{pmatrix} 19 & 5 \\ 14 & 4 \end{pmatrix}\begin{pmatrix} 13 & 15 \\ 14 & 5 \end{pmatrix}\begin{pmatrix} 25 & 14 \\ 15 & 23 \end{pmatrix}.$$

3. Next he uses a special procedure to "multiply" each group of numbers by his super encoder in the following super secret way.

$$\begin{pmatrix} 3 & 2 \\ 1 & 1 \end{pmatrix}\begin{pmatrix} 19 & 5 \\ 14 & 4 \end{pmatrix} = \begin{pmatrix} 3 \times 19 + 2 \times 14 & 3 \times 5 + 2 \times 4 \\ 1 \times 19 + 1 \times 14 & 1 \times 5 + 1 \times 4 \end{pmatrix} = \begin{pmatrix} 85 & 23 \\ 33 & 9 \end{pmatrix}$$

Now there are only 26 letters in the alphabet, so we reduce each element in the coded block modulo 26 and obtain $\begin{pmatrix} 7 & 23 \\ 7 & 9 \end{pmatrix}$.

Notice how two letters, S and E, have both ended up being represented by the same number 7. This is pretty clever stuff because it is hard for the enemy to guess which letter(s) the number 7 represents.

We treat the other two blocks in the same way and get our final three blocks of the message

$$\begin{pmatrix} 7 & 23 \\ 7 & 9 \end{pmatrix}\begin{pmatrix} 15 & 3 \\ 1 & 20 \end{pmatrix}\begin{pmatrix} 1 & 10 \\ 14 & 11 \end{pmatrix}$$

which we transmit as a single sequence 7, 23, 7, 9, 15, 3, 1, 20, 1, 10, 14, 11.

4. Back in London, Miss Moneypenny receives this string of numbers and reconstructs the three coded blocks above. Then she uses her super special decoder to unscramble the message. Her decoder is (surprise, surprise) the inverse of the encoder:

$$\begin{pmatrix} 1 & -2 \\ -1 & 3 \end{pmatrix}$$

so Miss Moneypenny now pre-multiplies the coded blocks by her decoder and obtains

$$\begin{pmatrix} -7 & 5 \\ 14 & 4 \end{pmatrix}\begin{pmatrix} 13 & -37 \\ -12 & 57 \end{pmatrix}\begin{pmatrix} -27 & -12 \\ 41 & 23 \end{pmatrix}.$$

5. Obviously some of the values lie outside the range 1 to 26, so we reduce those modulo 26 and hey presto, the original blocks reappear.

   Note how cleverly 007 chose an encoder which just happened to have a determinant of 1 so that the inverse exists and the elements in the inverse are integers.

A somewhat whimsical metaphor, but it is quite a clever application and we can just about appeal to 007's mystique for motivational purposes. Naturally, a secret code must use a pretty abstruse coding method, hence the need for a complicated method for multiplication.

Metaphor 5: Transformations

Although transformations are no longer in the O-level syllabus, students are still expected to learn that plane figures are congruent to their images under translation, reflection and rotation, and that plane figures are similar to their images under enlargement. However, this metaphor may still be too difficult for many students, but we include it here for pre-service teachers and as enrichment for some students.

Begin by reminding the students of some simple transformations of the plane, and show how they can be described by 2×2 matrices, reflection in the axes and easy lines, and rotations about the origin. Do not use translations for they are clumsy treated this way.

For instance, we initially treat a matrix as an algorithm, which given a certain point, produces another point:

New x-coordinate = $1 \times$ old x-coordinate + $0 \times$ old y-coordinate
New y-coordinate = $0 \times$ old x-coordinate + $(-1) \times$ old y-coordinate

So what happens to the point (5, 11)?

New x-coordinate = $1 \times 5 + 0 \times 11 \quad = 5$
New y-coordinate = $0 \times 5 + (-1) \times 11 = -11$

So the point (5, 11) is mapped to the point (5, –11). Repeat this with a few more points and then establish that this transformation is one the students already know; it is reflected in the x-axis. We take this approach so that the students can see that the only important part of the algorithm to remember is the arrangement of coefficients; our intention is they see that there is a reason for writing a matrix in this particular way. Further, since the students have already dealt with position vectors written as column vectors (at O-level), it is an easy step to identify the coordinates of a point with a position vector. Thus, we do not need to appeal to "convention" to explain multiplication; there is a perfectly good reason for writing the example above as

$$\begin{pmatrix} 1 & 0 \\ 0 & -1 \end{pmatrix}\begin{pmatrix} 5 \\ 11 \end{pmatrix} = \begin{pmatrix} 5 \\ -11 \end{pmatrix}$$

and thus a perfectly logical reason for the (apparently) strange way we multiply matrices.

This approach, beginning with (pre-)multiplying a column vector by a matrix, naturally extends from the example of a 2×2 matrix multiplying a 2×1 vector to a 2×2 matrix multiplying a $2 \times n$ matrix because we can interpret the $2 \times n$ matrix as an aggregation of n column vectors. Even better, we can also see that we may interpret multiplying a 2×2 matrix by another as one transformation followed by another.

Another nice feature of this metaphor is that there is a natural interpretation for the determinant. By establishing that the matrix $\begin{pmatrix} n & 0 \\ 0 & n \end{pmatrix}$ represents, in this metaphor, an enlargement scale factor n (which again the students have already met at O-level) and reminding them of the area properties of similar triangles, we can readily establish that the determinant of a 2×2 matrix is the area factor of the transformation, corresponding precisely to the relationship between areas of similar figures (the so-called $1 : k : k^2 : k^3$ property, also treated at O-level). Alternatively, you can draw out the unit square, transform it and calculate areas. If the determinant of a 2×2 matrix M happens to be negative, then this simply means that the transformation represented by M is a reflection (or more accurately is the product of an odd number of reflections).

The inverse of a 2×2 matrix M also has a nice interpretation: it is simply the transformation which "reverses" the effect of M.

One of the most mysterious properties of a matrix lies in its eigenvectors. If we think of a matrix M as a transformation of the plane, then this mystery goes away quite easily. For instance, suppose we consider a matrix M and look for its eigenvalues in the usual way:

$$\left| \begin{pmatrix} 4 & -1 \\ 2 & 1 \end{pmatrix} - \lambda I \right| = 0$$

From this we get $(4 - \lambda)(1 - \lambda) - (-1) \times 2 = 0$ and solving this we get $\lambda = 2$ or $\lambda = 3$.

Now consider the former case. We have, for any vector $\begin{pmatrix} x \\ y \end{pmatrix}$,

$$\begin{pmatrix} 4 & -1 \\ 2 & 1 \end{pmatrix} \begin{pmatrix} x \\ y \end{pmatrix} = 2 \begin{pmatrix} x \\ y \end{pmatrix}$$

from which we can get $4x - y = 2x$ which we simplify to $y = 2x$. What does this mean? It means that the line $y = 2x$ is invariant under the transformation M. What does the eigenvalue 2 mean? It means that any vector in the direction of $y = 2x$ is stretched by a factor of 2. For instance, the vector $\begin{pmatrix} 3 \\ 6 \end{pmatrix}$ (which lies along the line) is transformed by M to $\begin{pmatrix} 6 \\ 12 \end{pmatrix}$ (do the calculation and check for yourself) and we see this new vector also lies on $y = 2x$ and has been "stretched" by a factor of 2.

So powerful and satisfying is this metaphor that it is baffling why it is not specifically included in the syllabus any more. Nevertheless, it can still be used if the teacher so chooses and because it is so strong a metaphor it may well be worth the investment of time. There are, however, a few caveats to be born in mind with this metaphor.

- Some people call this metaphor *motion geometry*, thus implicitly suggesting to the students that these transformations involve moving something. They do not. Mathematical transformations take place in zero seconds – they are instantaneous, and demonstrating them with animations or with physically moving diagrams can be misleading unless the teacher is aware of this and makes appropriate provision.
- Many past O-level-type questions ask students to investigate the effects of transformations on particular sets of points. Often this results in students effectively learning that transformations just act on those points referred to. They do not. Mathematical transformations act on every point in the plane; it is just that in any particular circumstance, we are only interested in the effects on a particular few points. Teachers must be aware of this and act accordingly, for instance, by drawing two diagrams rather than superimposing one diagram on another.

Metaphor 6: Algebraic structure

In this metaphor we are not interested in what matrices represent: we merely bestow them with certain properties and examine the outcomes.

First, we *define* what we mean by a matrix: it is an array of m rows each of which contains n elements and we refer to each of these $m \times n$ elements by a doubly subscripted variable a_{ij} where $1 \leq i \leq m$ and $1 \leq j \leq n$ so that the element a_{ij} refers to the element in the ith row and the jth column. (We could define a matrix in terms of a function from the cross product of two vector spaces to the underlying field, but since students often do not understand it, there does not seem to be much point in doing so.)

Second, we define addition of two matrices: two matrices can be added together if and only if they have the same dimensions in the same order, in which case we define the sum C (with elements c_{ij} of two $m \times n$ matrices A and B (with elements a_{ij} and b_{ij})) by defining each $c_{ij} = a_{ij} + b_{ij}$.

Third, we define multiplication in the obvious way, which we will omit here because it is quite tedious.

We note that if m and n are different, we can add two $m \times n$ matrices but we cannot multiply them, but if two matrices have dimensions $m \times n$ and $n \times p$ we can multiply them but we cannot add them. If we wish to do both (and we do), we need to restrict our attention to square matrices. Furthermore, 3×3 matrices (and larger) are quite cumbersome to work with and so we also restrict ourselves to 2×2 matrices. So let us denote the set of all 2×2 matrices by T*, and let us consider two members of T*, say p and q. Further, we tacitly assume the elements of each member of T* are numbers of some kind. Let $\oplus$ denote matrix addition and $\otimes$ denote matrix multiplication. We note the following:

1. $p \oplus q = r$ (say) and $r \in T^*$ (closure).

2. $(p \oplus q) \oplus r = p \oplus (q \oplus r)$ (associativity).

3. There exists a unique member of T* denoted by **0** such that for any member s of T*, $\mathbf{0} \oplus s = s \oplus \mathbf{0} = s$ (identity; **0** is the zero matrix, all of its elements are 0).

4. For any $p \in T^*$ there exists a unique $u \in T^*$ such that $u \oplus p = p \oplus u = \mathbf{0}$ (p has an additive inverse).

We have thus shown that T* forms a group under matrix addition. This group turns out to be a pretty dull group, so we make a parallel argument for matrix multiplication. Unfortunately, when we do this, step 4 fails, for we cannot find an inverse for every member of T* under matrix multiplication. This is a shame but we can fix things by restricting the matrices to be non-singular, and so we denote the set of all such 2×2 matrices by T. Now T forms a group under matrix multiplication, and verifying this is left as an exercise.

All in all, while there is nothing wrong with this metaphor, it is not very enlightening for the students, and being completely abstract and not related to anything else (from the students' point of view), it is very hard for them to understand. On the other hand, this metaphor may be suitable for pre-service teachers.

APPLICATIONS OF MATRICES

For Additional Mathematics, there is only one real application: the solution of simultaneous linear equations. We illustrate the principle with an example. Before starting, be sure to write the equations in the standard form shown below:

$$5x - 3y = 34$$
$$3x - 4y = 16.$$

First, we rewrite the equations in matrix form:

$$\begin{pmatrix} 5 & -3 \\ 3 & -4 \end{pmatrix}\begin{pmatrix} x \\ y \end{pmatrix} = \begin{pmatrix} 34 \\ 16 \end{pmatrix}.$$

Now pre-multiply both sides by the inverse of the 2 × 2 matrix (what does it mean if this matrix is singular?):

$$\frac{-1}{11}\begin{pmatrix}-4 & 3\\ -3 & 5\end{pmatrix}\begin{pmatrix}5 & -3\\ 3 & -4\end{pmatrix}\begin{pmatrix}x\\ y\end{pmatrix} = \frac{-1}{11}\begin{pmatrix}-4 & 3\\ -3 & 5\end{pmatrix}\begin{pmatrix}34\\ 16\end{pmatrix}$$

$$\frac{-1}{11}\begin{pmatrix}-11 & 0\\ 0 & -11\end{pmatrix}\begin{pmatrix}x\\ y\end{pmatrix} = \frac{-1}{11}\begin{pmatrix}-88\\ -22\end{pmatrix}$$

$$\begin{pmatrix}1 & 0\\ 0 & 1\end{pmatrix}\begin{pmatrix}x\\ y\end{pmatrix} = \begin{pmatrix}8\\ 2\end{pmatrix}$$

So our solution is $x = 8$, $y = 2$. This is perhaps not the quickest way to solve this particular pair of equations, but for more complex equations, this method can be faster, especially if you have a powerful calculator. In fact, the main advantage of this method is that it can be extended to arbitrarily large sets of simultaneous equations, and there are some very efficient refinements which make this method particularly suitable for computer implementation.

One way of assessing whether students really understand the concept behind solving simultaneous equations using the matrix method (instead of just applying a routine procedure) is to reverse the process. For example,

(a) find the vector X if $\begin{pmatrix}5 & -3\\ 3 & -4\end{pmatrix}X = \begin{pmatrix}34\\ 16\end{pmatrix}$,

(b) hence, write down the equations of a pair of straight lines which intersect at the point (8, 2).

This type of questions has been tried out on many classes of students before, and you may be surprised to find that many students think that the answer for (b) is

$5x - 3y = 8$
$3x - 4y = 2.$

So this type of questions may suggest that many students may not really understand what they are doing.

CONCLUSION

As with any topic in mathematics, one metaphor will not cover every aspect of matrices. It is part of your job as the teacher to select the most appropriate metaphor for your class. It is important for you to know all the metaphors, for if you do not know them all, you cannot select the most appropriate one. You can only select the one(s) you happen to know and that may not be the optimal choice for your students. It is usually a mistake to assume that the way you were taught ten years ago is the best way to teach today, especially when you consider that you are a lot smarter than most of your students. Furthermore, one of the major weaknesses of our students is their failure to make links between different topics in mathematics. If you settle for one metaphor, you are contributing to this weakness. With matrices, the most common sequence is along the following lines. However, the sequence is *your choice.*

1. Metaphor 1 (football tables or something similar) to introduce the idea of a matrix, the terminology, addition and multiplication by a scalar.

2. Metaphor 2 or 4 (sweet shop arithmetic or 007) to introduce the idea of matrix multiplication and to add some variety, perhaps for homework if you like to set it.

3. Metaphor 3 (networks) for enrichment.

4. The application to the solution of simultaneous equations.

You would be wise to avoid metaphor 5 (transformations) and metaphor 6 (algebraic approach) for all except the cleverest students, and only then if they are so bright that the other metaphors are trivial for them.

FURTHER READING

Crowley, M.L. (1995). Transformations: Making connections in high school mathematics. In P.A. House (Ed.), *Connecting mathematics across the curriculum* (1995 Yearbook), 79–91. Reston, VA: National Council of Teachers of Mathematics.

Department of Mathematics and Computer Science, North Carolina School of Science and Mathematics. (1988). *New topics for secondary school mathematics: Matrices.* Reston, VA: National Council of Teachers of Mathematics.

Martin, G.E. (1982). *Transformation geometry: An introduction to symmetry.* NY: Springer-Verlag.

Okolica, S., & Macrina, G. (1992). Integrating transformation geometry into traditional high school geometry. *Mathematics Teacher, 85*, 716–719.

Rubenstein, R.N., & Thompson, D.R. (1995). Making connections with transformations in grades K-8. In P.A. House (Ed.), *Connecting mathematics across the curriculum* (1995 Yearbook), 65–78. Reston, VA: National Council of Teachers of Mathematics.

School Mathematics Project. (1981). *Matrix algebra and isometric transformations.* Cambridge, UK: Cambridge University Press.

School Mathematics Project. (1991). *Further matrices and transformations*. Cambridge, UK: Cambridge University Press.

Thompson, D.R., Senk, S.L., & Viktova, S.S. (1991). Matrices at the secondary school level. In M.J. Kenny & C.R. Hirsch (Eds.), *Discrete mathematics across the curriculum K-12* (1991 Yearbook). Reston, VA: National Council of Teachers of Mathematics.

REFERENCE

Li, Y., & Du, S. (1987). *Chinese mathematics: A concise history* (*Zhong guo shu xue*). Translated by J.N. Crossley & Anthony W-C Lun. Oxford: Clarendon Press.

Part II

Reading Resources

Chapter

16

Learning Theories for Mathematics Education

Wong Khoon Yoong

WHY LEARNING THEORIES?

Many trainees as well as practising teachers complain that learning theories are abstract and cannot be applied to real teaching situations. This negative perception is quite unfortunate because learning theories can actually serve several useful pedagogical functions.

a. Many psychological theories (http://tip.psychology.org/theories.html; Grouws and Cebulla, 2000; and Joyce, Calhoun, and Hopkins, 1997) attempt to explain how children develop intellectually, emotionally and socially. Understanding this development can help teachers decide on the strategies to use.

b. Theories provide the rationale behind common teaching practices, which goes beyond common sense. Thus, teachers will understand why certain techniques work and under what conditions, so that they do not just follow a technique blindly.

c. Theories can inspire teachers to develop different teaching techniques, and this leads to innovation.

d. The concepts and "jargons" used in educational theories form the special language of the teaching profession. This language facilitates discussion about education issues among colleagues and is used extensively in the education literature.

e. Most educational theories have been evaluated empirically, often in real classrooms. The findings of these research studies do not give unequivocal results, nevertheless, they still shed some light on how teaching and learning can be improved.

Mathematics educators have proposed many theories, some specific to mathematics instruction, while others are adaptations of psychological theories of learning and child development. Two crucial messages arise from the study of learning theories.

a. Teachers should borrow ideas from different theories and not be limited to one and only one theory. Trainees who ask "tell me the *best* way to teach ..." have missed this very important message!

b. These theories tell us that what the teachers have taught and what their students are able to learn may be two different but related things. Thus, the teacher's job is not just to complete the lesson plans, but also to check what the students have actually learned.

   Only a few of the theories, however, will be briefly discussed in this chapter. They are introduced through six teaching scenarios so that their applications will be more evident and realistic. These scenarios are given below:

Scenarios	Theorists
Traditional rule-based teaching	Thorndike, Skinner, Gagné; behaviourism
Types of mathematical understanding	Skemp
Multi-modal representation, discover ideas	Bruner; constructivism
Students' errors and stages of cognitive development	Piaget; constructivism
Cooperative learning	Vygotsky; social constructivism
Enhance memory	Information processing; cognitive science

SCENARIO 1: TRADITIONAL RULE-BASED TEACHING

The teacher explains and demonstrates how to perform a rule, for example, $(-2) \times 5 = -10$. The students listen silently and pay attention. Then they practise the rule with similar examples. The teacher monitors their work, rewards those who can do the work correctly and re-explains to those who have made mistakes. This is encapsulated as **explain → practice → feedback**.

This is the most common technique used to teach mathematics all over the world from primary to even tertiary levels. It has been called by different names, such as "chalk and talk", "drill and practice", "drill and kill", "whole class instruction", and so on. Its theoretical basis is *behaviourism*. There are many well-known behaviourist psychologists, the more influential ones being Pavlov (1849–1936; he won a Nobel Prize for Medicine on digestive glands), Thorndike (1874–1949) and Skinner (1904–1990). They proposed different versions of behaviourism.

The basic tenet of behaviourism is that learning consists of changes in observable or measurable behaviours based on stimulus (S) and responses (R). Teaching mathematics consists of helping students to establish appropriate bonds between S and R. For example, students learn to associate $(-2) \times 5$ with -10. These bonds are presented in small steps according to a hierarchy, for example, from easy to difficult. Questions (S) and answers (R) are used to check the establishment of the correct bonds.

Hierarchies of mathematical concepts and skills can be established based on logical analysis or what the students can understand, using evidence from personal experience or research, for example, the CSMS study (Hart, 1981). A simple hierarchy is given below (Figure 16-1).

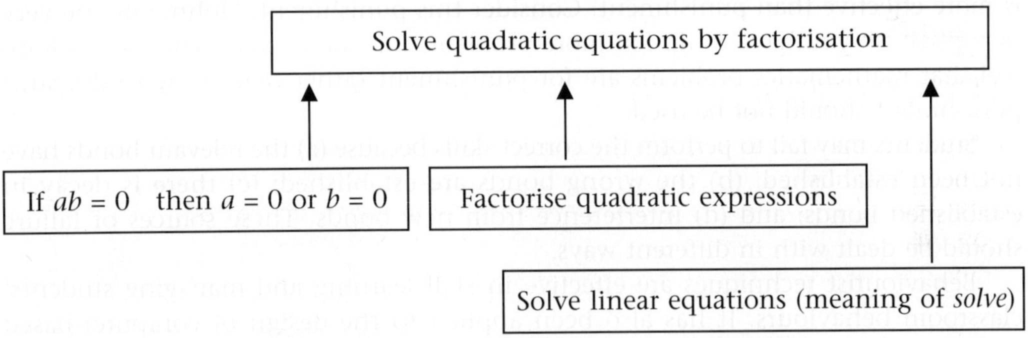

Figure 16-1 A simple hierarchy of solving quadratic equations

Such hierarchies can be used to plan lessons. Gagné provides a nine-step sequence:

a. Gain attention
b. Inform learners of the objective
c. Stimulate recall of prior learning
d. Present the stimulus
e. Provide learning guidance
f. Elicit performance
g. Provide feedback
h. Assess performance
i. Enhance retention and transfer

From behaviourist research, several laws on how to strengthen the S–R bonds have been widely established. Three well-known ones formulated by Thorndike are:

a. Law of exercise: Repetitions can strengthen bonds, but distributed practice is more effective than massed practice.

b. Law of effect: Any act that produces a satisfying effect in a situation tends to be repeated in that situation. This explains why positive reinforcement is preferred to punishment.

c. Law of recency: The most recent bond is likely to recur.

Thus, in teaching several skills, the teacher should follow the pattern: **teach skill 1 → practise skill 1 → teach skill 2 → practise skill 2**, and so on, rather than teach skills 1 and 2 → practise.

Practice can be reinforced *positively* (e.g. through praising or giving tangible rewards) or *negatively* (by removing an aversive stimulus). On the other hand, punishment presents an aversive stimulus (e.g. ordering a student to stand outside the class) or withdraws a desired stimulus (e.g. "Mary, you didn't finish the exercise, so you can't have your recess today"). Behaviourists stress that positive reinforcement is more effective than punishment. Consider this punishment: "John, you are very disruptive, so you have to do ten more problems for homework." This makes John feel that mathematics problems are for punishment rather than a joy to do; such punishment should not be used.

Students may fail to perform the correct skills because (a) the relevant bonds have not been established; (b) the wrong bonds are established; (c) there is decay in established bonds; and (d) interference from new bonds. These sources of failure should be dealt with in different ways.

Behaviourist techniques are effective in skill learning and managing students' classroom behaviours. It has also been applied to the design of computer-based tutorial programs. However, there are some criticisms about behaviourism: (a) over-emphasis on skills leading to rote learning, without attention to meanings; (b) heavy demand on memorisation, which makes learning difficult for students who have poor memory; and (c) too much reliance on external motivation such as giving star stickers and monetary rewards. External motivators may be appropriate under certain situations, but teachers should wean their students from external rewards and inculcate their intrinsic desire to learn. Behaviourism may not be a suitable theory to use if the aim is to develop higher-order thinking and problem solving.

SCENARIO 2: TYPES OF MATHEMATICAL UNDERSTANDING

The teacher tells the class that the curved surface area of a cone is πrl and shows a worked example. A student asks: "How do you know this formula is true?" The teacher replies: "Never mind, just memorise it!" What objective is the teacher trying to achieve?

This scenario highlights that teachers and students may hold different views about what learning mathematics is all about. Skemp (1979) proposed three types of understanding: (a) instrumental understanding as knowing the rules without reason, dependent on memory, and short term in effect; (b) relational understanding as knowing what to do and why, easily reconstructed from general principles, and more permanent; and (c) logical understanding as conforming to accepted conventions in mathematics and pertaining to logical proof. In this scenario, the mismatch in aims of the teacher and the student will hinder effective learning.

Skemp also explained that mathematical concepts of a higher order than those a person already knows cannot be communicated to that person by mere definition. At the secondary level, a definition with ample examples and non-examples must be used. This is illustrated below, where the teacher asks the students to discuss similarities and differences (using the thinking skill of *compare and contrast*) leading to the concept of a quadratic expression.

Definition	Examples	Non-examples
$ax^2 + bx + c$, where $a \neq 0$	$x^2 + x + 5$	$x^2 + x^3 + 5$
	$4 - x^2 + x$	$4 - x^2 + \frac{1}{x}$

In Scenarios 1 and 2, the teacher uses predominantly words, numbers and symbols. These modes of representation are quite abstract for many students. Failing to understand the abstract ideas, these students may feel bored or frustrated, and this leads to classroom misbehaviour. Scenario 3 below shows the use of multiple modes of representation that attempt to address this problem.

SCENARIO 3: MULTI-MODAL REPRESENTATION

To explain how to derive the formula for the curved surface area of a cone, the teacher can ask the students to cut a circle into two sectors and make two cones from the sectors (*concrete* mode); draw diagrams of the sectors and the cones (*pictorial* mode); and they derive the formula by considering the area of each sector and the curved surface area of its corresponding cone (*symbolic* mode). Students then apply the formula to each cone and appreciate the size of the area (*numerical* mode). Working through the different modes will enhance understanding of the formula.

This multi-modal approach is an extension of the ideas of Bruner and Dienes. Bruner proposed that to acquire mathematical concepts, the learner works through the three modes: **enactive** → **iconic** → **symbolic**. Dienes enunciated the principle of multiple embodiment (also called the perceptual variability principle), which states that several related models must be used to help students abstract the relevant mathematical concepts.

To put these principles into a practical form, we have designed a thinkboard consisting of six modes (Wong, 1999). Each mode is associated with a key action verb: (a) *Word* (communicate); (b) *Number* (calculate); (c) *Real thing* (do); (d) *Diagram* (visualise); (e) *Story* (apply); and (f) *Symbol* (manipulate). Figure 16-2 illustrates a thinkboard for the addition of integers. Each mode has its functions and limitations,

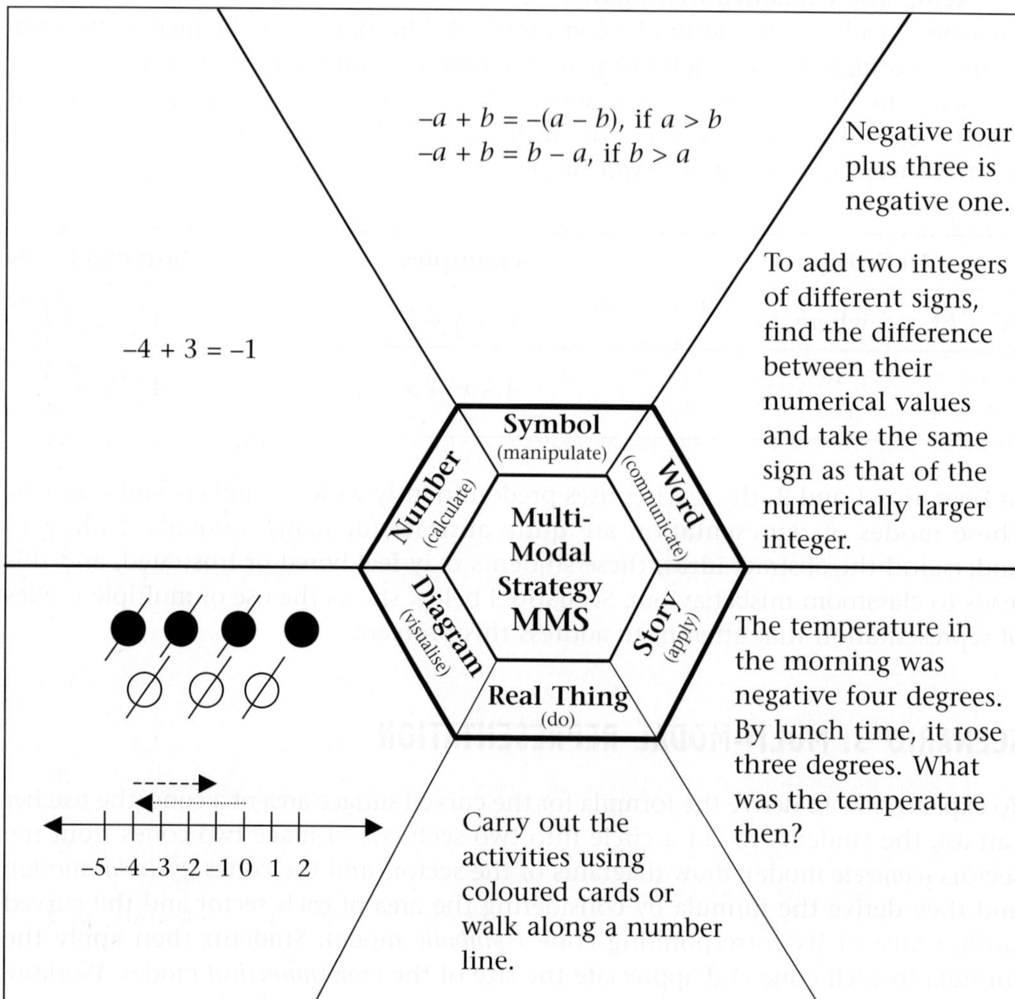

Figure 16-2 A thinkboard for the addition of integers

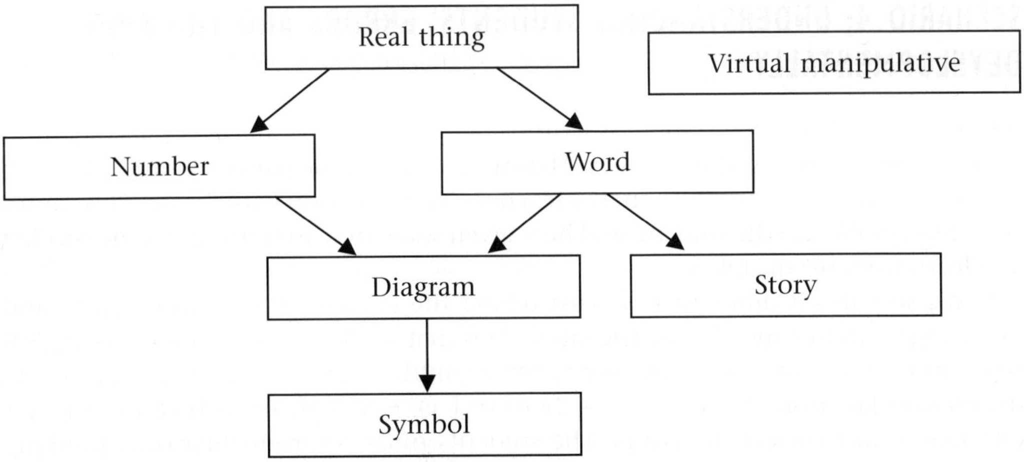

Figure 16-3 Suggested sequence for multi-modal teaching

so it is important for students to be able to translate from one mode to the other. A suggested teaching sequence using multi-mode is shown in Figure 16-3.

In the 1970s, Bruner introduced the guided discovery approach. Students try to discover mathematics on their own by working through various activities. It is believed that those who discover things for themselves will understand better and are more motivated. In addition, to quote Bruner, "*We teach a subject not to produce living libraries on the subject but rather to get a student to think mathematically for himself.*" Thus, guided discovery is an important way to help students think mathematically.

The discovery approach, however, has some shortcomings, namely, students may (a) discover the wrong mathematics; (b) feel frustrated at not knowing what to discover; or (c) just complete the activities or worksheets without thinking or becoming engaged with the mathematics. In addition, this approach requires more time than whole class teaching.

In terms of mathematics curriculum, Bruner advocated the spiral approach. This is also adopted by the Singapore mathematics curriculum:

> In the syllabus, the spiral approach is adopted to ensure, where possible, that each topic is covered at appropriate levels in increasing depth to enable pupils to consolidate the concepts and skills learnt and to develop further concepts and skills.
>
> Ministry of Education, 2001, p. 5

SCENARIO 4: UNDERSTANDING STUDENTS' ERRORS AND THINKING DEVELOPMENTALLY

A teacher observes that a student is writing $2^0 = 0$, $3^0 = 0$, etc. She asks the student to explain how he obtains those values. The student shows the pattern $2^1 = 2 \times 1 = 2$, $2^2 = 2 \times 2 = 4$, so $2^0 = 2 \times 0 = 0$. Then, the teacher challenges him with 2^3, etc. This causes cognitive conflict for the student, and he is given some time to think about the conflict and learn from his mistakes.

This scenario is different from just telling the students the correct answer and expecting them to remember it. The rationale is that students' errors often have logical basis and are *not* due to carelessness, for example, students often generalise the distributive law from $2(x + y) = 2x + 2y$ to $(x + y)^2 = x^2 + y^2$. In such cases, it is not effective to just correct the errors. The students must confront their own thinking related to the errors. Olivier (1989) provided further examples of common algebraic errors and argued that some errors arise from *correct* previous learning. For example, students who solve $(x - 1)(x - 3) = 0$ correctly with $x - 1 = 0$ or $x - 3 = 0$ will be puzzled why this correct procedure leads to the wrong answers with $(x - 1)(x - 3) = 5$, for instance.

Talking to students in order to understand their thinking is based on the technique of clinical interviews developed by Piaget (1896–1980). Clinical interviews are used to determine whether students have developed various types of conservation (e.g. conservation of number, of mass, of volume), which must be attained before they can understand the relevant mathematics. According to Piaget, cognitive development occurs in four stages: (a) sensori-motor (approximately 0–2 years); (b) pre-operational (2–7 years); (c) concrete operational (7–12 years); and (d) formal operational (>12 years). Later research shows that these year ranges are too optimistic. In fact, a large percentage of secondary school students (12–18 years) are still in the concrete operational stage, and only a small proportion of them reach the formal operational stage. This further supports the use of concrete materials in the multi-modal strategy mentioned earlier. According to Piaget, "*Manipulation of materials is crucial. In order to think, children in the concrete operational stage need to have objects in front of them that are easy to handle, or else to visualize objects that have been handled and that are easily imagined without any real effort.*" Using concrete manipulatives is especially important for students in the Normal streams because they prefer to learn using tangible objects.

Two other characteristics developed at the concrete operational stage are crucial for mathematics thinking. They are (a) reversal thinking, for example, given $2 + 7 = 9$, then $9 - 2 = 7$, as this applies to the study of functions and their inverses; and (b) transitivity, for example, if $a > b$, $b > c$, then $a > c$. This is required in the study of inequalities.

At the formal operational stage, students can think beyond concrete objects, and have developed deductive thinking (e.g. if-then statements, proofs) and combinatorial thinking (e.g. listing all possible cases). They are able to operate on operations (e.g. working on a family of functions and not just individual functions), formulate and test hypotheses, and explore "what if" questions. To lead students to reach this stage, ask divergent questions that have more than one correct answer, encourage students to develop hypotheses (e.g. search for patterns), ask them to justify their answers (right or wrong) and require them to verbalise their thinking process (metacognition).

Piaget described two cognitive processes when learners attempt to learn new materials. The *assimilation* process means that the learner can integrate new experience into existing cognitive structure (schema) without much difficulty. For example, it is quite easy to apply the meaning of multiplication as repeated addition from $2 \times 3 = 2 + 2 + 2$ to $-2 \times 3 = (-2) + (-2) + (-2)$. On the other hand, *accommodation* means that the learner has to modify existing schema or create new ones in order to learn new things. For example, when the multiplier is negative, the previously learned concept of repeated addition cannot be applied, for instance, what does it mean to add 2 *negative* three times in $2 \times (-3)$? In this case, a new model has to be learned and this causes cognitive conflict with the earlier model. If the students fail to accommodate the new model to existing ones, they may (a) resort to memorisation to pass tests but will soon forget what they have learned; (b) try to reason things out by over-generalising what they already know, and this is a common cause of mathematical errors; or (c) give up, hence losing interest and confidence in doing mathematics. Teachers need to be sensitive to these implications that arise from the different cognitive processes involved when students tackle new work.

Piaget cautioned that mathematical development cannot be accelerated because the students may not be ready for the new concept. According to him, *"This is why you cannot teach higher mathematics to a five-year-old. He does not yet have structures which enable him to understand."* This concept of *readiness* is quite controversial. Nevertheless, consider carefully Piaget's advice about giving adequate time for students to move to a higher stage of cognitive development: *"If we were willing to lose a bit more time and let the children be active, let them use trial and error on different things, then the time we seem to have lost we may have actually gained. Children may develop a general method that they can use on other subjects."* Consider this advice against the pressure that some teachers feel about not having enough time to complete the syllabus.

SCENARIO 5: COOPERATIVE LEARNING AND SOCIAL CONSTRUCTIVISM

A teacher organises the students to work in groups to promote cooperative learning. He gives them meaningful activities to work on, including contexts that are relevant to Singapore and National Education. The students discuss among themselves what they are doing but take responsibility for their own learning.

One rationale to support cooperative learning is social constructivism, advocated by Vygotsky (1896–1934). He coined the term "zone of proximal development (ZPD)" to mean the gap between what a learner can do independently (unassisted performance) and what he or she will be able to do under the guidance of a teacher or more capable peers (assisted performance). Learning activities fall under three levels: (a) activities already familiar to students, they can work independently to further practise skills; (b) activities within the students' ZPD, so scaffolding from the teacher or more capable peers is required; and (c) activities that are too hard and this leads to off-task behaviour and discipline problems (Tanner and Jones, 2000). Scaffolding provided in ZPD includes giving hints and cues, discussing heuristics, asking questions, giving encouragement and breaking problems into smaller steps. Group work and peer tutoring are other forms of scaffolding. For cooperative learning to be effective, the following four main factors must be present.

a. *Mutual dependence* or *positive interdependence*
Group members perceive that they need each other in order to accomplish the group's tasks. Thus, they have common goals, shared resources, assigned roles and joint rewards.

b. *Individual accountability*
Each member is responsible for completing the assigned tasks, mastering the material and explaining the group's work to the class.

c. *Face-to-face interaction*
Group members sit together to discuss and teach what they know to other members. Arranging students to sit together in groups but working on individual tasks is not cooperative learning.

d. *Interpersonal and group skills*
Students need to develop skills such as listening to others, respecting others, sharing responsibility and managing conflicts and disagreements in a constructive way.

Group activities are likely to be noisy, and the teachers need to be able to handle this constructively.

Vygotsky also stressed that students' private talk can guide their cognitive development. Meichenbaum and Goodman (1977, cited in Manning and Payne, 1996, p. 137) developed a five-step method that can help students master mathematics rules through a transition from public talk to self-talk.

a. Teacher models the rule and verbalises the steps aloud, while the students listen (external speech).

b. Teacher verbalises the steps and students perform the steps.

c. Students verbalise (talk aloud) and perform the steps, while the teacher observes and monitors.

d. Students whisper the instruction to themselves, while the teacher monitors.

e. Students internalise the rule (self-talk, silent).

This metacognitive technique is rarely practised in mathematics lessons, but it could be helpful for some students.

SCENARIO 6: INFORMATION PROCESSING

After practising a few examples in class, the students can carry out the rules correctly. However, two months later, most of them have forgotten what they could do earlier. The teacher has to re-teach the rules and feels that the students are too lazy to revise the work on their own. This is a very frustrating scenario for most teachers. What are the possible causes and how can this problem be avoided?

One approach to handle this scenario derives from information-processing models developed by cognitive scientists. They compare human thinking to how the computer works, with its components: input, processing, output and memory storage. Figure 16-4 illustrates the key ideas of the information-processing model. The behaviourists are interested in the bond between the input (e.g. solve the linear equation) and the output (the solution), without paying much attention to the internal cognitive processes involved (shown within the dotted box). However, the cognitive scientists study how the processes within the box work.

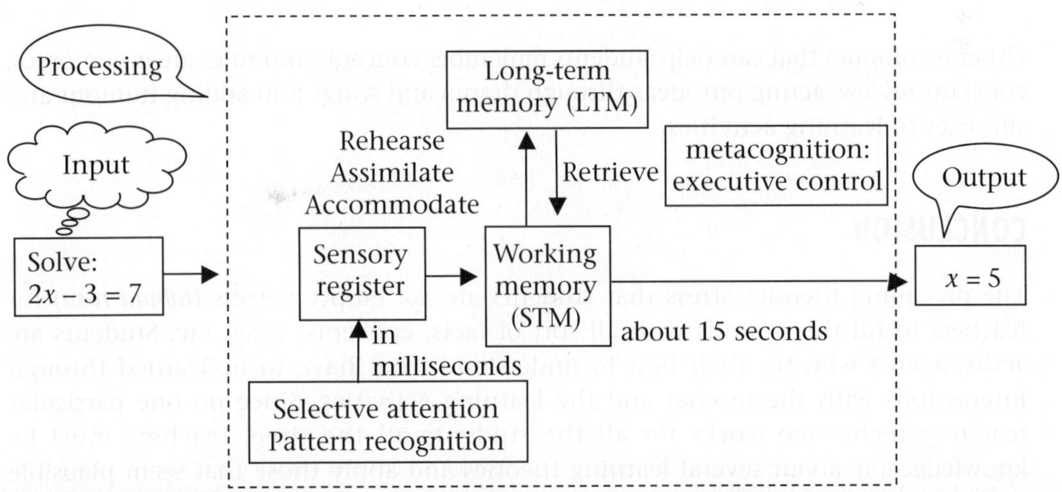

Figure 16-4 Key ideas of the information-processing model applied to solving simple equations

The human working memory has a limit of 7 ± 2 items. To improve processing, the items to be learned must be chunked together, for example, the discriminant, $b^2 - 4ac$, becomes one chunk instead of six items. Many students have short attention span, so the teacher needs to vary the activities every 10 to 15 minutes to hold their attention. Long-term memory can be improved by making the items meaningful and connected in as many ways as reasonable. Concept map is one way to show such links, as illustrated by Figure 16-5. This method works well if the students construct and compare their concept maps rather than memorise maps produced by the teacher.

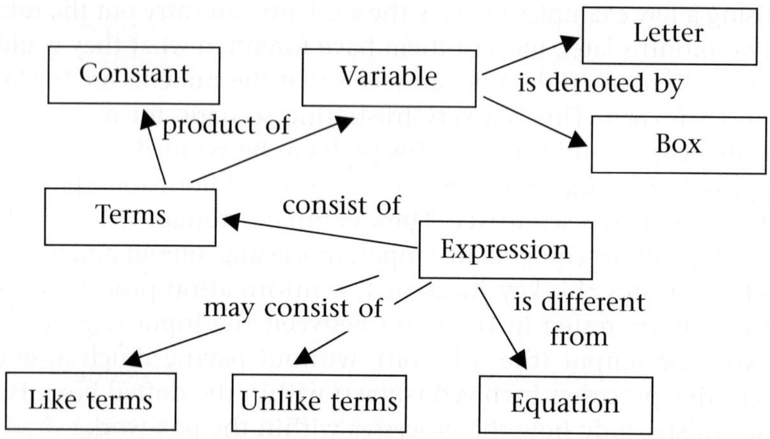

Figure 16-5 A concept map of basic algebra

Other techniques that can help students remember concepts and rules are mnemonics, constant review, acting out ideas through drama and songs and adding humour and surprises to learning activities.

CONCLUSION

The prevailing theories stress that students are *not* empty vessels (*tabula rasa*) for teachers to fill their minds with all sort of facts, concepts, rules, etc. Students are active agents who try their best to understand what have to be learned through interactions with the teacher and the learning activities. Since no one particular teaching technique works for all the students all the time, teachers must be knowledgeable about several learning theories and apply those that seem plausible under different contexts, then reflect on how well these theories work. With reflection, wisdom about teaching will grow with experience.

TUTORIAL DISCUSSION

1. Analyse the bonds and hierarchies that are involved when teaching a skill.

2. Write the following items on index cards: *examples, problem solving, non-examples, principles (theorems), concepts, skills, definition, practice.* Arrange them into the sequence in which you would use to teach a particular topic; include additional items if necessary. Share the sequences with other trainees.

3. All the theories mentioned above are developed by Westerners, but the mathematics achievement of students in some Western countries is not very high. Do we need Eastern theories of mathematics learning and teaching? If so, how are Eastern theories like?

4. Share your experience of discovering some mathematics on your own. What are the implications for teaching?

5. Discuss undesirable techniques teachers should not use when teaching mathematics.

6. How do you remember the mathematics you have learned? Share and develop suggestions to help your students remember mathematics better.

7. Discuss how errors can be used as springboards to deepen understanding.

8. Match the six learning outcomes with the appropriate learning processes (not complete).

Learning outcomes	Learning processes
Facts	Listen to explanation
Concepts	Discuss with others
Skills	Copy notes
Processes	Teach classmates
Metacognition	
Problem solving	
Attitude	

REFERENCES

Grouws, D.A., & Cebulla, K.J. (2000). *Improving student achievement in mathematics, Parts 1 and 2.* ERIC No. ED463952 and ED463953.

Hart, K.M. (Ed.). (1981). *Children's understanding of mathematics 11–16.* London: John Murray.

Joyce, B., Calhoun, E., & Hopkins, D. (1997). *Models of learning – Tools for teaching.* Buckingham: Open University Press.

Manning, B.H., & Payne, B.D. (1996). *Self-talk for teachers and students: Metacognitive strategies for personal and classroom use.* Boston, MA: Allyn and Bacon.

Ministry of Education. (2001). *Mathematics syllabus: Lower secondary.* Singapore: Ministry of Education.

Olivier, A. (1989). Handling pupils' misconceptions. *Pythagoras, 21,* 10–19. Available from http://www.sun.ac.za/mathed/HED/Misconceptions.pdf.

Skemp, R. (1979). Goals of learning and qualities of understanding. *Mathematics Teaching, 88,* 44–49.

Tanner, H., & Jones, S. (2000). *Becoming a successful teacher of mathematics.* London: Routledge Falmer.

Wong, K.Y. (1999). Multi-modal approach of teaching mathematics in a technological age. In E.B. Ogena & E.F. Golia (Eds.), *8th Southeast Asian conference on mathematics education, technical papers: Mathematics for the 21st century* (pp. 353–365). Manila: Ateneo de Manila University.

Internet. Common mathematical errors. http://www.math.vanderbilt.edu/~schectex/commerrs/.

Chapter

17

Mathematical Problem Solving in the Secondary Classroom

Berinderjeet Kaur & Yeap Ban Har

INTRODUCTION

Mathematical problem solving has been the primary goal of school mathematics curriculum in Singapore since 1990 (Ministry of Education, 1990; 2000; 2006). Such a goal is not a unique one as there has been a worldwide push for problem solving to be the central focus of school mathematics curriculum in the 1980s. In the UK, the Cockcroft Report of 1982 emphasised that

> "The ability to solve problems is at the heart of mathematics ... mathematics teaching at all levels should include opportunities for problem solving, including the application of mathematics to everyday situations."
>
> Cockcroft Report, 1982

Similarly the National Council of Teachers of Mathematics (NCTM) in the United States, in their document stating the principles and standards for school mathematics stated that:

> "Problem solving should be the central focus of the mathematics curriculum. As such, it is a primary goal of all mathematics instruction and an integral part of all mathematical activity. Problem solving is not a distinct topic but a process that should permeate the entire program and provide a context in which concepts and skills can be learned."
>
> NCTM, 1989

In Singapore, mathematical problem solving is central to mathematics learning at both the primary and secondary school levels. It involves the acquisition and application of mathematics concepts and skills in a wide range of situations, including non-routine, open-ended and real-world problems (Ministry of Education, 2006). Figure 17-1 shows the framework of the school mathematics curriculum.

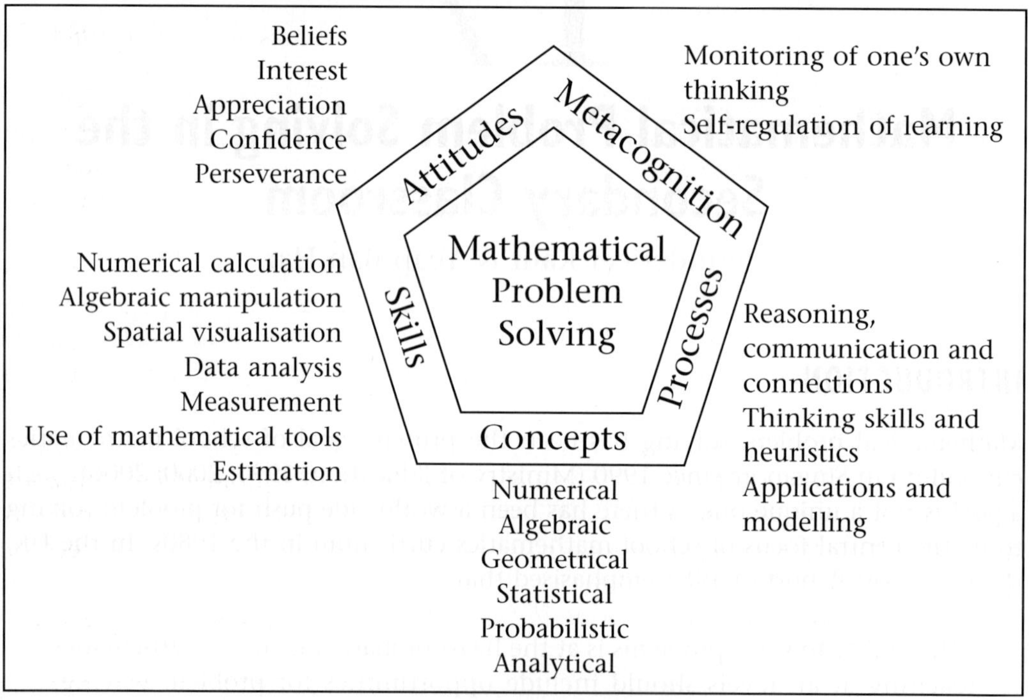

Figure 17-1 Framework of school mathematics curriculum

The framework highlights that the development of mathematical problem-solving ability is dependent on five inter-related components, namely, Concepts, Skills, Processes, Attitudes and Metacognition. Hence, it is important to note that while implementing the curriculum, a conscious effort must be made to draw on the inter-related components.

A PROBLEM AND PROBLEM SOLVING

The term "problem" is often very loosely used by many people. Let us first try to distinguish between tasks that are problems and those that are exercises.

What is a problem?

A problem is a task for which:

- The person confronting it wants or needs to find a solution.
- The person has no readily available procedure for finding the solution.
- The person must make an attempt to find a solution.

Charles and Lester, 1984

The above definition emphasises three crucial components of a problem. Firstly, a desire or need on the part of the problem-solver to find a solution to the problem; secondly the solution cannot be obtained directly or immediately by mere recall of knowledge; and thirdly the problem-solver must make a conscious attempt to arrive at the solution.

Following from the above definition, therefore, an exercise is a task for which a person, confronting it and desiring to resolve it, has a readily available algorithm to use and resolve it. As most textbook "problems" are practice tasks, which can be solved by the direct application of a procedure illustrated in the chapter to which they are appended, they are really mere exercises.

Owing to differences in knowledge, experience, ability or interest, a problem for one person may not be a problem for another. Also a problem for someone at a particular time may not be so at another time. In some contexts, as students develop their ability, what were problems initially may after some practice become mere exercises.

An example of a possible problem for secondary students would be as follows:

Cows, chickens and snakes

On a farm there are cows, chickens and snakes. Altogether they have 10 heads and 24 legs. How many cows, how many chickens and how many snakes are there? Explain how you worked it out.

An example of a possible exercise would be as follows:

Solve the following pair of simultaneous equations using the method of elimination:

$$x + y = 12$$
$$3x - 2y = 16$$

What is problem solving?

Problem solving is a complex process which requires an individual to coordinate previous experiences, knowledge, understanding and intuition, in order to satisfy the demands of a novel situation. In simple terms, it is the mental journey one takes to arrive at a solution starting with the givens of a situation. According to Charles and Lester (1984), generally three factors influence the problem-solving process of an individual. They are:

a. Experience factors, both environmental and personal, such as age, content knowledge, familiarity with solution strategies, familiarity with problem context and content;

b. Affective factors, such as interest, motivation, pressure, anxiety, tolerance for ambiguity and perseverance;

c. Cognitive factors, such as reading ability, spatial ability, analytical ability, logical ability, computational skill and memory.

PROBLEM-SOLVING STRATEGIES AND HEURISTICS

In problem solving, the terms "strategies" and "heuristics" are often used to describe certain approaches and techniques used in the solution process. These two terms are often used interchangeably or at times used jointly as "heuristic strategies" to mean the same. In this chapter, we will use the word "strategy" to mean an overall plan and "heuristic" to mean a specific technique or approach.

General strategies for problem solving

George Polya (1973), the father of problem solving, based on his extensive study of the problem-solving process, stated that there were four phases involved. They are:

First	Understand the problem
Second	Devise a plan
Third	Carry out the plan
Fourth	Look back

Polya's framework, as given in Figure 17-2, shows that in each of the phases, many questions an individual can ask himself or herself are apparent to guide him or her through the process. Such questions eventually lead one to engage in heuristic

First You have to *understand* the problem.	**1. Understand the problem** ■ What is the unknown? What are the data? What is the condition? ■ Is it possible to satisfy the condition? Is the condition sufficient to determine the unknown? Or is it insufficient? Or redundant? Or contradictory? ■ Draw a figure. Introduce suitable notation. ■ Separate the various parts of the condition. Can you write them down?
Second Find the connection between the data and the unknown. You may be obliged to consider auxiliary problems if an immediate connection cannot be found. You should eventually obtain a *plan* of the solution.	**2. Devise a plan** ■ Have you seen it before? Have you seen the same problem in a slightly different form? ■ Do you know a related problem? Do you know a theorem that could be useful? ■ Look at the unknown! Try to think of a problem you know which has the same or a similar unknown. ■ Here is a problem related to yours and solved before. Can you use it? Can you use its result? Can you use its method? Should you introduce some auxiliary element in order to make its use possible? ■ Can you restate the problem? Can you restate it still differently? Go back to definitions. ■ If you cannot solve the proposed problem, first try to solve some related problem. Can you imagine a more accessible related problem? A more general problem? A more special problem? An analogous problem? Can you solve a part of the problem? Keep only a part of the condition, drop the other part; how far is the unknown then determined, how can it vary? Can you derive something useful from the data? Can you think of other data appropriate to determine the unknown? Can you change the unknown or the data, or both if necessary, so that the new unknown data are nearer to each other? ■ Did you use all the data? Did you use the whole condition? Have you taken into account all essential notions involved in the problem?
Third *Carry out* your plan.	**3. Carry out the plan** ■ Carrying out your plan of the solution, check each step. Can you see clearly that the step is correct? Can you prove that it is correct?
Fourth *Examine* the solution obtained.	**4. Look back** ■ Can you check the result? Can you check the argument? ■ Can you derive the result differently? Can you see it at a glance? ■ Can you use the result, or the method, for some other problem?

Figure 17-2 Polya's framework of problem solving

thinking. It is important to note that these phases are not linear as a problem-solver may proceed from the first to the second, then return to the first to check for correctness of his understanding. A problem-solver may also proceed from the first to the second phase and on to the third before returning to the first again to clarify some doubts that may have surfaced due to the nature of the subsequent answers.

In *Mathematics Syllabus for Lower Secondary* (Ministry of Education, 2000), and *A Guide to Teaching and Learning of O-Level Mathematics 2007* (Ministry of Education, 2006), several suggestions are made for teachers regarding the four phases of problem solving and heuristics. A suggested guide for problem solving, which draws on both of the above resources is as follows.

Steps for Problem Solving

1. Understand the problem
- Look for information given
- Visualise the information
- Organise the information
  - *make a table*
- Connect the information

2. Devise a plan
- To make a representation
  - *draw a diagram*
  - *make a systematic list*
  - *use equations*
- To make a calculated guess
  - *guess and check*
  - *look for a pattern*
  - *make suppositions*
- To go through the process
  - *act it out*
  - *work backwards*
  - *before–after*
- To change the problem
  - *restate the problem*
  - *simplify the problem*
  - *solve part of the problem*

3. Carrying out the plan
- Use mathematical knowledge
- Use mathematical skills
- Use logical thinking

4. Look back (reflecting)
- Check solution – Is it reasonable?
- Improve on the method used
- Seek alternative solutions
- Extend the method to other problems

Some common heuristics used in problem solving at the secondary level

Draw a diagram

Using a diagram to model a situation or illustrate relationships in a problem is an effective way by which students clarify the problem and resolve it. The two examples that follow each show a different process that is being demonstrated by the drawings.

Example 1

At a party there are 10 people. If everyone at the party shakes hands with everyone else, how many handshakes would there be?

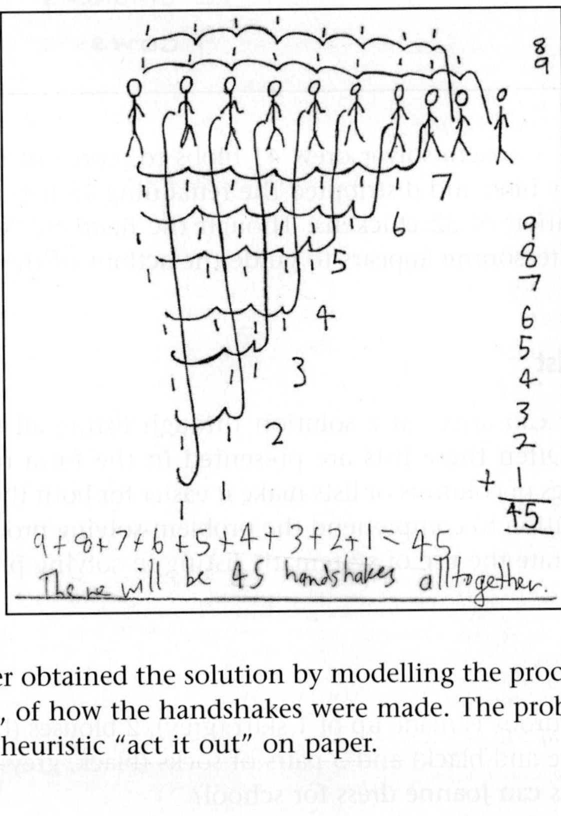

The problem-solver obtained the solution by modelling the process, on paper in the form of a diagram, of how the handshakes were made. The problem-solver has in a way executed the heuristic "act it out" on paper.

Example 2

On a farm there are cows and chickens. Altogether they have 41 heads and 100 legs. How many chickens are there?

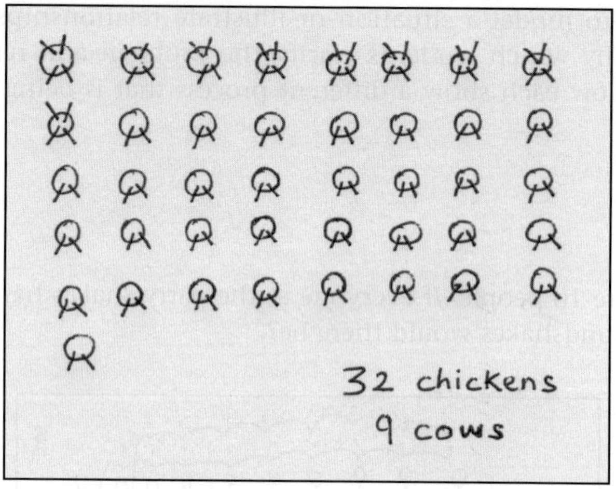

In this solution the problem-solver drew 41 blobs to represent the 41 animals. He stuck 2 legs to every blob and distributed the remaining 18 legs to 9 blobs, thereby arriving at the solution of 32 chickens. Though the heuristic "draw a diagram" is being used, logical reasoning appears to guide the actions of the problem-solver.

Make a systematic list

The problem-solver can arrive at a solution through listing all the possibilities in a systematic way. Often these lists are presented in the form of charts or tables. Appropriate headings of columns or lists make it easier for both the solver and others who review the solution to comprehend the problem-solving process. The following two examples illustrate the use of systematic listing in solving problems.

Example 3

Joanne's school wardrobe is made up of 1 skirt (grey), 2 blouses (blue and yellow), 2 pairs of shoes (white and black) and 3 pairs of socks (black, grey and blue). In how many different ways can Joanne dress for school?

Skirt	Blouse	Shoes	Socks
grey	blue	white	black
grey	blue	white	grey
grey	blue	white	blue
grey	blue	black	black
grey	blue	black	grey
grey	blue	black	blue
grey	yellow	white	black
grey	yellow	white	grey
grey	yellow	white	blue
grey	yellow	black	black
grey	yellow	black	grey
grey	yellow	black	blue

Through systematic listing it is found that Joanne can dress in 12 different ways for school.

Example 4

Ramli has 15 pebbles and he wishes to place them in 3 piles with an odd number of pebbles in each pile. In how many ways can he do it?

Pile 1	Pile 2	Pile 3
1	1	13
1	3	11
1	5	9
1	7	7
3	3	9
3	5	7
5	5	5

With the help of a systematic list it is found that Ramli can do it in 7 ways.

Guess-and-check

Guess-and-check, at times also known as "trial and error", is a very primitive heuristic. The simple idea of making a guess and checking it for correctness is always not a good means of arriving at a solution unless the guess leads to a better guess and ultimately the solution. There appears to be two types of guess-and-check: the systematic and the unsystematic. A systematic guess-and-check will steer the problem-solver to the solution after a few iterations while the unsystematic one will be a random journey which may or may not result in a solution. Shown below are an example each of systematic and unsystematic guess-and-check.

Example 5

On a farm there are cows and chickens. Altogether they have 41 heads and 100 legs. How many chickens are there?

a. Systematic guess-and-check
   The problem-solver keeps the number of animals constant and varies the number of cows and chickens to get a combination that gives 100 legs. His first attempt shows that the number of cows is larger than expected and so he systematically reduces the number of cows and increases the number of chickens accordingly and works towards the solution.

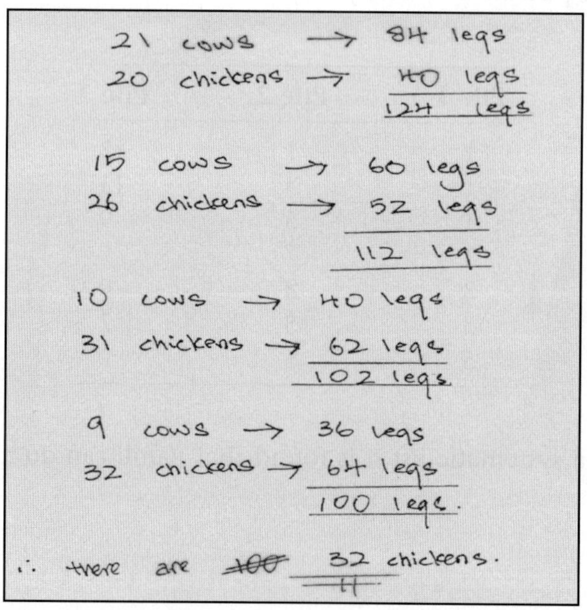

b. Unsystematic guess-and-check
The problem-solver makes a haphazard first attempt and gets 33 animals and 100 legs. She next manipulates the number of animals such that they total 41, and check for the number of legs. Her second attempt does not help to guide her subsequent attempts but she eventually arrived at the solution in her sixth attempt. Such an approach not only discourages productive thinking among the problem-solvers but also is very time-consuming and may lead to low morale amongst problem-solvers.

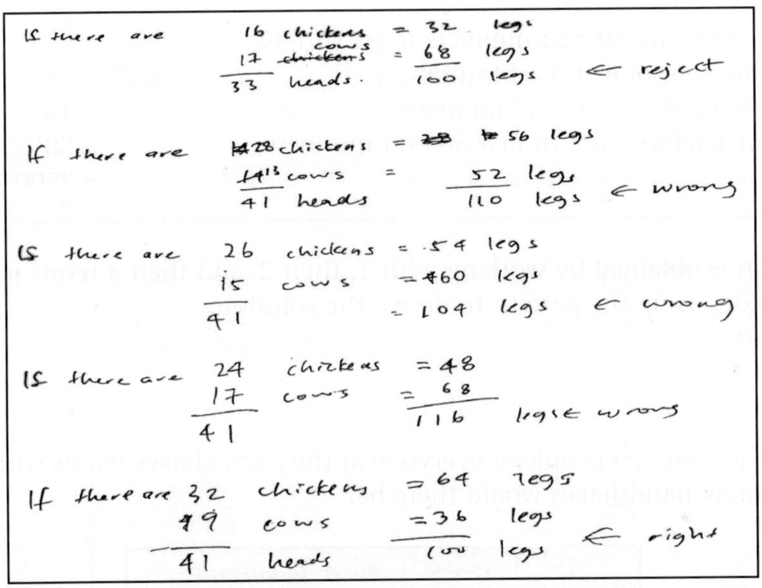
If there are 16 chickens = 32 legs
17 cows = 68 legs
33 heads. 100 legs ← reject

If there are 28 chickens = 56 legs
13 cows = 52 legs
41 heads 110 legs ← wrong

If there are 26 chickens = 54 legs
15 cows = 60 legs
41 = 104 legs ← wrong

If there are 24 chickens = 48
17 cows = 68
41 116 legs ← wrong

If there are 32 chickens = 64 legs
9 cows = 36 legs
41 heads 100 legs ← right

Look for a pattern

Mathematics is often known as the study of patterns. Looking for a pattern is a good problem-solving heuristic that enables one to reduce a complex problem to a pattern and then use the pattern to derive a solution. The two examples that follow show this heuristic at work.

Example 6

Find the sum of odd numbers from 1 to 99.

$1 + 3 + 5 + \ldots + 99 = ?$

$1 = 1 = 1^2$

$1 + 3 = 4 = 2^2$

$1 + 3 + 5 = 9 = 3^2$

There are 50 odd numbers from 1 to 99

So sum of first 5 odd numbers $= 25 = 5^2$

Sum of first 10 odd numbers $= 10^2$

Therefore, sum of first 50 odd numbers $= 50^2$

$= 2500$

The solution is obtained by working with 1, then 2, and then 3 terms to look for a pattern, before using the pattern to derive the solution.

Example 7

At a party there are ten people. If everyone at the party shakes hands with everyone else, how many handshakes would there be?

No. of people	No. of handshakes
2	1
3	3
4	6
5	10
⋮	⋮

A pattern is obtained.

$\frac{2(2-1)}{2} = 1.$

$\frac{3(3-1)}{2} = 3.$

$\frac{4(4-1)}{2} = 6.$

$\frac{5(5-1)}{2} = 10.$

$\therefore \frac{n(n-1)}{2}$ will be used to find out how many handshakes there would be.

$\therefore \frac{10(10-1)}{2} = 45.$

There would be 45 handshakes.

The solution is obtained by considering the number of handshakes if two, three, four or five people were at the party. The pattern obtained was generalised for n people at the party. The general form was finally used to find the number of handshakes if ten people were at the party.

Work backwards

As the name suggests this heuristic is used to work backwards from an endpoint of a situation to where it started. One of the most difficult parts of working backwards is keeping track of the information and organising it in a meaningful way. The following two examples illustrate the heuristic.

Example 8

Jane, Swee, Amina and Raj washed cars as part of their fund raising project on National Day. Jane washed twice as many cars as Swee. Swee washed 1 less than Amina. Amina washed 6 more than Raj. Raj washed 6 cars. How many cars did Jane wash?

Raj washed 6 cars.
Amina washed $6 + 6 = 12$ *cars.*
Swee washed $12 - 1 = 11$ *cars.*
Jane washed $2 \times 11 = 22$ *cars.*

The solution is obtained by working backwards, starting with Raj. Using the information given in the question and working backwards a step at a time, it was found that Jane washed 22 cars.

Example 9

A type of leaf growing on the surface of a pond covers twice as much of the pond surface every day, compared to the day before. If the water surface of a certain pond is completely covered by leaves on the 20th day, on what day was one-fourth of it covered?

20th day	*completely covered*
19th day	*half covered*
18th day	*one-fourth covered*

Working backwards, from the 20th day, it was found that on the 18th day one-fourth of the pond was covered.

Simplify the problem

This heuristic is also known as *Solve a Simpler Problem* or *Look at Simpler Cases*. It is a combination of sub-problems and patterns. The following two examples illustrate this heuristic.

Example 10

What is the sum of the first hundred whole numbers?

First break the problem into sub-problems.
Split the 100 numbers into groups of ten and compute the sum of each ten.
Do the first few and look for a pattern.

$1 + 2 + 3 + 4 + 5 + 6 + 7 + 8 + 9 + 10 = 55$
$11 + 12 + 13 + 14 + 15 + 16 + 17 + 18 + 19 + 20 = 155 = 100 + 55$
$21 + 22 + 23 + 24 + 25 + 26 + 27 + 28 + 29 + 30 = 255 = 200 + 55$

Can you see a pattern?

Therefore, the sum of the first hundred whole numbers
$= [55 \times 10 + (100 + 200 + 300 + 400 + 500 + 600 + 700 + 800 + 900)]$
$= 550 + 4500$
$= 5050$

Example 11

How many squares are there on a checker board?

A checker board has 8 squares on each side.

First break the problem into sub-problems.
Consider boards of sides 1, 2 and 3 squares and find the number of squares in each of them.

A board of side 1 square has only 1 square.

A board of side 2 squares has four 1 by 1 and one 2 by 2 squares, i.e. 5 squares.

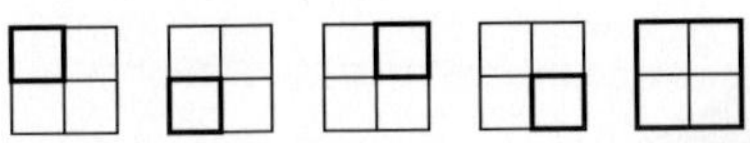

A board of side 3 squares has nine 1 by 1 squares, four 2 by 2 squares and one 3 by 3 square, i.e. 14 squares.

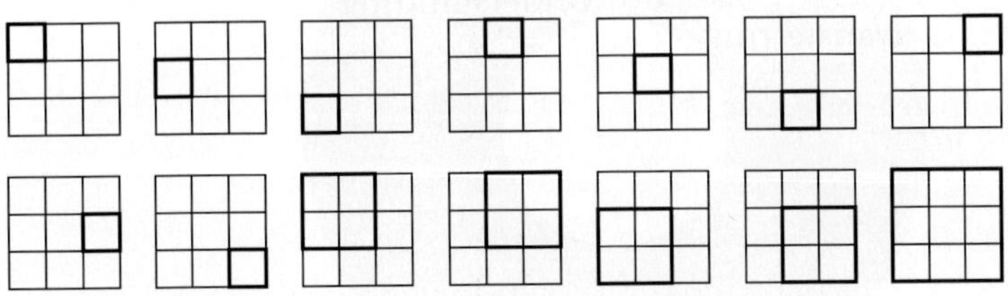

Can you see a pattern?

Size of board	Number of squares
1 by 1	$1 = 1^2$
2 by 2	$5 = 2^2 + 1^2$
3 by 3	$14 = 3^2 + 2^2 + 1^2$

Therefore, the number of squares on a checker board (8 by 8)
$= 8^2 + 7^2 + 6^2 + 5^2 + 4^2 + 3^2 + 2^2 + 1^2$
$= 204$

The above two examples show how a problem which may at first appear to be beyond resolution can be dealt with very systematically using the heuristic *Simplify the Problem,* which entails breaking the problem into sub-problems and looking for a pattern which in turn gives rise to the solution of the problem.

TYPES OF PROBLEM-SOLVING LESSONS

According to the teaching model (Ashlock, Johnson, Wilson, and Jones, 1983), shown in Figure 17-3, there are three phases in the teaching process. The first phase helps students develop an understanding of a concept or a skill. The second one provides students with opportunities to consolidate the concept or skill. The third provides opportunities for students to transfer their understanding to new situations. In this section, the focus is on lessons that concentrate on transfer. Problem solving involves students transferring their understanding of a concept or skill to familiar situations.

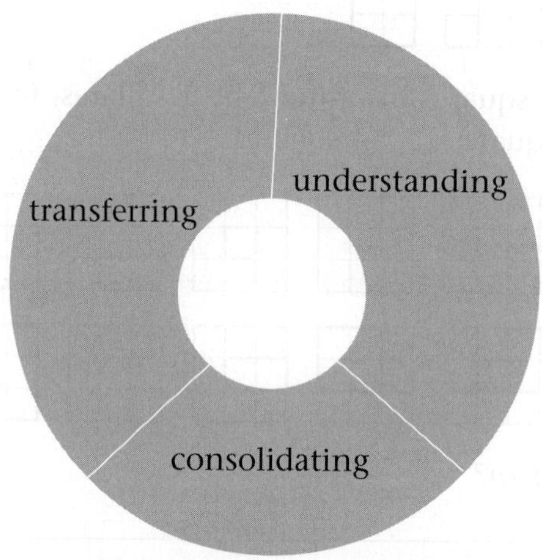

Figure 17-3 The teaching model

Three conceptions of problem-solving lessons will be discussed. The three conceptions are teaching through problem solving, teaching about problem solving, and teaching for problem solving. Three lessons are described to illustrate each of the conceptions.

Lesson I

Students were given a sheet containing several polygons as shown in Figure 17-4. The teacher asked the students to mark the interior angles of each polygon. The students were then required to find the fewest number of triangles that each polygon can be cut into. The solutions were then recorded in a table.

Number of sides	Number of triangles
4	2
5	3
6	4
8	6

The teacher then reminded the students of a well-known fact that the sum of interior angles of a triangle is 180°. The teacher then asked the students to use this fact to find the sum of interior angles in each of the polygon. Subsequently, students were led to make a generalisation to predict the number of triangles and, hence, the sum of angles in a 10-sided polygon and, finally, an *n*-sided polygon.

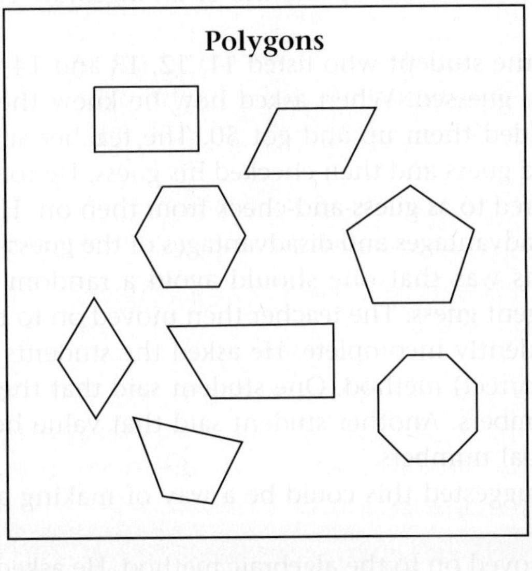

Figure 17-4 Polygon problem

In teaching through problem solving, problems are used to lead to the learning of a concept or skill. In Lesson 1, the Polygon Problem was used to lead students to a general method of finding the sum of interior angles in an *n*-sided polygon.

Lesson 2

The teacher posed a problem from the textbook and got a student to read the problem aloud.

> What are the four consecutive numbers whose sum is 50?
> Teh and Loh, 2007, p. 157

He then asked for someone to give examples of consecutive numbers. He also asked another student to explain the word "sum". Subsequently, he encouraged the students to solve the problem by thinking of a method that they would like to use and to try and use the method. He assured them that they could use any method.

After about ten minutes, the teacher selected a few responses and put them up on the board for a whole-class discussion. There was one response that merely listed four numbers, 11, 12, 13 and 14. Another response was to write a number sentence $50 \div 4$. Another uses a diagram, or commonly known as the "model" method. And there was one response that involved the use of an algebraic equation $a + b + c + d = 50$.

The teacher asked the student who listed 11, 12, 13 and 14 to tell what he did. He said that he simply guessed. When asked how he knew the guess was correct, the student said he added them up and got 50. The teacher summarised and said that the student made a guess and then checked his guess. He told the class that this method would be referred to as guess-and-check from then on. He then conducted a brief discussion on the advantages and disadvantages of the guess-and-check method. One of the conclusions was that one should avoid a random guess. Rather, one should make an intelligent guess. The teacher then moved on to the second method, $50 \div 4$, which was evidently incomplete. He asked the students to see the value of the incomplete (or incorrect) method. One student said that the answer 12.5 is the average of the four numbers. Another student said that value helped make a guess that is close to the actual numbers.

The teacher then suggested this could be a way of making an intelligent guess during guess-and-check.

The teacher then moved on to the algebraic method. He asked the students if the equation $a + b + c + d = 50$ is correct based on the information in the problem. The students concluded that although the equation was correct, it could not be solved because there were too many variables.

The teacher asked the students to consider the "model" method (Figure 17-5) that another student used.

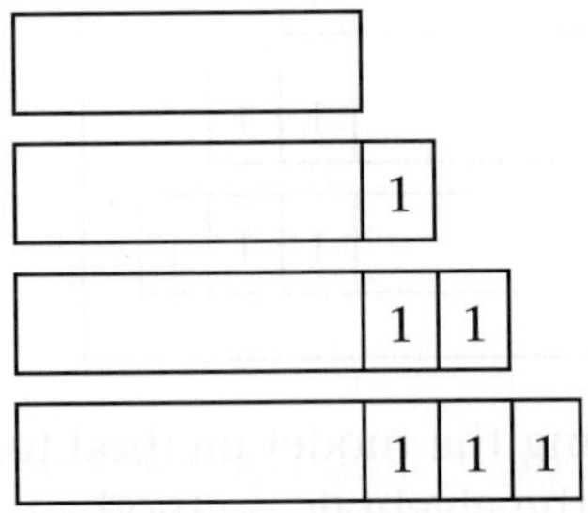

4 units → 50 – 6 = 44
1 unit → 11
The numbers are 11, 12, 13 and 14.

Figure 17-5 Model method

He asked the students to use the model to resolve the difficulty of having too many difficulties by suggesting that *a* could still represent the smallest number (Figure 17-6). The class then proceeded to construct a linear equation with one variable to solve the problem.

After solving this problem, the teacher asked each student to make up a similar problem where their friends need to find the unknown numbers given their sum. The students were asked how they could make sure they have found the correct set of numbers. It was not surprising that many of them said that they could simply check by adding up the numbers to see if the sum was the same as the one given in the problem.

The teacher ended the lesson by getting the students to name the methods that they have used to solve the problem. He also summarised the problem-solving process by indicating that when one solves a problem, one must understand the problem, plan the steps to be taken and look back to check after one has carried out the steps.

In this lesson, the focus is on the four-stage problem-solving process (Polya, 1973) and the different heuristics used to solve the problems. There was discussion on the types of heuristics and how to use them in a more efficient or elegant way. In teaching about problem solving, the focus is very much on the problem-solving process including the problem-solving heuristics and thinking habits rather than on the mathematical content.

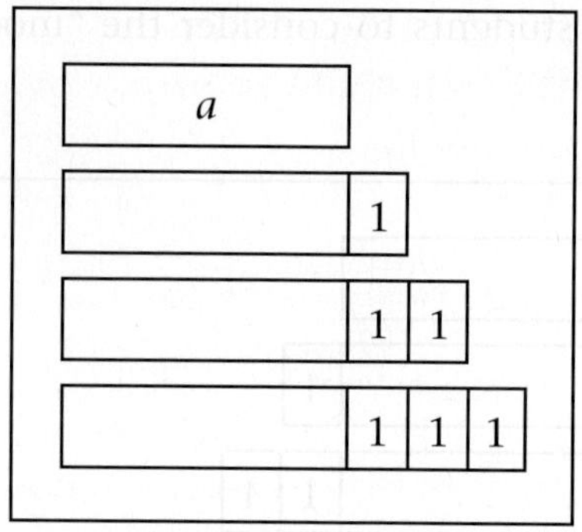

Figure 17-6 Using the model method to link to the algebraic method

Lesson 3

In teaching for problem solving, problem solving is preceded by the teaching of mathematics concepts or skills needed to solve the problems. For example, a teacher may spend a few lessons on vectors before presenting problems such as the one in Figure 17-5 to the students. It is often assumed that students are able to solve problems on, say, vectors, because they have been taught relevant concepts and skills required to solve the problem. In this conception of teaching problem solving, the content is taught for instrumental, relational and conventional understanding (Skemp, 1976) so that students are able to apply what they have been taught to problems associated with content. Students are provided with the problems and expected to transfer their understanding to the given situation.

After spending a few lesson on vectors where students were taught the concept of position vectors and the arithmetic of vectors, a teacher presented the fly and spider problem to the students.

Fly and spider problem

A fly, F, starts at the point with position vector (**i** + 12**j**) cm and crawls across the surface with a velocity of (3**i** + 2**j**) cm s^{-1}. At the instant that the fly starts crawling, a spider, S, at the point with position vector (85**i** + 5**j**) cm, sets off across the surface with a velocity of (–5**i** + k**j**) cm s^{-1}, where k is a constant. Given that the spider catches the fly, calculate the value of k.

Singapore Examinations and Assessment Board, 2005

As the students attempt to solve the problem, the teacher suggested that they sketch a diagram to help them picture the situation and, at some point, clarified the meaning of position vector.

STAGES IN A PROBLEM-SOLVING LESSON

Charles and Lester (1984) made several research-based practical suggestions in planning a problem-solving lesson. One of them is to plan for specific teaching actions before, during and after the solving of a given problem. The "before" stage refers to the time when the students discuss the given problem to understand it and to think about the strategies that could be used. The "during" phase refers to the time when the students are working on the problem solution individually or in groups. The "after" phase refers to the time when the students discuss their attempts at solving the given problem.

Charles and Lester (1984) suggested three teaching actions for the "before" stage. The first two teaching actions aim to get students to read and comprehend the problem. These include reading, or getting students to read, the problem, discussing words and phrases in the problem, as well as getting students to focus on important information in the problem. The third teaching action aims to get students to think of possible solution strategies. These teaching actions engage students in understanding the problem and planning a strategy.

Charles and Lester (1984) suggested four teaching actions for the "during" stage. One teaching action is to observe and question students to assess their strengths and difficulties in problem solving. The next section provides more details on the use of Newman's scheme (Newman, 1983) to assess students during the problem-solving process. The next two teaching actions aim to help students who experience blockage and to challenge those who have solved the problem faster than the rest of the students. The suggestions include providing hints in the first instance and giving problem extensions in the second. The other teaching action aims to get students to fit the solution into the problem situation. These teaching actions engage students in the carrying out of what they have planned to do. The teaching actions elicit both cognitive and metacognitive responses from the students. The teaching actions also help to provide students in a mixed-ability class with an appropriate level of challenge.

Charles and Lester (1984) suggested three teaching actions for the "after" stage. The teaching actions generally aim to help students learn about the problem-solving process. One set of teaching actions aims to help students know the various heuristics that could be used to solve the problem. Another aims for students to relate the current problem solved to previous ones to see problem structures. The last teaching action aims to emphasise any special features of the problem. These teaching actions engage students in looking back at and reflecting on what they have done, with the goal of helping them acquire some general problem-solving skills and habits.

In general, teachers use a combination of four instructional strategies to help students develop problem-solving ability. When students are new to problem solving, "modelling" is a useful strategy. Teachers using this strategy model by thinking aloud. For example, teachers may model reading techniques that can improve comprehension of the problem statement. Teachers may model metacognitive actions such as being aware that certain problem statements are difficult to comprehend, leading on to the cognitive strategies taken to overcome the difficulty.

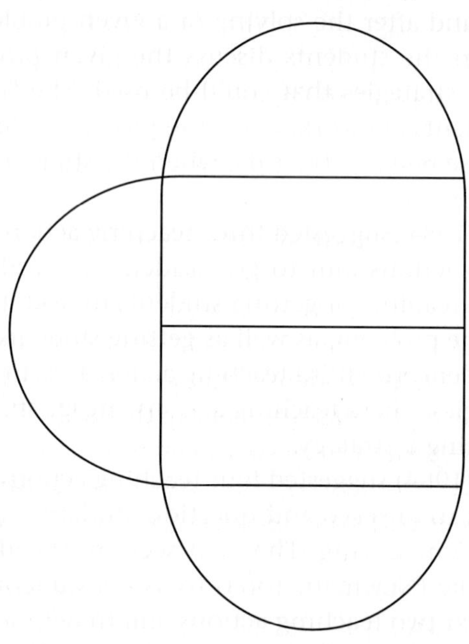

The figure comprises two identical rectangles and three identical semi-circles. The radius of the semicircle is 7 cm. Find the area of the figure.

Figure 17-7 Composite figure problem

Another instructional strategy that is useful to help students who are new to problem solving is "coaching". A teacher can use "coaching" to help students engage in visualisation in solving the composite figure problem shown in Figure 17-7. A teacher may say, "Look at a semicircle that is touching the length of the rectangle. The semi-circle and the rectangle share something in common." Or "Look at a semi-circle that is touching the width of the rectangle. Compare the width of the rectangle and the diameter of the semicircle." In coaching, teachers give instructions or ask questions to help students focus on one aspect of the problem.

These two instructional strategies complement another strategy that is commonly used in mathematics teaching – "explaining". In "explaining", teachers tell students the steps taken to solve a problem and the reasons behind the steps.

When students are more proficient in problem solving, a fourth instructional strategy, "providing", is used quite frequently. In "providing", teachers select suitable problems for students to solve independently. There is minimal modelling, coaching or explaining by the teacher.

At every stage in a problem-solving lesson, students may experience some difficulties. Newman (1983) suggested a useful scheme to help teachers identify students' difficulty during problem solving. According to this scheme, the difficulties could be in reading, comprehending, knowing strategies, transforming, carrying out procedures and making sense of the computation.

In a text-based problem, such as the fly and spider problem, a student may have difficulty reading or comprehending the text. Teachers can find out by asking the student to read and to answer some comprehension questions. Students with reading difficulties may not know how to read certain words. Students with comprehension difficulties may get many of the comprehension questions wrong.

Students who have no difficulty reading and comprehending the text may be unable to solve the problem because they do not know a suitable strategy to use. Teachers can find out by asking students what they want to do. Students who do not know any strategy may simply keep quiet or say that they do not have one. Students who do may say that they want to make a sketch or write a vector equation.

Another difficulty in problem solving is in transforming the situation into a mathematical model. Students who say that they want to write a vector equation may not be able to write the equation correctly or at all. They may lack the relational understanding that is necessary for the formulation of the vector equation. In this problem, students who are successful in transforming the situation into a mathematical model understand the meaning of position vector and its use in the identification of a location. These students are also able to interpret the idea of "the spider catches the fly" mathematically and construct the vector equation

$$\begin{pmatrix} 1 + 3t \\ 12 + 2t \end{pmatrix} = \begin{pmatrix} 85 - 5t \\ 5 + kt \end{pmatrix}$$

Another difficulty is in carrying out procedures. Some students may have difficulty solving the problem because they perform the procedure of solving vector equations wrongly. Otherwise, the values for t and k can be found easily.

In this problem, students are required to find the value of k. However, students can also be asked to find the position vector of the location where the spider catches the fly. Students who have difficulty making sense of the computation may give the value of k as the final solution. They could not make use of the value of k to obtain a solution.

FURTHER READING

Brown, S.I. (1990). *The art of problem posing.* Hillsdale, NJ: Lawrence Erlbaum.

Charles, R., & Lester, F. (1982). *Teaching problem solving – What, why & how.* London: Edward Arnold.

Charles, R., Lester, F., & O'Daffer P.G. (1987). *How to evaluate progress in problem solving.* Reston, VA: National Council of Teachers of Mathematics.

Halmos, P.R. (1991). *Problems for mathematicians, young and old.* Washington, DC: The Mathematical Association of America.

Herr, T., & Johnson, K. (1994). *Problem solving strategies: Crossing the river with dogs and other mathematical adventures.* (Text and Teachers' Resource). Emeryville, CA: Key Curriculum Press.

Krulik, S., & Reys, R.E. (Eds). (1980). *Problem solving in school mathematics.* Reston, VA: National Council of Teachers of Mathematics.

Krulik, S., & Rudnick, J.A. (1987). *Problem solving: A handbook for teachers.* (2nd ed.). Boston, MA: Allyn and Bacon.

Lenchner, G. (1983). *Creative problem solving in school mathematics.* Boston, MA: Houghton Mifflin.

Mason, J., Burton, L., & Stacey, K. (1985). *Thinking mathematically.* Wokingham, England: Addison-Wesley.

Morris, J. (1981). *How to develop problem solving using a calculator.* Reston, VA: National Council of Teachers of Mathematics.

O'Daffer, P.G. (Ed.). (1988). *Problem solving tips for teachers.* Reston, VA: National Council of Teachers of Mathematics.

Schoenfeld, A.H. (1985). *Mathematical problem solving.* FL: Academic Press.

Stacey, K., & Groves, S. (1990). *Strategies for problem solving.* Glen Waverley, Victoria: Latitude Publications.

REFERENCES

Ashlock, R.B., Johnson, M.L., Wilson, W.L., & Jones, W.L. (1983). *Guiding each child's learning of mathematics.* Columbus, OH: Charles E. Merill Publishing Company.

Charles, R.I., & Lester, F.K. (1984). *Problem solving: What, why and how?* Palo Alto, CA: Dale Seymour.

Cockcroft Report. (1982). *Mathematics counts.* London: Her Majesty's Stationary Office.

Ministry of Education. (1990). *Mathematics syllabus – Lower secondary.* Singapore: Ministry of Education, Curriculum Planning & Development Division.

Ministry of Education. (2000). *Mathematics syllabus – Lower secondary.* Singapore: Ministry of Education, Curriculum Planning & Development Division.

Ministry of Education. (2006). *A guide to teaching and learning of O-level mathematics 2007*. Singapore: Ministry of Education, Curriculum Planning & Development Division.

National Council of Teachers of Mathematics. (1989). *Principles and standards for school mathematics*. Reston, VA: National Council of Teachers of Mathematics.

Newman, A. (1983). *The Newman language of mathematics kit – Strategies for diagnosis and remediation*. Sydney. Australia: Harcourt Brace Jovanovich Group.

Polya, G. (1973). *How to solve it*. Princeton, NJ: Princeton University Press.

Singapore Examinations and Assessment Board. (2005). *Additional Mathematics Paper One*. Singapore: Dyna Publisher.

Skemp, R. (1976). Relational understanding and instrumental understanding. *Mathematics Teaching*, 77, 20–26.

Teh, K.S., & Loh, C.Y. (2007). *New syllabus mathematics 1* (6th ed.). Singapore: Shing Lee.

APPENDIX: A COLLECTION OF PROBLEMS

1. There are eight people in a room. Each person shakes hands with each of the other people once and only once. How many handshakes are there?

2. A bus from Singapore to Kuala Lumpur averages 80 km per hour. On its return trip from Kuala Lumpur to Singapore, it averages 100 km per hour. What is its average speed for the entire round trip?

3. A farmer has some cows and some chickens. He finds that together they have 70 heads and 200 legs. How many cows and how many chickens does he have?

4. How many squares are there on a standard (8×8) chessboard?

5. The Tans are having a party. The first time the doorbell rings, a guest enters. On the second ring, three guests enter. On the third ring, five guests enter, and so on. That is, on each successive ring, the entering group is two guests larger than the preceding group. How many guests will enter on the 15th ring? How many guests will be present after the 15th ring?

6. Find all rectangles with integral sides whose area and perimeter are numerically equal.

7. A new school has exactly 1,000 lockers and exactly 1,000 students. On the first day of school, the students meet outside the building and agree on the following plan: The first student will enter the school and open all of the lockers. The second student will then enter the school and close every locker with an even number (2, 4, 6, 8, etc.). The third student will then "reverse" every third locker. That is, if the locker is closed, he will open it; if the locker is open, he will close it. The fourth student will reverse every fourth locker, and so on until all 1,000 students in turn have entered the building and reversed the proper lockers. Which lockers will finally remain open?

8. In the "equation", $(he)^2 = she$, the letters represent digits and the configurations represent numerals in base 10. Find replacements for the letters that make the statement true.

9. a. Into how many different plane regions do n lines, no three of which are concurrent and none of which are parallel, separate the plane?
   b. What is the maximum number of regions into which n chords divide a circle?

10. The planet Klepton has only two types of creatures:

    Triads with 3 legs and Tetrads with 4 legs.

    Astronaut Janice could not bear to look at these ugly creatures and so she keeps her eyes on the ground so she would only see their legs. On her first day on Klepton, she sees some creatures and counts 31 legs.
    How many Triads and Tetrads has she seen?

11. A man takes a 5,000-km trip in his car. He rotates his tyres (four on the car and one spare) so that at the end of the trip each tyre has been used for the same number of kilometres. How many kilometres are covered on each tyre?

12. In a certain family, a boy has as many sisters as he has brothers. However, each sister has only one-half as many sisters as brothers. How many brothers and sisters are there in this family?

13. A curious biological fact is that a male bee has only one parent, a mother, whereas a female bee has both a mother and a father. How many second-generation ancestors (grandparents) does the male bee have? Third-generation ancestors (great-grandparents)? Fourth? Fifth? Tenth?

14. It costs to cut and weld a chain link. What is the minimum number of cuts needed to make a single chain from seven individual links?

15. How many triangles are there in the figure on the right?

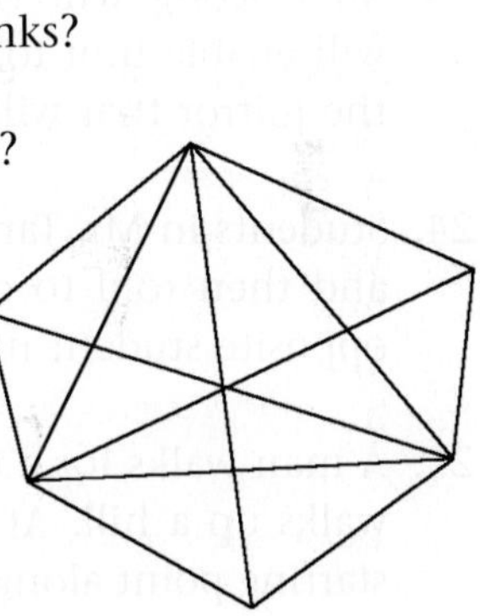

16. Karen has to number the 396 pages in her biology note-book. How many digits will she have to write?

17. Jeff and Mike breed tropical fish. Mike decides to abandon the hobby and give his fish away. First he gives half of them and half a fish more to Scott. Then he gives half of what is left and half a fish more to Billy. That leaves Mike with only one fish, which he gives to Jeff. How many fish did Mike start with?

18. To hang a picture on a bulletin board, Jim uses four thumb-tacks, one in each corner. If he overlaps the corners, Jim can hang two pictures with only six tacks. What is the minimum number of tacks Jim needs to hang six pictures?

19. A textbook is opened at random. To what pages is it opened if the product of the facing page numbers is 3192?

20. Remove

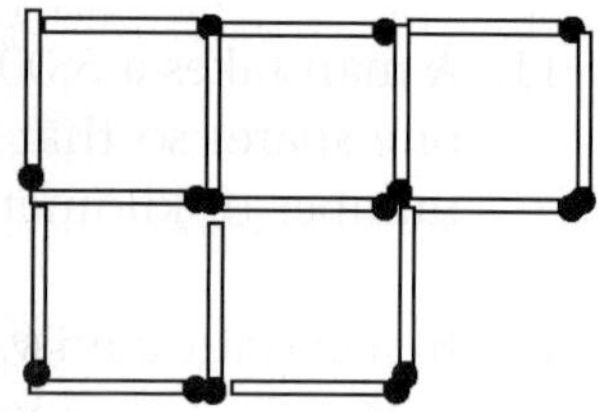

a. one match stick so that only four squares remain.
b. two match sticks so that only three squares remain.
c. three match sticks so that only three squares remain.
d. four match sticks so that only two squares remain.
e. five match sticks so that only three squares remain.

21. Tennis balls are packed in cylindrical cans of three. The balls just touch the sides, top and bottom of the can. How does the height of the can compare with the circumference of the top? What is the ratio of the volume of a ball to that of the can?

22. Find the last three digits of 1995^{1995}.

23. Mr. Cheong, who is 6 feet tall, wants to install a mirror on his bedroom wall that will enable him to see a full view of himself. What is the minimum length of the mirror that will serve his needs, and how should it be placed on his wall?

24. Students in Mr. Tan's physical education class are spaced evenly around a circle and then told to count off beginning with 1. Student number 16 is directly opposite student number 47. How many students are there in Mr. Tan's class?

25. A man walks for a total of five hours. First he walks along a level road, then he walks up a hill. At the top of the hill, he turns around and walks back to his starting point along the same route. Uphill, he walks at 3 km per hour; downhill he walks at 6 km per hour. On the level road, he walks at 4 km per hour. How far did the man walk?

26. The sum of two numbers is 2, and the product of these same numbers is 3. Find the sum of their reciprocals.

27. Two circles are concentric. The tangent to the inner circle forms a chord of 12 cm in the larger circle. Find the area of the "ring" between the two circles.

28. The total number of angles in two regular polygons is 13, while the total number of diagonals is 25. How many angles are there in each of the polygons?

29. A standard deck of playing cards contains 26 black cards and 26 red cards, or 52 cards in all. A deck is randomly divided into two unequal piles, such that the probability of drawing a red card from the small pile is $\frac{1}{3}$. At the same time, the probability of drawing a black card from the larger pile is $\frac{5}{14}$. How many cards are in the larger pile?

30. A wealthy philanthropist sets aside a certain amount of money to be distributed equally among the needy at a shelter each week. One week, he remarked, "If there are five fewer of you here next week, each will receive twenty dollars more." Unfortunately, instead of being fewer, there were actually four more people present the following week, and each received ten dollars less. How much does the philanthropist set aside each week?

31. Two towns lie to the south of a straight road, but they are neither connected to it, nor to one another. The citizens of the two towns decide to build two roads, one from each town, to the existing road. They are cost conscious in the choice of the roads. Find the shortest route connecting the two towns via the existing road.

32. A goat is tethered to a corner of a hut in the middle of a large field of grass. If the hut is rectangular, with dimensions 3 metres by 5 metres and the length of the tether is 2 metres, then on what area of grass can the goat graze?

33. A rectangle 4 by 3 has six squares passed through by a diagonal (see figure). Find the number of squares passed through by a diagonal for a rectangle of size m by n.

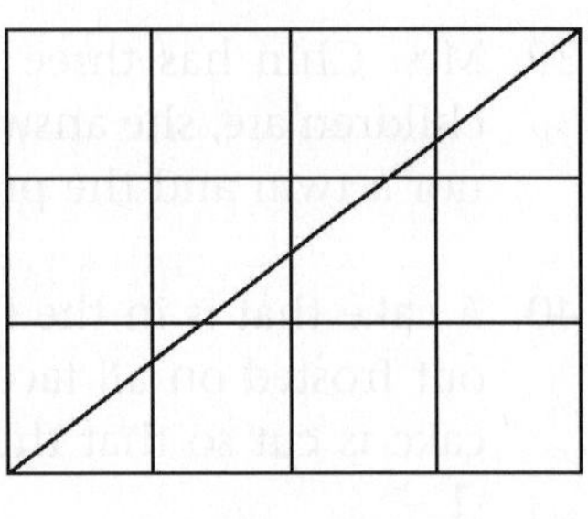

34. Sixty-four small cubes are assembled to form a large cube. The face of the large cube is then painted. How many of the small cubes are untouched by paint? How many of the small cubes have (a) one face, (b) two faces, and (c) three faces painted?

35. Five women are seated around a circular table. Mrs. Ong is sitting between Mrs. Lim and Miss Mah. Ellen is sitting between Cathy and Mrs. Ng. Mrs. Lim is between Ellen and Alice. Cathy and Doris are sisters. Betty is seated with Mrs. Png on her left and Miss Mah on her right. Match the names with the surnames.

36. The security guard at a bank caught a bank robber. The robber, the teller and a witness were arguing when the police arrived. This is what the police learned in the confusion.
    a. The names of the three men are Lee, Kim and Wong.
    b. Lee is the oldest of the three.
    c. The teller and Kim have been friends for many years.
    d. Lee is the brother-in-law of the witness.
    e. Wong completed secondary school education five years earlier than the robber.

    Who is the robber? Who is the teller? Who is the witness?

37. A lizard is at one ceiling corner of a rectangular room of dimensions 8 metres by 5 metres by 4 metres. Find the shortest path that the lizard can move from the ceiling corner A to the opposite floor corner B.

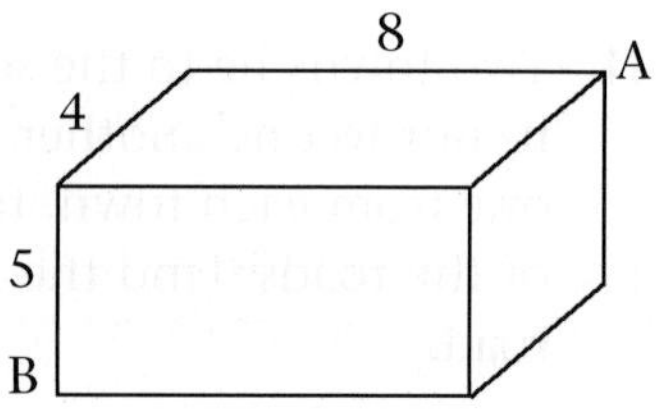

38. Three cylindrical oil drums of 2-metre diameter are to be securely fastened in the form of a "triangle" by a steel band. What length of band will be required?

39. Mrs. Chin has three children, two of them twins. When asked how old her children are, she answers with this riddle: "The youngest is neither one year old nor a twin and the product of their ages is 144." Find their ages.

40. A cake that is in the form of a cube falls into a large vat of frosting and comes out frosted on all faces. The cake is cut into small cubes of the same size. The cake is cut so that the number of pieces having frosting on three faces will be $\frac{1}{8}$ the number of pieces having no frosting at all. Find the total number of small cubes.

41. An alphametic is a mathematical puzzle where letters of the alphabet stand for digits of numbers and make meaningful words. Solve the following alphametic:

$$\begin{array}{r} \text{SEND} \\ +\ \text{MORE} \\ \hline \text{MONEY} \end{array}$$

42. If a hen and a half lay an egg and a half in a day and a half, how many hens are needed to lay a dozen eggs in one day?

43. After gathering a pile of coconuts one day, three sailors on a deserted island agreed to divide the coconuts evenly after a night's rest. During the night, one sailor got up, divided the coconuts into three equal piles with a remainder of one, which he tossed to a monkey that was conveniently near by, and, secreting his pile, mixed up the others and went back to sleep. The second sailor did the same thing, and so did the third. In the morning, the remaining pile of coconuts (less one) is again divisible by 3. What is the smallest number of coconuts that the original pile could have contained?

44. A palindrome is a number that reads the same backwards as forwards. How many 4-digit palindromes are there? Show that all 4-digit palindromes are divisible by 11.

45. Twelve golf balls appear identical but 11 weigh exactly the same while 1 ball is either lighter or heavier than the others. Determine the odd ball and whether it is lighter or heavier than the others in as few weighing of the balls on a balance as possible.

Chapter

18

Preparation of Schemes of Work and Lesson Plans

Lee Ngan Hoe

The mathematics syllabus is usually structured in units. The units can have themes and vice-versa, but they include many topics that are united by a common thread. The sequencing of the units is referred to as the scheme of work, while the units, which may involve work for days or weeks, are sub-divided into daily lesson plans.

SCHEME OF WORK

The scheme of work should serve as a blueprint for teachers to implement the mathematics instructional programme of the school. It should provide:

- continuity of progress in both syllabus content and approach,
- guidance on the approaches and resources to be used in the teaching of particular topics,
- examples on the type of work to be set for
  - consolidation of concepts,
  - increasing facility in computation,
  - developing problem-solving ability, and
- guidance on assessment and record keeping.

In preparing the scheme of work, the teacher should consider:

- the students' abilities,
- the students' experiences and interests,
- the link between mathematical concepts and syllabus requirements,
- materials and resources required,
- allocation of time to particular topics,
- formative and summative assessment, and
- diagnostic and remedial teaching.

LESSON PLANS

Lesson plans are written by teachers to help them structure the learning for themselves and for the students. Research shows that all students benefit from and appreciate well-structured lessons.

Furthermore, lesson planning enables the teacher to:

- establish specific goals and to ensure that essential concepts, skills and processes will be included,
- allow the work to be taught in a logical sequence and in feasible periods of time,
- have the lesson appropriately structured so that the opening will be interesting, the main body will be properly paced and the closure will highlight the key points,
- ensure that students are on task throughout the lesson,
- avoid omissions, mistakes and unnecessary repetition, while ensuring necessary reinforcement and consolidation during review and practice, and
- have a feeling of confidence and security.

In planning a lesson, the teacher should

- determine the specific instructional objective(s) of the lesson. A good specific instructional objective should include the four components: the targeted *audience*, the expected *behaviour* to be observed at the end of the lesson, the *condition* under which such behaviour is to be demonstrated, and the *degree* of performance of such behaviour,
- conduct a task analysis of the topic. A task analysis, the *identification* and subsequent *sequencing* of the *sub-skills* in an instructional objective, helps the teacher to identify the appropriate instructional sequence and select appropriate practice activities,
- identify the materials and resources required,
- determine the teaching strategies and time allocation for each part of the lesson,
- decide how students will be organised, and
- decide how the lesson will be evaluated.

Lesson plans are not written for teachers to read to the class. Lesson plans help teachers to structure and ensure smooth flow of the lessons, especially when something has occurred to distract everyone, including the teacher.

Thinking parts

Lesson plans involve thinking. This thinking process can be classified into four parts.

First, the teacher determines the curriculum; that is, what the children will learn, and what they will be able to do at the end of the lesson.

Secondly, the teacher determines what the students already know, before the beginning of the lesson, that can lead into the new curriculum of the day.

Thirdly, the teacher determines at least one way to assist the students in learning the new curriculum.

Fourthly, the teacher determines at least one way to evaluate the learning outcomes of the students.

Written format

There are many different formats that are being used by teachers to write daily lesson plans. The most useful ones are those that are very easy to follow and are well structured.

The following is one suggested format for writing daily lesson plans.

Teacher ____________________________

Subject ____________________________

Level/Class ____________________________

Date ____________________________

Time ____________________________

Duration ____________________________

i. Content
Indicate what you intend to teach, and identify which forms of knowledge (concept, academic rule, skill, law and law-like principles and/or value knowledge) will be included in the lesson.

ii. Specific instructional objective
Indicate specifically what the students will be able to do upon completing the lesson, and thus what will be evaluated as a result.

iii. Prerequisites
Indicate what the students must already know or be able to do in order to be successful with this lesson (you would want to list one or two specific behaviours necessary to begin this lesson).

iv. Instructional procedures
Description of what you will do in teaching the lesson, and, as appropriate, includes a description of how you will introduce the lesson to the students, what actual instructional techniques you will use, and how you will bring closure to the lesson. Include what specific things students will actually do during the lesson.

Teaching/Learning activities	Materials	Time
Introduction The introduction could begin with an assessment of students' mastery of the prerequisites, or an interesting problem that could be solved by the concepts to be learned in the lesson. It could also begin with an interesting story or situation involving the concepts to be learned. **Development** This is the heart of the lesson where the concept(s) are developed and explained, where the activities which lead to learning are carried out. Major questions which lead to the concept or which check for understanding and important points to make should be recorded. **Consolidation** Class work can be included here for consolidation and practice. In mathematics, it is particularly important that students be given opportunity to internalise the new concept through applying it to problems. Teachers need to show how to apply concepts in a range of problems related to the concepts. Teachers are to first model how problems are to be tackled and solutions to be presented. This is followed by some guided practice whereby teachers provide prompts to guide students through the process. The modelling and guided practice will familiarise students with the necessary heuristics and expectations to handle independent practices. **Closure** The teacher can summarise the main ideas, set homework* or prepare students for the next lesson, such as a follow-up activity which indicates how other activities/materials will be used to reinforce and extend this lesson.		

* See Homework assignment on p. 342.

v. Materials and equipment
List all materials and equipment to be used by both the teacher and learner and how they will be used.

vi. Extra material
Extra material may include enrichment or additional exercises to fill up the time in case you have under-planned. However, new teachers usually tend to over-plan and put too much into the time given.

vii. Self-assessment (to be completed after the lesson is presented)
Address the major components of the lesson plan, focusing on both the strengths and areas of needed improvement. A good idea is to analyse the difference between what you want (the objective) and what is attained (the results of the assessment).

Homework assignment

- Problems given for homework should be carefully chosen to provide practice for consolidation. These should be planned along with the lesson and is directly connected to the behaviour called for in the instructional objective.

- Although challenging problems can be assigned for strong students, teachers should take care that weaker students should be able to cope with a great portion if not all of the homework assignment.

- It is good practice for teachers to work out similar examples during class before assigning such problems as homework.

The homework is for the students to practise and provide feedback as to the students' understanding of the lesson. Teaching the curriculum should be the job of teachers, not the job of parents and private tutors.

Mistakes in lesson planning

The following are common mistakes made in lesson planning:

- The objective of the lesson does not specify what the student will actually do that can be observed.

- The lesson assessment is disconnected from the behaviour indicated in the objective.
- The materials specified in the lesson are extraneous to the actual described learning activities.
- The instruction in which the teacher engages is not efficient for the level of intended student learning.
- The student activities described in the lesson plan do not contribute in a direct and effective way to the lesson objective.

A lesson plan that contains one or more of these mistakes needs rethinking and revision.

A SAMPLE CHECKLIST FOR WRITING LESSON PLANS

Stage	Component	Check	Component	Check
Curriculum	Objective(s) is/are realistic and measurable	☐		
Prerequisite(s)	Identified through task analysis	☐		
Introduction	Assess students' mastery of prerequisites or use motivational materials to set the stage for learning	☐	Include exact examples and non-examples to be used	☐
Development	Determine at least one way to assist the students in learning the new curriculum	☐	Include questions prompts that are to be used to lead and guide students along	☐

Stage	Component	Check	Component	Check
Consolidation	Teacher modelling → Guided practice → Independent practice	☐	Include sample expected students' response, including response that may arise out of misconception	☐
Closure	Summary of lesson, set homework that is aligned with the lesson objectives, and possibly assign follow-up activity to set the stage for next lesson	☐		

SUMMARY

Lesson plans can include much more than indicated here. For example, materials needed, assessments, evaluation procedures, etc. The information given here is meant to provide a quick and efficient yet effective way to develop daily lesson plans. Notice that the thinking and mental structuring parts of lesson plans are completed before the written format is begun.

It is very important that the exact examples needed are actually written in the lesson plan. This is important for several reasons. Poorly selected examples and non-examples that are given to students can be confusing, and can actually lead students to false conclusions that the teacher never intended.

Remember to always write the exact examples and non-examples in the lesson plan. This gives the teacher a quick reference whenever he or she loses her place or train of thought due to any reason. Citing of poor examples due to bad or insufficient planning can also be avoided in this way.

Of course, there is an immense difference between being able to plan and actually being able to carry out the plan. However, if you have thought carefully about where you are going before you begin writing your plan, the chances of your success, as well as the success of your students, are much greater.

APPENDIX 18A1: SAMPLE SCHEME OF WORK – SECONDARY 1 EXPRESS

Week	Topic	Specific instructional objectives	Exer.	Maths communication	Maths investigation	Problem solving	NE	IT	Resources
Term 1 1 & 2	Chapter 1 Whole Numbers	■ State the different types of numbers: natural numbers, whole numbers, even and odd numbers.	1a	Pg 2, 3, 7 Pg 13 (text)	Pg 12, 16 19	Pg 11, 20 23	Pg 5 (Ex. 1a, q1)	Website address (refer to TRM)	Textbook
		■ Differentiate the various types of numbers and classify them accurately.	1a		Pg 13 (text)		pg 18 (Ex. 1h, q5)		
		■ Use the number line to represent the different types of numbers and order them.							
		■ Use the symbols =, ≠, >, <, ≤ and ≥ correctly.							
		■ Identify place value of any digit in a given whole number.							

- Perform addition, subtraction, multiplication and division of whole numbers.
- State and use the three arithmetic properties: commutative, associative, distributive.
- Perform mental calculation.
- State the order of operations involving brackets and calculations involving the four basic operations.
- Round off a whole number to a specific degree of accuracy.
- Use the relevant keys of a calculator to perform operations on whole numbers.
- Make estimates of results of calculations.

Legend: Pg – Page; 1a, q1 – Exercise (a), Question (1); and TRM: Teachers' Resource Manual.

APPENDIX 18B: SAMPLE SCHEME OF WORK – SECONDARY 2 NORMAL (ACADEMIC)

Topic	Time	Specific instructional objectives	Exercises	Initiatives suggested
Chapter 1 Ratio, Proportion, Percentages, Simple Financial Transactions and Standard Form	3 weeks	By the end of the unit, the students will be able to:		
		1.1 (a) use a ratio to compare two quantities (b) write a ratio as a fraction (c) write a ratio in its simplest form (d) write the ratio of the two measurements (e) solve word problems involving ratio	Ex.1A	NE: Cost of Desalination
		1.2 (a) solve word problems involving direct proportion (b) solve word problems involving inverse proportion	Ex. 1B	
		1.3 (a) calculate the actual distance between two places on a map, given its scale (b) calculate the distance on a map, given the scale and actual distance (c) find the scale of a scale drawing	Ex. 1C	
		1.4 convert one currency to another	Ex. 1D	IT: DMS – The Business of Graphs B(CD-ROM)
		1.5 (a) express a percentage as a fraction or decimal (b) express a decimal or fraction as a percentage and express the number in words (c) express a quantity as a percentage of another (d) find the value of a percentage of a quantity	Ex. 1E	

1.6 (a) solve word problems involving profit, percentage profit loss, percentage loss.	Ex. 1F & 1G	
(b) solve problems involving discount	Ex. 1H	
(c) solve problems involving commission	Ex. 1I	
(d) use the simple interest formula I = PRT/100 to solve problems	Ex. 1J	
(e) solve problems involving simple interest and compound interest	Ex. 1K	
(f) solve problems involving hire purchase	Ex. 1L	
(g) solve problems involving taxation and service charge	Ex. 1M	IT: Road Tax Charges (surf the Web)
1.7 Express numbers in standard form and vice-versa	Ex. 1N	TS: Induction NE: CPF

Legend: TS – Thinking skills; NE – National Education; DMS – Dynamic Maths Series; and CPF – Central Provident Fund.

APPENDIX 18C: SAMPLE LESSON PLAN

Topic:	2-D Cartesian plane	Unit:	Straight line graphs
Class:	Secondary 2C2 (Express)	Date:	____________
Time:	35 minutes (1 period)		

Prerequisite knowledge:

a. Students are able to mark numbers (including negative numbers) on a number line.
b. Students have encountered map reading in social studies or geography.

Objectives:
At the end of the lesson, students should be able to:

a. State the Cartesian coordinates of points marked on the 2-D Cartesian plane.
b. Mark points on the 2-D Cartesian plane, given the Cartesian coordinates.
c. Interpret the x- and y-coordinates as the perpendicular distances of the point from the y- and x-axes respectively.
d. Interpret points with the same x-coordinates lying on a vertical line and points with the same y-coordinates lying on the same horizontal line.

Key concepts: Cartesian coordinates of points, the 2-D Cartesian plane

Procedure:

Teaching /Learning activities	Materials	Time
Introduction (Game of location) The students are seated in 6 rows of six or seven students each. Explain that the rows will be numbered 1 to 6 and the students of each row 1 to 7. The teacher has two stacks of cards, one with cards numbered 1 to 6 for the rows and the other with cards numbered 1 to 7 for the students. Draw on the board a table with three columns labelled Row No., Student No. and Student with a fourth column blank. The teacher picks up one card from each pile and announces, say, Row 4, Student 6. She explains that the sixth student (from the front) in the fourth row must stand up and announce the two numbers as a pair, that is, 4, 6. The teacher will fill in the two numbers in the table on the board and write the student's name. After calling three or four students, she will tell the class that instead of saying row and student, it can write as a short form a pair of numbers enclosed in brackets. She fills in Column 4 with the ordered pairs, for example, (2, 4) and say "Will the student stand up?" Ask the following questions: ▪ "Do the two pairs (2, 4) and (4, 2) identify the same student?" ▪ "If all of you change desks for tomorrow's lesson, will the pair (2, 4) still be called (2, 4)? So the pair identifies the location, not the student." ▪ "If I give you a pair of numbers, will there be any ambiguity as to who will stand up?" (This is to bring out the idea of unique identification of location.)	Number cards, board	10 min

Teaching /Learning activities	Materials	Time
Development Using a projector, show transparency 1 of the school's location and landmarks around it on a white board. Tell the students to imagine they have a robot bird which can only fly in the directions of north, south, east and west but it has to fly in the east or west directions before north or south directions. How would they direct the bird to fly to the various locations from the school? Let several students try the various locations. For example, fly 1 km west and 0.5 km north. Let students see that it is difficult to gauge the distances. Now show overlay with the axes marked in where the school is located at the origin. Tell students that the axes are like two number lines with north and east being the positive directions and south and west negative directions. Now ask the students to specify the locations again but to use positive and negative directions instead of the N, S, E, W directions. Ask questions like "Will the bird get lost?" to emphasise the uniqueness of the point identified. Emphasise the importance of order and that the location of a point can be expressed as an ordered pair. Show the students that the first number tells how far the point is from the vertical axis and the second from the horizontal axis. This means we are actually moving along the horizontal axis and then up or down. Emphasise again that the two numbers given in brackets give the location of the point. Tell them these are called Cartesian coordinates. From the overlay, tell the names of the two axes as *x*- and *y*-axes and the coordinates *x*- and *y*-coordinates.	OHT 1 white board	10 min

Teaching /Learning activities	Materials	Time
Consolidation Project transparency 2 of the Cartesian plane on the white board and show how to mark a point (–3, –2) by moving left by 3 from origin and moving down by 2. Get the students to mark in the points with a cross (or using the magnetic buttons). They should put the coordinates next to the point. (2, 3), (3, –1), (–2, 4), (–2, –1), (2, –0.5), (3, –4). Mark in some points (–1.5, 4), (–3, –2.5) on the board and get the students to give the coordinates. Now mark in (3, 0) and ask them what the coordinates of the point marked are. Repeat with (0, –1). Ask them what they think the coordinates of the origin are. Using magnetic buttons of the same colour, put them on points with the same *x*-coordinate and ask the students what they have noticed (they have the same *x*-coordinate, they lie in a vertical line). Similarly for the *y*-coordinate.	White board, OHT2; markers (or magnetic mark buttons to the points)	10 min
Closure Recap the concepts of 2-D Cartesian coordinates and how they help us to locate points on the 2-D plane. Tell the class to bring graph paper for the next lesson. Give out worksheets for homework. If there is time, let the students begin on their homework.		5 min

Evaluation:

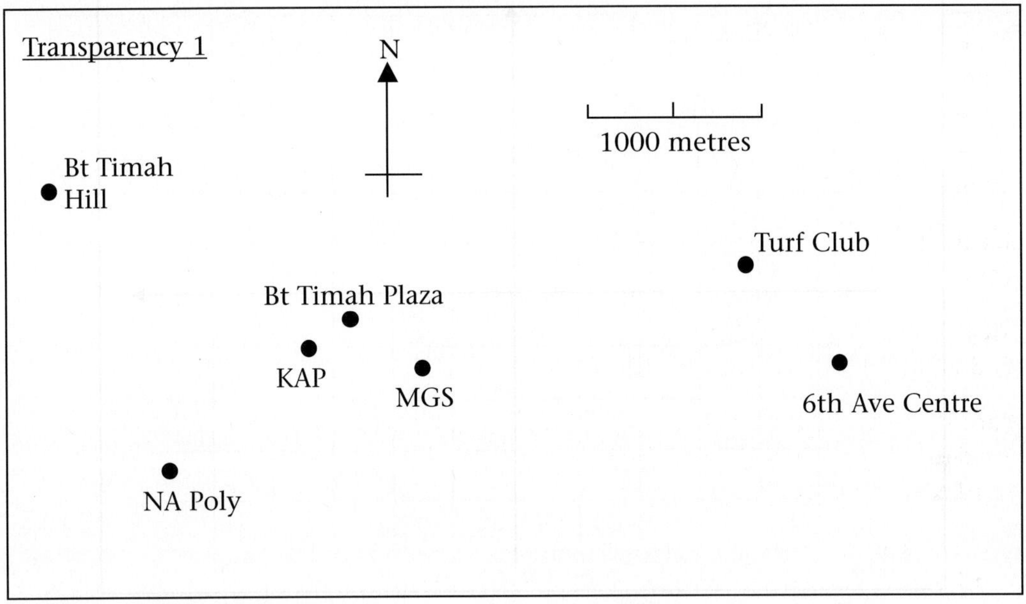
Transparency 1
N
1000 metres
Bt Timah Hill
Turf Club
Bt Timah Plaza
KAP
MGS
6th Ave Centre
NA Poly

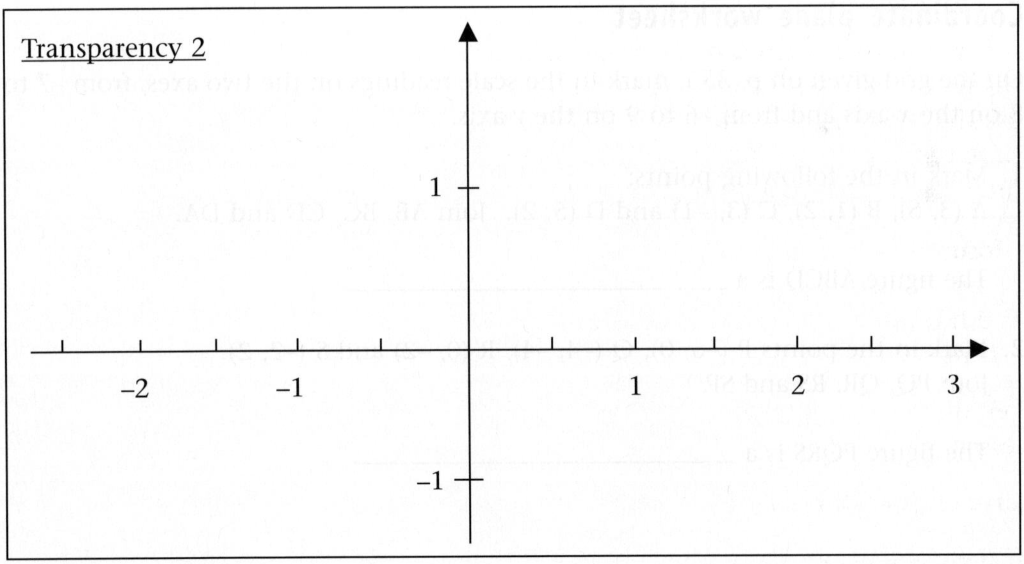
Transparency 2
1
−1
−2
−1
1
2
3

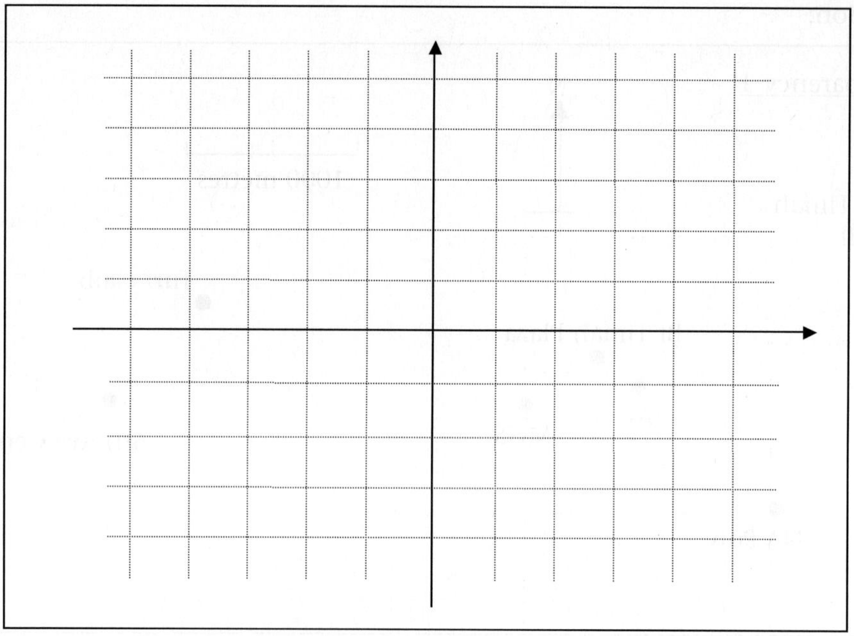

Coordinate plane worksheet

On the grid given on p. 355, mark in the scale readings on the two axes, from –7 to 8 on the *x*-axis and from –6 to 9 on the *y*-axis.

1. Mark in the following points:
   A (3, 5), B (1, 2), C (3, –1) and D (5, 2). Join AB, BC, CD and DA.

   The figure ABCD is a ______________________________.

2. Mark in the points P (–6, 0), Q (–4, –4), R (0, –2) and S (–2, 2).
   Join PQ, QR, RS and SP.

   The figure PQRS is a ______________________________.

3. Mark in the points K (–2, 7), L (1, –2), M (8, –3) and N (4, 9).
   Join KL, LM, MN and NK.

   The figure KLMN is a ______________________.

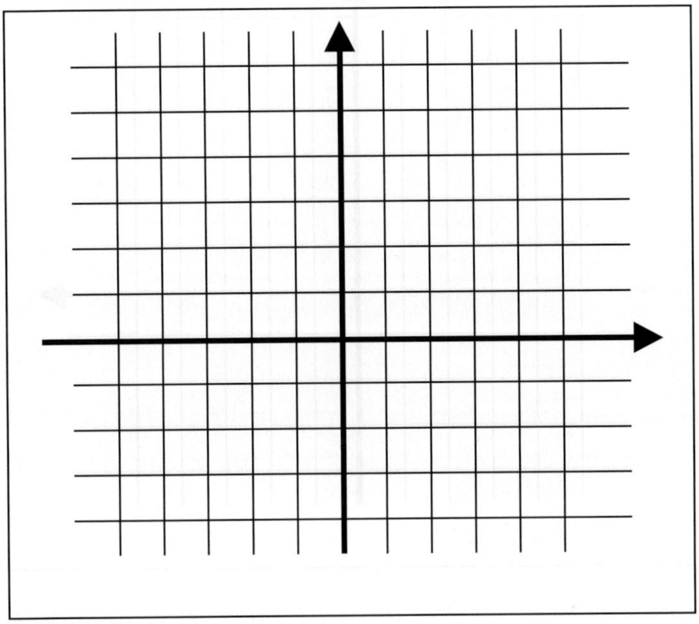

In the grid on p. 356, do the following:

a. Join the following points in order and colour the figure formed in red.
   (–1, –2), (1, –2), (2, –0.5), (1, –1), (–1, –1), (–2, –0.5), (–1, –2).

b. Join the following points in order and colour the figure formed in green.
   (–1, 2), (–2, 3), (–3, 2), (–2, 1) and (–1, 2).

c. Join the following points in order and colour the figure formed in green.
   (1, 2), (2, 3), (3, 2), (2, 1) and (1, 2).

d. Join the following points in order and colour the figure formed in black.
   (0, 1), (1, 0), (–1, 0) and (0, 1).

e. Join the following points in order.
(–4, –1), (–4, 6), (–2, 4), (2, 4), (4, 6), (4, –1), (2, –3), (–2, –3) and (–4, –1).

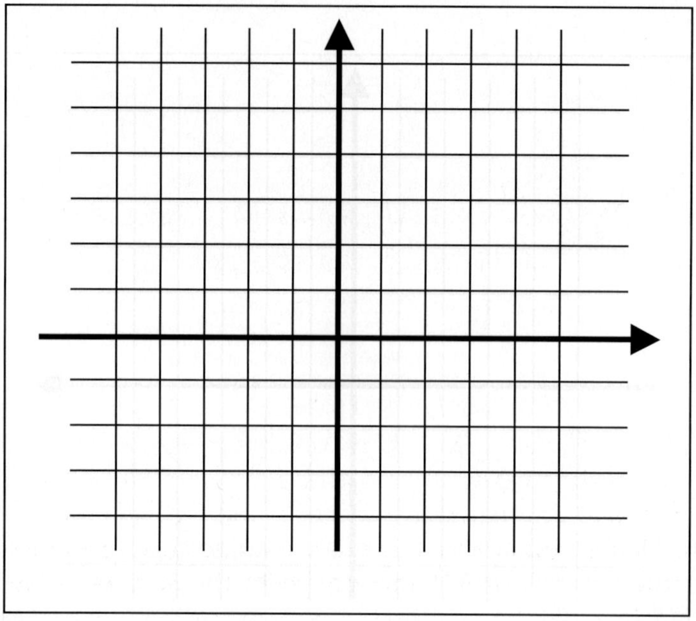

Chapter 19

ICT and Mathematics Education

Wong Khoon Yoong

Information and communications technology (ICT) refers to technology that uses computer software or the Internet. It can affect how mathematics is taught and may change the contents of the mathematics curriculum. This chapter begins with the four modes of ICT use in mathematics education and then examines with specific examples how the six uses of ICT mentioned in the Singapore lower secondary mathematics syllabus may be achieved. The final section gives some ideas about organising ICT mathematics lessons. Since ICT continues to expand at a tremendous rate, only a few key ideas can be covered here.

MODES OF ICT

Four modes of ICT are used in mathematics education. They are:

1. *Tutor* mode
   The computer acts as a tutor to teach students using pre-programmed activities. These activities include explanations and practice with feedback. Attractive multimedia features such as sound, video-clips and animation are used to motivate learning and enhance interactivity. This tutor mode is effective for weak students who need repeated instruction and structured practice to master routine skills.

2. *Tool* mode
   This refers to using the computer as a tool for learning, presentation and assessment. Many types of software are used in this mode. Tools that help students learn and apply mathematics include: spreadsheets (e.g. Excel), Computer Algebra Systems (CAS) (e.g. Maple), graphing software (e.g. Graphmatica), dynamic geometry (e.g. Geometer's Sketchpad) and mathematics applets. Mathematics

educators generally recommend this tool mode because it helps to develop conceptual and relational understanding of mathematics. Word processor with mathematical and drawing features (e.g. Equation Editor and FXDraw) and presentation software (e.g. PowerPoint) are useful tools for preparing high-quality materials. Online assessment may be used, for example, the locally developed Math Explorer (http://iqexplorers.com), can mark and grade students' answers to open-ended mathematical questions.

3. *Tutee* mode

   This treats the computer as a "tutee" which obeys the commands issued by the students when they write computer programs. The most popular programming language in mathematics education is Logo. This language is rarely used in Singapore schools nowadays, but it is recommended by the mathematics curriculum in the United States, UK and Australia. When writing Logo programs, students apply geometry and algebra to solve problems and develop mathematical reasoning. Dealing with program bugs in a non-threatening way reduces students' anxiety about making mistakes, which is often part of the learning process.

4. *Co-learner* mode

   Under this mode, teachers and students form a community of learners. They can learn from one another by using various communication resources, for example, e-mail, Internet and e-learning.

OBJECTIVES OF ICT USE IN THE SINGAPORE MATHEMATICS CURRICULUM

The overall aim of ICT use is spelt out in the lower secondary mathematics syllabus as follows:

> The integration of IT can help develop in students their interest in mathematics, enrich their learning experience and help fulfil their potentials by becoming independent thinkers and learners.
>
> Ministry of Education, 2001, p. 16

Six specific objectives of ICT use are also mentioned, and they are discussed as follows.

1. Bridge the gap between abstract concepts and concrete experiences

   The influential work of Piaget and Bruner suggests that students should work with concrete materials before they develop abstract mathematical concepts. ICT can provide semi-concrete (cyber) experiences to bridge the gap between concrete experiences and abstraction (Figure 19-1). However, the transition from concrete to semi-concrete to abstract does not happen automatically, and this requires the teachers to plan appropriate activities carefully. Furthermore, computer manipulatives should not replace concrete experiences because there is still a need for students to see the links between mathematics and the real world.

Figure 19-1 ICT bridges the gap between abstract concepts and concrete experiences

When learning about *median*, students often forget to arrange the values in ascending (or descending) order before they read the middle value. After working with sticks or other suitable materials, the following Excel template (Figure 19-2) may be used to link the concept of median represented in numbers and charts. The numbers are sorted using a pre-programmed macro, and the median can be readily read from the sorted column.

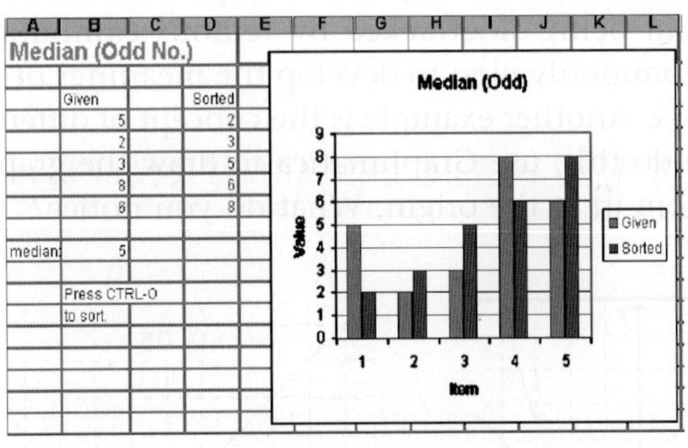

Figure 19-2 An Excel template for the concept of median

Doing geometric transformations on Geometer's Sketchpad has also become very popular, but students should begin with the real actions. In Figure 19-3, triangle A′B′C′ is the image of ABC under reflection in the y-axis. Students are asked to find the relationship between the coordinates of the vertices of the object and coordinates of the image. One student's response is: "The x-coordinate becomes negative."

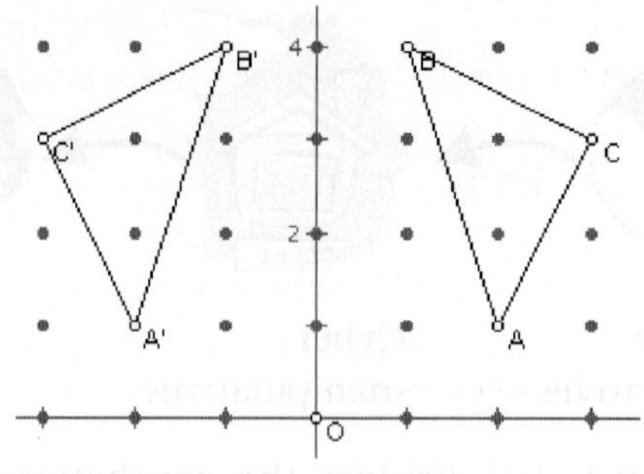

Figure 19-3 Reflection of ABC in the *y*-axis

This is only partially correct because this student focuses on only *positive* coordinates. The teacher should tell the students to also explore negative coordinates, thus leading to a more correct conclusion.

2. Consolidate concepts and skills

   ICT allows students to actively explore concepts with many examples and non-examples, without being sidetracked by tedious computations. For example, Graphmatica is commonly used to develop the meanings of m and c in the linear equation $y = mx + c$. Another example is the concept of differentiability and "local straightness". To do this, use Graphmatica to draw the graphs of $|x|$ and $y = x^2$ (Figure 19-4). Zoom in at the origin. What do you notice?

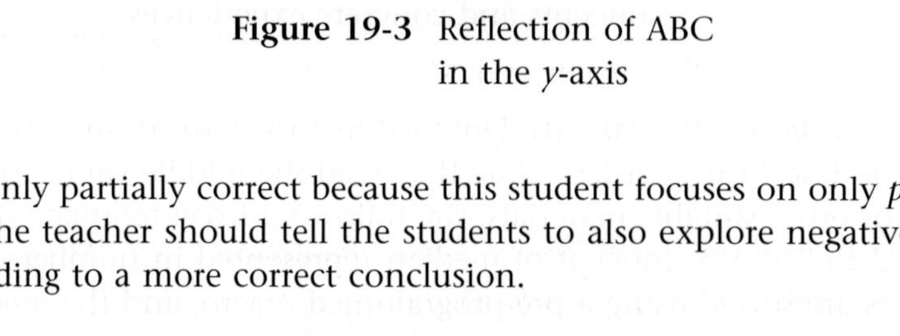

Figure 19-4 Local straightness of graphs

To consolidate skills, ICT programs can be used as tutors to provide numerous routine exercises with feedback, following the behaviourist theory. The *Dynamic Series* and *Treefrog*, which is a drill-and-practice program about algebraic skills, are examples of this use. More interestingly, some ICT applets provide challenging practices that require higher-order thinking. One example is the strategic factor game available from the National Council of Teachers of Mathematics (NCTM) Illuminations website (see References).

Students should apply learned mathematical skills to real-life situations. Real-life data are usually quite large, but a spreadsheet can be used here. For example, a survey can be conducted about the body mass index (BMI) of all the students in a class, and the data displayed using Excel. The relationships between BMI and mathematics scores can be explored using scatterplot and correlation, computed using Excel.

Since ICT can be used to handle many types of arithmetic and algebraic skills, a controversy regarding whether students should still be required to master these skills manually (also called paper-and-pencil skills) has arisen. In other words, should spreadsheets (and calculator) replace arithmetic algorithms and CAS replace algebraic manipulations? In general, basic paper-and-pencil skills involving small values should be mastered, and they should not be replaced by pushing buttons or clicking screen icons only. Psychologically speaking, working through an algorithm manually produces the so-called "generation effect", which is a foundation for deeper understanding (McNamara, 1995). The difference is illustrated in Figure 19-5. Some teachers also believe that carrying out simple skills with calculators or ICT make students mentally "lazy".

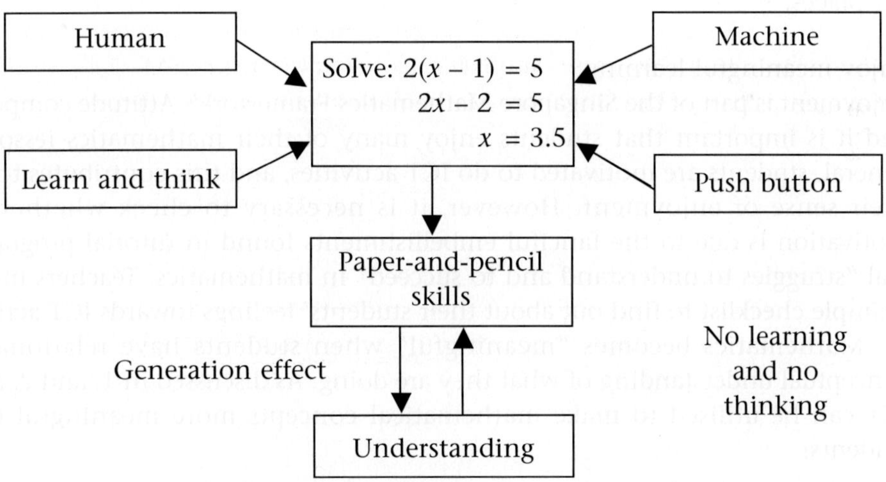

Figure 19-5 ICT versus manual skills

If ICT is allowed in examinations, then assessment requirements will have to be changed. At the moment, only scientific calculators are allowed at school level and graphing calculators at junior college level. In the future, teachers may have to create ICT-free, ICT-neutral, ICT-optional and ICT-active items. Examples of these types of items are given below.

i. ICT-free items, where basic skills are required, for example,
   a. Calculate 4×12.
   b. Expand $2(x + y)$.
   c. Make r the subject: $A = 4\pi r^2$.

ii. ICT-neutral items, where ICT is allowed, but has little advantage over manual skills because the focus is on concepts rather than skills.
   a. John bought x footballs and y tennis balls. Altogether he bought 19 balls. Write an equation in x and y.
   b. The lowest common multiple of 6, 15 and x is 90. Find two possible values of x, which is an odd number. (Cambridge O-level question)

iii. ICT-optional items, where the manual skills or ICT methods are equally acceptable, and the students decide which method to use. Example: The volume $V(t)$ of a solid at time t seconds is given by $\frac{dV}{dt} = V - 0.5V^2$. For which value of V is the change in volume greatest?

iv. ICT-active items, which are very difficult to solve without ICT. Example: Let $f(x) = (20 - x)\lg x$. Find the maximum value of $f(x)$, correct to three decimal places.

3. Enjoy meaningful learning
Enjoyment is part of the Singapore Mathematics Framework's Attitude component, and it is important that students enjoy many of their mathematics lessons. In general, students are motivated to do ICT activities, and this contributes towards their sense of enjoyment. However, it is necessary to check whether their motivation is due to the fanciful embellishments found in tutorial programs or real "struggles to understand and to succeed" in mathematics. Teachers may use a simple checklist to find out about their students' feelings towards ICT activities.
   Mathematics becomes "meaningful" when students have relational and conceptual understanding of what they are doing. As discussed in 1. and 2. above, ICT can be utilised to make mathematical concepts more meaningful to the students.

4. Participate in cooperative work and broaden learning styles
Under the traditional mode, students work on mathematics problems individually by following the procedures that have been demonstrated by the teachers. There is little discussion among the students. Using ICT can change this scenario. Students are encouraged to work in pairs or small groups as they work through ICT worksheets that require thinking and sharing of ideas. An example is for students to study the

number of factors of natural numbers by using a Logo microworld that outputs the factors so that the students can concentrate on looking for patterns, without being hindered by mistakes made when finding the factors manually. They may use a table like the following to explore what types of natural numbers have even or odd number of factors.

Number of factors

	1	2	3	4	5	6	7	8
Enter the numbers in the correct column	1	2 3 5	4					

Similar examples will extend the students' learning styles from rote practice to guided discovery and social construction of mathematical ideas.

5. Explore and attempt different approaches to tasks and problems, and hence observe a variety of consequences
According to Dienes' principle of multiple embodiment, a multi-modal approach should be used in teaching concepts. These include verbal, pictorial, kinaesthetic, symbolic and numerical modes of representation (See Chapter 16). ICT can facilitate this multi-modal approach. For example, a quadratic function is uniquely determined by any three points on its curve. Given the three points, the function can be determined in several different ways: (a) solve algebraic equations, (b) use Excel and the "difference" method, and (c) guess-and-check with Graphmatica. Students should be encouraged to compare and contrast these different methods.

6. Shift towards tasks and problems which require higher level of competencies
This objective fits in with the initiative to promote higher-order thinking. Engaging students in investigations as project work has become increasingly important in mathematics. For example, after learning about linear graphs, students may explore the outcome if two linear graphs are "added" or "multiplied" together. Students can use Graphmatica to explore many examples and search for patterns in the graphs generated. The exploration should not stop at this pictorial level; the students should explain the mathematics underlying the patterns found.

To summarise, when the above six objectives are put into action, students will have been exposed to a variety of learning experiences ranging from routine practice to explorations and working individually and in groups. These experiences, under the proper guidance of the teachers, will hopefully help the students to become more independent as learners of mathematics.

ORGANISING ICT MATHEMATICS LESSONS

Potential shortcomings of ICT

Before planning an ICT mathematics lesson, the teacher should decide whether or not the use of ICT will make the lesson more effective. The teacher must be aware of some potential shortcomings of ICT use such as the following:

1. Inappropriate use of PowerPoint in mathematics lessons. PowerPoint may be used if the teacher wants to demonstrate special effects such as photographs or complicated diagrams that cannot be readily done otherwise. The potential drawbacks of PowerPoint are: (a) it is difficult to demonstrate problem-solving processes; (b) the sequence is controlled by the pre-prepared slides and this discourages the teacher from following students' suggestions that deviate from the prepared sequence; (c) the teacher tends to read from the slides with the back facing the class, hence, there is no eye contact with students; and (d) a dimmer classroom will induce sleepiness among the students.

2. Inaccuracies in screen output. Figure 19-6 shows a distorted graph of $y = \sin 30x$. This is due to the limitations of the pixels on the screen. Students should be alerted to these problems.

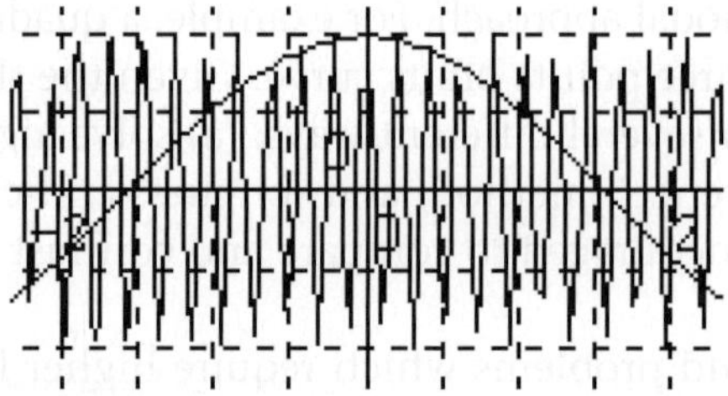

Figure 19-6 Inaccuracy in graphing

3. Some notations used in various software differ from those used in mathematics lessons, for example, $2x$ as 2*x; x^2 as x^2, etc. Matlab interprets *solve* without a complete equation (see below), and this may confuse students about the difference between an *equation* and an *expression.*

```
> solve (2*x – 4);
                                        2
```

Some considerations about incorporating ICT in mathematics lessons

1. Identify the cognitive, affective and psychomotor objectives of the lesson. Is ICT necessary to achieve these objectives?

2. Select the software to be used and consider which of the following four levels of ICT use is suitable.

   a. Teacher demonstrates to the whole class, preferably with a question-and-answer session and discussion.
   b. Students use templates (as black boxes) that require minimum software skills. The teachers prepare the templates and worksheets, including expected answers to the worksheet problems. These worksheets may be completed individually, in pairs or small groups.
   c. Students learn simple software skills to solve mathematics problems, for example, enter formulae into a spreadsheet. Time has to be set aside for the students to learn the necessary software skills, and this may reduce curriculum time for mathematics.
   d. Students learn more about the software and use their skills to carry out extended investigations. This is suitable for project work.

3. Situate the ICT lesson within an off-line → on-line → off-line sequence. The first off-line lesson deals with basic ideas so that the students know what to pay attention to when they work on the computer. The second off-line lesson provides reinforcement of the ICT activities.

4. Rehearse the lesson plan to check that everything works as planned.

5. Train students to work actively in ICT lessons. For example, they should scribble their thoughts and calculations on paper rather than stare at the computer screen, ask themselves "what if" questions, compare answers with their classmates, and so on.

6. Observe what the students are doing. Are they on task? Do they complete the worksheets mindfully or mindlessly? Some students have been found to check e-mails and play computer games during ICT mathematics lessons, and they should be reprimanded for doing so.

7. Give careful feedback on the students' work. Can they relate the ICT activities to work taught earlier in normal lessons? For example, a class was asked to use Graphmatica to plot the graphs of $(x + 2)^2$ and $x^2 + 4$ and to deduce whether

$(x + 2)^2 = x^2 + 4$ and whether they have the same line of symmetry and minimum values. A student gave the following response:

$(x+2)^2 \neq x^2+4$ They have the same line of symmetry but different minimum values.

The teacher did not spot the mistake in this answer. Did you? What comments will you give on this student's work?

TUTORIAL TASKS

1. Discuss sample ICT lesson plans. Which of the six objectives are being achieved?
2. Share one example of Internet resources that you (or your team) find to be pedagogically sound and of local relevance. What modifications do you need to make?
3. Design some test items that are ICT-free, ICT-neutral, ICT-optional or ICT-active.
4. Discuss factors that may facilitate or hinder your decision to use ICT to teach mathematics.
5. What criteria would you use to evaluate software for mathematics lessons, when it is used in the tutor, tool and tutee modes?

CONCLUSION

Teachers should not let ICT replace them in the mathematics classrooms. ICT tools should be used to serve significant mathematical learning objectives. Teachers should be bold and creative to experiment with new ways of using ICT. Sharing experiences of ICT use with colleagues will raise the instructional standards in classes. Indeed, teachers are the catalysts to ensure the success of ICT use in mathematics and the Singapore IT Master Plan (mp2).

REFERENCES

Internet

Do not just download the files! Try each example and write down your views about how it can be used.

Archimedes Laboratory (http://www.archimedes-lab.org/atelier.html), puzzles to solve and make on your own.

edHelper.com (http://www.edhelper.com), many worksheets; subscribers can automatically create worksheets in various topics, answers included.

Math Forum (http://www.mathforum.org), with free e-newsletter and many links.

Maths Encyclopedia (http://planetmath.org/encyclopedia) gives definitions and examples.

National Library of Virtual Manipulatives (http://matti.usu.edu), including information for teachers.

NCTM Illuminations (http://illuminations.nctm.org/tools/index.aspx)

Project Interactivate (http://www.shodor.org/interactivate), with many applets and activities.

PurpleMath with algebra resources (http://purplemath.com/index.htm), with tutorial lessons.

Walter Fendt applets (http://www.walter-fendt.de/m11e/)

Webmath.com (http//www.webmath.com/index.html); user chooses a problem type and enters the parameters; explanations, intermediate steps and final answer will be given.

Books

Ameis, J.A. (2002). *Mathematics on the Internet: A resource for K-12 teachers.* (2nd ed.). Upper Saddle River, NJ: Prentice Hall.

Healy, J.M. (1999). *Failure to connect: How computers affect our children's mind and what we can do about it.* NY: Simon & Schuster.

Humble, S. (2002). *The experimenter's A-Z of mathematics: Maths activities with computer support.* London: David Fulton.

McNamara, D.S. (1995). Effects of prior knowledge on the generation advantage: Calculators versus calculation to learn multiplication. *Journal of Educational Psychology, 87*(2), 307–318.

Ministry of Education. (2001). *Mathematics syllabus: Lower secondary.* Singapore: Ministry of Education.

Oldknow, A., & Taylor, R. (2000). *Teaching mathematics with ICT.* London: Continuum.

Chapter 20

Designing Test Items

Wong Khoon Yoong

Practising examination-style questions is important for consolidating skills and problem solving. However, for many students, these questions soon become routine work and they no longer seem interesting or motivating. At this junction, the teacher needs to modify the questions to make them more enchanting, meaningful and challenging. This idea applies not only to the better students; it should also be relevant to the average or weaker ones. It is probably wrong to think that the weaker students are not capable of working on challenging problems; what might be true is that the routine exercises are so boring that these students have lost interest and, hence, do not exert themselves intellectually to meet the challenge. To apply this idea in teaching, teachers need to develop a repertoire of interesting and meaningful problems that are not too different from the work covered in the syllabus. There are several ways to modify standard examination questions to make them more interesting and challenging. Five main themes with examples are given below to help teachers get started to compile their own "favourite" problems for classroom use. The problems are not original, and the presentation has been adapted here to suit school situations.

THEME 1: CHANGING THE GIVENS

Many mathematical problems involve several pieces of information and steps of computation. We can change what is given in the problems. When all the givens are on the same side, the problem is usually relatively easy. However, when the givens appear on different sides of an equation, the problem becomes more difficult.

Example 1

a. (Direct) Find 15% of 200. This percentage problem gives the base and percent in the general formula, *base* × *percent* = *quantity*. This is quite easy to solve.

b. (Change) Give the percent and quantity instead: If 15% of a number is 200, find the number. Here the givens appear on both sides of the equation; students may have some difficulty solving it. The problem may also give the base and quantity and ask for the percent. The teacher should discuss all these possible cases so that the students do not get "stuck" with the difficult ones.

Example 2

a. (Direct) An arc subtends an angle 30° at the centre of a circle of radius 5 cm. Calculate the arc length.

b. (Change) If an arc of length 4 cm subtends an angle 30° at the centre of a circle, find the radius of the circle. What other changes to the problem can you think of?

The above two examples illustrate how to cover all possible changes to the givens and the unknown when the problem involves a formula. Take any formula and make up examples of a similar kind.

Some examples of changing the givens without involving a specific formula are given below. These examples also illustrate the idea of *reversing* the role of operations and givens and unknowns.

Example 3

a. (Typical) Given that $h = 3$ and $k = -2$, find the value of $3h + 4k$.

b. (Change) Given that $h = 3$ and $3h + 4k = 6$, find the value of k.

Example 4

a. (Typical) Find the next number: 1, 3, 6, 10, _, …

b. (Change) Find the beginning number: _, 3, 6, 10, ...; or the middle number: 1, 3, _, 10, ...

A more tricky reverse problem is as follows.

Example 5

a. Consider shape 1 in Figure 20-1, which is divided into four equal parts. Remove one quarter of shape 1 to obtain shape 2. What fraction of shape 2 must be added to get back to shape 1? A common answer is $\frac{1}{4}$. Is it right?

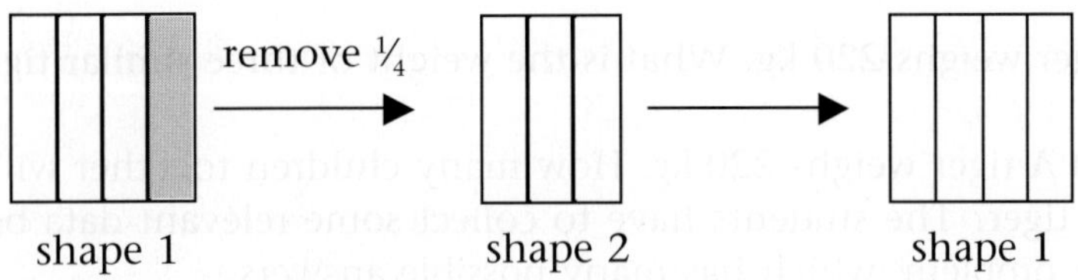

Figure 20-1 Changes to a shape

b. (Generalise) Suppose you remove $\frac{1}{n}$ of a rectangle to obtain a new shape. What fraction of the new shape do you need to add to get back the shape you started with?

THEME 2: USING MORE OPEN-ENDED TASKS

A closed problem is one that has only one correct answer and possibly also one most efficient method of solution that the students are trained to master. On the other hand, an open-ended problem has several or infinitely many solutions and may be solved using many different methods. These open-ended problems can be used to probe deeper understanding of concepts and to promote creative thinking. Their use also helps to change the common perception that mathematics problems always have only one right answer or one correct method of solution.

Example 1

a. (Closed) Round 34.56 to the nearest one decimal place.

b. (Open-ended) Which number when rounded off becomes 34.6? What are the largest and smallest possible such numbers?

Example 2

a. (Closed) Solve $2x - 3 = 7$. The answer is $x = 5$.

b. (Open-ended) Write down at least two linear equations whose solution is 5. In this case, teach students how to check their answers by substitution.

Example 3

a. (Closed) A tiger weighs 220 kg. What is the weight of three similar tigers?

b. (Open-ended) A tiger weighs 220 kg. How many children together will weigh as much as one tiger? The students have to collect some relevant data before they can solve this problem, which has many possible answers.

Example 4

a. (Closed) Calculate the hypotenuse of the triangle in Figure 20-2(a).

b. (Open-ended) Find out everything you can about this triangle. Give another triangle as in Figure 20-2(b). and ask students to find out everything they can about both triangles (after Clarke, 1992).

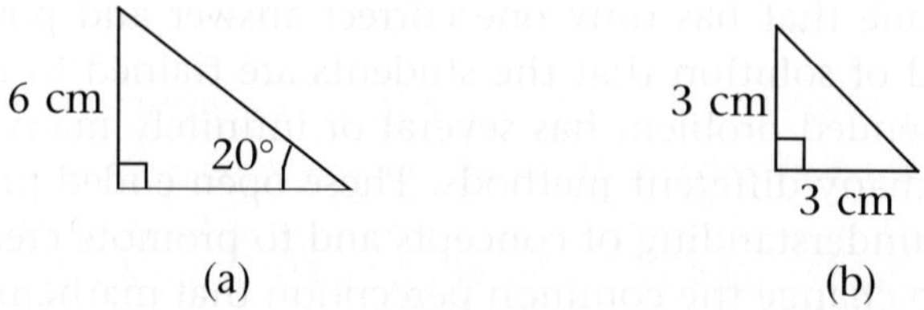

Figure 20-2 (a) Right-angled triangle;
(b) An isosceles right-angled triangle

Example 5

Given a diagram, most textbooks will ask just one type of question. For example, in Figure 20-3, the common problem is to calculate the area enclosed between the two circles. What other questions can you ask about this diagram (see Walter, 1987a)? What questions can your *students* ask about this diagram, and can they solve *their* own questions?

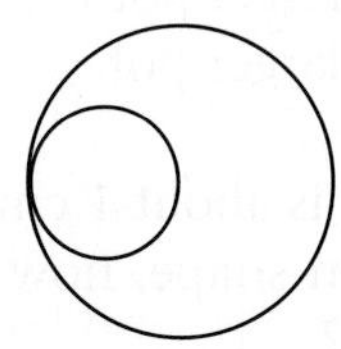

Figure 20-3 Two circles

Since these open-ended questions involve strategies and planning, it will be useful to ask the students to describe their problem-solving process or to explain how they would go about solving the problem (Stenmark, 1991). Also ask them to explain how they know they have obtained the correct answer, how they feel about solving the problems and what they think the purpose of this exercise is!

A management problem arises when open-ended problems are used, that is, how can a busy teacher check all the given answers? In some cases, a computer can be used to do the checking. Training students to self-check their answers is more difficult; however, this has the advantage of not only reducing checking by the teachers but also encouraging students to take more responsibility for their own learning.

THEME 3: INCLUDING INTERESTING OR MEANINGFUL CONTEXTS

> Problem solving in school is for the sake of solving problems in life. Other things being equal, problems where the situation is real are better than problems where it is described in words. Other things being equal, problems which might really occur in a sane and reasonable life are better than bogus problems and mere puzzles.
>
> Thorndike, 1923, cited in Bell, 1993, p. 80

Real-life problems are set in some contexts. The contexts may be everyday situations (meaningful), current affairs, historical events (heritage) and cultural practices. Including real contexts in problems will widen students' perspectives of their local environments and the wider world and provide links to other subjects. For problems embedded in these contexts, the methods may be hidden, so the students have to find the correct method before they can solve a problem. Some examples of locally rich mathematics problems are given in Wong (1997). Here we look at other examples.

Example 1

a. (Context-free) Two plant pots are geometrically similar. The height of the smaller pot is 5 cm. The height of the larger pot is 15 cm. Find the ratio of the volume of the smaller pot to that of the larger pot.

b. (Context) A hummingbird egg is about 1 cm long. An ostrich egg is about 18 cm long. If both eggs are similar in shape, how many hummingbird eggs will equal the volume of one ostrich egg?

Example 2

a. (Context-free) Calculate the area of the annulus between two concentric circles of radii 4 cm and 7 cm.

b. (Context) Estimate the length of a toilet roll. Using area, it can be shown that the estimated length is $L = \frac{\pi(R^2 - r^2)}{d}$, where d is the thickness of the paper. Make an estimate of the values of R, r and d. Work out the value of L. [In practice, there will be measurement errors, especially if one presses the paper too hard.]

The following values were obtained: $r = 2.1$ cm, $R = 5.1$ cm, $d = \frac{0.6}{1.8}$ cm, so $L = 2{,}035$ cm. The length of each sheet was 11.5 cm and there were 178 sheets, making $L = 2{,}047$ cm. [Both measurements were very close. However, the percentage error will change drastically if one makes larger measurement errors.]

A more mathematical approach is as follows (Swetz and Hertzler, 1991):

> Let N denote the number of times the toilet paper completely wraps around the toilet roll. Using arithmetic progression, one can find the sum
>
> $$\begin{aligned} L &= 2\pi r + 2\pi(r + d) + 2\pi(r + 2d) + \ldots + 2\pi[r + (N - 1)d], \\ &= 2\pi\{r + (r + d) + (r + 2d) + \ldots + [r + (N - 1)d]\} \\ &= 2\pi \times \frac{N}{2}(r + R). \end{aligned}$$

Since $N = \dfrac{R - r}{d}$, we have $L = \dfrac{\pi(R - r)(R + r)}{d} = \dfrac{\pi(R^2 - r^2)}{d}$, as before. Note that this can be written as $N \times 2\pi\dfrac{(r + R)}{2}$, where $\dfrac{(r + R)}{2}$ is the average of the inner and outer radii and $2\pi\dfrac{(r + R)}{2}$ the circumference of this "average radius".

c. How long does a roll last? The students will realise that answers to such questions depend on the assumptions made and only an approximate value can be given.

Example 3

a. Every time a heart beats, it ejects about 56 g of blood. Given that the heart beats about 72 times per minute, calculate the amount of blood ejected from the heart into the aorta.

b. How does the amount in a. compare to the body weight of a person? What can you conclude from the above calculation?

[William Harvey (1578–1657) used this calculation to formulate the hypothesis that the same blood was constantly recycled through the heart! It took him another nine years of careful experimentation and observations to prove his theory (Hart, 1978).]

Example 4

a. (Context-free) The number of apples is twice the number of oranges. Write this in algebra.

b. (Context) The circumference of a person's neck is approximately twice the circumference of the wrist. Write this in algebra. Check that it is true for you! Anthropometry is the study of human sizes and proportions. The information is used to design clothes and furniture and in forensic science.

c. Here is an example taken from Knill (1991). When a skeleton is found, a forensic scientist can estimate the height of the living person (h cm) by measuring the length of the thighbone (or femur, F cm). The formula is:

For male: $h = 69.089 + 2.238\ F$

For female: $h = 61.412 + 2.317\ F$

i. The femur of a man is 46.8 cm. What is his estimated height?
ii. What is the estimated length of the femur of a person whose height is 165 cm?
iii. Measure the length of your thigh. Does the formula work for you and your classmates?

d. Other formulae about the human body can be found on the website http://tqjunior.advanced.org/4116/science/science.html.

Example 5

Up to O-level, most of the probability questions involve tossing coins or dice, drawing cards or beads from bags and applying tree diagrams to compute the probability of compound events. Rarely do the questions ask for interpretations, especially when they involve *subjective* probability. The following illustrate probability in a scientific situation.

a. What do you think is the probability that the engines of a space shuttle will break down?

b. After the disaster of *Challenger* on 28 January 1986, Professor Richard Feynman was involved in a presidential commission to investigate the causes of the disaster (Feynman, 1989). He asked the engineers and NASA managers to give an estimate of the above probability. He was given values like 1 in 200 or 1 in 300 (by the engineers) and 1 in 100 000 (by the managers). What do these figures mean in terms of the number of successful flights?

c. Assume that the probability of failure of any flight is 1 in 200. What is the probability of at least one disaster in every two flights? What is this probability if you use the managers' value?

In Singapore, the problem contexts can encompass national and current issues, the history and geography of Singapore and the world, and the daily life of the students. This is referred to as National Education into mathematics lessons. A simple example follows.

Example 6

a. (Context-free) Find 985762 – 985595.

b. (National Education context) Before Chinese New Year, Mei Lin's mother gives her a bundle of $2 notes. The notes have serial numbers from 985595 to 985762. She puts $6 into each *ang pow*.

   i. How many *ang pow* can she prepare?
   ii. Mei Lin donates $87.60 to the Community Chest of Singapore. If this is 24% of her *ang pow* money, how much is her *ang pow* collection?
   iii. Malay parents give green packages during Hari Raya Puasa. What are they called?

More examples of problem contexts involving Singapore National Education are discussed by Wong (2003).

THEME 4: USING CREATIVE IMAGINATION

> Imagination is more important than knowledge. It is the supreme art of the teacher to awaken joy in creative expression and knowledge.
>
> Albert Einstein

Not all mathematics problems need to include real contexts. They may involve fantasy and imagination to create some fun and make mathematics more enchanting. It is, indeed, very rare that teachers help students develop creative imagination in mathematics lessons. Because of this shortcoming, school mathematics is predominantly left-hemispheric thinking, leaving little opportunity to develop right-hemispheric visualisation, even in geometry work that is supposed to develop our intuition about objects in space.

In a book published in 1903, Mary Boole, the wife of the famous algebraist George Boole who established the algebra of sets, used mental pictures in the teaching of mathematics. She would begin her lessons with the instruction: *sit slack, shut your eyes, and rest ... I am going to give you a mental picture* (for example, five lines and a dot). At the end of the lesson, she would ask the students to open their eyes, draw the mental picture and write about it. Some interesting examples are given in the book *Geometric Images* (Association of Teachers of Mathematics, 1982). Try it! Before teachers can use this approach to help their students develop imagination, they have to experience this first!

Take a line, a circle and a triangle as shown in Figure 20-4(a). Close your eyes and try to mentally assemble these three shapes into a recognisable figure. The shapes can vary in size, position, orientation, but they must not be altered in shape. An example of this arrangement is an ice cream shown in Figure 20-4(b). Give students other shapes to work with.

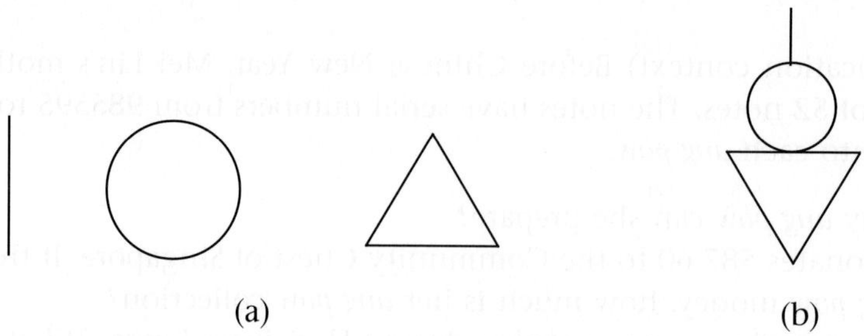

Figure 20-4 (a) Three shapes for creative imagination
(b) An ice cream

A more mathematical example is described in Walter (1987b). Imagine a large white equilateral triangle. At each corner imagine a small black equilateral triangle, as in Figure 20-5(a). Close your eyes and slowly enlarge each small triangle. Describe the shape of the interior of the white triangle. Repeat with a square, as in Figure 20-5(b).

Figure 20-5 (a) Triangle with black corners
(b) Square with black corners

THEME 5: USING DIFFERENT FORMATS

The same question may be given in a combination of different modes, for example, symbols, diagrams, numbers or words. The mode of presentation can have significant effects on student achievement. Plant (1985) found that among Singapore students, a problem presented with a diagram and a "simple" explanation was easier than the same problem stated in words only. To help the weaker students master problem solving, it is helpful to start with problems presented in a "diagram + explanation" form and slowly move to a verbal format. In fact, public examinations are now giving more problems in a combination of diagrams and words. In some cases, the students have to obtain the relevant information from the diagrams.

Example

a. (Words only) Villages B and C are each 5 km from village A and $\angle BAC = 150°$. The village C is due south of a point X and the villages A and B are both due east of X.

b. Now add a diagram to the above description. Does it make the problem easier?

CONCLUSION

There are other ways to design interesting test items that we have not dealt with here. These may involve using students' errors, asking for specific cases of a general rule, generalising from specific cases and applying the Structure of Observed Learning Outcomes (SOLO) taxonomy to develop items that have increasing levels of complexity (Collis and Romberg, 1992). Whichever ways are used, the test items must cover a range of low- to high-order skills so that students of different abilities and interests can demonstrate what they understand and can do. This requires teachers to acquire new mathematical knowledge as well as knowledge of other fields that make use of mathematics, such as the sciences, technology, social sciences and psychology. This is the exciting challenge for the teachers in this new millennium!

REFERENCES

Association of Teachers of Mathematics. (1982). *Geometric images*. London: Association of Teachers of Mathematics.

Bell, M. (1993). Modelling and applications of mathematics in the primary curriculum. In T. Breiteig, I. Huntley, & G. Kaiser-Messmer (Eds.), *Teaching and learning mathematics in context* (pp. 71–80). NY: Ellis Horwood.

Clarke, D. (1992). *Assessment alternatives in mathematics*. Canberra: Curriculum Development Centre.

Collis, K.F., & Romberg, T.A. (1992). *Collis-Romberg mathematical problem solving profiles*. Hawthorn: Australian Council for Educational Research.

Feynman, R.P. (1989). *"What do you care what other people think?": Further adventures of a curious character.* NY: Bantam Books.

Hart, M.H. (1978). *The 100: A ranking of the most influential persons in history.* NY: A&W Visual Library.

Knill, G. (1991). Mathematics in forensic science. In J.D. Austin (Ed.), *Applications of secondary school mathematics: Readings from the mathematics teacher* (pp. 31–32). Reston, VA: National Council of Teachers of Mathematics.

Plant, E. (1985). *Presentation influences problem solving in mathematics*. Unpublished report. Singapore: Institute of Education.

Stenmark, J.K. (1991). *Mathematics assessment: Myths, models, good questions, and practical suggestions*. Reston, VA: National Council of Teachers of Mathematics.

Swetz, F., & Hartzler, J.S. (Eds.). (1991). *Mathematical modeling in the secondary school curriculum: A resource guide of classroom exercises*. Reston, VA: National Council of Teachers of Mathematics.

Walter, M. (1987a). Generating problems from almost anything: Part 1. *Mathematics Teaching, 120*, 3–7.

Walter, M. (1987b). Generating problems from almost anything: Part 2. *Mathematics Teaching, 121*, 2–6.

Wong, K.Y. (1997). Mathematics in CONTECH. *Science and Mathematics Education, 12*, 6–9.

Wong, K.Y. (2003). Mathematics-based national education: A framework for instruction. In Tan, K.S., & Goh, C.B. (Eds.), *Securing our future: Sourcebook for National Education ideas and strategies for secondary schools and junior colleges* (pp. 117–130). Singapore: Pearson Education Asia.

Chapter 21

Making Alternative Assessment an Integral Part of Instructional Practice[1]

Fan Lianghuo

The past two decades or so have witnessed the growing acceptance and use of alternative assessment in mathematics classrooms in many countries including the United States, Canada and Australia. In Singapore, alternative assessment as a new way of assessing students' learning has also received mounting attention from educational policy makers, administrators, researchers and practitioners, particularly since the mid-1990s (e.g. Fan and Yeo, 2000; Seto, 2002; Yazilah and Fan, 2002; Ministry of Education, 2004a, 2004b; Mathematics Assessment Project, 2004; Chow and Fan, 2005; Fan and Yeo, 2006). Nevertheless, it seems reasonable to say that mathematics educators are still at the early stage of understanding and implementing alternative assessment in pedagogy and practice, and there is much need to share experiences, reflect on practices, identify relevant issues and seek further improvement in this area.

CONCEPTION OF ASSESSMENT AND ALTERNATIVE ASSESSMENT

Traditionally, the concept of assessment was largely equated with classroom written test, and it seems that this conception still exerts profound influence on many teachers' cognition and practices (Fan, 2002). Under this traditional and narrower conception, what students are assessed on are purely their academic achievements, mainly their

---

[1] An earlier version of this article appeared on an online journal, *Mathematics Newletter* (Issue No. 6, 2003), published by the Ministry of Education of Singapore. Minor modifications and updates were made for this publication.

knowledge on topics well defined in the textbooks and skills on solving routine and conventional problems. Students are assessed dominantly by administering time-limited (in a block of time), tool-limited (paper-and-pencil) and venue-limited (within classrooms) tests, and the most important purpose is to grade and report students' learning results.

The newer and broader conception of assessment goes beyond the boundary of tests. A widely-accepted description of the modern concept of assessment in mathematics was given by the National Council of Teachers of Mathematics (NCTM) in its publication *Assessment Standards for School Mathematics*, which defined assessment as "the process of gathering evidence about a student's knowledge of, ability to use, and disposition towards mathematics and of making inferences from that evidence for a variety of purposes" (NCTM, 1995, p. 3). According to this conception, assessment means gathering information and making inferences, and the attention should be paid to students' achievement in both cognitive and affective domains, and most importantly assessment should serve various purposes in teaching and learning.

It should be noted that the traditional concept of assessment as test virtually excludes students "disposition", which NCTM's *Standards* interpreted as students' interest in and appreciation for mathematics, tendency to think and act in positive ways, and confidence, curiosity, perseverance, flexibility, inventiveness and reflectivity in doing mathematics. The disposition to be assessed should not be only about mathematics itself as a discipline, but also about mathematics teaching and learning. In addition, what is to be assessed should include not only students' learning results, but also students' learning process, that is, how they learn.

In a relative sense, the main features of the traditional and newly developed concepts of student assessment can be summarised in Table 21-1.

The development of the concept of alternative assessment can be roughly traced through three stages, though some so-called novel assessment techniques, for example, classroom observation, oral discussion, and student interview, have been discussed since as early as the 1940s (e.g. see Lambdin, 1993). In the 1970s, education reformers particularly in the United States begun to see more clearly the inadequacy of purely employing standardised tests, which dominantly used multiple-choice questions, to assess students' learning, and they suggested a number of alternatives to standardised tests. The list recommended includes the so-called performance contract (or contract grading), classroom observation, interviews, etc. At this stage, researchers also treated teacher-developed test as an alternative to the standardised ones, which were the main target of criticism for assessment reform (e.g. see Quinto and McKenna, 1977).

In the 1980s, much attention was shifted to teachers' classroom assessment, and alternative assessment was meant to be different from traditional paper-and-pencil tests, including large-scale standardised and teacher-developed ones. Performance-based assessment (also called performance assessment), journal writing assessment (also called journal assessment) and portfolio assessment were increasingly utilised in the reform practice.

Table 21-1 Comparing the main features of the traditional and new concepts of assessment

Student assessment	Traditional concept	New concept
What to be assessed	Cognitive domain (mainly knowledge and skill) and the results of learning	Both cognitive and affective domains (knowledge, skill, ability and disposition) and both the results and process of learning
Where it is conducted	Within classrooms	Within and/or outside classrooms
When students work on the tasks	During in-class time	During and/or after class time
How it is conducted	Conventional way (paper-and-pencil or written test)	Both conventional and alternative ways
How long the process takes	A block of time (e.g. one or two class periods)	It depends on the tasks. It could be days, weeks, months or even years
What purpose(s) it usually serves	Single (most important: grading and reporting students' learning results)	Multiple (most important: improving teaching and learning)

In the last decade, the list of alternative assessment has been further expanded. The most recent development indicates that educators are focusing more on directly exploring new ways to assess students, and less on the relative meaning of "alternatives"; this could be partially seen from the fact that people are increasingly using a more neutral term – "new ways (modes) of assessment" – instead of "alternative assessment" in describing their assessment concept and practice, and in some extreme cases, people even argued that the labels "traditional" and "alternative" are meaningless (Romagnano and Long, 2001).

Although educators have different views about alternative assessments and there seems no single definition of alternative assessment, people generally agree that alternative assessment is different from traditional paper-and-pencil or written tests, and it can include any type of assessment in which students create a response to a question or task rather than simply recall an answer from memory or choose a response from a given list as typically seen in traditional multiple-choice, true/false, or matching test items. Moreover, in alternative assessment, the tasks are expected to be consistent with curriculum goals and often embedded in real-world situations, and teachers need to employ a variety of ways or procedures for observing, collecting and evaluating students' learning.

According to Hatfield, Edwards and Bitter (1997, p. 107), alternative assessment usually has one or more of the following characteristics: (1) Students perform, create and produce (procedures, answers or even questions); (2) Tasks require problem solving or higher-order thinking; (3) Problems are contextualised; (4) Tasks are often time-consuming and need days to complete; and (5) Scoring rubrics or scoring guides are required. Nevertheless, it is not difficult to note that those characteristics are mainly applicable to assessment tasks in the cognitive domain rather than the affective domain.

In recent years, the term "alternative assessment" in mathematics has been generally used to include the following specific techniques in student assessment: performance-based assessment, authentic assessment, portfolio assessment, journal writing, project assessment, oral presentations, interviews, classroom observation, student self-assessment, student-constructed assessment, among others. Those specific ways of assessment have been better defined and increasingly used in practices. In this sense, the general label "alternative assessment" is still meaningful to reflect the difference between these new ways of assessment and the paper-and-pencil test. It also appears clear that the traditional written test can be designed in a way so some kinds of test items can to a degree reflect and accommodate certain ideas of the so-called alternative assessment.

WHY ALTERNATIVE ASSESSMENT?

Why is alternative assessment needed in classroom practice? There are mainly three inter-related reasons. The first is that the traditional paper-and-pencil test has its limitations. The second is that our educational goals and values have changed. The third, following the second reason, is a reflection of the development of the new conception of pedagogy and assessment.

Regarding assessing students' learning of mathematics, undoubtedly the traditional written classroom test has its advantages; however, it also has serious inadequacies, which have become more evident under the new paradigms of educational goals and values. Table 21-2 summarises the potential advantages and disadvantages of using traditional paper-and-pencil tests in student assessment.

Table 21-2 Advantages and disadvantages of traditional paper-and-pencil tests in student assessment

Advantages	Disadvantages
1. Can have good coverage in content.	1. Exclude affective domain.
2. Good for testing factual knowledge and specific skills.	2. Often test what is easy to test, not what is important to test.
3. Easy to design.	3. Emphasise more on memorisation, less on understanding.
4. Easy to administer.	4. Emphasise more on lower-level skills, less on higher-order skills and abilities.
5. Easy to mark and grade.	5. Often test what students don't know, not what they do know.
6. More objective.	6. Students might have test anxiety which will affect their performance in test.
7. Easy to analyse and report.	7. Can be destructive, making students dislike mathematics and learning.
8. Well established.	8. Emphasise more on the product, less on the process of learning.
9. Well accepted.	9. Hard to be an integral part of the teaching and learning process.

Because of its advantages, it is clear that the paper-and-pencil test should and can still play an important role in teachers' daily practice in assessing students, and because of its limitations, new ways of assessment are needed to compensate for what the traditional written test cannot achieve.

As teachers, the ultimate reason for our educational practice is to help students achieve the educational goals. Assessment as a tool and as an activity in education is no exception. In Singapore, as in many other countries, the goals of education have undergone significant changes for the last decades along with the rapid economic and social development and change. Developing students' problem-solving ability and higher-order thinking, interpersonal and cooperative skills, oral and written communication skills, among other objectives, are increasingly valued in education in modern societies. Those changes must be reflected in classroom practice, and teachers need to measure how their students achieve and make progress against those important goals. As the traditional written test largely cannot serve this aspect, there is a necessity to introduce alternative assessment to better reflect the changed goals.

According to the well-known pentagon curriculum framework in Singapore's mathematics syllabus (Ministry of Education, 2000), the primary aim of mathematics curriculum is to enable students to develop their ability to solve mathematical problems. Around the centre are five components: concepts, skills, processes, attitudes and metacognition. Moreover, the syllabus clearly states that "teachers should assess different aspects of thinking, learning and behaviour", which include mental calculation, mathematical communication, practical uses of mathematics, investigative work, problem solving, critical thinking, creative work and use of information technology. Given the broad objectives and range of contents in mathematics and the inadequacies of traditional written tests discussed above, there is much real reason to employ new approaches to assess students' learning.

Alternative assessment can also be regarded as a reflection of the newly developed conception of pedagogy and assessment. For the last decades, people have gained much knowledge about the importance of students' affect (e.g. attitude and interest), of the ways of students' learning (e.g. cooperative learning and constructivism learning), and of teachers monitoring students' learning behaviour and process (e.g. their learning habit and thinking process) in improving the teaching and learning of mathematics. Correspondingly, the concept of assessment has expanded to include both students' cognitive and affective domain, and both the results and process of students' learning, as mentioned earlier. In the light of such new development, the traditional paper-and-pencil test is far from enough and therefore different methods are needed to provide new tools for student assessment.

In short, the alternative assessment techniques are developed to better reflect the new desired instructional goals and shifted values in education, and are a reflection of the newly developed conception of pedagogy and assessment.

IMPLEMENTING ALTERNATIVE ASSESSMENT

There is plenty of literature available concerning the implementation of alternative assessment concepts and techniques in teaching practice, particularly in the United States and some other western countries (e.g. see Clarke, 1992; Kulm, 1994; Mayer and Hillman, 1996; Hargreaves, Earl, and Schmidt, 2002).

In Singapore, the Ministry of Education has made much effort in promoting the use of project work to develop students' problem-solving ability and other desirable skills. According to the Ministry, a trial carried out in all junior colleges and centralised institutes has affirmed that project work is a valuable learning activity, though it found that teachers and students needed more time than originally scheduled to be familiar with the processes involved in project work. As a result, it decided that project work would be included as part of the student assessment package for admission into local universities from 2005 instead of 2004 as recommended earlier (Ministry of Education, 2001).

For the last few years the National Institute of Education has offered in-service training modules in alternative assessment to local primary mathematics teachers. The main objective of the in-service training is to help teachers keep abreast of the new developments in assessment and to be equipped with the necessary knowledge and skills for implementing a variety of alternative assessment methods in their teaching (also see Fan, 2002). Hundreds of teachers have participated in the training. They were required to design, implement and analyse an alternative assessment task in the class they were teaching. Various ways of doing alternative assessment were employed by those in-service teachers in an authentic way, including project work, journal writing, interviews, oral presentations, performance tasks, student self-assessment and classroom observation.

More structured (though small-scale) research work in this line in Singapore educational settings can be found in Yeo (2001) on journal writing in junior college classrooms (also see Fan and Yeo, 2000), Seto (2002) on oral presentation with Primary 4 pupils in a neighbourhood school, Yazilah and Fan (2002) on journal writing with Primary 5 pupils in a high-performing school and Chow and Fan (2005) on using open-ended problem solving with Secondary 1 students in an autonomous secondary school.

Since the end of 2003, a team consisting mainly of university professors, researchers, educational administrators and school teachers have been conducting a major research project known as the Mathematics Assessment Project (MAP) under the Centre for Research in Pedagogy and Practice (CRPP), National Institute of Education. Four types of new assessment strategies: project-based assessment, performance-based assessment, communication-tasks-based assessment (on both written and oral communications tasks) and student self-assessment, have been implemented in more than 50 mathematics classrooms in 16 schools – including both primary and secondary schools and high-performing and non-high-performing schools – involving a total of 55 mathematics teachers and more than 2,300 students. The implementation lasted about one-and-a-half years, and the purpose is to investigate the influence of those assessment strategies on students' learning of mathematics in both academic and affective domains and to explore the effective ways of implementing those strategies in mathematics classrooms (Fan and Quek, 2005).

The results from the in-service teachers' experiences, the small-scale studies and the MAP project, have been quite consistent and very positive overall. They prove that alternative assessment is within teachers' ability to grasp and implement, and both teachers and students benefit from these new methods of assessment in a variety of ways. They can effectively overcome the weakness of traditional paper-and-pencil tests as described earlier in Table 21-2. In addition, it has been found that alternative assessment can not only help students develop their problem-solving ability and higher-order thinking skills and foster positive dispositions towards mathematics learning, but also help them achieve more, measured using conventional written tests, which is particularly notable in Seto's study (also see Nirmala, 2002).

On the other hand, it should be pointed out that, compared with the traditional teacher-made test, alternative assessment also presents practical challenges for teachers and students. The main problems or challenges can be generally described in the following four aspects. Some relevant suggestions are given accordingly.

1. Time-consuming
   Designing, administering, evaluating and reporting alternative assessment are often very time-consuming. It requires not only teachers' innovation and creativity, but also more importantly their determination and persistence. Doing alternative assessment tasks, such as project work and oral presentation, could be also very time-consuming for students. Therefore, teachers should be cautious in deciding the frequency of using such tasks. It could be unrealistic or even counterproductive for teachers and students to implement too many different ways of alternative assessment or use a single way too often in a short period of time. The ideal situation would be that teachers integrate alternative assessment into their instructional practice so as to avoid disrupting the process of teaching and learning or imposing unnecessary additional work on both the teachers themselves and students.

2. Difficulty in getting started
   Teachers and students often have substantial difficulty at the beginning and need time to be familiar with the new approaches to assessment. Hence, it is often necessary that teachers start using alternative assessment methods gradually and carefully. It is also essential that enough guidance be given to students at the initial stage.

3. Lack of resources
   There are not many resources available in this area. The current textbooks do not reflect alternative assessment concepts and contents well. Nevertheless, the amount of supporting alternative assessment resources, especially online resources, has been growing rapidly in recent years. It would be helpful if teachers can exchange more with their colleagues and be provided with more professional development opportunities in this area, such as participating in seminars, workshops and in-service training courses.

4. Less well accepted
   This is particularly true at the introduction of alternative assessment. Being used to paper-and-pencil work, students may question why they need to work on new types of tasks, and parents may doubt if the teachers' evaluation of their children's work is fair, valid and reliable. In this regard, it is important for teachers to bear in mind and make clear that the main purpose of employing these new ways of assessment is not for teachers to grade and report students' learning results, instead it is to help improve teaching and learning.

To make alternative assessment successful, it is also vital that teachers realise different alternative assessment methods serve different purposes. It would be naive to think that there is a single best way, be it the traditional written test or a new alternative method, that can serve all the purposes of mathematical instruction. Table 21-3 indicates some alternative assessment methods and the different purposes of assessment they can reasonably serve. The list is neither exclusive nor exhaustive.

CONCLUSION

There are two basic principles relevant to the theme of this chapter about teachers' classroom assessment. First, assessment must serve the purpose of teaching and learning; and second, assessment must be an integral part of instructional practice. Given those two principles and the limitations of the traditional paper-and-pencil assessment, it is quite natural to see the necessity and values of employing new ways of assessing students in mathematics instruction.

Although the traditional assessment still has its advantages and values to offer, and, hence, we should improve rather than abolish it, alternative assessment does provide us new hope and give us new tools in our teaching practices. It can help us make assessment more consistent with educational goals and curriculum objectives, more constructive in promoting students' learning and more integral in the process of teaching and learning, though the extent of its helpfulness depends on how we can implement it effectively in mathematics classrooms.

Table 21-3 Alternative assessment methods and different purposes of assessment

Alternative method	What can be better assessed
Performance-based assessment	Cognitive domain, particularly students' higher-order thinking process and problem-solving ability
Authentic assessment	Cognitive domain, particularly real-life problem-solving ability
Portfolio assessment	Both cognitive and affective domains, particularly the development of students' learning over a period of time or represented in a variety of aspects
Journal writing	Both cognitive and affective domains, particularly students' deep thinking and written communication skills, and their disposition concerning learning of mathematics
Project assessment	Cognitive domain, particularly students' problem-solving ability and creative thinking skills
Oral presentation	Cognitive domain, particularly students' organisational and oral communication skills
Interview	Both cognitive and affective domains, particularly for getting information from a few students
Classroom observation	Affective domain, particularly students' learning behaviours in classroom
Student self-assessment	Both cognitive and affective domains, particularly students' disposition concerning learning of mathematics, and their participation in the learning process (e.g. doing group activity)
Student-constructed assessment	Cognitive domain, particularly at the evaluation level in Bloom's taxonomy of educational objectives in cognitive domain

REFERENCES

Chow, Y.P., & Fan, L. (2005). *Impact of open-ended problem solving as an alternative assessment on Secondary One mathematics students*. Paper presented at the "Redesigning the Pedagogy: Research, Policy, Practice" conference. Centre for Research in Pedagogy and Practice, National Institute of Education, Singapore.

Clarke, D.J. (1992). Activating assessment alternatives in mathematics. *Arithmetic Teacher, 39*(6), 24–29.

Fan, L. (2002). In-service training in alternative assessment with Singapore mathematics teachers. *The Mathematics Educator, 6*(2), 77–94.

Fan, L., & Quek, K.S. (2005). Integrating new assessment strategies into mathematics classrooms: What have we learned from a CRPP mathematics assessment project. Paper presented at the "Redesigning the Pedagogy: Research, Policy, Practice" conference. Centre for Research in Pedagogy and Practice, National Institute of Education, Singapore.

Fan, L., & Yeo, S.M. (2000). Journal writing as an alternative assessment. *Scientas, 34*, 16–25.

Fan, L., & Yeo, S.M. (2006). Integrating oral presentation into mathematics classrooms: A study in Singapore secondary schools. Paper presented at the annual meeting of the American Educational Research Association, San Francisco, USA.

Hargreaves, A., Earl, L., & Schmidt, M. (2002). Perspectives on alternative assessment reform. *Educational Researcher, 39*(1), 69–95.

Hatfield, M.M., Edwards, N.T., & Bitter, G.G. (1997). *Mathematics methods for elementary and middle school teachers*. Boston, MA: Allyn and Bacon.

Kulm, G. (1994). *Mathematics assessment: What works in the classroom*. San Francisco, CA: Jossey-Bass.

Lambdin, D.V. (1993). The NCTM's 1989 evaluation standards: Recycled ideas whose time has come? In Web, N.L., & Coxford, A.F. (Ed.), *Assessment in mathematics classroom* (pp. 7–16). Reston, VA: National Council of Teachers of Mathematics.

Mathematics Assessment Project. (2004). *Annotated bibliography of alternative assessment in mathematics*. Singapore: Centre for Research in Pedagogy and Practice, National Institute of Education.

Mayer, J., & Hillman, S. (1996). Implementing the assessment standards for school mathematics: Assessing students' thinking through writing. *Mathematics Teacher, 89*(5), 428–432.

Ministry of Education. (2000). *Mathematics syllabus – Lower secondary*. Singapore: Curriculum Planning and Development Division, Ministry of Education.

Ministry of Education. (2001). Project work to be included for university admission in 2005. Press Release (20 June), Singapore: Ministry of Education (also see http://www1.moe.edu.sg/press/2001).

Ministry of Education. (2004a). *Assessment guides to primary mathematics*. Singapore: Ministry of Education.

Ministry of Education. (2004b). *Assessment guides to lower secondary mathematics*. Singapore: Ministry of Education.

National Council of Teachers of Mathematics. (1995). *Assessment standards for school mathematics*. Reston, VA: National Council of Teachers of Mathematics.

Nirmala, M. (2002, May 18). Pupils talk about maths in this class. *The Straits Times*, H11, Singapore.

Quinto, F., & McKenna, B. (1977). Alternatives to standardized testing. Washington, DC: National Education Association.

Romagnano, L., & Long, V. (2001). The myth of objectivity in mathematics assessment. *Mathematics Teacher, 94*(1), 31–37.

Seto, C. (2002). Oral presentation as an alternative assessment in mathematics. In Edge, D., & Yeap, B.H. (Eds.), *Mathematics education for a knowledge-based era* (Vol. 2, pp. 33–39). Singapore: Association of Mathematics Educators.

Yazilah, A., & Fan, L. (2002). Exploring how to implement journal writing effectively in primary mathematics in Singapore. In Edge, D., & Yeap, B.H. (Eds.), *Mathematics education for a knowledge-based era* (Vol. 2, pp. 56–62). Singapore: Association of Mathematics Educators.

Yeo, S.M. (2001). *Using journal writing as an alternative assessment in junior college mathematics classrooms*. Unpublished Master's dissertation, Nanyang Technological University, Singapore.

Chapter

22

The Model-drawing Method with Algebra

Kho Tek Hong

INTRODUCTION

One of the main objectives of mathematics education in Singapore is to enable students to develop their abilities in problem solving. The model-drawing method was introduced in the 1980s by the Primary Mathematics Project of the Ministry of Education. It involves the construction of pictorial models, namely the part-whole model and the comparison model, to help students visualise abstract mathematical relationships and various problem structures through pictorial representations (Kho, 1987). It is a powerful visual aid for solving complex problems involving fractions, ratios and percentages. Above all, it is closely related to the algebraic method for solving algebra word problems (Kho, 1987; Fong, 1994; Ng, 2001; Cheong, 2002; Beckmann, 2004).

This chapter[1] demonstrates how the model-drawing method can help students visualise and conceptualise a problem so that they can formulate an algebraic equation to solve it.

---

[1] The original version (October 2005) was an internal document of the Ministry of Education, and was issued to heads of department and teachers at workshops and meetings.

MATHEMATICAL MODELS

The Part-Whole Model

The part-whole model (also known as the "part-part-whole" model) shows the relationship between a whole and its parts, e.g.

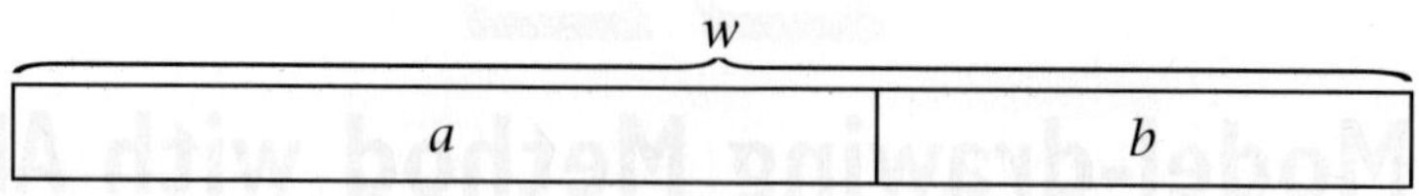

The pictorial model shows that the whole w is divided into two parts a and b. That is, $w = a + b$.

In the part-whole model, we may divide the whole into a number of equal parts, e.g.

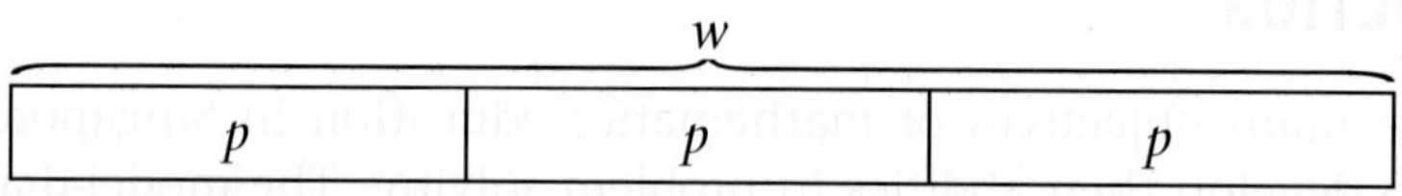

The pictorial model shows that the whole w is divided into 3 equal parts, and each part is p. That is, $w = 3p$.

The Comparison Model

The comparison model shows the relationship between two quantities when they are compared, e.g.

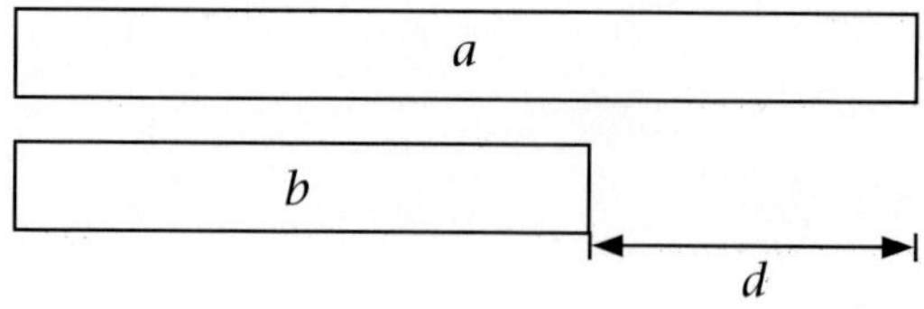

The pictorial model shows that the quantity a is more than the quantity b, and the difference between a and b is d. That is, $d = a - b$.

Also,

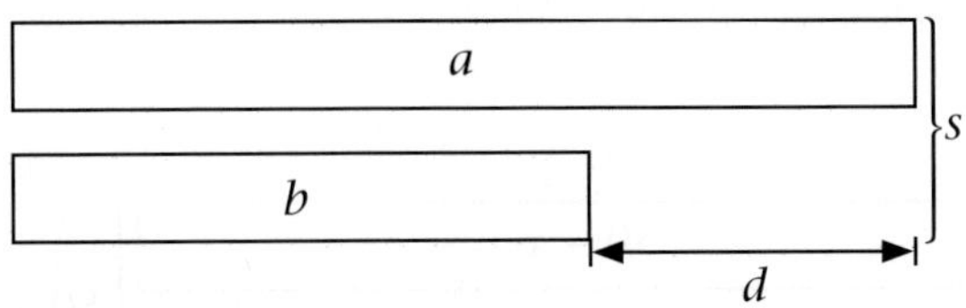

The sum of a and b is s. That is $s = a + b$.

In the comparison model, we may express one quantity as a multiple of the other, e.g.

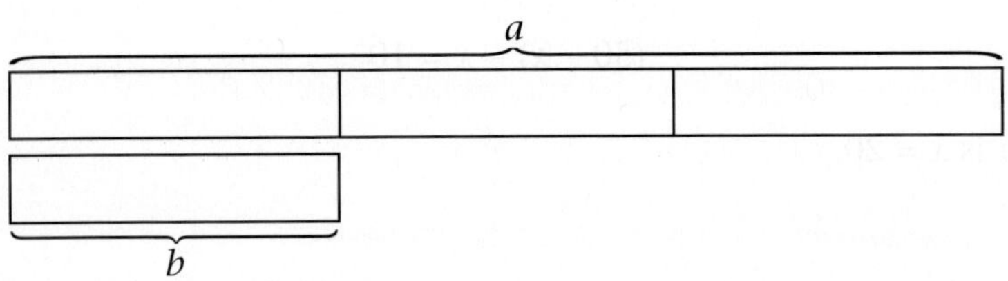

The pictorial model shows that the quantity a is 3 times as much as the quantity b. That is, $a = 3b$.

Example 1

There are 50 children in a dance group. If there are 10 more boys than girls, how many girls are there?

Method 1:

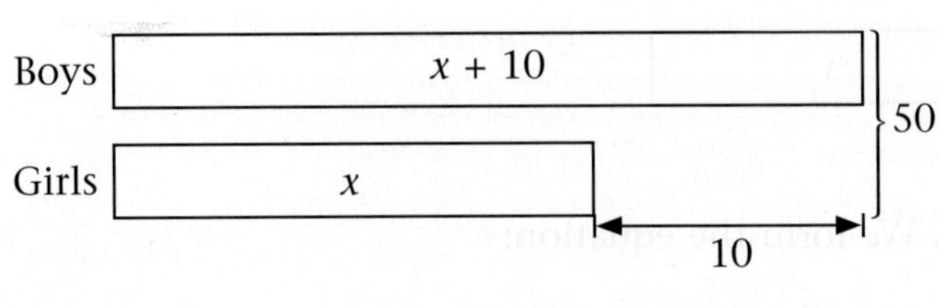

Let the number of girls be x. We form the equation:

$$x + (x + 10) = 50$$

The solution is $x = 20$.
There are 20 girls.

The same problem can be solved by formulating a different equation as shown in the alternative method below:

Method 2:

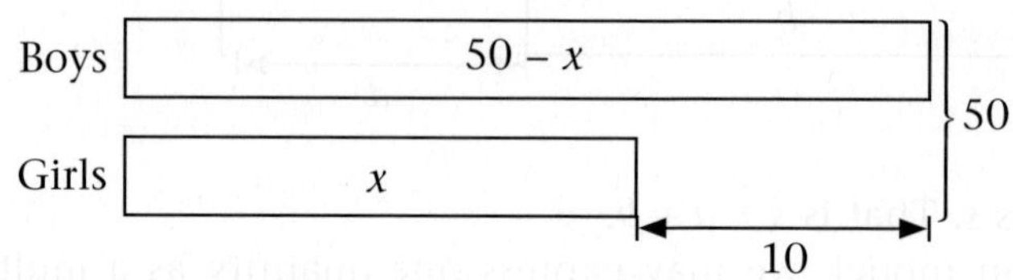

Here we form the equation:

$$(50 - x) - x = 10$$

The solution is $x = 20$.

Example 2

\$120 is shared among 3 persons *A*, *B* and *C*. If *A* receives \$20 less than *B*, and *B* receives 3 times as much money as *C*, how much money does *C* receive?

Method 1:

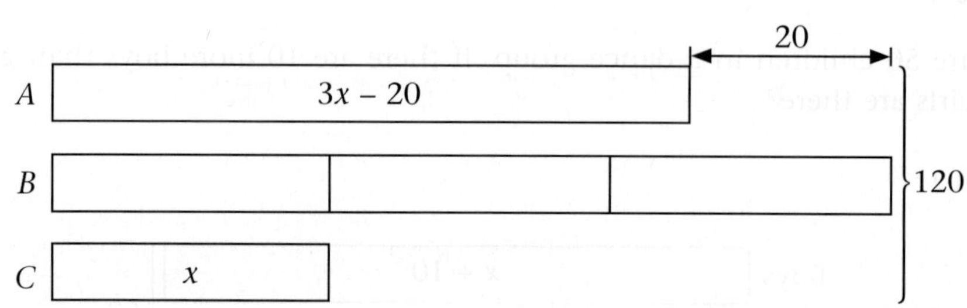

Let *C* receive \$$x$. We form the equation:

$$(3x - 20) + 3x + x = 120$$

The solution is $x = 20$.
C receives \$20.

Method 2:

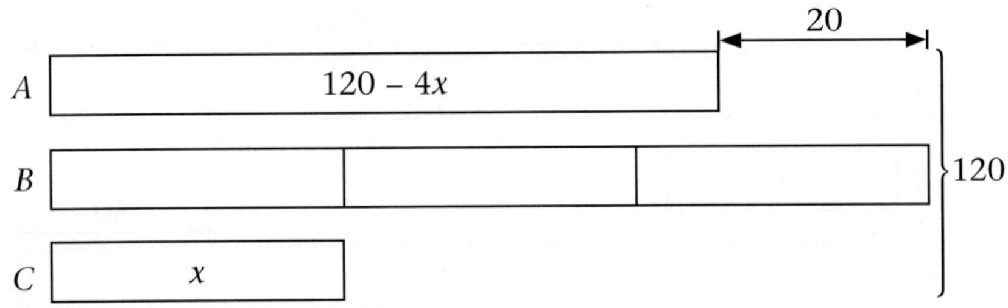

Here we form the equation:

$$3x - (120 - 4x) = 20$$

The solution is $x = 20$.

Example 3

A has 3 times as much money as *B*. *B* has \$200 less than *C*. *C* has \$50 more than *A*. Find the total amount of money that *A*, *B* and *C* have.

Method 1:

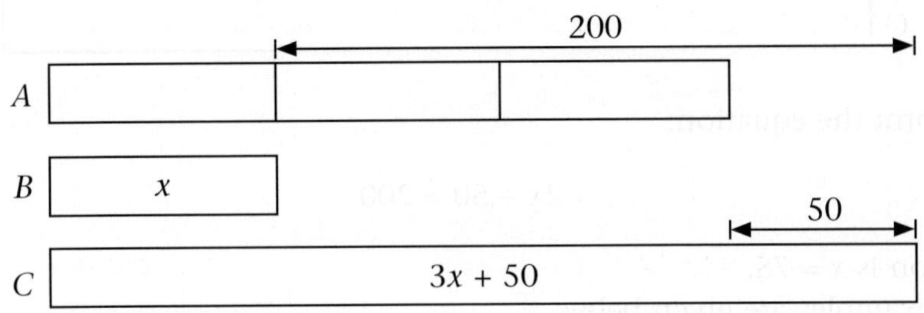

Let *B* have $\$x$. We form the equation:

$$(3x + 50) - x = 200$$

The solution is $x = 75$.
Total amount of money = $\$(3x + x + 3x + 50) = \$575$.

Method 2:

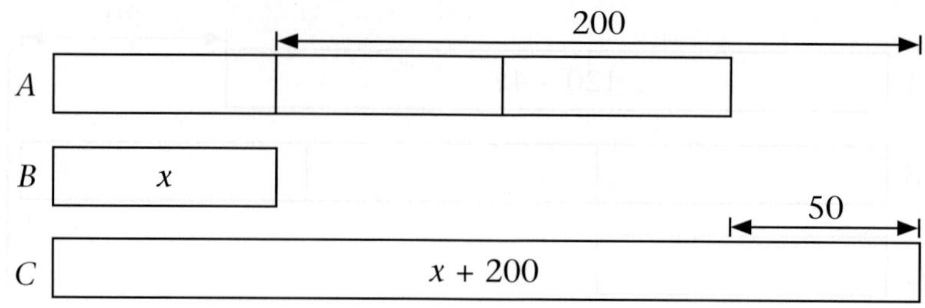

Here we form the equation:

$$(x + 200) - 3x = 50$$

The solution is $x = 75$.

Method 3:

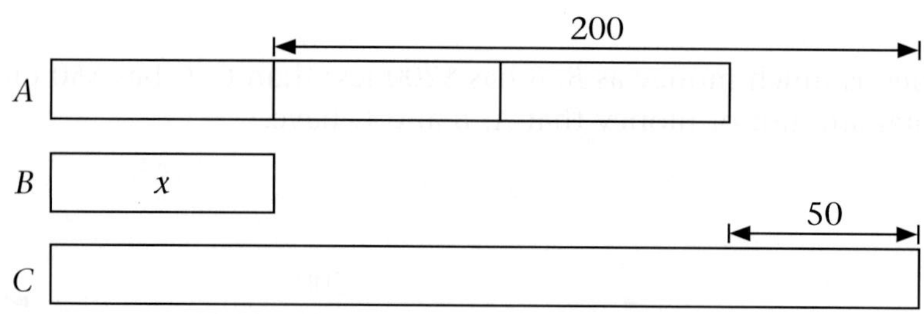

Here we form the equation:

$$2x + 50 = 200$$

The solution is $x = 75$.

More examples are given below.

Example 4

John is 4 times as old as his son. If their total age 10 years ago was 60, find their present ages. [16, 64]

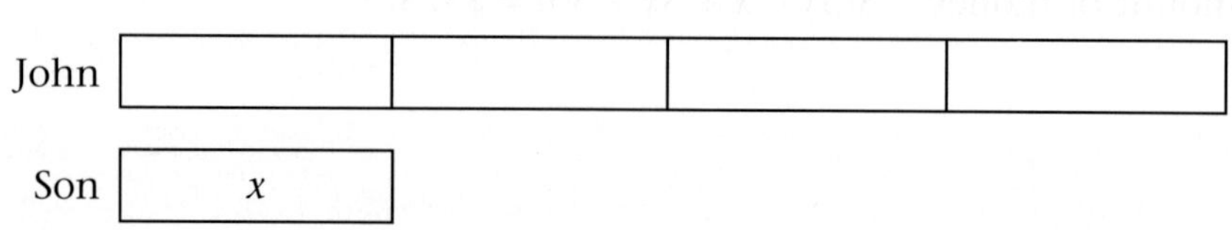

10 years ago:

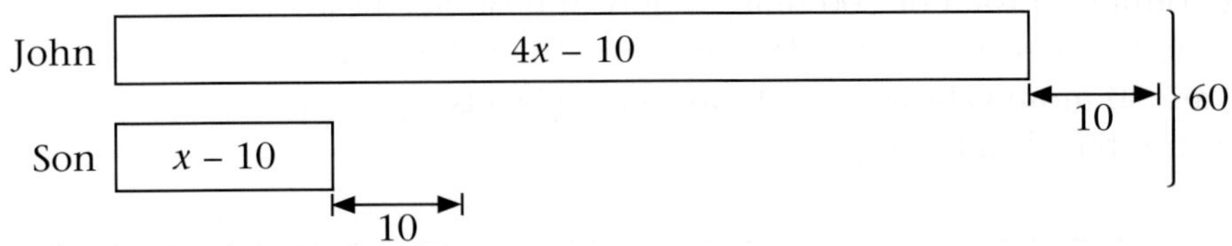

[$(4x - 10) + (x - 10) = 60$]

Example 5

Raju had 3 times as much money as Gopal. After spending \$60 each, Raju had 4 times as much money as Gopal. How much money did Raju have at first? [\$540]

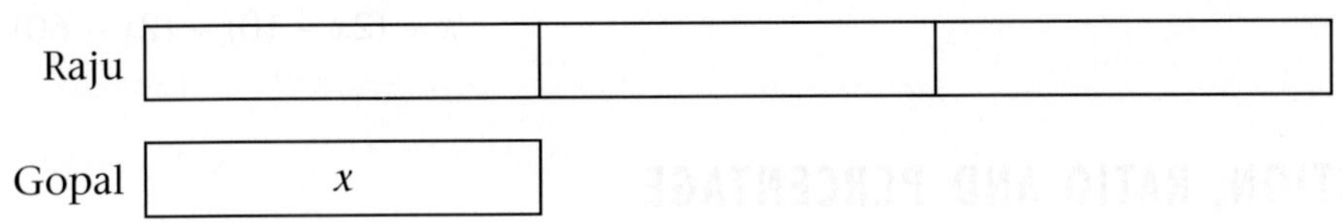

After spending \$60 each:

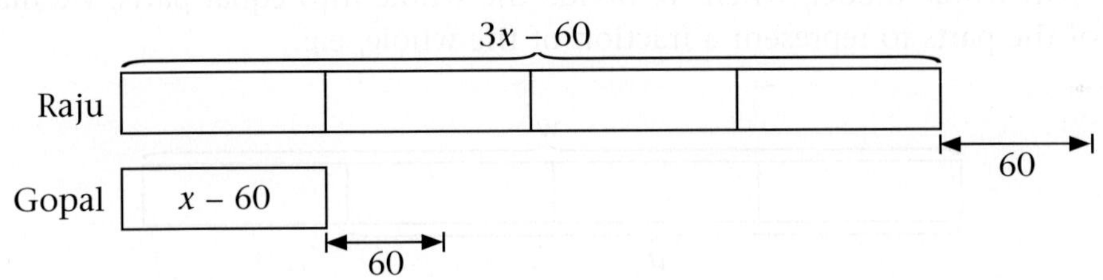

[$3x - 60 = 4(x - 60)$]

Example 6

A box contains a total of 200 blue, yellow and orange beads.
Twice the number of blue beads is 10 more than the number of yellow beads.
There are 50 more yellow beads than orange beads.
How many blue beads are there? [54]

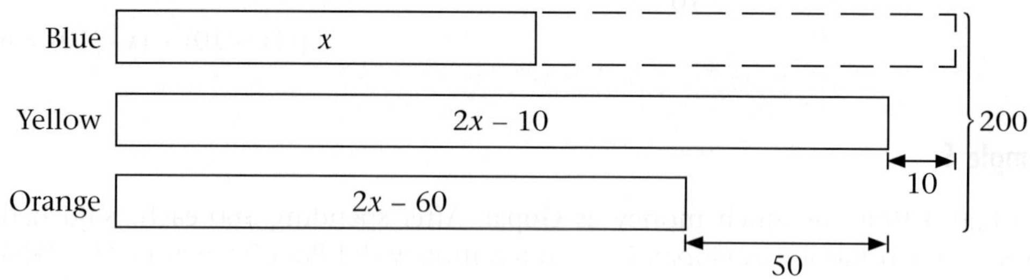

$$x + (2x - 10) + (2x - 60) = 200$$

FRACTION, RATIO AND PERCENTAGE

The part-whole model for fraction

In the part-whole model, when we divide the whole into equal parts, we may use some of the parts to represent a fraction of the whole, e.g.

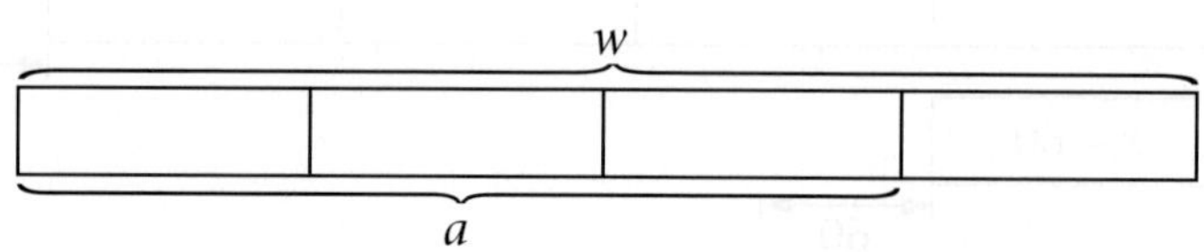

The pictorial model shows that a is $\frac{3}{4}$ of w.

In this case, w comprises 4 units, and a is equal to 3 units.

We write: $a = \frac{3}{4}w = \frac{3w}{4}$.

For example, the following model shows $\frac{3}{4}$ of a whole.

i.

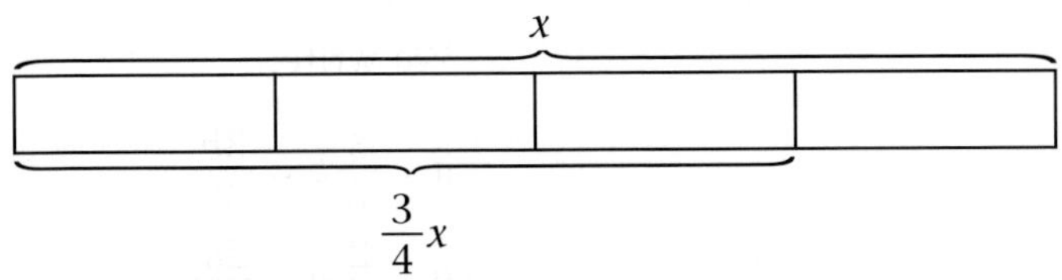

ii. If we let $\frac{3}{4}$ of the whole be x, then the whole is $\frac{4x}{3}$.

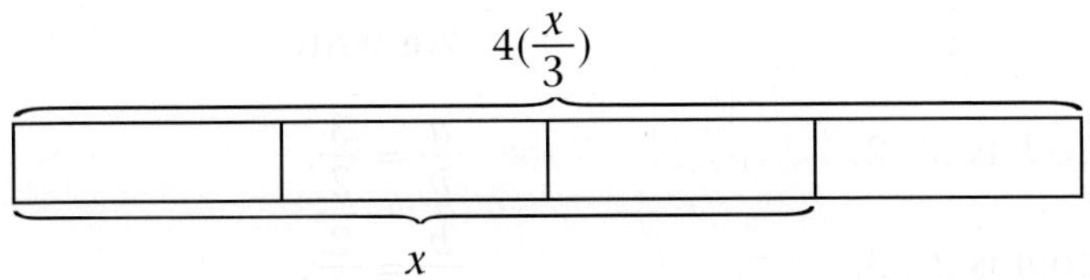

iii. If we let the whole be $4x$, then $\frac{3}{4}$ of the whole is $3x$.

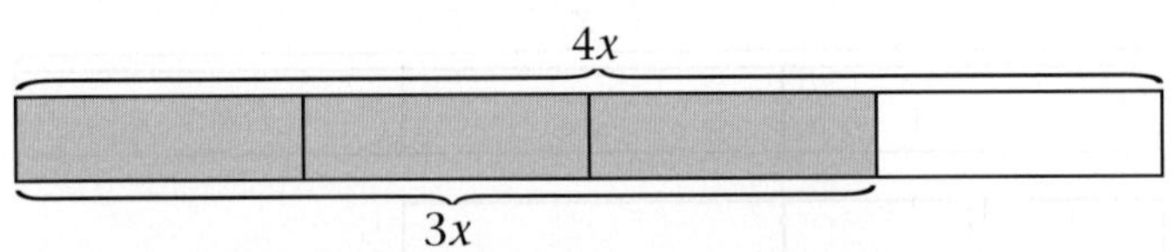

The comparison model for fraction and ratio

In the comparison model, we may express one quantity as a fraction of the other, e.g.

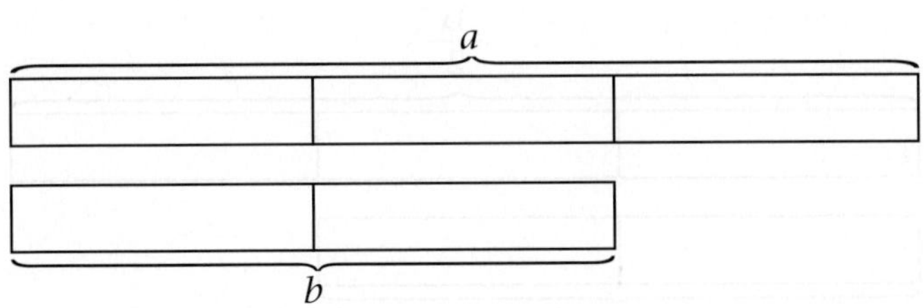

The pictorial model shows that two quantities a and b are 3 units and 2 units respectively.

We say:	We write:
a is $\frac{3}{2}$ of b.	$a = \frac{3}{2}b = \frac{3b}{2}$.
b is $\frac{2}{3}$ of a.	$b = \frac{2}{3}a = \frac{2a}{3}$.

The relationship between a and b can also be expressed as a ratio. In this case,

We say:	We write:
The ratio of a to b is 3 : 2.	$\frac{a}{b} = \frac{3}{2}$.
The ratio of b to a is 2 : 3.	$\frac{b}{a} = \frac{2}{3}$.

For example, the following model shows one quantity is $\frac{2}{3}$ of the other.

i.

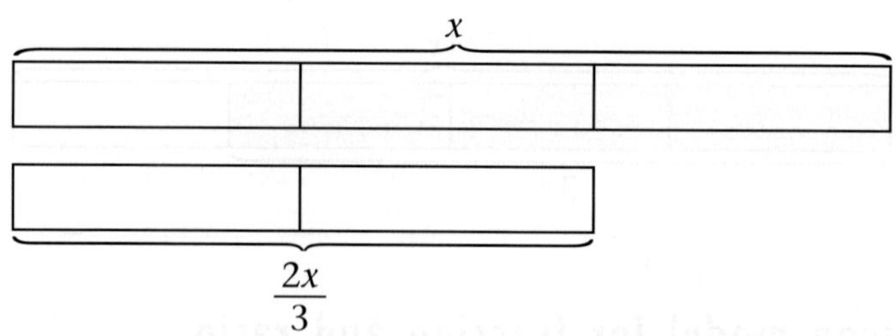

ii. The same model shows one quantity is $\frac{3}{2}$ of the other.

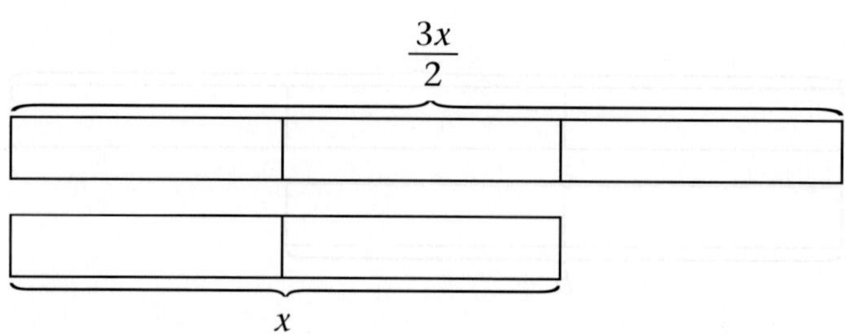

iii. The same model shows two quantities in the ratio 3 : 2.

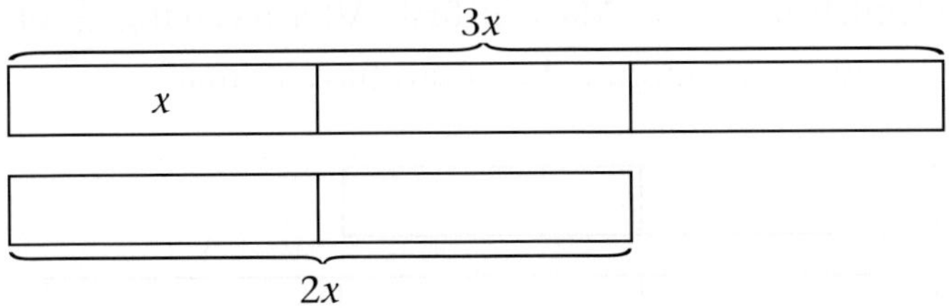

Example 7

Susan had $\frac{2}{3}$ as much money as Mary at first. After receiving $\frac{1}{2}$ of Susan's money, Mary had \$210. How much money did Susan have at first?

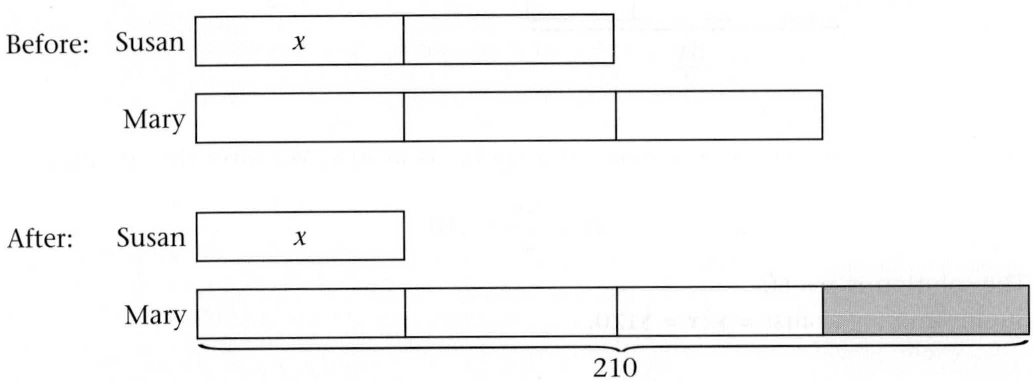

Let Susan's money be $2x$ and Mary's money be $3x$ at first. We form the equation:

$$4x = 210$$

The solution is $x = 52.5$.
Susan's money at first = $\$2x = \$105$.

Example 8

Susan had $\frac{2}{3}$ as much money as Mary at first. After receiving $\frac{1}{2}$ of Mary's money, Susan had $210. How much money did Susan have at first?

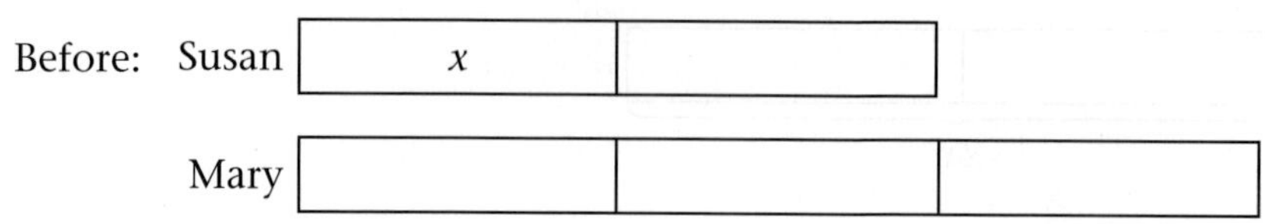

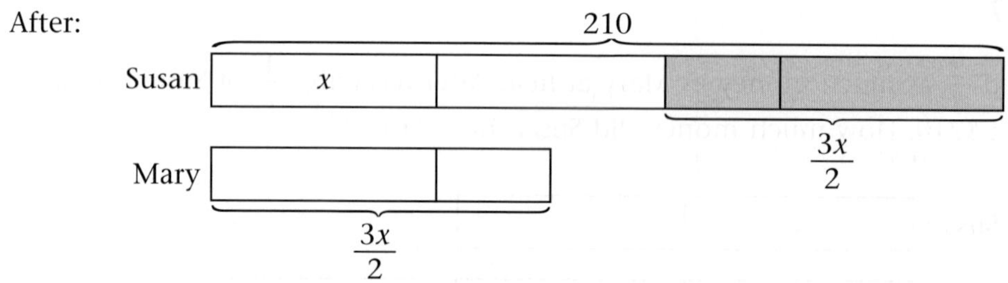

Let Susan's money be $2x$ and Mary's money be $3x$ at first. We form the equation:

$$2x + \frac{3x}{2} = 210$$

The solution is $x = 60$.
Susan's money at first = $\$2x = \$120$.

Example 9

$\frac{3}{5}$ of the beads in a box are yellow beads. The rest are orange and blue beads. The ratio of the number of orange beads to the number of blue beads is 4 : 5.
If there are 30 blue beads, how many yellow beads are there?

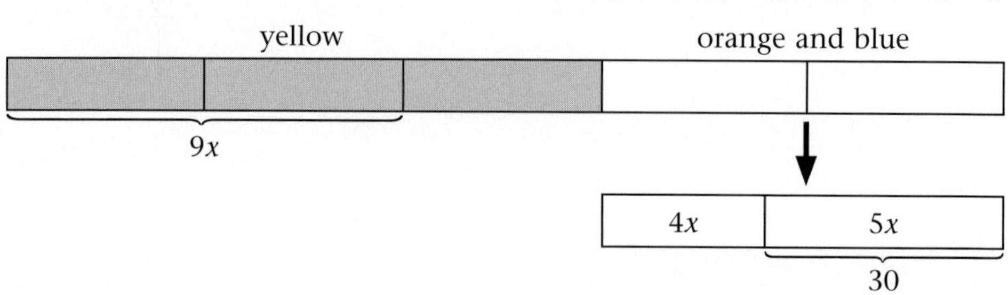

Let the number of orange beads and blue beads be $4x$ and $5x$ respectively. We form the equation:

$$5x = 30$$

The solution is $x = 6$.
Number of yellow beads $= 3(\frac{9x}{2}) = \frac{27x}{2} = 81$.

More examples are given below.

Example 10

A box contains a total of 200 blue and yellow beads. $\frac{2}{3}$ of the blue beads and $\frac{1}{2}$ of the yellow beads are taken out and used to make a necklace. If there are 30 fewer blue beads than yellow beads in the necklace, how many beads are left in the box? [90]

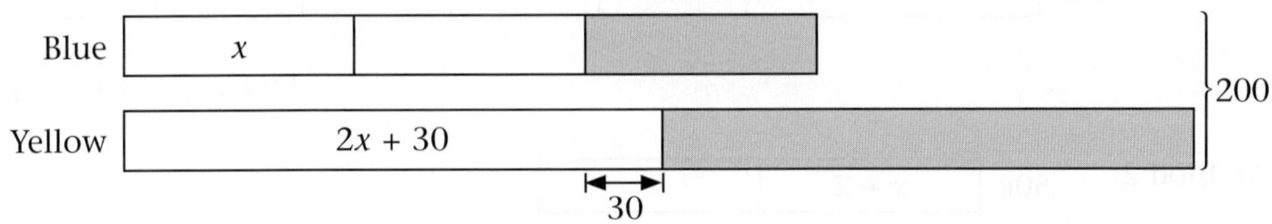

$[3x + 2(2x + 30) = 200]$

Example 11

$\frac{3}{5}$ of the students in Sec 1A and $\frac{2}{3}$ of the students in Sec 1B are girls. Both classes have the same number of girls. Sec 1A has 4 more boys than Sec 1B. How many students are there in Sec 1A? [40]

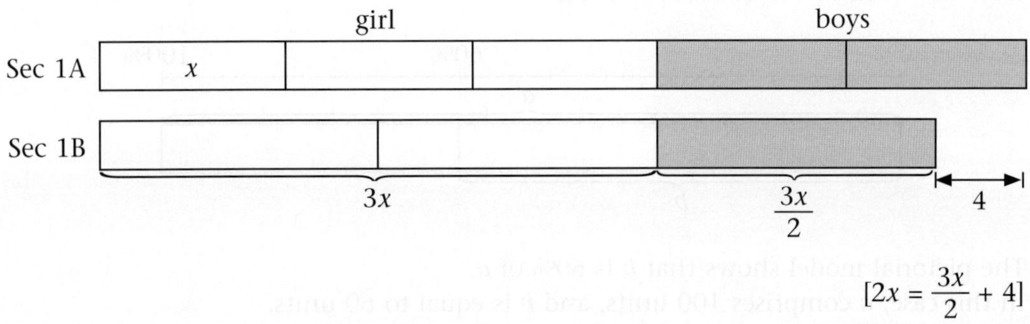

$[2x = \frac{3x}{2} + 4]$

Example 12

The number of fifty-cent coins and twenty-cent coins are in the ratio 2 : 3. If 4 of the fifty-cent coins are exchanged for twenty-cent coins, the ratio will become 2 : 7. What is the total value ($) of the set of coins? [$9.60]

Method 1:

Before:

After:

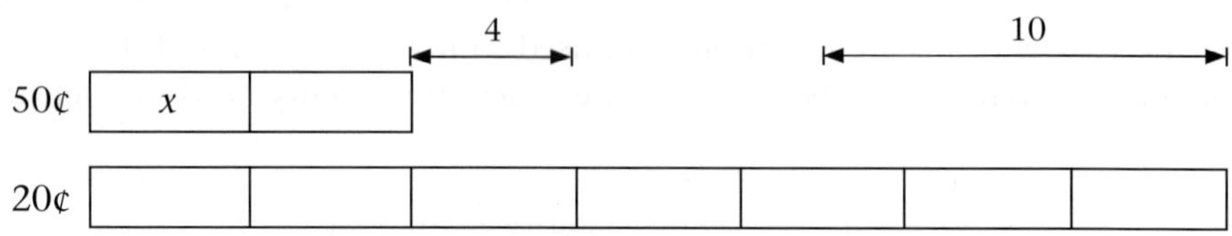

$[3(x + 2) + 10 = 7x]$

Method 2:

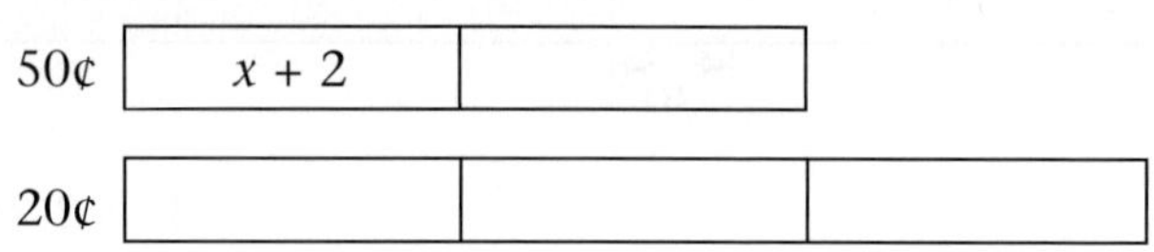

$[\frac{2x - 4}{3x + 10} = \frac{2}{7}]$

The part-whole model for percentage

In the part-whole model, we may express a part as a percentage of the whole. We take the whole as the base (100%), e.g.

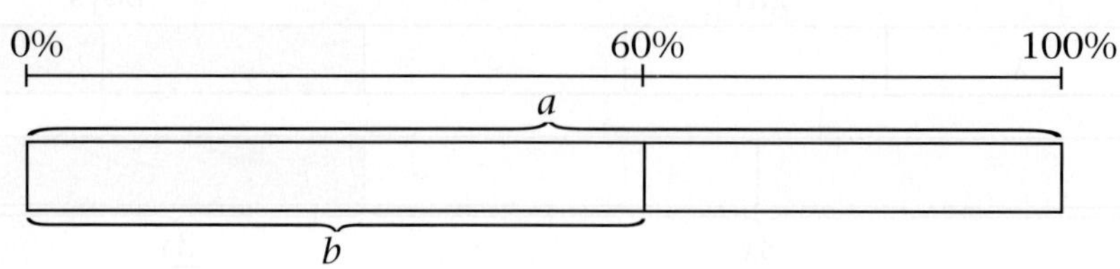

The pictorial model shows that b is 60% of a.
In this case, a comprises 100 units, and b is equal to 60 units.

We write:

$$b = 60\% \text{ of } a = 0.6a$$

The part-whole model can be used to show the relationship between the new value of a quantity and its original value after an increase or a decrease.

Let the original value be x.

a. The following model shows an increase of 20%.

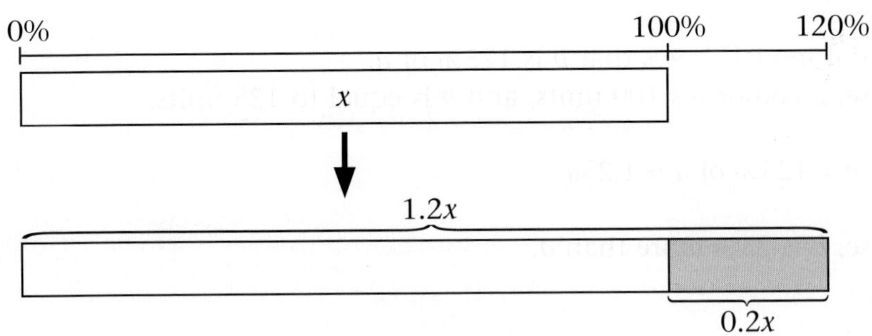

Here the increase is $0.2x$ and the new value is $1.2x$.

b. The following model shows a decrease of 40%.

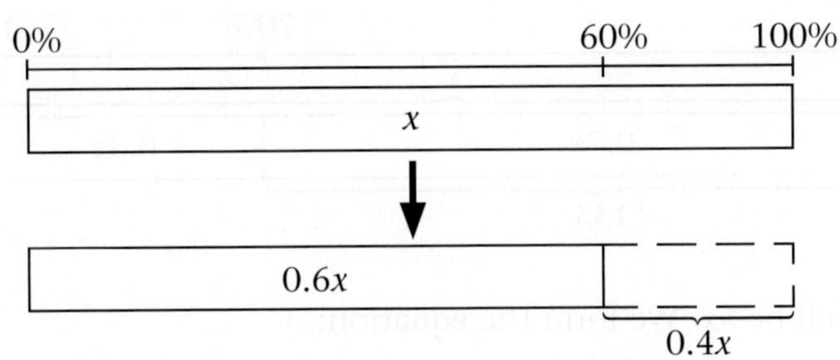

Here the decrease is $0.4x$ and the new value is $0.6x$.

The comparison model for percentage

In the comparison model, we may express one quantity as a percentage of the other. For example, to compare b with respect to a, we take a as the base (100%), e.g.

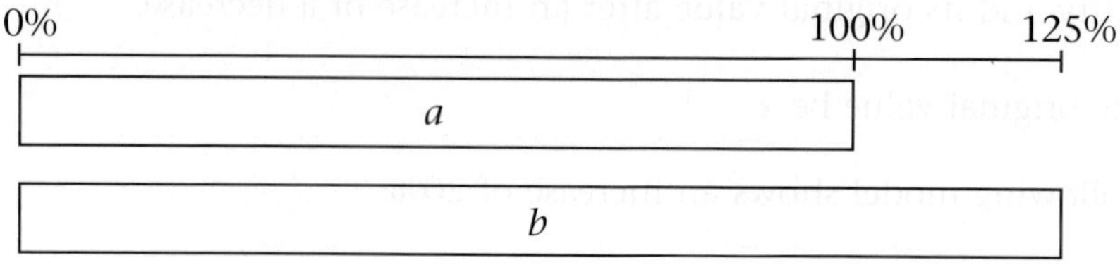

The pictorial model shows that b is 125% of a.
In this case, a comprises 100 units, and b is equal to 125 units.

We write: $b = 125\%$ of $a = 1.25a$.

In this case, b is 25% more than a.[2]

Example 13

Mrs. Tan has a VIP card that entitles her to a discount of 30% off her dinner bill. If she pays $133 for her dinner, how much is the original bill?

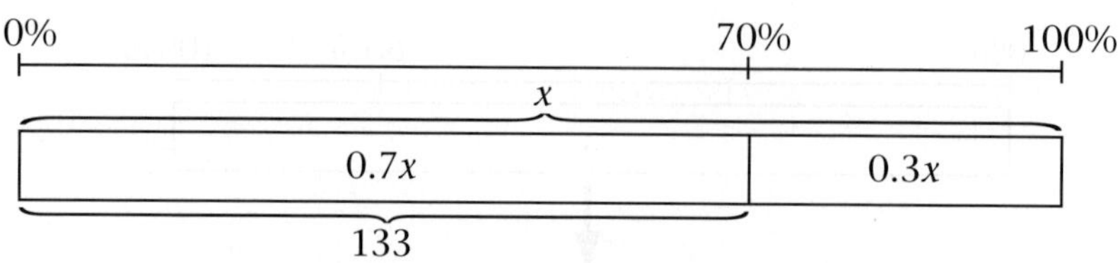

Let the original bill be $\$x$. We form the equation:

$$0.7x = 133$$

The solution is $x = 190$.
The original bill is $190.

---

[2] It is not true that "b is 25% more than a" will imply "a is 25% less than b". Indeed, in this case, a is 20% less than b.

Example 14

Jane saved 20% more in January than in February. If she saved a total of \$330 in the two months, how much did she save in February?

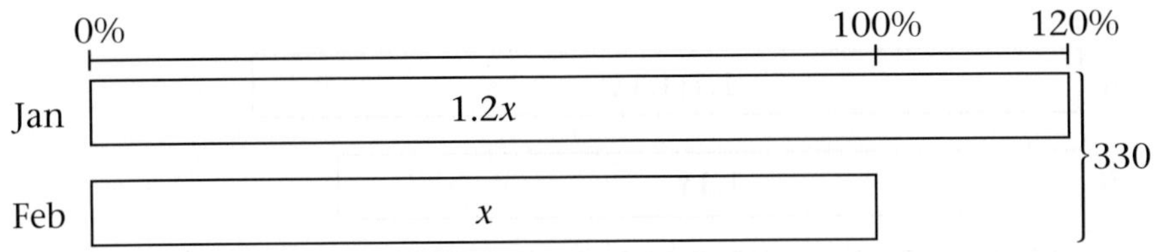

Let Jane save \$$x$ in February. We form the equation:

$$x + 1.2x = 330$$

The solution is $x = 150$.
Jane saved \$150 in February.

Example 15

Mrs. Tan spent $\frac{2}{3}$ of her money on a handbag. She spent 40% of the remaining money on a dress. If the handbag cost \$80 more than the dress, how much money did she have at first?

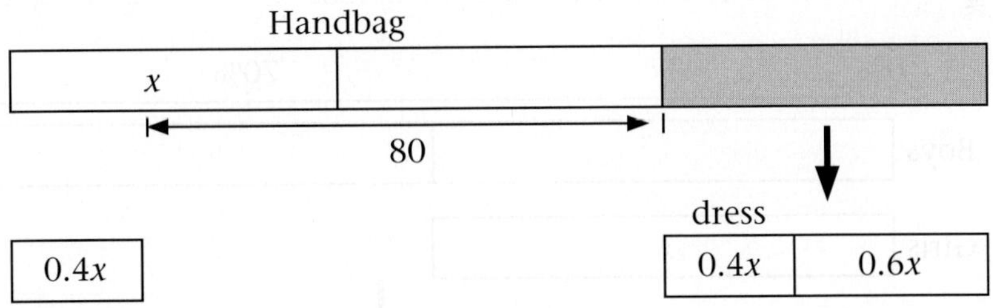

Let Mrs. Tan have \$$3x$ at first. We form the equation:

$$2x - 0.4x = 80$$

The solution is $x = 50$.
Mrs. Tan's money = \$$3x$ = \$150.

Example 16

A sum of money is shared among 3 persons, A, B and C, so that A receives 10% more than B, and B receives 10% more than C. If A receives \$525 more than C, find the sum of money.

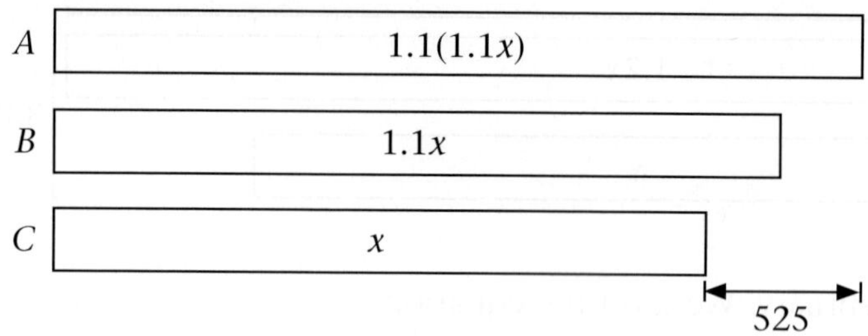

Let C receive \$$x$. We form the equation:

$$1.1(1.1x) - x = 525$$

The solution is $x = 2500$.
Sum of money = \$$(1.21x + 1.1x + x)$ = \$8275.

Example 17

There are twice as many boys as girls in a choir. If the number of boys is decreased by 30%, by what percentage must the number of girls be increased (or decreased) so that there will be an equal number of boys and girls in the choir?

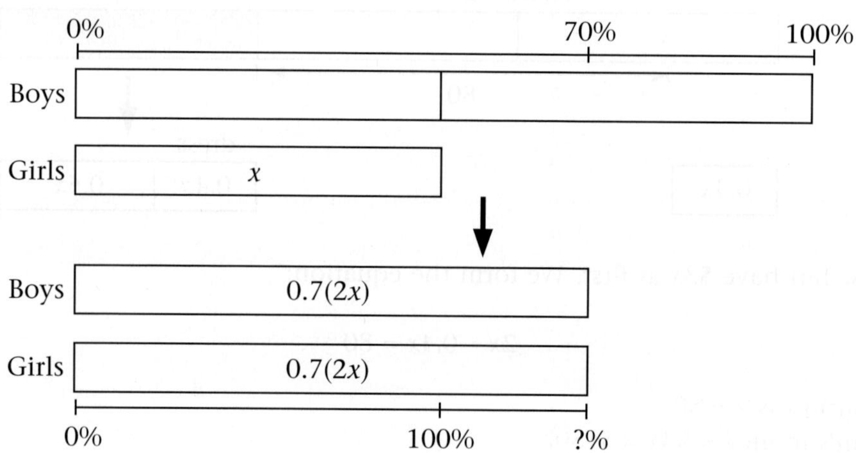

$$\text{Percentage increase} = \frac{0.7(2x) - x}{x} = 0.4 = 40\%.$$

Example 18

The ratio of the number of boys to the number of girls is 5 : 6. It is given that 30% of the boys wear glasses, and there is an equal number of boys and girls who wear glasses. What percentage of the girls wear glasses?

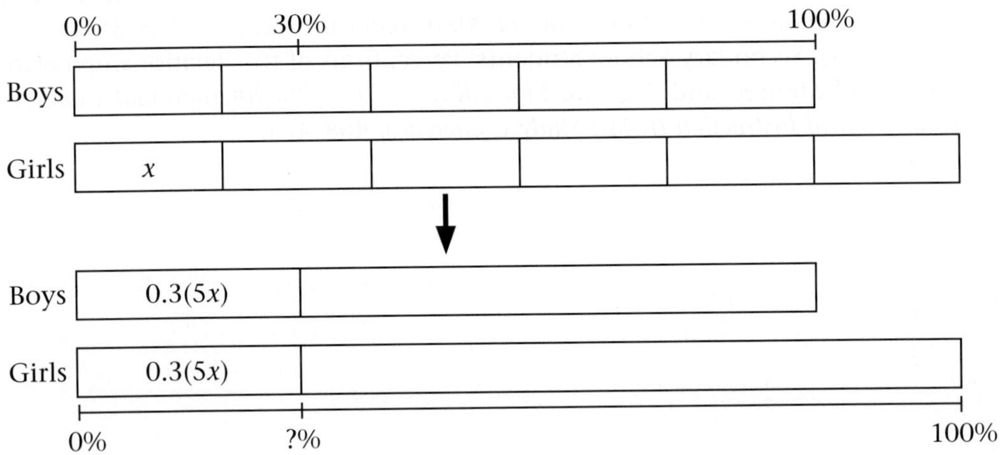

$$\text{Percentage} = \frac{0.3(5x)}{6x} = 0.25 = 25\%.$$

CONCLUSION

Algebra is the key to the learning of higher mathematics. Nevertheless, it is a worldwide concern that many students have difficulties making the transition from arithmetic to algebra, especially when they attempt to formulate algebraic equations for solving problems. The integration of the model-drawing method and the algebraic method provides an enriching opportunity for students to engage in the construction and interpretation of algebraic equations through meaningful and active learning. We hope that this approach will help more students develop their competence and confidence in using the algebraic method.

REFERENCES

Beckmann, S. (2004). Solving algebra and other story problems with simple diagrams: A method demonstrated in Grade 4–6 texts used in Singapore. The *Mathematics Educator, 14*(1), 42–46.

Cheong, N.P. (2002). The teaching of primary mathematics and the model approach to problem solving. *Mathematics Newsletter* (Issue No. 4, 2002), Ministry of Education, Singapore.

Fong, H.K. (1994). Bridging the gap between secondary and primary mathematics. *Teaching and Learning, 14*(2), 73–84.

Kho, T.H. (1987). Mathematical models for solving arithmetic problems. *Proceedings of the 4th Southeast Asian Conference on Mathematical Education,* 345–351.

Ng, S.F. (2001). Secondary School Students' Perceptions of the Relationship between the Model Method and Algebra. *Proceedings of the 12th International Congress of Mathematical Instruction (ICMI) Study Conference,* 468–474.

Index